Net Zero+

CLIMATE AND ECONOMIC RESILIENCE IN A CHANGING WORLD

OECD
BETTER POLICIES FOR BETTER LIVES

Please cite this publication as:
OECD (2023), *Net Zero+: Climate and Economic Resilience in a Changing World*, OECD Publishing, Paris, https://doi.org/10.1787/da477dda-en.

ISBN 978-92-64-99669-4 (print)
ISBN 978-92-64-86879-3 (pdf)
ISBN 978-92-64-60464-3 (HTML)
ISBN 978-92-64-64873-9 (epub)

Photo credits: Cover © Baseline Arts.

Corrigenda to OECD publications may be found on line at: www.oecd.org/about/publishing/corrigenda.htm.

Preface

The need to act on climate change, in a way that is globally effective, is urgent and real. Climate impacts – and the risk of crossing irreversible tipping points – are increasing, foreshadowing the catastrophic changes to come should policy efforts fail. Indeed, the Sixth Assessment Report of the Intergovernmental Panel on Climate Change (IPCC) shows that human-induced climate change is under way and accelerating, and that action to first achieve a peak and then a steep reduction in global emissions towards net-zero needs to rapidly accelerate, starting now.

Climate change is not the only challenge governments face. The scars left by the COVID-19 pandemic and Russia's unprovoked, unjustifiable and illegal war of aggression against Ukraine have demonstrated the social and economic vulnerability of human systems and the threat that economic disruptions can pose to climate policy resilience. At the same time, the world is grappling with longer-term structural challenges such as a rapidly changing labour market, aging societies, digital transformation of economies and of course environmental impacts related to biodiversity loss, degrading ocean health and others.

Addressing these challenges is the focus of the OECD-wide project *Net Zero+: Climate and Economic Resilience in a Changing World*. Outcomes achieved in countries across the world will improve more quickly if we all more systematically share data and information about what we are each doing to bring our emissions down. These efforts are at the heart of our work at the OECD – developing and using verifiable data sets based on mutually agreed methodologies to support better policy making.

The *Net Zero+* synthesis report sits alongside three other flagship OECD initiatives on climate action. First, the OECD's Inclusive Forum on Carbon Mitigation Approaches, which looks to improve data and information sharing about the comparative effectiveness of different carbon mitigation policy approaches. Second, the International Programme for Action on Climate (IPAC) – developed as part of the *Net Zero+* project – has established a detailed set of headline indicators to track and monitor both the impacts of climate change and our climate action responses – adaptation and mitigation – across OECD and non-OECD countries annually. Third, the OECD's work to track progress toward the goal of donor countries providing and mobilising USD 100 billion climate finance annually for developing countries under the UNFCCC and the Paris Agreement.

Net Zero+ draws on the full breadth of the OECD's multidisciplinary expertise to provide policy makers with a cohesive set of recommendations for accelerating resilient, whole-of-government climate policy making. This report brings together findings from the first phase of the *Net Zero+* project. Spanning work from 17 OECD policy committees, it is a central contribution to the OECD's organisation-wide efforts to support climate action in practice. The report is structured around three distinct but interlinked parts that together provide a complete picture of the policy needs for resilient climate action.

- Part I sets the scene of the current context for climate policy making, underlining the urgency of the climate crisis alongside the myriad other disruptions governments are facing. Despite recent progress, climate change is not yet sufficiently mainstreamed into core economic policy. Mitigation and adaptation also remain largely compartmentalised from each other and are dealt with separately from other environmental challenges such as biodiversity.

- Part II focuses on how to ensure the transition to net-zero emissions is not only accelerated but also itself resilient. This means making sure climate policies are durable even under changing circumstances, but also that they do not engender negative impacts in other policy domains. The analysis identifies potential bottlenecks to the transition and how policies can be designed to anticipate them across public and private finance, innovation, jobs and social policy, as well as the particular circumstances of developing countries.
- Part III shifts the focus towards building systemic resilience to climate impacts, highlighting the intrinsic synergies between mitigation, adaptation and other environmental concerns. It shows that adaptation efforts are necessary to avoid losses and damages, and how, here too, a systemic approach is needed, moving away from adapting individual systems' components in response to specific climate risks, in favour of building overall resilience. In this light, the analysis includes a specific deep dive into building resilience in key sectors and systems.

The stakes are high. We know some climate impacts are already "baked in". In 2021 alone, the global direct costs of extreme climate-related events were estimated at around USD 290 billion (EUR 265 billion) and IPAC data highlights observable changes. At the same time, the benefits from faster, more co-ordinated action are clear.

The richness of approaches that countries are using, or plan to use, is important and justified. The challenge in translating ambition and efforts into real actions and real outcomes is to ensure that all these individual policy efforts are globally as effective and as fair as possible.

Mathias Cormann
OECD Secretary-General

Foreword

This report presents findings from the first phase of the OECD Horizontal Project *Net Zero+: Climate and economic resilience in a changing world* (Net Zero+). It offers governments recommendations across diverse policy areas in order to ensure a resilient transition to net-zero emissions while simultaneously building resilience to climate impacts. It is not a comprehensive synthesis of all existing climate-relevant work across the OECD, but rather a curated selection to support climate policy making today and in the future.

The report was prepared under the work programme of the Environment Policy Committee (EPOC) as the lead committee. It also draws on work carried out under the Regional Development Policy Committee (RDPC), Committee on Fiscal Affairs (CFA), Insurance and Private Pensions Committee (IPPC), Working Party on Responsible Business Conduct (WPRBC) under the Investment Committee (IC), Development Assistance Committee (DAC), Economic Policy Committee (EPC), Public Governance Committee (PGC), Regulatory Policy Committee (RPC), Committee of Senior Budget Officials (SBO), Committee on Statistics and Statistical Policy (CSSP), Committee for Scientific and Technological Policy (CSTP), Committee for Industry Innovation and Entrepreneurship (CIIE), Committee for Agriculture (COAG), Trade Committee (TC), Employment, Labour and Social Affairs Committee (ELSAC). The report also draws on the work of the International Energy Agency (IEA) and the Nuclear Energy Agency (NEA).

The report is structured in three parts.

Part I presents the complex challenge that climate policy makers face today: how to accelerate climate action while dealing with equally urgent priorities such as crisis relief, upended global markets and value/supply chains, geopolitical tensions, and economic recovery. This is demonstrated through a review of the most recent science on climate system tipping points (Chapter 2), and a look at the challenges and opportunities for climate action brought by recent global disruptions such as the COVID-19 pandemic and Russia's war on Ukraine (Chapter 3). In order to meet this challenge, Chapter 4 argues for an overarching approach to climate policy making centred on systemic resilience and "future-proofing" climate and economic policies, including through the use of tools such as strategic foresight.

Climate policies can only be successful if they themselves are resilient to potential future crises, including the socio-economic effects that may arise as a consequence of their implementation. Part II thus further explores systemic resilience in the transition to net-zero emissions. Chapter 5 spotlights climate mitigation and the immense transformation necessary to reach net zero, including bottlenecks and potential barriers. Chapter 6 considers the implications of climate policies on public finances. Chapter 7 explores the essential role of innovation in mitigating transition risks, notably in reducing overall mitigation costs to ensure that the necessary pace of emissions reductions can be maintained. Chapter 8 stresses the need to consider the distributional outcomes of climate policies on household income and expenditure and on labour markets, in order to ensure a fair and equitable transition and secure crucial public support. Chapter 9 addresses the importance of aligning financial flows with climate policy and the role of the private sector in driving the net-zero transformation. Chapter 10 considers the critical importance of developing countries in shaping progress on net zero globally.

Part III emphasises that the bifurcation of climate policy into mitigation and adaptation does little to build systemic resilience, again calling for a more holistic approach. Given that severe climate impacts are already happening and projected to intensify, Chapter 11 flags that there are limits to societies' ability to adapt to the impacts of runaway climate change. Chapter 12 points out the interlinkages between mitigation, adaptation, and other environmental concerns such as biodiversity, and the need to better harness synergies between these areas. Chapter 13 addresses the importance of finance for building resilience, while Chapter 14 provides specific examples of what building resilience means across three distinct sectors (cities, food and energy systems).

Finally, Chapter 15 collects key policy recommendations from across the report's three parts, identifying commonalities and interlinkages across policy domains. These recommendations provide practical options for how to integrate systemic resilience across climate-relevant policy areas, lighting the way for policy makers as they navigate the complexities of the climate crisis going forward.

Acknowledgements

This report profited from the support of colleagues throughout the OECD. Drafting was overseen and co-ordinated by the Environment Directorate (ENV), with inputs from colleagues in the Centre for Entrepreneurship, SMEs, Regions and Cities (CFE), Centre for Tax Policy and Administration (CTP), Directorate for Financial and Enterprise Affairs (DAF), Development Co-operation Directorate (DCD), Economics Department (ECO), Directorate for Employment, Labour and Social Affairs (ELS), Directorate for Public Governance (GOV), Public Affairs and Communications Directorate (PAC), Statistics and Data Directorate (SDD), Directorate for Science, Technology and Innovation (STI), Trade and Agriculture Directorate (TAD), Office of the Secretary-General (OSG/SF), International Energy Agency (IEA), and the Nuclear Energy Agency (NEA), as well as external contributors.

The project was overseen by OECD Deputy Secretary-General Kerri-Ann Jones and ENV Director Jo Tyndall, as well as ENV Deputy Director Kumi Kitamori. It was co-ordinated and managed by a core team in ENV comprising Andrew Prag (Team Lead), Stephanie Venuti, Kilian Raiser, Cian Montague, and Amelia Smith.

The main authors of *Net Zero+: Climate and Economic Resilience in a Changing World* were:

Chapters	Authors
I.Chapter 1	**Andrew Prag, Stephanie Venuti, Kilian Raiser, Cian Montague, Amelia Smith**
Chapter 2	**Kilian Raiser**, Coline Pouille, Marcia Rocha
Chapter 3	**Andrew Prag, Kilian Raiser**
Chapter 4	**Kilian Raiser, Amelia Smith**, Dexter Doherty, Trish Lavery, William Hynes
Chapter 5	**Andrew Prag,** Cian Montague, Ben Henderson, Camila Saffirio, Gillian Dorner, Mateo Ledesma Bohorquez, Tadashi Matsumoto
Chapter 6	**Kilian Raiser,** Anasuya Raj, Assia Elgouacem, Elisa Lanzi, Jean Fouré, Kurt van Dender, Rob Dellink
Chapter 7	**Antoine Dechezleprêtre,** Kilian Raiser
Chapter 8	**Cian Montague, Kilian Raiser,** Antoine Dechezleprêtre, Camila Saffirio, Gillian Dorner, Herwig Immervoll, Luca Marcolin, Tobias Kruse
Chapter 9	**Stephanie Venuti,** Benjamin Katz, Benjamin Michel, Catriona Marshall, David Gaukrodger, Iris Mantovani, Jolien Noels, Raphael Jachnik
Chapter 10	**Stephanie Venuti,** Cian Montague, Giorgio Gualberti, Jens Sedemund, Manon Fortemps, Özlem Taskin, Shashwat Koirala
Chapter 11	**Simon Touboul,** Cian Montague
Chapter 12	**Simon Touboul,** Cian Montague
Chapter 13	**Simon Touboul,** Cian Montague, Kilian Raiser, Leigh Wolform, Michael Mullan,
Chapter 14	**Cian Montague,** Jinsun Lim, Koen Deconinck, Mateo Ledesma Bohorquez, Simon Touboul, Tadashi Matsumoto
Chapter 15	**Andrew Prag, Stephanie Venuti, Kilian Raiser, Cian Montague, Amelia Smith**

Many other colleagues provided inputs, comments and suggestions and their contributions are gratefully acknowledged:

- CFE: Tadashi Matsumoto, Mateo Ledesma Bohorquez, Aziza Akhmouch
- CTP: Kurt van Dender, Assia Elgouacem, Anasuya Raj, Jonas Teusch
- DAF: Leigh Wolfrom, Timothy Bishop, Iris Mantovani, David Gaukrodger, Benjamin Katz, Benjamin Michel, Sophia Gnych, Rashad Abelson, Barbara Bijelic, Catriona Marshall
- DCD: Giorgio Gualberti, Jens Sedemund, Manon Fortemps, Özlem Taskin, Shashwat Koirala
- ECO: Alain de Serres, David Turner, Filippo Maria D'Arcangelo, Jean Chateau, Luca Marcolin (former-ELS), Mauro Pisu, Tobias Kruse, William Hynes, Yvan Guillemette
- ELS: Herwig Immervoll, Luca Marcolin, Mark Keese
- ENV: Abenezer Zeleke Aklilu, Beth Del Bourgo, Catherine Gamper, Edward Perry, Elisa Lanzi, Jean Fouré, Jolien Noels, Katia Karousakis, Mark Mateo, Michael Mullan, Mikaël Maes, Nathalie Girouard, Raphael Jachnik, Rob Dellink, Rodrigo Pizarro, Ruben Bibas, Sarah Miet, Shardul Agrawala, Simon Touboul, Susan Gonzalez, Walid Oueslati, William Foster
- GOV: Camila Saffirio, Charles Baubion, Gillian Dorner, Monica Brezzi, Sara Fyson
- PAC: Flora Monsaingeon-Lavuri, Janine Treves
- SDD: Santaro Sakata
- STI: Antoine Dechezlepretre, Chiara Criscuolo, Dirk Pilat, Frida Aulie, Guy Lalanne, Hélène Dernis, Mario Cervantes, Philippe Larrue
- TAD: Ben Henderson, Grégoire Garsous, Guillaume Gruère, Hugo Valin, Julia Nielson, Koen Deconinck, Lee Ann Jackson
- SGE/SF: Dexter Doherty, Duncan Cass-Beggs, Rafal Kierzenkowski, Trish Lavery
- IEA: Christopher McGlade, Jinsun Lim, Paul Hugues, Sara Moarif, Stephanie Bouckaert
- ITF: Stephen Perkins
- NEA: Michel Berthélemy
- external contributors: Ben Trump, Cathal O'Donoghue, Denisa Sologon, Igor Linkov, Jules Linden, Patrick Love

Amelia Smith and Clara Young provided editorial support. Beth Del Bourgo (ENV Communications Manager), Stéphanie Simonin-Edwards, and Willam Foster were essential to the publication and communications process. Thanks also to Andrew Esson, Chelsea Carter, Flora Monsaingeon-Lavuri, Janine Treves, Juliet Lawal, Teresa Trallori, and Yasmine Amrioui.

Former ENV senior management were instrumental in shaping and directing the project, including Anthony Cox, Alain de Serres, Ingrid Barnsley and Rodolfo Lacy, as well as former Deputy Secretary-General Masamichi Kono.

The Net Zero+ project benefits from the expertise and guidance of a High-level External Advisory Panel comprising Amal Lee Amin, Peter Bakker, Sharan Burrow, Vibha Dhawan, Sandrine Dixson-Declève, Ottmar Edenhofer, Zaheer Fakir, Connie Hedegaard, Rachel Kyte, Martin Lees, Mariana Mazzucato, Ann Mettler, Helen Mountford, Nicholas Stern, Hans-Jörn Weddige and Ji Zou, as well as former members Carmen Reinhart and Will Steffen.

The project is overseen by a Committee Leadership Group comprising the chairpersons of all contributing OECD committees, led by the Environment Policy Committee Chair.

The first phase of the Net Zero+ project was generously supported through voluntary contributions from the governments of Germany and Portugal.

Table of contents

FIGURES

TABLES

Executive Summary

The substantial global upheavals of recent years have come at a time of unprecedented urgency for faster action on climate change. Addressing this challenge is the focus of *Net Zero+: Climate and Economic Resilience in a Changing World*. The project draws on the breadth of the OECD's multidisciplinary expertise to present resilience as the backbone of effective, whole-of-government climate policy. *Net Zero+* is about *how* we reach net zero in a rapidly changing world – it is about not only making sure climate policies are as ambitious as they need to be but also resilient in a world of overlapping disruptions. This means building resilience to the impacts of climate change itself, as well as designing policies that fully take into account socio-economic implications and considerations of fairness and equity. This report is the final output of the first phase of this project.

Turbulent times call for a more systemic approach to climate policy making

The climate crisis is more pressing than ever. The threat of crossing climate system tipping points means overshooting 1.5°C of warming will likely result in catastrophic consequences. Avoiding this requires a much faster transformation of economies and systems than has so far been achieved or is projected. Reaching global net-zero emissions by 2050 is not enough by itself: the shape of the pathway to get there will be critical to whether tipping points are triggered or not. Rapid and deep emissions cuts are required already this decade, with a parallel emphasis on improving resilience to climate impacts.

The scale and speed of the net-zero transition will have profound economic and social implications. Designing climate policies with these in mind is key to building economic resilience while ensuring that the net-zero transition is itself resilient. Climate policies are not carried out in isolation, however. The disruptive events of recent years, including the COVID-19 pandemic and the widespread implications of Russia's war of aggression in Ukraine, have highlighted the importance of maintaining a focus on climate priorities while responding to other urgent social and economic needs. These disruptions have also underlined the need to pursue resilience, ensuring that systems can anticipate, absorb, recover and adapt to potential future shocks. Strategic foresight tools and techniques can help to anticipate disruptions, building in buffers to absorb initial impacts and ensuring the capacity to invest in recovery efforts.

An accelerated net-zero transition must be resilient for the long term

A successful net-zero transition needs to combine an increase in the scale and speed of policy action with a focus on resilience. Governments can do more to get the policy basics right in the near-term, including the mix of price-based and other instruments and reform of fossil fuel subsidies. A resilience lens requires an awareness of potential bottlenecks that could slow down or derail the transition, and the development of strategies to anticipate and overcome such challenges. Materials shortages, supply-chain vulnerabilities, skills gaps, rising costs of capital, and clean energy supply are just a few examples where policy action is required to avoid bottlenecks that could pose barriers to accelerated climate action.

One important pre-requisite for a resilient net-zero transition is the long-term sustainability of public finances. Governments need to consider public finance resilience as part of their efforts to develop comprehensive and resilient climate policy frameworks. New OECD modelling carried out for this project shows that different climate policy mixes, and how they interact with the domestic economic structures in different countries, result in highly heterogeneous implications for public finances, and in some cases considerable public finance risks.

Public finances alone are not enough to meet transition needs. Aligning investment and financial markets and getting private sector buy-in is critical but current commitments too often lack credibility. Environmental Social and Governance (ESG) investing could become a conduit for change but is held-back by a lack of standardisation and prevalent greenwashing. In addition to aligning finance and investment flows, businesses outside of the financial sector have an essential role to play in turning climate policy commitments into resilient action across the real economy, and governments' responsible business conduct tools are an important pillar in that regard.

Widespread public support will be essential for a resilient transition. Climate policies have considerable distributional impacts, whether directly (on household incomes and labour markets) or indirectly (on consumption baskets and economic activity), as well as implications for gender equality. Identifying and carefully communicating on distributional outcomes and means to manage these is integral to building support and ensuring a fair and equitable transition. Revenue from carbon pricing can be substantial and used to balance distributional concerns. Similarly, labour market shifts require a careful balance between labour market flexibility and worker protection as well as enhanced assessments of skills needs in order to inform vocational training and education policies.

The net-zero transition cannot be cost-effectively achieved with existing technologies. Technological innovation is an essential pillar of a resilient transition. Current policies focus too much on technology deployment and not enough on research and development. To fully harness innovation potentials, governments will need to do more than just redirect their science, technology and innovation policies, shifting instead towards a mission-oriented approach to technology development and deployment to ensure that efforts are streamlined across policy areas.

Climate change is a global problem requiring globally co-ordinated responses and strong trust internationally. A global response is critically dependent on the ability of developing countries to meet development needs whilst simultaneously decarbonising. Development co-operation has a key role to play in supporting the design of policies that align development priorities with climate objectives.

Building systemic resilience to climate impacts

Some climate impacts are already "baked in" and adaptation efforts will be necessary to avoid losses and damages. Here too, a systemic approach is needed, moving from adapting individual systems components to specific climate risks towards building overall resilience. There are limits to adaptation, however. This reinforces the need to overcome the compartmentalisation of climate policy into adaptation and mitigation. Reducing emissions is essential to minimising climate risks and adaptation to climate impacts are both essential to a resilient transition to net-zero. Synergies between the two abound, also considering other natural systems such as biodiversity. Nature based solutions offer one example of how such synergies can be harnessed to produce cost-effective win-win policy options, but implementation remains sparse.

To meet adaptation needs, finance flows and investments need to be aligned with resilience objectives. Governments can be instrumental in creating an enabling environment for enhanced adaptation spending. The strategic use of grant or concessional finance by multilateral development banks can be highly impactful but will require institutional reforms. The insurance sector, as both a provider of financial protection and major portfolio investor, has a particular role to play in enhancing adaptation efforts, including development of risk assessment tools and providing important risk signals and incentives.

Accelerating action: 12 steps for governments to build climate and economic resilience

1. Faced with threat of **climate tipping points,** do everything possible to limit overshoot beyond 1.5C – faster reductions and shape of the pathway matters.
2. Ensure spending for **crisis relief and economic stimulus** is aligned with climate goals and sufficiently targeted.
3. Make climate strategies as **"future-proofed"** as possible, stress-testing using **strategic foresight techniques** and **anticipating bottlenecks** to the transition: e.g., on public finance, cost-of-capital, energy and materials supply, skills, innovation.
4. Focus policy making on **the systems level**, rather than considering individual components or outcomes, to accelerate transition and improve systemic resilience.
5. Get the **climate policy basics right**, including a mix of price-based and other instruments tailored to **regional, national and local contexts** and greening of public governance.
6. **Mainstream climate change adaptation** throughout national policy processes and exploit synergies between interlinked mitigation and adaptation policy objectives, while minimising trade-offs.
7. Address public finance implications of transition through careful **fiscal planning**, assessing direct and indirect effects of policies, and transition to net-zero aligned **tax instruments.**
8. **Accelerate innovation** through a mission-oriented, outcome-based approach to drive the whole innovation cycle. Target support measures for **early-stage innovation** and R&D.
9. Carefully assess direct and indirect **distributional impacts** of climate policy; consider multiple options for revenue recycling and employ **effective, accurate, clear, and easily accessible communication** with the public about how policies work.
10. Support **new employment patterns** by ensuring reasonable labour market flexibility and mobility while promoting job quality and protecting workers; identify **skills needs and bottlenecks** and prioritise up- or re-skilling.
11. Better **align financial system policies with both climate mitigation and adaptation goals,** including improved market practices, alignment of core investment policies, use of responsible business conduct tools, and harnessing the double role of the insurance sector as both investor and insurance provider.
12. Embed a global approach that recognises the interlinkages between climate and development transitions, drawing on all levers of development co-operation support to converge on a **'common approach' that aligns development and climate objectives.**

1 Net Zero+: Introduction and extended summary

This overview chapter highlights key messages and summarizes relevant findings from each of the reports three substantive parts drawing on the full breadth of the OECD's multidisciplinary expertise, and synthesises policy recommendations for accelerating resilient action on climate change.

Addressing climate change has never been more urgent. The Intergovernmental Panel on Climate Change's Sixth Assessment Report makes it clear that human-induced climate change is under way and accelerating, and that concerted action to rapidly reduce global emissions towards net zero, and to adapt to mounting climate impacts, is imperative.

Climate policies are not designed, nor carried out, in isolation, however. The unprecedented and disruptive events of recent years, including the COVID-19 pandemic and far-reaching implications of Russia's war of aggression in Ukraine, demonstrate the challenge policy makers face today: how to increase momentum on long-term climate priorities while responding to urgent social and economic needs.

This is the focus of ***Net Zero+: Building climate and economic resilience in a changing world***. ***Net Zero+*** collates climate-relevant findings from across the OECD's multidisciplinary expertise – for example on environment, economic and tax policy, financial and fiscal affairs, development, science and technology, and employment and social affairs – to provide cohesive recommendations for making the transition to net zero emissions resilient, and as well as building resilience to the impacts of climate change. As such, the project is a major step forward for the OECD's whole-of-government approach to climate policy.

Figure 1.1. Net Zero+: Climate-relevant policy expertise from across the OECD

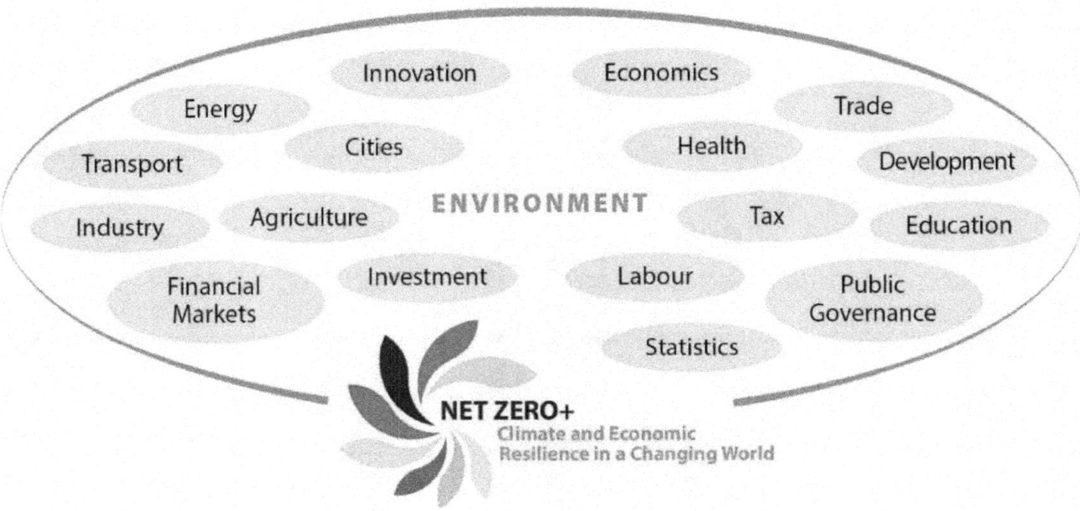

Sounding the alarm: Increased likelihood of crossing climate system tipping points

The urgency of the climate crisis is exemplified by the growing risk of crossing climate system tipping points. At certain levels of warming, these "points of no return" for elements of the global climate system would result in irreversible and potentially abrupt changes to our environment. These could occur in timeframes short enough to defy the ability and capacity of human societies to adapt, leading to widespread and catastrophic impacts.

The latest science shows that climate system tipping points are likely to occur at lower levels of warming than previously thought. Already, at current levels of warming, some tipping points cannot be ruled out (Figure 1.2). This has stark implications for near-term policy making. Action on climate change needs to accelerate fast. It is not just about getting to net zero by a particular date; the shape of the pathway to get there matters hugely for lowering the risks of tipping points. Doing everything possible to limit temperature overshoot beyond 1.5°C is therefore essential to minimising tipping point risks.

Figure 1.2. Warming thresholds at which the crossing of climate system tipping points becomes likely

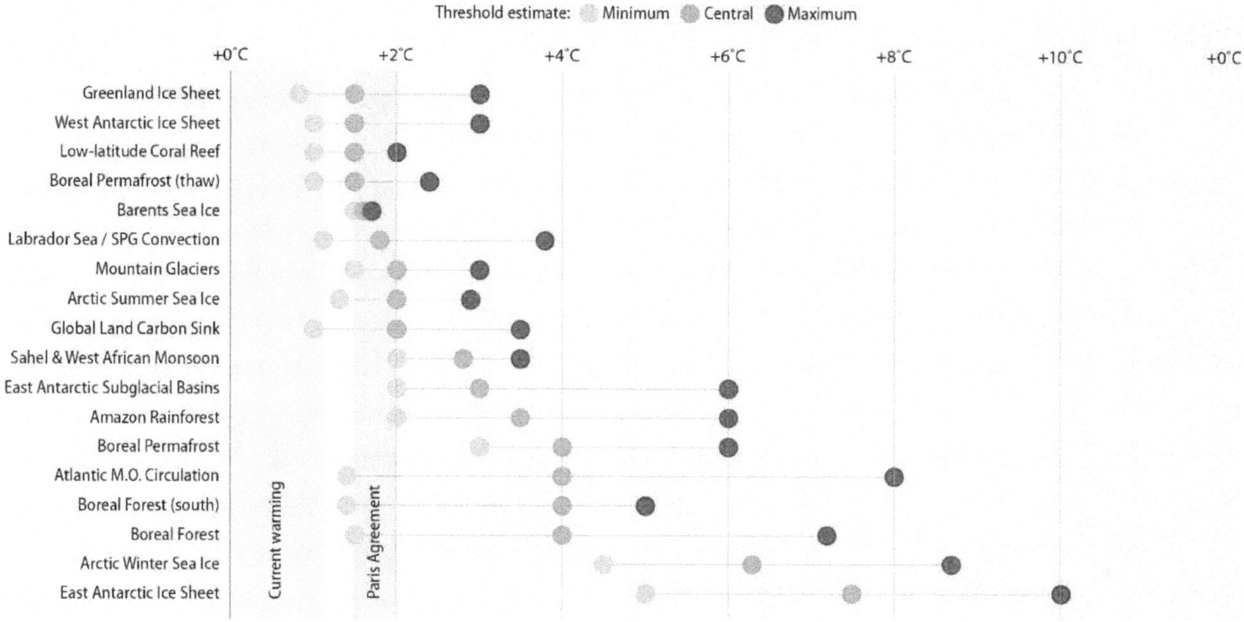

Source: OECD (2022) adapted from (McKay et al., 2022[1]).

Despite recent progress on emissions reductions, the current pace of action is far too slow. A rapid acceleration is needed. At the same time, COVID-19 and the war in Ukraine have demonstrated the social and economic vulnerability of human systems and the threat that socio-economic disruptions can pose to climate policy resilience.

The systemic nature of climate risks and overlapping crises requires a systemic response

Recovery spending following the COVID-19 pandemic presented an opportunity to enhance climate policy efforts, but evidence shows that, in terms of the environment, it has not quite lived up to the promise of "building back better". The OECD Green Recovery Database shows that only around one third of total COVID-19 recovery spending was environmentally friendly, and almost 15% of total recovery spending went towards environmentally harmful activities (OECD, 2022[2]). Efforts across countries to address the immediate social and economic consequences of the war in Ukraine offer a similarly mixed picture. Although a shift in government priorities towards energy security has significantly galvanised efforts to decarbonise the energy sector, short-term measures to secure energy supply and offer households untargeted relief from rising living costs – in the form of price support – risk encouraging and locking in longer-term fossil-fuel use, counteracting the net-zero transition.

In addition, the scale and speed of the net-zero transition itself will have profound economic implications on public finances, labour markets and income distribution. Meanwhile, the world grapples with other pressing mega-trends such as a rapidly changing labour market, aging societies, digital transformation of economies and of course environmental impacts related to climate change, biodiversity loss, degrading ocean health and others, and the potential for tipping points within these, all of which will come with their own challenges and opportunities. Designing climate policies with all these implications in mind is key to building economic resilience while also ensuring the resilience and durability of the net-zero transition.

While climate impacts can be foreseen to some degree, the extent of overlap and interaction with other global changes is less clear. This calls for a "resilient by design" systems approach – seeking to be prepared for, and to respond to, multiple disruptions without knowing their exact nature. This requires foresight tools and techniques to help anticipate future shocks, building in buffers to absorb initial impacts and ensuring the availability of resources to invest in recovery efforts. It also requires acknowledgment that some changes may be irreversible and require permanent adaptation to new circumstances.

Figure 1.3. What is systemic resilience?

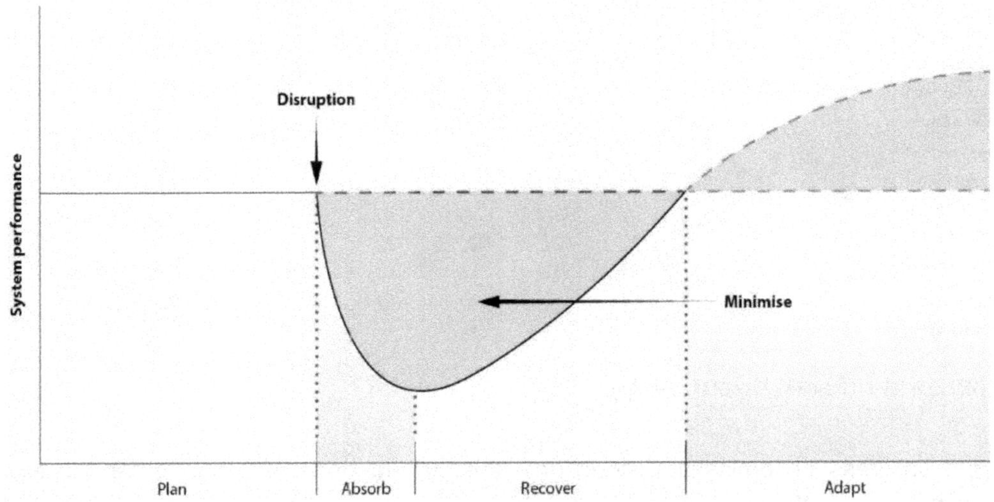

Source: (OECD, 2020[3]).

Despite recent progress, climate change is not yet sufficiently mainstreamed into core economic policy. Mitigation and adaptation remain largely compartmentalised from each other and are dealt with separately from other environmental challenges such as biodiversity. A systemic approach to resilience requires breaking down these silos, and identifying interactions and joint opportunities, for example across climate change mitigation, adaptation and tackling biodiversity loss.

Box 1.1. Policy recommendations: Responding to increasing climate risks amidst concurrent global crises

- **Act now to avoid potential catastrophic impacts from climate system tipping points (Chapter 2)**
  - Take all possible measures to limit global warming to 1.5°C with limited or no overshoot.
  - Strengthen Nationally Determined Contributions (NDCs) before 2025, prioritising accelerated emissions reductions now.
  - Prepare for the possibility of climate system tipping points being triggered even if 1.5°C is achieved.
  - Enhance monitoring and early warning systems and modelling of likely impacts. Consistently review and evaluate implemented policies.
- **Make climate action resilient in the face of unpredictable and overlapping global disruptions (Chapter 3)**

- Ensure that spending for crisis relief and economic stimulus is aligned with, rather than acting in opposition to, climate goals.
- **Make climate strategies as "future-proofed" as possible (Chapter 4)**
  - Focus policy making on system-wide alignment with climate goals rather than individual components or outcomes.
  - Look beyond short-term efficiency in order to better absorb future shocks and limit the need for emergency intervention.
  - Stress test net-zero strategies through tools such as strategic foresight.

Mitigation, no matter what: A resilient net-zero transition

A resilient net-zero transition necessitates a fair and globally co-ordinated response, with policy approaches tailored to differing national circumstances, and including financial and non-financial support to developing countries.

Governments first need to get the policy basics right. This means establishing clear long-term policy frameworks, setting overarching goals and interim targets that align with these, and ensuring regular monitoring and review of progress. It also means considering the full range of climate policy instruments and tailoring the policy mix to national circumstances, including phasing out fossil-fuel subsidies.

These policy basics can be supported by public governance tools such as employing "green budgeting" to better orient public expenditure towards the transition and using public procurement to drive demand for green products and services. A successful transition requires a genuinely "whole of government" approach, and institutions at the centre of government can play a key role in co-ordinating and aligning policies across departments. Subnational governments are equally important and are often the driving force behind implementing specific policy instruments on the ground.

A resilient net-zero transition requires more than just increasing the scale and speed of policy action, but also an awareness of potential bottlenecks that could slow down or derail the transition, and the development of strategies to anticipate and overcome such challenges. Materials shortages, supply-chain vulnerabilities, skills gaps, lengthy permitting processes and rising costs of capital are just some areas where potential bottlenecks could slow down climate action. As just one example, the transition towards net-zero emissions needs a reliable supply of critical materials, which are currently highly concentrated geographically, not only in terms of their origin but also in processing and production (Figure 1.4) Governments therefore need to encourage increased diversity of supply chains, particularly considering lessons learned from the energy crisis induced by the war in Ukraine.

Figure 1.4. Regional shares of global production of selected critical materials, 2021

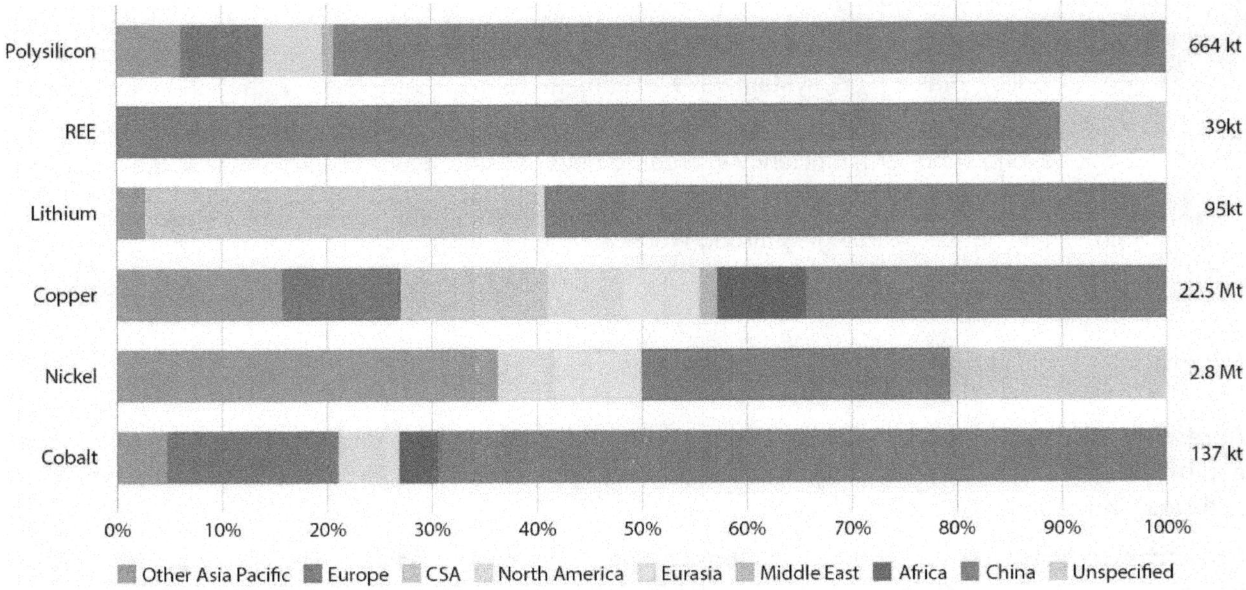

Source: (IEA, 2023[4]).

Public finance risks cannot be overlooked

The net-zero transition will cause significant shifts in economic activity and require substantial mobilisation of public resources. It is therefore imperative to consider the longer-term financial implications of different climate policy approaches. Recent crises have further underlined the importance of public finances to enable economic recovery and leverage private investment, but the large fiscal deficits incurred in the last few years cannot be sustained over coming decades.

New OECD modelling of the public finance implications of a transition to net zero shows that the interaction between different climate policy mixes and domestic economic structures results in highly heterogeneous implications for public finances. While some policy measures increase public revenue over time, others decrease it. Overall, public revenues in the modelled scenario decrease by amounts equal to between 0.7 and 3.4% of GDP (Figure 1.5). This implies that governments will need to find alternative sources of revenue to make up for changes in the fiscal base due to the transition. For instance, if mitigation policy is designed to be growth-enhancing, new revenues could compensate for the erosion of tax bases. Differences due to varying policy tools, as well as across regions, underline the role of careful fiscal planning as part of climate policy design. The modelling also highlights the importance of taking interactions between policies, and their potential indirect effects on public revenues, into account.

Figure 1.5. Changes in net public revenues in a net-zero scenario range from -0.7% to -3.4% of baseline GDP in 2050, depending on the region

Changes in net public revenues compared to baseline in 2050 (% of baseline GDP)

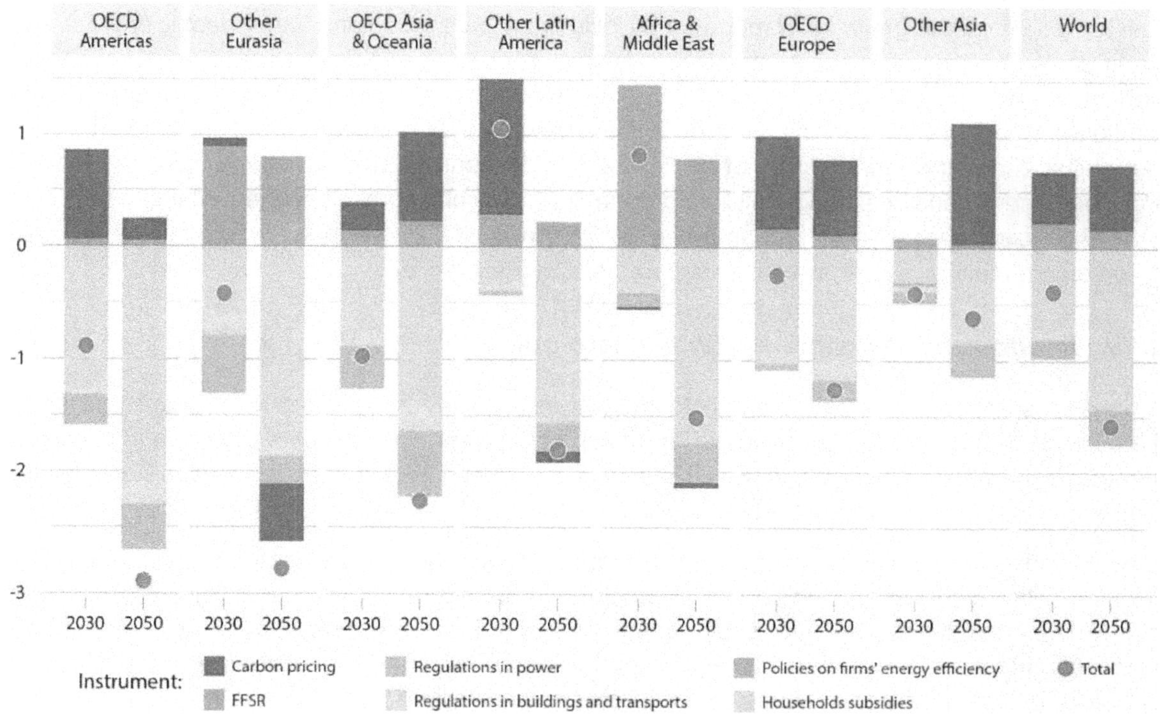

Note: Note: The black diamonds correspond to the full Net-Zero Ambition scenario, which implements the policy instruments altogether. It differs from the sum of the effects of individual policy instruments depicted in the bars due to interactions between the different policy instruments. FFFR=fossil fuel subsidy reform.
Source: OECD ENV-Linkages model.

Mission-driven innovation is essential

According to the International Energy Agency's Net-Zero Emissions by 2050 Scenario, half of the global reductions in energy-related CO_2 emissions through 2050 will need to come from technologies that are not yet fully commercialised (IEA, 2021[5]). Yet recent trends indicate that innovation is not keeping pace. Low-carbon technology patents are declining while trademarks increase, implying that new innovations are slowing as more mature technologies come onto the market. Similarly, venture capital investments in climate-relevant technologies focus predominantly on early and late-stage technologies rather than seed money critical to supporting innovation efforts. Analysis shows that current policy portfolios put too much emphasis on deployment and not enough on research and development.

To reverse these trends, governments need to reorient policies towards research and development and take a mission-oriented approach to drive outcomes across the whole innovation chain, also considering the effects that core climate policies such as carbon pricing and standard setting can have on innovation.

A successful net-zero transition will be fair, equitable and publicly supported

Achieving net zero by 2050 requires important changes across society and the economy, predicated on the actions and attitudes of governments and citizens. Ensuring that the transition is effective, fair and equitable will maintain strong and widespread public support for ambitious action, a key prerequisite for resilient policies. For governments, this means implementing policies that make credible progress towards environmental objectives; ensuring trust in government itself; addressing and communicating the distributional effects of climate policies and of climate impacts; and assessing and acting on the labour market shifts induced by these policies.

The impacts of climate policies on people are widespread and complex, with implications for gender inequality, and intersecting with other megatrends including digitalisation and demographic change, as well as the impacts of climate change themselves. Climate policies have indirect as well as direct effects on household income. These can be similar in magnitude, but the indirect effects are often overlooked in distributional assessments. Regional heterogeneity is also an important consideration. In terms of labour market shifts, a better understanding of skills needs in the transition is essential, including identifying potential bottlenecks and designing reskilling programmes to avoid them. Reasonably flexible employment and social policies, based on careful analysis, will play a critical role in both facilitating the low-carbon transition and in maintaining strong public support for climate action.

Aligning finance and investment with net zero goals

Public finances alone will not be enough to meet transition needs. Aligning investment and financial markets and securing private sector buy-in is critical, but current commitments too often lack credibility. Environment, Social and Governance (ESG) investing could become a conduit for change but is held back by a lack of standardisation and evidence of greenwashing.

Businesses have a key role in scaling up climate ambition and implementing net-zero transitions, channelling policy commitments and related finance and investment into aligned activities across the real economy. The contribution of private-sector commitments to a resilient transition relies on commitments being implemented with environmental integrity, avoiding greenwashing and safeguarding against adverse impacts across other areas of business' operations or responsibilities.

The need for a global response

Given the global nature of climate change and highly interconnected economies, a resilient and durable transition to net-zero requires a global response. Developing countries – both the source of the majority of future emissions and most exposed to future impacts of climate change – will require international support to meet development needs while decarbonising their economies and building resilience to climate impacts, as captured in IPAC data (Figure 1.6). This implies international co-operation at several levels, which is of increasing importance in the current context of heightened international tensions.

Figure 1.6. Per-capita emissions have fallen in the OECD but are increasing in non-OECD countries

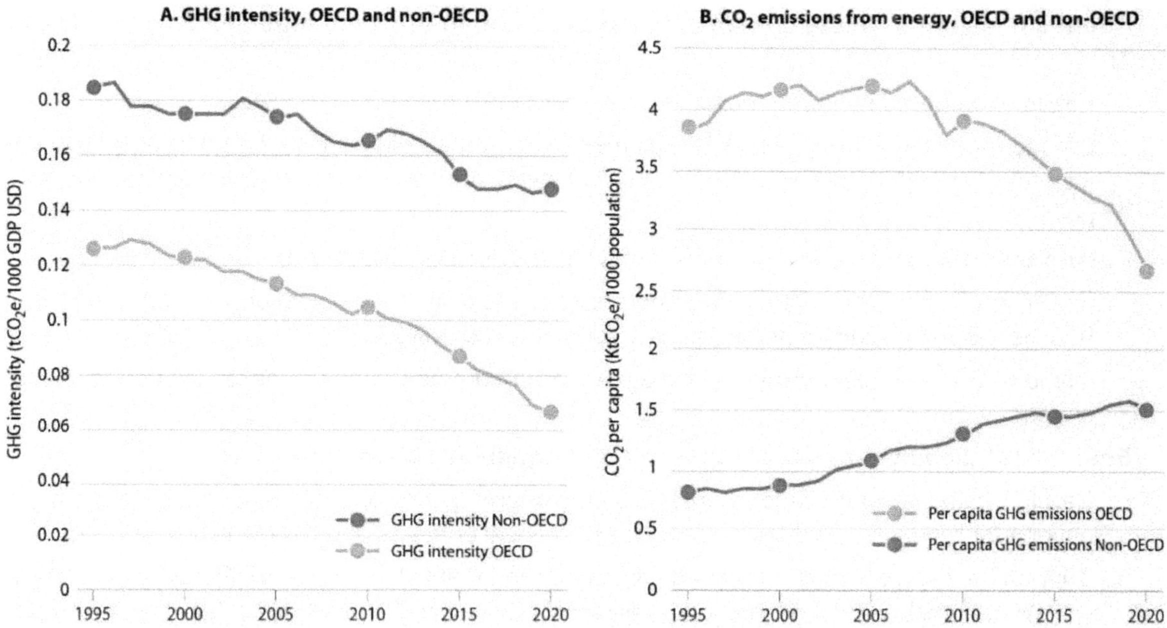

Note: The underlying GDP data used for this chart stems from (OECD, 2023[6]); the underlying CO2 emissions data stems from (IEA, 2022[7])..
Source: (IEA, 2022[6]).

The UNFCCC process remains central and delivered important agreements at the COP26 and COP27 climate conferences in 2021 and 2022, covering mitigation, adaptation, finance, and loss and damage. Beyond multilateralism, strategic partnerships to ensure necessary support to developing countries, including just transition partnerships, and to diversify clean energy supply chains, remain crucial. Development assistance can play an essential role here, but is currently not sufficiently aligned with climate objectives. Moreover, developing countries continue to face much higher capital costs for low-carbon technology investments. Overcoming this barrier is paramount to climate policy success. The OECD's Inclusive Forum on Carbon Mitigation Approaches (IFCMA) can also play a key role to improve trust and transparency in countries' policy approaches.

Box 1.2. Policy recommendations: Safeguarding the resilience of the net-zero transition

- **Get policy basics right**
  - Consider the full range of policy tools, including price-based and non-priced-based instruments, including reforming fossil-fuel subsidies, tailoring climate policy mixes to regional, national and local circumstances.
  - Integrate climate policy making across all of government, making use of public governance tools such as "green budgeting" and including sub-national institutions and governments to foster implementation.
- **Identify and address potential bottlenecks to the net-zero transition (Chapter 5)**
- **Address public finance implications (Chapter 6)**
  - Employ careful fiscal planning to ensure the resilience of public finances in the net-zero transition, taking the direct and indirect effects of policy instruments into account.

- Plan for the gradual introduction of new tax instruments designed to maintain fiscal resilience during the transition, such as distance-based vehicle charges.

- **Adopt a mission-oriented, outcome-based approach to drive the innovation cycle (Chapter 7)**
  - Focus on targeted support measures for early-stage innovation and R&D.
  - Embed innovation policy within complementary climate policies including carbon pricing and technology support and standards and implement related education and skills development policies.
- **Ensure that the net-zero transition is publicly supported (Chapter 8)**
  - Prioritise effective, accurate, clear, and easily accessible communication with the public about how policies work and what their distributional impacts will be.
  - Combat dis- and mis-information by agreeing on common data standards to monitor climate change.
- **Ensure that the net-zero transition is fair and equitable (Chapter 8)**
  - Carefully assess direct and indirect distributional impacts of climate and consider multiple options for revenue recycling, tailoring these to local contexts and clearly communicating.
  - Support new employment patterns by ensuring reasonable labour market flexibility and mobility while simultaneously promoting job quality and protecting workers from unfair practices.
  - Identify skills needs and bottlenecks through long-term planning and prioritise up- or re-skilling workers to meet such needs through targeted support.
- **Align finance and private sector action with climate mitigation goals (Chapter 9)**
  - Prioritise further research, improved data collection, and strengthened co-ordination to support better climate alignment of finance.
  - Harness market practices such as ESG investing to accelerate the mobilisation and reallocation of capital towards net zero-aligned investments and ensure that both FDI and investment treaty policies are aligned with climate objectives.
  - Recognise and address the barrier presented by rising costs of capital to low-carbon investments.
  - Leverage responsible business conduct tools and due diligence guidance to drive private sector-led climate action.
- **Leverage the interlinkages between climate action and development (Chapter 10)**
  - Draw on all levers of development co-operation to develop a 'global approach' that aligns climate and development objectives.

Building systemic resilience to unavoidable climate impacts

Some climate impacts are already "baked in". In 2021 alone, the global direct costs of extreme climate-related events were estimated at EUR 265 billion (Munich Re, 2022[7]), and IPAC data highlights observable changes (Figure 1.7).

Figure 1.7. Mean annual change in the number of unusually warm days over the period 1979-2021

Mean annual change in the number of unusually warm days over the period 1979-2021 where (a) Tmax> 95thpercentile and (b) Tmin< 5thpercentile of the reference period (1981-2010)

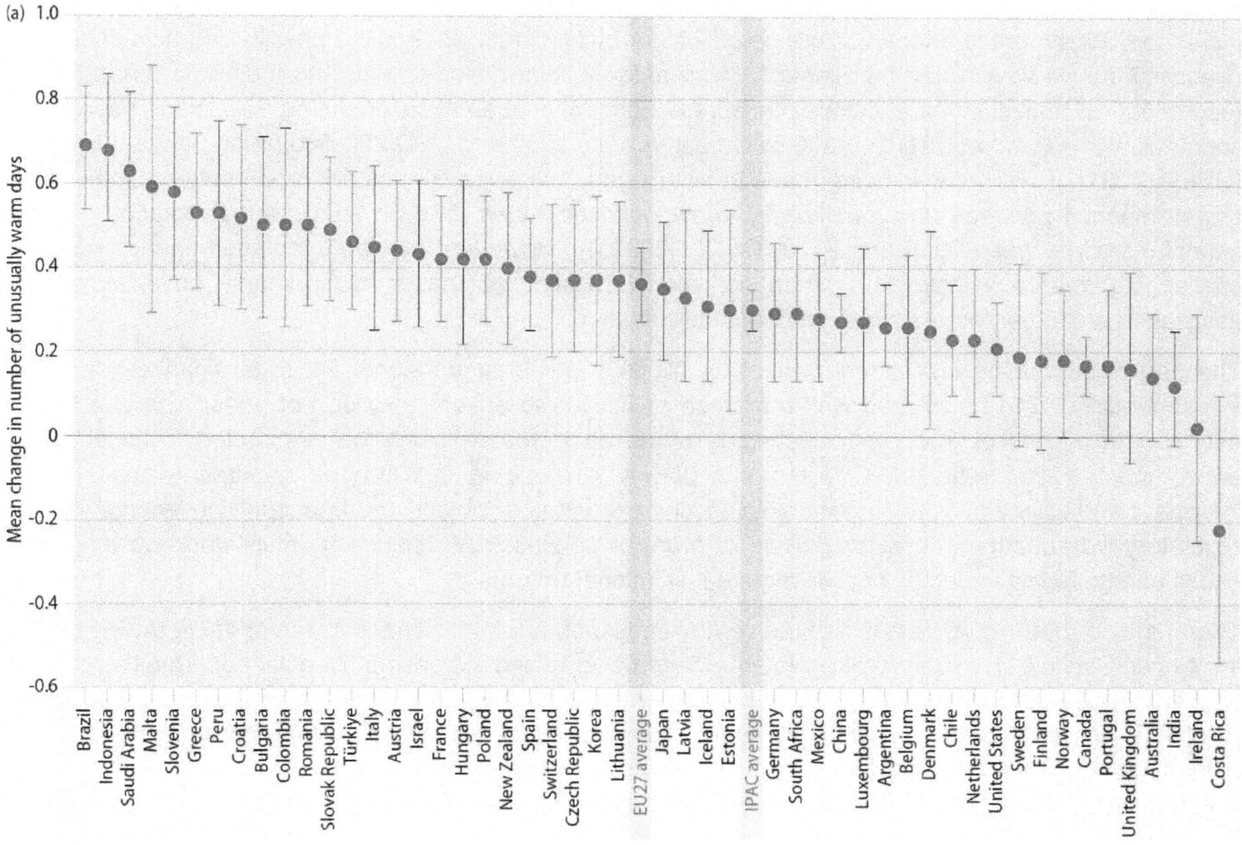

Source: (Maes et al., 2022[8]).

Increased adaptation efforts will be necessary to limit losses and damages resulting from climate change impacts. Here too, a systemic approach is needed, shifting from responses to specific climate risks in favour of building overall resilience. This requires continuous and thorough assessment of hazard, exposure and vulnerability risks, taking regional circumstances into account. Adaptation efforts and overarching governance frameworks must be proactive and dynamic.

There are limits to adaptation, however. The threat of climate tipping points reinforces the urgent need for mitigation. Synergies between the two abound, and there is a clear need to overcome the division of climate policy between adaptation and mitigation. For example, efforts to restore forests or mangroves create an opportunity to increase ecosystems' carbon storage capacity, while also contributing to the reduction of weather-related risks, such as landslides or coastal storm surges.

There are also important linkages between climate action and other environmental crises such as biodiversity loss. Marine and terrestrial ecosystems are natural carbon sinks, with an annual gross sequestration equivalent to about 60% of global anthropogenic emissions (IPBES, 2019[9]). Conserving, restoring and improving the management of forests, grasslands, wetlands and agricultural lands, could deliver an estimated 23.8 gigatonnes of cumulative CO_2 emission reductions by 2030 (OECD, 2021[10]). Nature-based solutions offer one example of how such synergies can be harnessed to produce cost-effective win-win policy options, but implementation remains minimal due to a lack of awareness regarding their effectiveness, challenges in quantifying costs and benefits, and their omission from climate policy taxonomies and legal structures.

Aligning finance and investment with building resilience

Increased investment in adaptation will be critical for building resilience to the physical impacts of climate change. Finance flows must be aligned with climate-resilient development, and mobilised as additional resources for necessary adaptation measures. Estimated adaptation financing needs for developing countries alone stand at USD 140-300 billion per year by 2030 and USD 280-500 billion per year by 2050 (UNEP, 2021[11]). Progress is being made to fill this gap. Mitigation finance still represents the majority of climate finance provided and mobilised by developed countries (58% in 2020), but adaptation finance almost tripled between 2016 and 2020 (OECD, 2022[12]). However, tracking adaptation finance remains challenging due to a lack of common definitions. Existing estimates rely primarily on development assistance and other forms of international public finance.

The gap in adaptation investment cannot be filled by public funds alone. Thus, all finance flows and investments need to be aligned with resilience objectives to ensure they do not undermine adaptation efforts. The trillions of euros in investments made each year will only be re-directed if the enabling environment is strengthened. Governments play a key role in this through generating and sharing information on climate risks, communicating clear adaptation objectives, and applying economic and regulatory instruments. The strategic use of grant or concessional finance by multilateral development banks can be highly impactful but will require institutional reforms.

There is also growing interest in climate resilience issues within the financial sector itself, driven by the increasingly visible costs of climate-related extreme events and increasing financial opportunities offered by a changing climate. The insurance sector, in particular, has a unique role to play in building resilience to climate impacts, acting as both investor and provider of protection. Governments' role includes mandating adequate climate risk monitoring in the insurance sector and reviewing regulation that impedes insurers' ability to set risk-reflective premiums. With increasing global temperatures and mounting impacts, the global risk landscape is changing and incentives to invest in adaptation are rising. In order to harness this interest, investors themselves will need to demonstrate demand for adaptation-aligned investment opportunities and articulate frameworks and minimum standards for what information they require from investees. Several initiatives are under way, but challenges around the measurement of financial flows and collection of data persist.

Box 1.3. Policy recommendations: Building systemic resilience to climate impacts

- **Assess climate impacts and adaptation needs (Chapter 11)**
  - Continue mainstreaming climate change adaptation throughout national policy processes. Establish comprehensive adaptation planning and careful monitoring and review of implemented policies.
  - Develop appropriate measurement tools. Make and regularly update hazard, exposure and vulnerability assessments.
- **Apply a systems approach (Chapter 12)**
  - Conduct careful analysis to exploit synergies and minimise trade-offs between interlinked mitigation and adaptation policy objectives, and between climate and other environmental objectives.
  - Identify opportunities for, implement, and monitor nature-based solutions (NbS) to foster adaptation-mitigation synergies.

- Take a systems-level view of climate resilience in key systems. For example, beyond providing incentives and education for farm-level adaptation, assess and act on vulnerabilities across the entire food system.

- **Financing adaptation in a world of rising risks (Chapter 13)**
  - Scale up funding for the wide range of adaptation measures needed to respond to the impacts of climate change.
  - Support the alignment of financial flows with adaptation needs.
  - Consider the role of government in harnessing the double role of the insurance sector as both investor and insurance provider, for example through regulation of climate-risk assessment.

Box 1.4. Development and structure of the OECD Horizontal Project on Climate and Economic Resilience

OECD horizontal projects take full advantage of the OECD's multidisciplinary expertise by engaging multiple committees to work on topics that cut across policy areas.

Guided by cross-OECD governance and co-ordination structures, in addition to an external high level Expert Advisory Panel[1], and overseen by the OECD Environment Policy Committee, *Net Zero+* is a key example of the OECD's organisation-wide response to climate action in practice.

The *Net Zero+* synthesis report brings together work carried out under the first phase of the OECD's horizontal project on climate and economic resilience, launched by OECD Council in 2021.

The project's first phase, carried out over (2021 and 2022) was structured around four modules.

- Module 1: framing climate and economic resilience post-COVID-19.
- Module 2: accelerating the transition to net-zero emissions and making it resilient.
- Module 3: building systemic resilience to impacts of climate change.
- Module 4: initial phase of the International Programme for Action on Climate (IPAC).[2]

The project's second phase will take place over 2023-24. Phase 2 will continue to focus on climate and economic resilience, covering both resilience of the net-zero transition and building resilience to climate impacts. In addition, a new work area has begun with a focus on enabling transitions and supporting governments in identifying and removing barriers that prevent faster climate action. In parallel, the IPAC programme will continue to develop data and indicators for tracking progress. Overall, the work will embrace a number of cross-cutting themes including implications for gender equality, representing the perspectives of developing countries and focusing on capacity building of policy makers and government capabilities.

Reaching net zero in a rapidly changing world

Climate policy makers today face conflicting and competing needs for immediate and accelerated climate action at the same time as they must respond to social and economic crises, upended global markets and value/supply chains, geopolitical tensions, and a slow economic recovery. The Net Zero+ project and report speak to these tensions and offer a way through them.

Net Zero+ is about **how** we reach net zero in a rapidly changing world – it is about making sure climate policies are both ambitious and resilient in a world of overlapping disruptions. This means building resilience to the impacts of climate change itself, and designing policies that fully take socio-economic implications and considerations of fairness and equity into account.

The task is momentous and the stakes could not be higher – but through bold and deliberate policy making a resilient net-zero future is possible.

Notes

1 See list of panel members at https://www.oecd.org/climate-change/net-zero-resilience/

2 IPAC provides governments with comparable and comprehensive datasets, annual evaluation of action and best practices on progress towards the transition to net-zero emissions. While IPAC has delivered its own set of deliverables, IPAC data and indicators underpin the analysis in the wider project. See https://www.oecd.org/climate-action/ipac/

References

IEA (2023), *Energy Technology Perspectives 2023*. [4]

IEA (2022), *Greenhouse Gas Emissions from Energy*. [6]

IEA (2021), *Net Zero by 2050: A Roadmap for the Global Energy Sector*, OECD Publishing, Paris, https://doi.org/10.1787/c8328405-en. [5]

IPBES (2019), *Global assessment report on biodiversity and ecosystem services of the Intergovernmental Science-Policy Platform on Biodiversity and Ecosystem Services*, https://doi.org/10.5281/zenodo.6417333. [9]

Maes, M. et al. (2022), "Monitoring exposure to climate-related hazards: Indicator methodology and key results", *OECD Environment Working Papers*, No. 201, OECD Publishing, Paris, https://doi.org/10.1787/da074cb6-en. [8]

McKay, A. et al. (2022), "Exceeding 1.5°C global warming could trigger multiple climate tipping points", *Science*, Vol. 377/6611, https://doi.org/10.1126/science.abn7950. [1]

Munich Re (2022), *Hurricanes, cold waves, tornadoes: Weather disasters in USA dominate natural disaster losses in 2021*, https://www.munichre.com/en/company/media-relations/media-information-and-corporate-news/media-information/2022/natural-disaster-losses-2021.html. [7]

OECD (2023), "Labour Force Statistics: Population and vital statistics", *OECD Employment and Labour Market Statistics* (database), https://doi.org/10.1787/data-00287-en (accessed on 3 February 2023). [13]

OECD (2022), *Aggregate Trends of Climate Finance Provided and Mobilised by Developed Countries in 2013-2020*, Climate Finance and the USD 100 Billion Goal, OECD Publishing, Paris, https://doi.org/10.1787/d28f963c-en. [12]

OECD (2022), "Assessing environmental impact of measures in the OECD Green Recovery Database", *OECD Policy Responses to Coronavirus (COVID-19)*, OECD Publishing, Paris, https://doi.org/10.1787/3f7e2670-en. [2]

OECD (2021), "Biodiversity, natural capital and the economy: A policy guide for finance, economic and environment ministers", *OECD Environment Policy Papers*, No. 26, OECD Publishing, Paris, https://doi.org/10.1787/1a1ae114-en. [10]

OECD (2020), *A Systemic Resilience Approach to dealing with Covid-19 and future shocks*, New Approaches to Economic Challenges, Paris, https://read.oecd-ilibrary.org/view/?ref=131_131917-kpfefrdfnx&title=A-Systemic-Resilience-Approach-to-dealing-with-Covid-19-and-future-shocks (accessed on 26 July 2022). [3]

UNEP (2021), *Adaptation Gap Report 2021 The Gathering Storm - Adapting to Climate Change in a Post-pandemic World*. [11]

Part I Climate policy making in a volatile world

2 Climate system tipping points and the need for urgent climate action

Emerging evidence on the potential crossing of climate systems "tipping points" at lower levels of warming than previously thought makes clear that immediate and accelerated emissions reductions are needed to avoid potentially catastrophic climate impacts. This chapter reviews the latest scientific evidence, providing an overview of major climate tipping points, their projected impacts if crossed, and the warming thresholds at which this becomes likely. It also considers policy options for managing tipping point risks: while efforts to keep global warming to 1.5°C with minimal overshoot are paramount, some tipping points may be crossed at lower warming thresholds and so transformational adaptation may also be necessary.

This chapter draws on contributions to the Horizontal Project carried out under the responsibility of the Environment Policy Committee.

The Intergovernmental Panel on Climate Change (IPCC) delivered a stark warning of the extreme urgency of the climate challenge in its Sixth Assessment Report, projecting that severe climate impacts could occur in many regions of the world at lower levels of warming than previously thought (IPCC, 2021[1]). Climate change will lead to an increased frequency and intensity of extreme weather events as well as "slow onset" effects such as sea-level rise and changes in precipitation. A less well-understood impact of climate change are "tipping points" in the climate system and the potential for the thresholds of these critical points to be crossed.

What are climate system tipping points and how soon could they occur?

Overview and evolution of the scientific understanding of tipping points

The IPCC defines a tipping point as "a critical threshold beyond which a system reorganises, often abruptly and/or irreversibly". A tipping element is "a component of the Earth system that is susceptible to a tipping point" (Chen et al., 2021[2]). Climate system tipping points may lead the global or regional climate to change from one stable state to another, or result in changes that occur non-linearly and faster than the rate of change expected from climate forcing (Alley et al., 2003[3]; Lee, 2021[4]).[1] Such abrupt and/or irreversible changes are particularly dangerous because they can occur in timeframes short enough to defy the ability and capacity of human societies to adapt. As such, the impacts of crossing climate tipping point thresholds would be severe and widespread, with potentially catastrophic consequences for human and natural systems.

Tipping elements have been identified in three types of climate sub-systems: the cryosphere (ice bodies); circulations of the oceans and the atmosphere (circulation patterns); and the biosphere. Key examples include the collapse of the West Antarctic and Greenland ice sheets and the melting of the Arctic permafrost (cryosphere); the slowdown or collapse of the Atlantic Meridional Overturning Circulation (circulation patterns); and the dieback of the Amazon rainforest and destruction of coral reefs (biosphere). (For more detail on major tipping elements see Box 2.1.)

Figure 2.1. Candidate tipping elements in climate subsystems

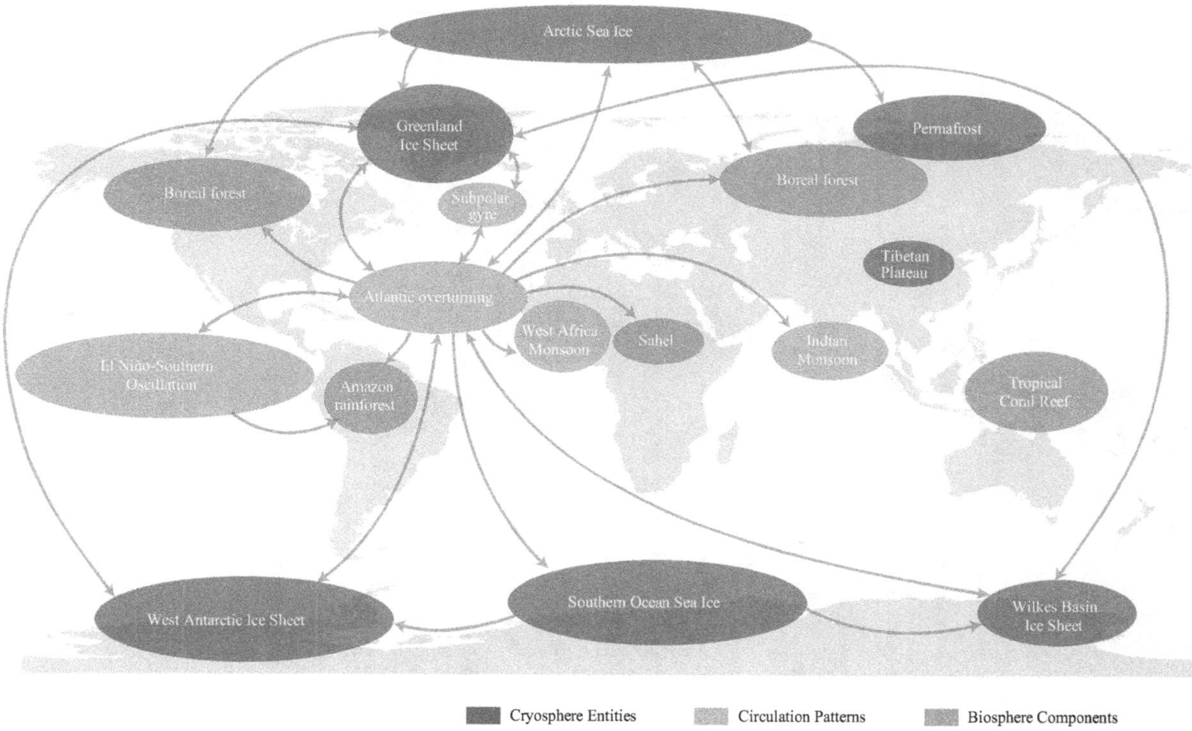

Note: Arrows show potential interactions among the tipping elements that could generate tipping cascades, based on expert elicitation.
Source: (OECD, 2021[5]) (Kriegler et al., 2009[6]; Cai, Lenton and Lontzek, 2016[7]; Wunderling et al., 2021[8]).

The issue of climate tipping points was first introduced by the IPCC over two decades ago, when they were projected to possibly occur in "the next few centuries if greenhouse gas concentrations continue to increase" (IPCC, 2001[9]). More recent IPCC reports recognise the risk of crossing tipping point thresholds at much lower levels of warming and therefore within considerably shorter timescales (IPCC, 2018[10]; IPCC, 2019[11]). Indeed, the latest IPCC report recognises that the possibility of crossing the thresholds of climate tipping points cannot be ruled out this century and must be an integral part of risk management strategies (IPCC, 2021[1]).

A recent synthesis of the most up-to-date evidence on tipping points shows that current global warming of ~1.1°C could already be within the lower end of the uncertainty range of five climate system tipping points, including the collapse of the Greenland and West Antarctic ice sheets, die-off of low-latitude coral reefs, and widespread abrupt permafrost thaw (McKay et al., 2022[12]). This means that crossing the thresholds of these tipping points is already "possible" (Ibid). The same study shows that within the Paris Agreement range of 1.5 to < 2°C warming, these climate tipping points and two others (abrupt Barents Sea ice loss and Labrador-Irminger Seas/SPG convection collapse) become "likely". While not yet scientific consensus, these findings challenge the previously well-accepted assumption that climate system tipping points are low likelihood outcomes (OECD, 2022[13]).

To restate: the most recent findings thus suggest that the thresholds of many climate tipping points could be crossed with a considerably higher probability and at much lower levels of warming than previously thought. Scientific advances increasingly and systematically point to the potentially catastrophic impacts of continued warming, with evidence that irreversible tipping elements in Earth systems could already be triggered this century. This will have long-lasting effects over a timeframe of centuries to millennia (Lee, 2021[4]).

Figure 2.2. Global warming threshold estimates for global core and regional impact climate tipping elements

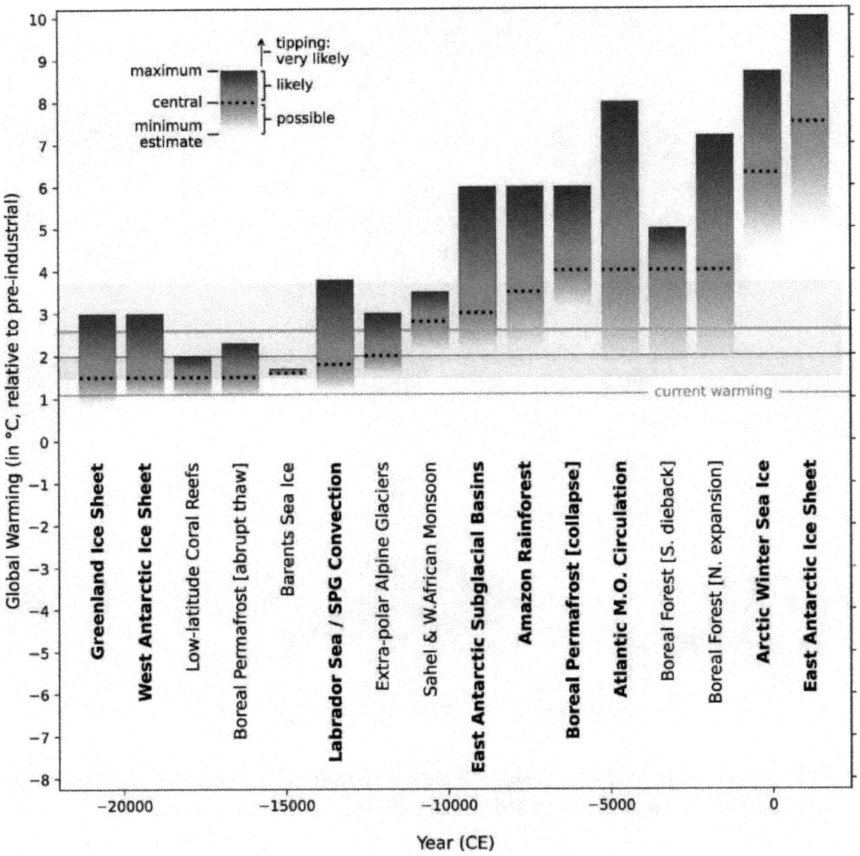

Note: Shadowed in green is the 1.5°C-2°C Paris Agreement range of warming. The shadowed area in grey shows the estimated 21st-century warming under current policies (horizontal line shows central estimates). Bars show the minimum (base, yellow); central (line, red); and maximum (top, dark red) threshold estimates for each tipping element (bold font, global; regular font, regional).
Source: (McKay et al., 2022[12]).

Figure 2.1 and Table 2.1 show the temperature range at which a number of tipping elements may be triggered – that is, ranges of temperature within which change in these tipping elements is strong enough to self-propel them.[2] Despite significant scientific advances in reducing these ranges over past decades, uncertainty remains. Considering that larger uncertainties can potentially lead to a larger range of potential climate risks, they should amplify – not weaken – the case for strong climate action (OECD, 2021[5]).

Table 2.1. Temperature thresholds and uncertainty ranges of tipping points

Impact scale	Type	Tipping point	Temperature threshold (°C)		Potential for Abrupt Change?	Irreversibility if forcing reversed
			Central estimate	Range		
Global	Cryosphere	Greenland Ice Sheet collapse	1.5°C	0.8 - 3°C	No (high confidence)	Irreversible for millennia (high confidence)
Global	Cryosphere	West Antarctic Ice Sheet collapse	1.5°C	1 - 3°C	Yes (high confidence)	Irreversible for decades to millennia (high confidence)
Global	Ocean-atmospheric circulation	Labrador-Irminger Seas / SPG Convection collapse	1.8°C	1.1 - 3.8°C		
Global	Cryosphere	East Antarctic Subglacial	3°C	2 - 6°C		

Impact scale	Type	Tipping point	Temperature threshold (°C)		Potential for Abrupt Change?	Irreversibility if forcing reversed
			Central estimate	Range		
		Basins collapse				
Global	Biosphere	Amazon rainforest dieback	3.5°C	2 - 6°C	Yes (low confidence)	Irreversible for multidecades (medium confidence)
Global	Cryosphere	Boreal Permafrost collapse	4°C	3 - 6°C	Yes (high confidence)	Irreversible for centuries (high confidence)
Global	Ocean-atmospheric circulation	AMOC collapse	4°C	1.4 - 8°C	Yes (medium confidence)	Reversible within centuries (high confidence)
Global	Cryosphere	Arctic Winter Sea Ice collapse	6.3°C	4.5 - 8.7°C	Yes (high confidence)	Reversible within years to decades (high confidence)
Global	Cryosphere	East Antarctic Ice Sheet collapse	7.5°C	5 - 10°C		
Regional	Biosphere	Low-latitude coral reefs die-off	1.5°C	1 - 2°C		
Regional	Cryosphere	Boreal Permafrost abrupt thaw	1.5°C	1 - 2.3°C		
Regional	Cryosphere	Barents Sea Ice abrupt loss	1.6°C	1.5 - 1.7°C		
Regional	Cryosphere	Mountain Glaciers loss	2°C	1.5 - 3°C		
Regional	Biosphere	Sahel greening	2.8°C	2 - 3.5°C		
Regional	Biosphere	Boreal Forest southern dieback	4°C	1.4 - 5°C	Yes (low confidence)	Irreversible for multidecades (medium confidence)
Regional	Biosphere	Boreal Forest northern expansion	4°C	1.5 - 7.2°C		

Note: Literature-based temperature threshold estimates, including a central estimate and an uncertainty range for crossing of key tipping elements of the climate system. Central estimate column colour codes: red, dark orange and light orange denoting, respectively, central global warming threshold are within the Paris Agreement range of 1.5-2°C, within temperature range in line with current policies (2-4°C) and 4°C and above. Range column colour codes: red, dark orange and light orange denote respectively that current warming already within uncertainty range, levels in line with the Paris Agreement range within uncertainty range and range above Paris Agreement range. Compared to previous characterisation of tipping elements in the literature, the following tipping elements had not yet been featured: Labrador-Irminger Seas /SPG Convection (collapse), East Antarctic Subglacial Basins (collapse), Barents Sea Ice (abrupt loss). Information on potential to cause abrupt change and irreversibility, including timescales, and timescales from IPCC AR6 ((Lee, 2021[4]), Table 4.10). IPCC confidence levels of potential to cause abrupt change reflect the author team's judgement about the validity of the findings by an evaluation of evidence and agreement (Lee, 2021[4]).
Source: (McKay et al., 2022[12]; Lee, 2021[4]).

Evidence that climate tipping points may be approaching is increasing and has led scientists to declare a climate and ecological emergency (Lenton et al., 2019[14]; Ripple, 2020[15]).. For example, irreversible loss of part of the West Antarctic ice sheet may have already begun (Good et al., 2018[16]) and the Greenland ice sheet may also reach a tipping point whereby irreversible loss begins at 1.5°C of warming (Lenton et al., 2019[14]). Ocean ecosystems are already experiencing large-scale changes. For example, ocean heatwaves and acidification are causing mass bleaching of warm-water coral reefs; at warming above 2°C, 99% of coral reefs are projected to be lost (Lenton et al., 2019[14]). In addition, the Atlantic Meridional Overturning Circulation (AMOC) has been slowing over the past two decades (Good et al., 2018[16]) and is at its weakest for over a millennium (Caesar et al., 2021[17]; Boers, 2021[18]). Recent evidence that deforestation – itself a key contributor to climate change – combined with a warming climate, raises the probability that the Amazon will already shift from a humid to dry state during the 21st century (Lenton et al., 2019[14]; Arias et al., 2021[19]). If triggered, these tipping points would lead to often abrupt and irreversible impacts with potentially cascading global implications, including triggering of further tipping points, with dramatic effects on human and natural systems (Lenton et al., 2019[14]).

The possibility of tipping point cascades

If triggered, climate system tipping points may lead to changes in the regional or global climate. At a regional level, individual tipping points are associated with potentially severe local impacts such as extreme temperatures and higher frequency of droughts, forest fires and unprecedented weather. At the global level, due to atmospheric and ocean circulation, tipping elements are not isolated systems; rather, they interact. This means that the tipping of one element has the potential to trigger others (Lenton et al., 2019[14]; Wunderling et al., 2021[8]). Such cascading effects – when crossing the threshold of one tipping point triggers further tipping elements – could lead to a "hothouse" global climate that would be less suitable for human existence (Steffen et al., 2018[20]; Lenton et al., 2019[14]). The potential impacts of selected climate tipping points are summarised in Table 2.2.

Table 2.2. Potential impacts of selected tipping points

Tipping point	Timescale (years)	Weather	Sea-level rise	Carbon feedbacks	Maximum impact on global temperature	Socio-economic	Interaction with other tipping points
Greenland ice sheet meltdown	10 000	Local warming, local shifts in rainfall	+ 1 m by 2100	Flooding of permafrost, CO_2, CH_4	0.13C	Indirect negative impacts (through sea-level rise)	Trigger AMOC collapse Flooding of permafrost
West Antarctic ice sheet collapse	2 000	Local warming, local shifts in rainfall	+1 m by 2100	Flooding of permafrost, CO_2, CH_4	0.05C	Indirect negative impacts (through sea-level rise)	Destabilising/stabilising impact on AMOC
Year-round collapse of Arctic sea ice	20	Arctic warming amplification through loss of surface albedo effect	No significant effect	Increased permafrost thawing, CO_2, CH_4	0.60C	Arctic coastal hazards; Arctic communities food security and autonomy	Contribute to northern permafrost and ice sheet decline; increase ocean acidification
Atlantic overturning (AMOC) collapse	50	Increase in temperatures in the Northern Hemisphere, drier Europe, storm surges in North America, disruption to precipitation patterns in the tropics	Increased along North American coast	CO_2 from ocean and land, biome changes	-0.50C	Critical threat to global food security	Increase WAIS disintegration, stabilising effect on Greenland ice sheet
Permafrost abrupt collapse	50	Local warming		Permafrost Carbon Feedback: CO_2 and CH_4 release; Up to >800 Gt CO_2	0.4C	Damages to infrastructure Release of infectious diseases	Increases risk of other tipping points with increased warming
Boreal forest dieback	100	Decrease winter local temperatures and increase in	-	Increased CO_2, potential	-0.18C	Major disruption of ecosystem	

Tipping point	Timescale (years)	Weather	Sea-level rise	Carbon feedbacks	Maximum impact on global temperature	Socio-economic	Interaction with other tipping points
		global temperatures, potential decrease in regional precipitation		increased permafrost thawing		services for local communities	
Amazon rainforest dieback	100	Local and regional warming, lower local precipitation	-	Increased CO_2	0.2C	Major disruption of ecosystem services, migration, food security and health	Potential contribution to the weakening of the AMOC

Source: (OECD, 2021[5]; McKay et al., 2022[12]).

The impacts of crossing tipping point thresholds can also cascade through socio-economic and ecological systems, often rapidly. They would intensify a range of climate hazards such as droughts, floods and other extreme weather events, causing direct damage to infrastructure and impacts on ecosystems, and water and food systems. These would, in turn, affect socio economic systems with impacts that could then propagate across sectors and international borders via global trade, financial flows and supply networks. Socio-economic responses to such impacts may themselves be non-linear, tipping socio-economic subsystems into a different state, inducing migration or political instability. Socio-economic responses can also result in positive or negative feedback effects with the climate system, either increasing emissions or accelerating mitigation action, thus potentially affecting further tipping elements.

Box 2.1. Overview of selected tipping points and their impacts

Collapse of the Atlantic Meridional Overturning Circulation (AMOC)

The Atlantic Meridional Overturning Circulation (AMOC) drives part of the ocean circulation through fluxes of heat and freshwater. While the AMOC has been relatively stable for several millennia, recent observations reveal that it is weakening and is currently at its weakest point in over 1 000 years. Early-warning signals suggest that the AMOC is losing stability and is close to a critical transition (Boers, 2021[18]). This is driven by high melt rates of the Greenland ice sheet, demonstrating the interlinkages between tipping elements and potential for cascading effects (Wunderling et al., 2021[8]).

A collapse of the AMOC would represent a complete reorganisation of ocean circulation, with dramatic impacts on the climate system (OECD, 2021[5]). It would lead to a redistribution of heat around the planet and shifting rainfall patterns affecting sea ice, global sea levels, agricultural systems, and marine and terrestrial ecosystems (OECD, 2021[5]). Paleo records show that, in the past, changes in the strength of the AMOC have played a prominent role in transitions between warm and cool climatic phases (OECD, 2021[5]). In addition, changes in surface temperatures and precipitation patterns induced by an AMOC collapse or weakening have the potential to affect other tipping elements of the climate system, specifically the stability of the Amazon and boreal forests as well as the global monsoon system (Wunderling et al., 2021[8]). Even if a collapse does not occur, further weakening of the AMOC would still have major impacts, essentially a scaled-down version of those resulting from a complete collapse (OECD, 2021[5]).

Amazon and boreal forest dieback

The close association between land surface and water cycles makes the Amazon potentially susceptible to abrupt change (Douville et al., 2021[21]). A number of studies indicate that climate change (Cox et al., 2000[22]) and deforestation (Boers et al., 2017[23]), especially when combined, can lead to changes that would push the Amazon past a critical threshold beyond which a wide-scale ecosystem collapse becomes inevitable and tropical forest would gradually turn to a drier savannah state. While there is uncertainty regarding temperature thresholds at which this would occur, it is projected that continued Amazon deforestation, combined with a warming climate, raises the probability of crossing a tipping point in the state of the Amazon already this century (Arias et al., 2021[19]). The impacts associated with the dieback of the forest could be severe and of global scale. This has profound implications for biodiversity and ecosystem function, and dire consequences for local communities, in particular indigenous populations (Pörtner et al., 2022[24]).

Boreal forests are an integral component of regional and global climate systems that affect biosphere-atmosphere interactions as well as large-scale circulation patterns. They are expected to experience the largest increase in temperatures of all forest biomes during the 21st century. The latest IPCC report assesses with high confidence that warmer and drier conditions have increased tree mortality and forest disturbances in many temperate and boreal biomes, negatively impacting provisioning services (Pörtner et al., 2022[24]). The impacts associated with a potential dieback of the boreal forest would be severe locally and globally. Local communities and economies that rely on the forests are particularly at risk. At the global level, boreal forest dieback would have implications for the long-term provisioning of global climate regulation through the exchange of energy and water.

Abrupt permafrost collapse

The release of carbon dioxide and methane from permafrost thaw into the atmosphere due to global warming and its impacts leads to an amplification of surface warming. Known as permafrost carbon feedback (PCF), carbon release following permafrost thaw is irreversible over centennial timescales (Canadell et al., 2021[25]). The PCF has been hypothesised to have substantial implications for greenhouse gas (GHG) emissions and the potential for abrupt permafrost thaw is considered a major tipping element of the Earth system (Lenton et al., 2019[14]). A total collapse of permafrost would release up to 888 Gt of carbon dioxide and 5.3 Gt[3] of methane over this century (Canadell et al., 2021[25]). By comparison, the remaining carbon budgets for maintaining warming below 1.5°C and 2°C[4] are respectively 400 and 1150 Gt CO_2 (Canadell et al., 2021[25]). Alongside the global PCF and its contribution to global GHG emissions and warming, a permafrost collapse would also pose risks to local ecosystems, human livelihoods, health and infrastructure. Permafrost thaw interacts with other climatic and human factors and leads to geomorphological alterations, hydrological regime shifts and biome shifts, with regional implications for the frequency and magnitude of floods and landslides, coastal erosion, and hydrological dynamics.

The Arctic is both the largest permafrost region and the fastest warming region on Earth. High Arctic regions have seen global warming levels more than double those of the global average and virtually all climate scenarios project widespread permafrost warming and thawing in the future. In addition to global warming, wildfires and heatwaves currently drive abrupt permafrost thaw processes, exposing several meters of permafrost carbon on very short timescales. These are projected to increase in frequency in the Arctic region. There is also evidence that a synchronous large-scale permafrost collapse could occur due to abrupt permafrost drying and self-sustained internal heat production inside carbon-rich permafrost grounds – also known as "compost-bomb instability" (Hollesen et al., 2015[26]; McKay et al., 2022[12]). It is estimated that the temperature threshold for an abrupt regional permafrost thaw lies between 1°C and 2.3°C (best estimate at 1.5°C), while the large-scale collapse of permafrost is estimated to likely occur at higher warming levels of 3 to 6°C (McKay et al., 2022[12]).

Greenland ice sheet meltdown and West Antarctic ice sheet collapse

Improved data and models of ice sheet behaviour have recently revealed unexpectedly high melt rates in the Earth's ice sheets. The Greenland and Antarctic ice sheets are being destabilised by several processes linked with global warming. There is now high scientific agreement on the existence of tipping points after which the Greenland and West Antarctic ice sheets irreversibly disintegrate. Different models have given critical temperature thresholds for a collapse of the Greenland ice sheet ranging from 1.5°C to 2.7°C (McKay et al., 2022[12]). Several studies highlight increasing evidence of an instability threshold for the West Antarctic ice sheet already at warmings levels of 1°C to 3°C, with a most probable estimate at 1.5°C (McKay et al., 2022[12]). The Greenland and Antarctic ice sheets are already major contributors to sea level rise. In the case of a collapse, these two tipping elements combined will lead to more than one additional metre of sea-level rise over this century. Additionally, the Greenland ice sheet and AMOC tipping elements are intimately interlinked, and Greenland ice sheet mass loss is already contributing to the weakening of the AMOC, with further mass loss potentially leading to an AMOC tipping point.

Arctic sea ice loss

Arctic summer and winter sea ice are declining fast under global warming. At warming levels of 1.5°C to 5°C, the Arctic will remain covered by winter sea ice over the course of this century, though to a lower extent. Above these warming levels, an abrupt collapse of the Arctic winter sea ice has been projected by several models. Such abrupt changes are driven by local positive feedbacks as the loss of sea ice reduces solar radiation reflection and increases temperatures locally. This makes Arctic winter sea ice collapse a credible tipping-point candidate. The likely threshold at which this tipping point would be crossed has been estimated at 6.3°C (McKay et al., 2022[12]). There are, however, many other models that show that the Arctic Sea ice responds linearly to global warming levels without any irreversibility in changes (Fox-Kemper et al., 2021[27]). There is therefore still a debate on whether the Arctic sea ice is susceptible to a tipping point or not.

Changes in sea ice impact exchanges of energy fluxes between the atmosphere and the ocean, thereby influencing atmospheric, oceanic and climatic conditions. Through changes to the surface-albedo feedback, which results from solar radiation reflection on the Earth's surface, sea ice loss amplifies warming. A collapse of year-round Arctic sea ice could lead to up to 0.6°C of additional warming globally. Surface-albedo feedbacks due to the loss of sea ice have already played an important role in the amplification of warming in the Arctic. Arctic sea ice loss is thereby contributing to losses in other components of the cryosphere, accelerating permafrost thaw rates and Arctic ice sheet surface melt The loss of Arctic sea ice will also contribute to ocean acidification (Canadell et al., 2021[25]) and threaten polar ecosystems and local livelihoods.

Source: Summary of more extensive literature review provided in (OECD, 2022[28]).

Incorporating climate tipping points into economic modelling[5]

Socio-economic systems also exhibit non-linearities and their own potential tipping points when subjected to worsening climate impacts. Yet models that underpin most economic analyses of climate change rarely include the possibility of abrupt changes to climate or economic systems (Rose, 2022[29]).

A comprehensive review of the literature highlights that economic modelling that includes tipping points has not informed climate policy in a substantive way (Kopits, Marten and Wolverton, 2013[30]). This is largely because modelling efforts that included large-scale singular events were based on Integrated Assessment Models (IAMs) that used ad hoc parameters without empirical bases and typically without considering the multi-decade time horizons at which such large-scale events could unfold. Recent efforts have attempted to more accurately incorporate physical science into economic models and better capture the dynamics of Earth systems and their associated uncertainties (Nordhaus, 2019[31]; Yumashev et al., 2019[32]; Kikstra et al., 2021[33]). As an interesting example, Dietz et al. (2021[34]) provide estimations for the impacts of different tipping points on the social cost of carbon (SCC),[6] proposing a meta-analytic IAM that includes eight climate tipping points under a unified framework. They find that, taken collectively, tipping points increase the SCC by around 25% and, importantly, that they increase global economic risk.

Efforts have also been made to take interactions between tipping points into account. Models wherein the crossing of one tipping point threshold increases the probability of another tipping point result in substantially increased SCC (Cai, Lenton and Lontzek, 2016[35]) (Lemoine and Traeger, 2016[36]). Given the uncertainties in the timing and biophysical effects of tipping points in the scientific literature, factoring uncertainty into economic models is also essential. Models that include the uncertainty of economic and climate risks also result in large effects on the social cost of carbon (Cai and Lontzek, 2019[37]) (Cai, Lenton and Lontzek, 2016[35]).

To better understand the cost of climate system tipping points, economic models of climate tipping points should account not only for changes in global mean temperature but also for other physical climate or weather elements (e.g. water cycle, radical changes in the seasonality of extreme events, etc.). There is also a need for improved tipping metrics that consider, for instance, some interval of temperatures. Finally, to improve the coupling of economic and geophysical models, researchers should start with a recursive/simulation model and only then move to optimisation models. There seems to be merit in performing simulation, not optimisation-based models, to achieve a better sense of expected damages.

Finally, climate impacts including tipping points are also inextricably linked to socio-economic systems. There is a clear need to better understand these interlinkages. This includes, for example, modelling the impacts of climate change on financial stability (Kiley, 2021[38]) (Lamperti et al., 2020[39]) (Lamperti et al., 2019[40]); the macroeconomic implications of the transition to net zero (Pisani-Ferry, 2021[41]); regional differences in macroeconomic impacts (Batten, forthcoming[42]); and interactions between impacts across different economic sectors.

Policy responses to address the risk of climate tipping points

Global policy efforts and actions that explicitly target risks associated with the triggering of climate system tipping points and their potential cascading effects remain intangible and highly insufficient. It is imperative to assess how the latest knowledge on climate tipping points can inform risk-management strategies today, including the mitigation of greenhouse gas emissions and net-zero transition strategies; adaptation to climate change and building resilience to accelerating potential climate impacts; and technological development and innovation.

Accelerating mitigation strategies

Fully integrating the risks associated with climate tipping points into climate risk management strategies requires a precautionary approach to mitigation. Considering that some tipping points may already be triggered between 1.5 and 2°C of warming, this means limiting the temperature increase to 1.5°C, with no or very limited overshoot. Indeed, an overshoot of the 1.5°C limit could result in a considerably higher risk of crossing climate tipping-point thresholds even if temperatures return to 1.5 °C levels by the end of this century (OECD, 2022[28]).

The estimated possibility of climate system tipping points effectively limits the number and shape of emissions pathways towards 1.5°C of warming and renders lenient interpretations of the Paris Agreement goal significantly more dangerous. Limiting warming to 1.5°C with no or very limited overshoot requires urgent acceleration of near-term action to reach net-zero CO_2 emissions. It is therefore no longer "only" about achieving net-zero emissions by mid-century but how this can be achieved: rapid and deep emissions cuts must be made already this decade. As is, current policies in line with meeting countries' Nationally Determined Contributions (NDCs) will not limit warming to 1.5°C without overshoot. It is critical that NDCs are strengthened before 2025, and that commensurate policies are implemented at relevant timescales to meet revised targets (OECD, 2022[28]).

It is also important to note that, if triggered, some climate tipping points would effectively reduce the remaining carbon budget for reaching temperature objectives. Indeed, loss of sea ice and ice sheets leads to a decrease of solar radiation reflection, raising surface temperatures. If these tipping points are crossed, emissions reductions would need to be even larger than previously thought to meet stated temperature targets. In addition, permafrost carbon emissions have already lowered the estimated remaining carbon budgets for achieving the 1.5°C and 2°C warming objectives, even without having reached the threshold for an abrupt tipping point (Canadell et al., 2021[25]). As most of these tipping elements are likely to be tipped already within the 1.5 to 2°C range, temperature feedback loops further stress how crucial it is to avoid or limit overshooting 1.5°C.

Moreover, for some tipping elements, climate and human disturbances outside GHG emissions can potentially interact with global warming and contribute to surpassing critical thresholds. For example, land use and hydrological changes alongside climate change could lead to widespread dieback of the Amazon rainforest in the near term. In the Arctic, wildfires are increasingly contributing to abrupt permafrost thaw and carbon release from boreal forests.

Collective ambitious action to keep warming below 1.5°C is the safest and most cost-effective way to mitigate climate change and minimise the risk of triggering climate tipping points. The latest economic assessments show that when faced with the risk of cascading tipping points and their non-linear and irreversible impacts, the additional costs of implementing stringent climate policies earlier are worth paying. A rise of 1.5°C can still be achieved with very limited or no overshoot, although this requires a very rapid transformation of economies and societies, and a focus on a resilient and orderly transition (see Part II of this report). As emissions continue to rise, however, this window of opportunity is closing swiftly.

Building transformational resilience to climate impacts

Given the lower levels of warming at which the thresholds of climate system tipping points may be crossed, adaptation planning must account for the possibility of climate tipping points and their cascading impacts. The sheer magnitude of these possible impacts, coupled with their possibly abrupt and non-linear nature, requires more than just incremental adaptation efforts. To remain resilient, policy makers need to consider transformational adaptation actions. Even if the Paris Agreement's temperature target is met, it is likely that some transformational adaptation will be needed (Ara Begum, 2022[43]). If mitigation efforts fall short of the 1.5°C target, transformational adaptation will be all the more important as impacts become more severe, and the risk of crossing tipping points increases (Ara Begum, 2022[43]).

Transformational adaptation means changing the fundamental characteristics of human and natural systems to increase their capacity to cope with potential hazards (IPCC, 2022[44]). In light of the threat of climate system tipping points, transformational adaptation could necessitate stringent and even drastic measures to reduce impacts and avoid losses. Such drastic measures, potentially transforming whole communities and economic sectors, will undoubtedly result in short-term disruptions. However, considering the immense cost of inaction in the face of tipping point impacts, transformational adaptation is worthwhile.

Transformational adaptation measures can be technological, for example, implementing water capture and storage solutions in areas at risk of drought. They can also be behavioural or include fundamental changes in institutional arrangements, priorities, and norms (Kates, Travis and Wilbanks, 2012[45]). They can also target the spatial development of human activities, such as managed retreat of communities and settlements, relocation of assets and infrastructure to less at-risk areas, long term spatial planning, and urban and agricultural zoning. Other examples include international co-operation among governments to manage migrations, the deployment of nature-based solutions (NbS), and livelihood transformation in land systems (New, 2022[46]).

A specific example is adapting energy planning and zoning in the Amazon region, which is heavily reliant on large-scale hydropower, to anticipate the impacts on the region's hydrological cycle should the Amazon turn from rainforest to savannah. This includes decentralisation of energy production, diversification of energy sources focusing on small-scale hydropower and solar power, and investments in energy saving (Lapola et al., 2018[47]). A transformational approach to adaptation in the Amazon would also mean livelihood transformation, i.e. encouraging farmers to switch to crop varieties and livestock suitable for drier conditions in order to protect the agricultural sector (ibid).

Transformational adaptation measures that are beneficial or low-cost even if tipping points do not occur are "no-regret" policies (Heltberg, Siegel and Jorgensen, 2009[48]). Some may come with large co-benefits by contributing to reductions in GHG, supporting the advancement of other sustainable development goals (e.g. energy and water access), and building the resilience of systems and populations to future climate shocks. This is especially the case for investment in rehabilitating ecosystems and ecosystems services and the implementation of nature-based solutions, which are also important for accelerating mitigation efforts (Schipper et al., 2022[49]). (NbS are discussed further in Chapter 12.)

Many current adaptation initiatives prioritise near-term climate risk reduction and may even clash with efforts to bring about transformational adaptation (IPCC, 2022[37]). For example, building flood defences may lock in infrastructure development in areas that would be untenable if tipping points were crossed. Instead, to ensure societies' resilience to climate-change impacts, especially those brought about by the crossing of tipping-point thresholds, transformational adaptation efforts must be pursued alongside stringent mitigation efforts to limit climate risk. Implementing transformative actions that support sustainable development goals is a key opportunity for climate resilient development.

Technology and innovation

Technological developments and innovation can also help to reduce and manage the risks associated with climate tipping points.

First, technologies for better monitoring and modelling of the climate system are essential to assess how climate-related hazards resulting from tipping points may evolve over time. In addition, it is difficult to predict the thresholds at which tipping points may be crossed, as the parameters that induce a shift often show only incremental changes before the system makes a sudden or persistent transition. Climate modelling and remote sensing are improving in their ability to detect early warning signals, but these new findings are not yet feeding into the risk management strategies informing policy makers. Greater efforts to make this information readily accessible is essential to addressing the threat of climate tipping points.

Second, technologies can help develop and implement ways to reduce and manage the risks of climate system tipping points. Carbon-dioxide removal (CDR) technologies are key, as scenarios that limit warming to 1.5°C with no or very limited overshoot all include some deployment of CDR. It is essential to note that CDR technologies are needed to accelerate early and deep emissions reductions and balance out harder to-abate sectors that continue to produce residual emissions during the first half of the century, but CDR technologies should not justify delayed mitigation action (Riahi et al., 2021[50]).

Moreover, there are legitimate concerns regarding CDR technologies, for example the immense demand for land and resulting implications for land-use practices that bioenergy with carbon capture and storage (BECCS) requires (Creutzig et al., 2021[51]). Questions also remain over the scalability of CDR. The potential trade-offs between the risks of employing CDR technologies – in particular BECCS – and the risks of triggering climate system tipping points if CDR technologies are not employed are poorly understood. Investments are needed to better understand these trade-offs and evaluate the risks associated with scaled-up use of CDR technologies or failure to employ them altogether.

Chapter conclusions

Mounting evidence that climate tipping point thresholds may be crossed sooner and at lower warming levels than previously thought means that every effort must be made to avoid this scenario. This requires an immediate acceleration of climate mitigation efforts, as even the most optimistic projections of current policy commitments are insufficient. Focusing solely on the goal of net-zero emissions by 2050 is not enough. Even if net-zero emissions by are achieved by 2050, it is still possible that certain tipping point thresholds will be crossed this century, even more so if the target of 1.5°C warming is overshot. Drastic, transformational adaptation efforts must be considered to ensure the resilience of climate policies in the face of future disruptions.

Notes

[1] Climate or radiative forcing is the change in energy flux in the atmosphere caused by natural or anthropogenic factors of climate change, such as greenhouse gas emissions or increased water vapour. It is a direct measure of the amount that the Earth's energy budget is out of balance due to external drivers of change.

[2] The latest IPCC report does not provide temperature thresholds for tipping per tipping element, but summarises levels of change according to different levels of temperature increase. For example, the report estimates that it is likely that under temperature levels of 1.5°C, 2.0°C or 3.0°C relative to 1850–1900, the Atlantic Meridional Overturning Circulation (AMOC) will continue to weaken for several decades by about 15%, 20% and 30% of its strength. In addition, at sustained warming levels between 2°C and 3°C, there is evidence, albeit limited, that the Greenland and West Antarctic ice sheets will be lost almost completely and irreversibly over multiple millennia. The probability of their complete loss and the rate of mass loss increases with higher surface temperatures (high confidence) (Arias et al., 2021[19])

[3] Or 143 Gt CO_2-eq.

[4] The IPCC's remaining carbon budgets from 2020 onwards for maintaining warming below these levels by the end of the century with a 67% chance.

[5] This sub-section draws partially on the results of the *OECD Expert workshop on Economic Modelling of Climate and Related Tipping Points* held under the Net Zero+ project on 18-19 October 2021: https://www.oecd.org/env/indicators-modelling-outlooks/Workshop-Tipping-Points-Summary-Report.pdf.

[6] The social cost of carbon (SCC) is the central concept for the inclusion of climate change damages in the cost-benefit analysis of public policy and public investments. It measures the present value in

monetary terms of the damages incurred when an additional tonne of carbon (or any other greenhouse gas) is released into the atmosphere.

References

Alley, R. et al. (2003), "Abrupt Climate Change", *Science*, Vol. 299/5615, pp. 2005-2010, https://doi.org/10.1126/science.1081056. [3]

Ara Begum, R. (2022), "Point of Departure and Key Concepts", in H.-O. Pörtner, D. (ed.), *Climate Change 2022: Impacts, Adaptation, and Vulnerability. Contribution of Working Group II to the Sixth Assessment Report of the Intergovernmental Panel on Climate Change*, Cambridge University Press, In Press. [43]

Arias, P. et al. (2021), "Technical Summary", in Masson-Delmotte, V. et al. (eds.), *Climate Change 2021: The Physical Science Basis. Contribution of Working Group I to the Sixth Assessment Report of the Intergovernmental Panel on Climate Change*, Cambridge University Press, Cambridge, United Kingdom and New York, NY, USA. [19]

Batten, S. (forthcoming), "The impact of the weather on the UK economy", *Mimeo*. [42]

Boers, N. (2021), "Observation-based early-warning signals for a collapse of the Atlantic Meridional Overturning Circulation", *Nature Climate Change*, Vol. 11/8, pp. 680-688, https://doi.org/10.1038/s41558-021-01097-4. [18]

Boers, N. et al. (2017), "A deforestation-induced tipping point for the South American monsoon system", *Scientific Reports*, Vol. 7/1, https://doi.org/10.1038/srep41489. [23]

Caesar, L. et al. (2021), "Current Atlantic Meridional Overturning Circulation weakest in last millennium", *Nature Geoscience*, Vol. 14/3, pp. 118-120, https://doi.org/10.1038/s41561-021-00699-z. [17]

Cai, Y., T. Lenton and T. Lontzek (2016), "Risk of multiple interacting tipping points should encourage rapid CO2 emission reduction", *Nature Climate Change*, Vol. 6/5, pp. 520-525, https://doi.org/10.1038/nclimate2964. [7]

Cai, Y., T. Lenton and T. Lontzek (2016), "Risk of multiple interacting tipping points should encourage rapid CO2 emission reduction", *Nature Climate Change*, Vol. 6/5, pp. 520-525, https://doi.org/10.1038/nclimate2964. [35]

Cai, Y. and T. Lontzek (2019), "The Social Cost of Carbon with Economic and Climate Risks", *Journal of Political Economy*, Vol. 126/6, pp. 2684-2734, https://www.journals.uchicago.edu/doi/full/10.1086/701890. [37]

Canadell, J. et al. (2021), "Global Carbon and other Biogeochemical Cycles and Feedbacks", in Masson-Delmotte, V. et al. (eds.), *Climate Change 2021: The Physical Science Basis. Contribution of Working Group I to the Sixth Assessment Report of the Intergovernmental Panel on Climate Change*, Cambridge University Press, Cambridge, United Kingdom and New York, NY, USA. [25]

Chen, D. et al. (2021), "Framing, Context, and Methods.", in Masson-Delmotte, V. (ed.), *Climate Change 2021: The Physical Science Basis. Contribution of Working Group I to the Sixth Assessment Report of the Intergovernmental Panel on Climate Change*. [2]

Cox, P. et al. (2000), "Acceleration of global warming due to carbon-cycle feedbacks in a coupled climate model", *Nature*, Vol. 408/6809, pp. 184-187, https://doi.org/10.1038/35041539. [22]

Creutzig, F. et al. (2021), "Considering sustainability thresholds for BECCS in IPCC and biodiversity assessments", *GCB Bioenergy*, Vol. 13/4, pp. 510-515, https://doi.org/10.1111/gcbb.12798. [51]

Dietz, S. et al. (2021), "Economic impacts of tipping points in the climate system", *{Proceedings of the National Academy of Sciences*, Vol. 118/34, https://doi.org/10.1073/pnas.2103081118. [34]

Douville, H. et al. (2021), "Water Cycle Changes", in Masson-Delmotte, V. et al. (eds.), *Climate Change 2021: The Physical Science Basis. Contribution of Working Group I to 45 the Sixth Assessment Report of the Intergovernmental Panel on Climate Change*, Cambridge University Press. [21]

Good, P. et al. (2018), "Recent progress in understanding climate thresholds", *Progress in Physical Geography: Earth and Environment*, Vol. 42/1, pp. 24-60, https://doi.org/10.1177/0309133317751843. [16]

H.-O. Pörtner, D. (ed.) (2022), *Cross-Working Group Box ECONOMIC: Estimating Global Economic Impacts from Climate Change*, Cambridge University Press. [29]

H.-O. Pörtner, D. (ed.) (2022), *Decision Making Options for Managing Risk*, Cambridge University Press. [46]

Heltberg, R., P. Siegel and S. Jorgensen (2009), "Addressing human vulnerability to climate change: Toward a 'no-regrets' approach", *Global Environmental Change*, Vol. 19/1, pp. 89-99, https://doi.org/10.1016/j.gloenvcha.2008.11.003. [48]

Hollesen, J. et al. (2015), "Permafrost thawing in organic Arctic soils accelerated by ground heat production", *Nature Climate Change*, Vol. 5/6, pp. 574-578, https://doi.org/10.1038/nclimate2590. [26]

IPCC (2022), "Summary for Policymakers", in H.-O. Pörtner et al. (eds.), *Climate Change 2022: Impacts, Adaptation, and Vulnerability. Contribution of Working Group II to the Sixth Assessment Report of the Intergovernmental Panel on Climate Change . In Press.*, Cambridge University Press. [44]

IPCC (2021), "Summary for Policymakers", in Masson-Delmotte, P. et al. (eds.), *Climate Change 2021: The Physical Science Basis. Contribution of Working Group I to the Sixth Assessment Report of the Intergovernmental Panel on Climate Change*, In Press. [1]

IPCC (2019), "Summary for Policymakers", in H.-O. Pörtner et al. (eds.), *IPCC Special Report on the Ocean and Cryosphere in a Changing Climate*, Intergovernmental Panel on Climate Change, Geneva. [11]

IPCC (2018), "Summary for Policymakers", in Masson-Delmotte, V. et al. (eds.), *Global Warming of 1.5°C. An IPCC Special Report on the impacts of global warming of 1.5°C above pre-industrial levels and related global greenhouse gas emission pathways, in the context of strengthening the global response to the threat of climate....*, Intergovernmental Panel on Climate Change, Geneva. [10]

IPCC (2001), *Climate Change 2001: Synthesis Report. A Contribution of Working Groups I, II, and III to the Third Assessment Report of the Integovernmental Panel on Climate Change*, Watson, R.T. et al. (eds.), Cambridge University Press, Cambridge, United Kingdom, and New York. [9]

Kates, R., W. Travis and T. Wilbanks (2012), "Transformational adaptation when incremental adaptations to climate change are insufficient", *Proceedings of the National Academy of Sciences*, Vol. 109/19, pp. 7156-7161, https://doi.org/10.1073/pnas.1115521109. [45]

Kikstra, J. et al. (2021), "The social cost of carbon dioxide under climate-economy feedbacks and temperature variability", *Environmental Research Letters*, Vol. 16/9, p. 094037, https://doi.org/10.1088/1748-9326/ac1d0b. [33]

Kiley, M. (2021), "Growth at Risk From Climate Change", *Finance and Economics Discussion Series*, Vol. 2021/054, pp. 1-19, https://doi.org/10.17016/feds.2021.054. [38]

Kopits, E., A. Marten and A. Wolverton (2013), "Moving Forward with Incorporating "Catastrophic" Climate Change into Policy Analysis", *NCEE Working Paper Series, Working Paper 13-01*. [30]

Kriegler, E. et al. (2009), "Imprecise probability assessment of tipping points in the climate system", *Proceedings of the National Academy of Sciences*, Vol. 106/13, pp. 5041-5046, https://doi.org/10.1073/pnas.0809117106. [6]

Lamperti, F. et al. (2019), "The public costs of climate-induced financial instability", *Nature Climate Change*, Vol. 9/11, pp. 829-833, https://doi.org/10.1038/s41558-019-0607-5. [40]

Lamperti, F. et al. (2020), "Climate change and green transitions in an agent-based integrated assessment model", *Technological Forecasting and Social Change*, Vol. 153, p. 119806, https://doi.org/10.1016/j.techfore.2019.119806. [39]

Lapola, D. et al. (2018), "Limiting the high impacts of Amazon forest dieback with no-regrets science and policy action", *Proceedings of the National Academy of Sciences*, Vol. 115/46, pp. 11671-11679, https://doi.org/10.1073/pnas.1721770115. [47]

Lee, J. (2021), "Future Global Climate: Scenario-Based Projections and NearTerm Information", in [Masson-Delmotte, V. (ed.), *Climate Change 2021: The Physical Science Basis. Contribution of Working Group I to the Sixth Assessment Report of the Intergovernmental Panel on Climate Change*, Cambridge University Press, Cambridge, United Kingdom and New York, NY, USA, pp. 553–672. [4]

Lemoine, D. and C. Traeger (2016), "Economics of tipping the climate dominoes", *Nature Climate Change*, Vol. 6/5, pp. 514-519, https://doi.org/10.1038/nclimate2902. [36]

Lenton, T. et al. (2019), "Climate tipping points — too risky to bet against", *Nature*, Vol. 575/7784, pp. 592-595, https://doi.org/10.1038/d41586-019-03595-0. [14]

Masson-Delmotte, V. et al. (eds.) (2021), *Ocean, Cyroshphere and Seal Level Change*, Cambridge University Press, Cambridge, United Kingdom and New York, NY, USA. [27]

McKay, A. et al. (2022), "Exceeding 1.5°C global warming could trigger multiple climate tipping points", *Science*, Vol. 377/6611, https://doi.org/10.1126/science.abn7950. [12]

Nordhaus, W. (2019), "Economics of the disintegration of the Greenland ice sheet", *Proceedings of the National Academy of Sciences*, Vol. 116/25, pp. 12261-12269, https://doi.org/10.1073/pnas.1814990116. [31]

OECD (2022), *Climate tipping points: insights for effective policy action*. [13]

OECD (2022), *Climate Tipping Points: Insights for Effective Policy Action*, OECD Publishing, Paris, https://doi.org/10.1787/abc5a69e-en. [28]

OECD (2021), *Managing Climate Risks, Facing up to Losses and Damages*, OECD Publishing, Paris, https://doi.org/10.1787/55ea1cc9-en. [5]

OECD (2018), *"The social cost of carbon"*, OECD Publishing, Paris, https://doi.org/10.1787/9789264085169-17-en. [52]

Pisani-Ferry, J. (2021), "Climate policy is macroeconomic policy, and the implications will be significant", *PIIE Policy Brief 21-20*, https://www.piie.com/publications/policy-briefs/climate-policy-macroeconomic-policy-and-implications-will-be-significant. [41]

Pörtner, H. et al. (2022), "Technical Summary", in Pörtner, H. et al. (eds.), *Climate Change 2022: Impacts, Adaptation, and Vulnerability. Contribution of Working Group II to the Sixth Assessment Report of the Intergovernmental Panel on Climate Change*, Cambridge University Press. [24]

Riahi, K. et al. (2021), "Cost and attainability of meeting stringent climate targets without overshoot", *Nature Climate Change*, Vol. 11/12, pp. 1063-1069, https://doi.org/10.1038/s41558-021-01215-2. [50]

Ripple, W. (2020), "World scientists' warning of a climate emergency.", *Bioscience*, Vol. 70/1, pp. 8-12. [15]

Schipper, E. et al. (2022), "Climate Resilient Development Pathways", in H.-O. Pörtner et al. (eds.), *Climate Change 2022: Impacts, Adaptation, and Vulnerability. Contribution of Working Group II to the Sixth Assessment Report of the Intergovernmental Panel on Climate Change.*, Cambridge University Press. [49]

Steffen, W. et al. (2018), "Trajectories of the Earth System in the Anthropocene", *Proceedings of the National Academy of Sciences*, Vol. 115/33, pp. 8252-8259, https://doi.org/10.1073/pnas.1810141115. [20]

Wunderling, N. et al. (2021), "Interacting tipping elements increase risk of climate domino effects under global warming", *Earth System Dynamics*, Vol. 12/2, pp. 601-619, https://doi.org/10.5194/esd-12-601-2021. [8]

Yumashev, D. et al. (2019), "Climate policy implications of nonlinear decline of Arctic land permafrost and other cryosphere elements", *Nature Communications*, Vol. 10/1, https://doi.org/10.1038/s41467-019-09863-x. [32]

3 Unpredictable and overlapping global crises: risks and opportunities for climate policy

Climate change is not the only crisis governments face. Events of recent years have highlighted how global socio-economic shocks can severely change the landscape for climate policy implementation. This chapter reviews evidence on COVID-19 recovery spending and efforts taken to address the socio-economic consequences of Russia's war on Ukraine, assessing associated challenges and opportunities for the net-zero transition.

This chapter draws on work carried out under the Environment Policy Committee (the Green Recovery Database) and the Committee on Industry, Innovation and Entrepreneurship (forthcoming work on innovation and recovery), as well as a background paper prepared for the OECD Round Table on Sustainable Development.

Global events of recent years have highlighted how global socio-economic shocks can dramatically change the landscape for climate policy implementation, even as evidence of the severity of the climate emergency continues to mount. The COVID-19 pandemic, the lingering measures taken to contain it, and stimulus packages aimed at launching economic recovery continue to have profound implications for climate policy globally. The impacts of Russia's war of aggression against Ukraine have exacerbated these pressures and come with their own climate policy implications. Such crises highlight the need to ensure the resilience of the net-zero transition in the face of shocks, while also seizing opportunities to accelerate climate ambition and build resilience to climate impacts.

The COVID-19 pandemic and its consequences for climate policy

The COVID-19 pandemic has posed major challenges and offered numerous opportunities for global climate action. Lockdown measures initially enacted to limit the spread of the virus temporarily pushed down global emissions trajectories but emissions have since rebounded to their highest-ever levels as economies recover. With some exceptions, supply chains proved to be resilient during the initial waves of the pandemic, but rapid economic recovery in some parts of the world coupled with ongoing virus restrictions elsewhere – particularly in major manufacturing regions – led to supply-chain bottlenecks. This raised commodity prices and exerted inflationary pressures, unsettling economies worldwide even before Russia's invasion of Ukraine.

As the virus became more manageable, government spending switched from emergency rescue measures to recovery plans. These aimed to restart economies in the near term while building resilience to future shocks, emphasising an opportunity to "build back better". The immense scale of these recovery packages enables government support for restructuring economies in line with net-zero trajectories. At the same time, recovery stimulus spending has helped spur demand and broad inflationary pressures. Recovery spending in the wake of the war in Ukraine also has an important role to play in improving energy security and diversifying the energy mix.

The following section reviews the most recent evidence from the OECD Green Recovery Database[1] and Low-Carbon Technology Recovery Database to assess what lessons can be drawn from COVID-19 recovery spending as governments turn from stimulus measures towards regular policy making.

Does COVID-19 recovery spending align with climate ambitions?

The OECD Green Recovery Database collects and tracks information on measures related to COVID-19 recovery for which a clear positive or negative environmental impact can be identified. It includes new measures specifically targeting COVID-19 recovery and prior measures that were enhanced, accelerated or extended as part of recovery plans. At its last update in 2022, the database contained 1832 measures from 44 countries and the European Union (OECD, 2022[1]).

The most recent data show that green or environmentally friendly spending increased into 2022, from USD 677 billion in September 2021 to USD 1 090 billion in April 2022, amounting to 33% of total recovery spending (up from 21% in 2021). Spending with "mixed" and "negative" impacts on the environment also increased, though to a lesser extent, accounting for only 14% of recovery spending. The remaining half of recovery spending was not found to have a direct environmental impact (OECD, 2022[1]). These estimates are supported by other recovery trackers developed separately, such as the International Energy Agency

(IEA) Sustainable Recovery Tracker and the Oxford Global Recovery Observatory (O'Callaghan et al., 2021[2]).

The increase in greener spending linked to COVID-19 recovery does not account for other government expenditure with environmental implications. According to pre-COVID-19 estimates, environmentally harmful government support together annually amounted to more than USD 680 billion globally,[2] including subsidies for fossil fuel production and consumption[3] and potentially environmentally harmful agricultural practices (OECD, 2022[1]; OECD, 2021[3]). Although not directly comparable, these numbers indicate that in just over two years, harmful support measures were similar in magnitude to the total amount of green recovery spending identified in the database (which itself accounts for more than 90% of total global economic stimulus packages adopted in response to the pandemic). As recovery packages will be spent over multiple years, these estimates highlight the stark climate implications of policies intended to shield households and affected sectors from high-energy prices in the wake of crises such as COVID-19 and the war in Ukraine. Careful consideration is needed to ensure energy affordability for those in need without derailing climate-policy ambitions.

Although 20% of measures cover all economic sectors, most recovery measures in the database target specific sectors. Energy and ground transport are the most targeted sectors, receiving 26% and 21% of recovery spending with environmental implications respectively (OECD, 2022[1]).

A key gap in recovery efforts is the lack of spending targeting innovation and skills development. Only 8% of measures focus on promoting research and development (R&D), and 2% on job skills upgrades (OECD, 2022[1]). Innovation and skills development are key components of an accelerated transition to net zero while also providing key economic stimulus to help withstand shocks. This is clearly reflected in the fact that the few R&D measures identified in the database almost all have a positive impact on the environment. Although recovery efforts only provide a partial picture of overall green innovation support by governments, this gap nonetheless warrants further exploration.

Building on the OECD Green Recovery Database and the Oxford University Global Recovery Observatory database, the OECD Low Carbon Technology Recovery Database (LTRD) assesses the impact of recovery spending specifically on low-carbon technologies across 51 countries (members of the OECD, the European Union and G20). These collectively represent 89% of global GDP and 79% of global annual CO_2 emissions. In total, 1149 measures involving government spending toward low-carbon technologies have been identified, amounting to USD 1.3 trillion. This includes measures that are not considered in the most recent data in the Green Recovery Database such as the US Inflation Reduction Act (IRA), which was initially announced in 2021 as the Build Back Better Act but was then amended and finally passed into law as the IRA in August 2022. The IRA adds an additional USD 412 billion to overall recovery spending (accounting for almost 50% of green recovery spending covered by the Green Recovery Database).

The vast majority of technology-related recovery spending is focused on scaling up existing technologies. Compared to the recovery packages following the 2007-2008 global financial crisis, the response to the COVID-19 crisis appears to have placed more emphasis on R&D and demonstration. Among measures for which the innovation stage could be determined, roughly 5% of total green recovery funding was channelled towards support for R&D (2.5%) and demonstration projects (2.8%). An additional USD 34 billion (2.5% of low-carbon recovery spending), while not specifically mentioning R&D or demonstration, is channelled at technologies at the pre-adoption stage based on their Technology Readiness Level (TRL). In total therefore, around 8% of recovery funding targets pre-commercialisation phases, and 92% adoption and deployment phases, again with significant country differences (Aulie et al., Forthcoming 2023[4]). This appears to be a very significant contribution to closing the USD 90 billion funding gap in R&D and demonstration until 2030 highlighted by the IEA Net Zero Emissions Scenario.

Nine percent of low-carbon technology recovery funding is specifically dedicated to supporting emerging technologies with a clear priority on hydrogen, and to a lesser extent on carbon capture and storage, smart grids, zero-emission buildings and advanced batteries. Again, the regional prioritisations here differ, where hydrogen has been the main priority in many EU countries (including France, Germany and Belgium), New Zealand and the United Kingdom, while CCUS received priority in Norway, Australia and Denmark. Smart grid technology played an important role in Hungary, Estonia, Italy, Korea and Canada, while low-emission buildings dominate in Korea. In contrast to other countries, the United States manage to spread efforts across several emerging technologies, including hydrogen, CCUS, smart grid, nuclear innovation and advanced batteries (Aulie et al., Forthcoming 2023[4]).

How does this technology spending compare to investment needed to reach carbon neutrality? The IEA estimates that USD 3.3 trillion and USD 4.2 trillion would need to be invested in clean energy annually by 2030, in the Sustainable Development Scenario (SDS) and the Net Zero Emission 2050 Scenario (NZE), respectively. Existing policies are expected to induce USD 2 trillion of annual investments by 2030 (IEA Stated Policies scenario), implying that USD 1.3 trillion and USD 2.2 trillion is needed in additional annual investments by 2030 to achieve the SDS and NZE scenarios, respectively, including both private and public financing. As such, total recovery funding targeting low-carbon technologies equals about the additional annual investments needed to reach net zero, keeping in mind that recovery spending is one off and will be spent over multiple years. This implies that, while recovery spending makes a welcome contribution to closing the carbon neutrality investment gap, it falls short of being on track to meeting net zero needs. It is also important to note that projections of additional annual investment needs include both public and private sector investments. The public sector (including recovery spending) is only anticipated to directly contribute 30% of the necessary finance for meeting net zero globally (Vivid Economics, UNFCCC Race to Zero campaign and the Glasgow Financial Alliance for Net Zero, 2021[5]). Assessing the capacity for recovery spending on low-carbon technologies, and indeed other public technology finance, to crowd-in private investment is therefore paramount.

The role of recovery spending in making up the investment gap differs across technology groups, time periods and scenarios (Figure 3.1). Between 2021 and 2025, low-carbon recovery spending makes a significant contribution to global investment needs projected by the Sustainable Development scenario and the Net Zero scenario for CCUS (over 40% of average needs in the SDS scenario), hydrogen-based fuels (30% of investment needs) and, to a lesser extent, nuclear energy and energy efficiency (between 10% and 20% of investment needs). The contribution of recovery spending to investment needs in electric vehicles, energy storage, electricity networks and renewables is significantly smaller at about 5%-7%, and marginal in biofuels and CCUS for industry specifically. Therefore, while recovery packages make a significant contribution – in particular for CCUS, nuclear, energy efficiency and hydrogen – they fall short of filling the potential annual average investment gap towards 2030 to be on track with net-zero targets (Aulie et al., Forthcoming 2023[4]).

Figure 3.1. Annual average low-carbon recovery spending in selected technologies as a share of annual investment needs in IEA scenarios, 2021-2025 and 2026-2030

SDS = Sustainable Development Scenario; NZE = Net Zero Emission Scenarios

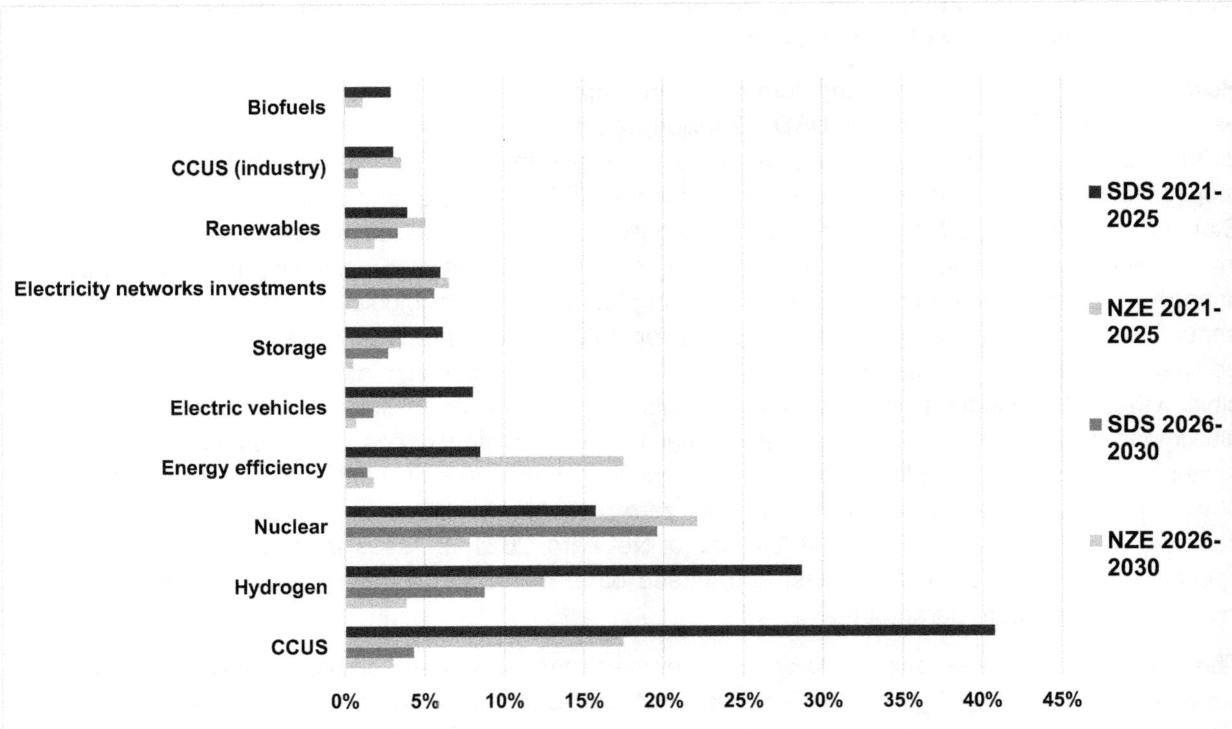

Note: Some of the technologies are summed across sectors, such as energy efficiency (from buildings and industry) and renewables (industry and power generation/fuel supply) and hydrogen (industry, fuel supply (clean fuels) and transport).
Source: OECD Low-carbon Technology Recovery database (version March 2023); IEA.

Lessons on net-zero spending for governments

- COVID-19 recovery spending offered a clear opportunity to channel investment towards the net zero transition and climate action more broadly. Although spending has become increasingly green over time, clear gaps remain, with a substantial number of measures entailing a negative environmental impact, and the green portion of total recovery spending only at one-third.
- As governments move from one-off recovery spending to annual budget policies, it is important to ensure that support measures intended to shield vulnerable households from high-energy prices do not work against green spending.
- While post-COVID-19 stimulus packages have oriented investment towards sectors and key technologies key for a low-carbon transition, they cannot by themselves close the investment gap needed by 2030. They must now be accompanied by more ambitious complementary climate policies that would induce private investment and trigger the deeper structural changes made necessary by net-zero targets and the current fossil-fuel energy price crisis.

The impact of COVID-19 on global supply chains and investment

The COVID-19 pandemic placed unprecedented stress on global supply chains. International logistics constraints, supply shocks due to bottlenecks in labour markets, trade and transport, manufacturing, and food systems, and radically shifting demand and consumption patterns worldwide were all disruption factors (OECD, 2020[6]; OECD, 2022[7]; OECD, 2020[8]; Brenton, Ferrantino and Maliszewska, 2022[9]).

These stresses also have implications for the net-zero transition, particularly as they restrict the flow of critical minerals for low-carbon technologies and the diffusion of low-carbon goods themselves. Key technology deployment such as solar photovoltaic (PV) installations suffered a considerable dip during the pandemic because of supply-chain bottlenecks and local mobility restrictions (OECD, 2020[8]; Goldthau and Hughes, 2020[10]).

Government responses to the pandemic have often hinted at increasing trade protectionism. Recovery strategies aim to shore up domestic production and manufacturing in order to stimulate national job creation and growth. Although increasing supply chain resilience is a key policy priority, particularly in the wake of the war in Ukraine (see below), protectionism could jeopardise the global trade and investment networks that brought down low-carbon technology costs in the past decade (Goldthau and Hughes, 2020[10]). To ensure resilience, governments must build an enabling environment for domestic industries while continuing to reap the benefits of international trade and investment, including diversification (OECD, 2022[7]).

Supply chain stresses in food systems highlight the importance of an open and predictable international trade environment to ensure continued access to key goods (OECD, 2020[6]). Rather than shortages, accessibility (including trade barriers and concerns around affordability) has been the primary stressor in food systems. This underlines the need for safety nets (e.g. stockpiling) to safeguard short-term accessibility in times of shock or crisis. A similar lesson can be drawn for the resilience of low-carbon supply chains: i.e. maintain international trade openness to drive continued long-term cost decreases and innovation while also diversifying supply chains and maintaining necessary domestic safety nets (e.g. stockpiling key minerals and other inputs to low-carbon production).

In addition to supply-chain bottlenecks and the threat of protectionist response policies, government stimulus spending has contributed substantially to global demand surges and associated inflation. This has been exacerbated by the war in Ukraine. While it remains difficult to untangle the exact extent of COVID-19 recovery stimulus in driving inflation, the resulting high investment costs are a clear obstacle to accelerated and resilient climate action (for more detail on this see Chapter 5). Governments will need to carefully target recovery efforts following future shocks to minimise inflationary pressures.

Implications of the war in Ukraine for climate policy

Russia's war of aggression against Ukraine has had far-reaching consequences well beyond the severe suffering in Ukraine itself. Impacts on global energy and food markets, as well as the broader economic situation, have created serious short-term challenges with implications for longer-term policy, including climate change policy. This section considers policy responses taken in the first six months following the invasion of Ukraine, with a focus on the implications of energy and macroeconomic policies for the transition to net-zero emissions. The section draws on a background paper prepared for the October 2022 meeting of the OECD Round Table on Sustainable Development.[4]

Energy supply disruptions due to the war in Ukraine have spurred a strong political focus on energy security that could in fact accelerate the transition away from fossil fuels, especially as renewable electricity sources become competitive with thermal power generation. However, near-term policy responses, including those aimed at managing high energy prices and costs of living, risk running counter to the transition. Governments need to ensure that necessary short-term deviations from net-zero paths do not lock in carbon for decades ahead.

The reduction in energy supplies from Russia and Ukraine due to sanctions and war-related supply disruptions initially led to sudden and sharp increases in energy prices. In mid-2022, European gas prices rose to about ten times their average over the previous five years. Although prices have since fallen due to successful campaigns to fill gas storage facilities, efforts to reduce energy demand, and a relatively mild winter in Europe, it is likely that price pressures will remain for several quarters ahead given Europe's constraints in accessing alternative sources of gas supply. Global food prices also surged by nearly 20% in the months following Russia's invasion of Ukraine due to war-related disruptions and concerns about possible impacts on global markets. These have since eased (FAO, 2022[11]).

These price increases have been responsible for the majority of the increase in headline inflation rates, reaching levels not seen in most countries since the two great oil shocks of the 1970s and inflation spike in 1988. Annualised consumer price index (CPI) inflation in OECD countries was over 10% in July 2022, its highest in over three decades. Higher energy prices, together with restrictions on energy supplies, are bearing down on the level of activity of many economies and the world as a whole. The OECD's March 2023 interim economic outlook showed that global GDP growth was down to 3.2% in 2022 with a further fall to 2.6% projected for 2023 with a distinct change of a recession – a marked slowdown relative to expectations prior to the war – with a distinct chance of a recession (OECD, 2023[12]).

Energy and macroeconomic policy responses

Widespread sanctions have been imposed on Russia following its invasion of Ukraine. In parallel, many countries have taken urgent steps to develop new or modified energy policies. Some of these are well aligned with climate goals, such as focusing on demand-side policies to encourage or enforce reduced demand and ramping up clean energy deployment through enhanced support programmes and streamlined planning processes. Others are less so, such as a push for new investment in liquefied natural gas (LNG) terminals and pipelines, and turning to fossil-based thermal power generation.

On the macroeconomic side, central banks have consistently been raising interest rates to prevent initial inflation due to higher energy and food prices from triggering a generalised price/wage spiral. Monetary policy has been tightening in most advanced economies and in a majority of emerging market economies. Until very recently, fiscal policy was also being tightened in most countries, following the large fiscal expansions of the COVID-19 stimulus policies discussed above. Measures of discretionary fiscal policy (as measured by changes in the cyclically adjusted budget position) indicate that, in 2021, G7 economies were set to tighten their collective fiscal position by a substantial 5.2% of GDP, largely driven by the magnitude of the change in the United States.

Since mid-2022, however, the situation has changed quickly and dramatically. Several countries, including across the EU and the UK, have introduced policies to offset a significant part of the effect of higher energy prices on household users and, in many cases, industry. By late 2022, the European package was some 2.2% of EU GDP, and larger still in the UK and Germany as a proportion of GDP, with the total across the EU and UK estimated at EUR 500 billion.

Changing political circumstances

In recent years, climate change policies have become increasingly interrelated with social and political considerations. For example, regions dependent on fossil fuel production are concerned not only about job insecurity but also the distributional impacts of climate policies on lower income groups. Such distributional effects have been brought into sharp focus following the rise in energy prices due to the war in Ukraine. The impacts of higher costs of living are unequally distributed (Blake and Bulman, 2022), disproportionately impacting people on low incomes – especially with respect to household energy use – leading to significant pockets of poverty in many OECD countries and grave poverty in parts of the non-OECD world. Policies are being put in place to protect the poorest in many societies from increases in costs of living they could not otherwise bear, but the design of these measures matters greatly, as discussed below.

Such measures are being taken in an increasingly fractured international political environment. Beyond the breakdown of relations between most OECD countries and Russia, the war in Ukraine has stoked tensions with other non-OECD countries, including over sanctions. These tensions are affecting collaboration on climate change and clean energy, including through the UNFCCC process. This was apparent at COP27 in 2022, where significant progress on accelerating the transition to net zero was mostly lacking, though notable progress was made on adaptation finance and through the establishment of a "loss and damage" fund.

Better aligning near-term policy responses with the climate challenge

Some macroeconomic and energy-related policies enacted in response to near-term developments resulting from the war in Ukraine are indeed consistent with longer-term energy and macroeconomic aims. In other cases, however, there are important inconsistencies between evolving near-term and long-term objectives. This includes the risk of locking in fossil fuel infrastructure that could last decades, running counter to needed net-zero pathways, or creating stranded assets if forced into early retirement.

Energy policies broadly aligned with net zero

Many energy policies implemented since the beginning of the war in Ukraine have been well-aligned. Despite the current crisis, most countries have not backtracked on their overall climate goals and ambitions. Many have stated aims to progressively phase out fossil fuels and accelerate the transition towards clean energy while promoting and supporting energy efficiency. Moreover, the war in Ukraine has increased the desire of many countries to reduce dependency on imported fossil fuels and spur development of home-grown clean energy supply chains. A key example is the US Inflation Reduction Act (IRA), which contains a range of measures and incentives designed to reduce the demand for energy and increase its supply from renewable sources. Faced with the consequences of Russia's war on Ukraine, many near-term energy policies seek to accelerate the penetration of renewables, energy efficiency and other clean-energy technologies, thereby broadly aligning with longer-term energy goals.

On the energy supply side, cases of policy changes that are broadly aligned with long-term goals include accelerating the scaling-up of renewable electricity by supporting deployment of mature technologies; ramping up investment in energy innovation; and deployment of new technologies during the early stage of their development. Ramped-up policies for clean energy have also been oriented towards supporting new infrastructure, in particular power networks, storage, hydrogen, and initiating and accelerating new nuclear power programmes. Energy-supply policies also require a speeding-up of enabling regulation, pricing, planning, and investment. Time-consuming legal processes are often cited as a major obstacle to rapid deployment of renewables (McWilliams et al., 2022[13]). In response, the EU and the UK, for example, have recently announced plans to simplify their permission policies on rooftop PV in order to promote self-consumption (Climate Action Tracker, 2022[14]). Likewise, the German government has initiated major reforms aimed at the expansion of solar and wind, pledging to make additional sites available for renewable energy projects and to remove bureaucratic barriers in order to accelerate planning and approval processes (McWilliams et al., 2022[13]).

Energy policies not aligned with net zero

While a number of recent energy policies are broadly consistent with longer-term energy aims, there are a number of initiatives whose perceived near-term imperatives are not aligned with, and may even impede, longer-term net-zero objectives.

On the energy supply side, this includes cases where efforts to diversify from Russian fossil fuels has led investment in supply and infrastructure of other fossil fuels. It is important that governments take necessary steps to ensure that measures taken to ease immediate, urgent supply concerns are genuinely temporary and do not lock in supply over the longer term. There are plans for new LNG terminals in Germany, the Netherlands, Italy, and Greece, which, if they all come on stream, could significantly increase Europe's LNG import capacity (Financial Times, 2022[15]).

Given development lead-times, this Europe-wide rush to build new LNG import terminals will not deliver instantly and risks prolonging reliance on fossil fuel energy supply beyond what is feasible for a net-zero emissions trajectory. It also increases the risk of creating stranded assets should demand for gas fall away before the expected lifetimes of terminals as the net-zero transition gathers pace. In addition, the overall cost of imported LNG will need to cover more than regasification and storage infrastructure in importing countries: it must reflect the need for more expensive infrastructure upgrades to LNG terminals in exporting countries. As accountability for net-zero commitments intensifies, costing of the climate change implications of methane leaks in the supply chain must also be taken into account.

In the near term, meeting energy demands will require recommissioning, extending the life of, or even investing in additional capacity in thermal fossil fuel plants, with the risk of locking in exposure to future risks of energy unaffordability and insecurity, and of growing damage from local air pollution and climate change. This effect was strong in mid-2022 due to it being a poor year for hydropower (due to droughts) and nuclear (due to heatwaves and extensive maintenance outages in France). Examples of thermal revival include Germany, which is delaying the closure of some coal- and oil-fired power plants, and Austria, where a retired coal power station is being renewed. The Netherlands is lifting its limit on power from coal, and France is preparing a coal plant as a reserve for the winter. While the immediate emissions impact of coal recommissioning in Europe may not be significant, it is important that their operation remains temporary (Ember, 2022[16]).

Further risk of locking in high carbon production comes from the granting of new exploration rights or permits, and initiating and accelerating new domestic oil and gas production infrastructure. The United States overturned the Biden administration's 2021 pledge to suspend new leases for oil and gas companies by allowing oil and gas drilling to resume on federal lands as part of the Inflation Reduction Act (Reuters, 2022[17]). The UK is also looking to expand licencing of North Sea oil and gas fields.

On the demand side, policies to reduce consumer energy costs in the near term (e.g. price caps, non targeted reductions in excise duty, or policies that reintroduce fossil-fuel subsidies) may encourage longer-term fossil-fuel energy use. The design of such measures is important to ensure that they reach those who most need them and that they are aligned with longer-term climate goals. OECD analysis shows that measures need to be targeted, and that measures designed around income support are preferable to those focusing on price support: their fiscal cost tends to be lower, and they also better preserve incentives to reduce energy demand (OECD, 2022[18]). However, recent data show that policies implemented to date have mostly been untargeted price-support measures (OECD, 2022[18]).

In addition, reduced support for renewable energy investment funded through energy bills may curtail funds for the deployment of low-carbon technologies and systems. For example, the UK temporarily scrapped the "green levy" that typically accounted for around 8% of household energy bills (FT Adviser, 2022[19]).

Alignment of macroeconomic policies with climate goals

Concerted action by central banks to raise official interest rates is important to contain inflation in the near term, but also to ensure the medium-term economic stability necessary for investment. However, higher rates do not necessarily align with the longer-term aim of promoting the strong investment needed for the net zero transition and sustainable economic growth. This is important, as some clean energy technologies are likely to remain vulnerable to higher nominal interest rates for a period. These technologies tend to be capital-intensive with their full profit potential yet to be realised, meaning that future benefits are discounted more highly and carry less weight when assessing the business case. They are therefore more vulnerable to higher costs of capital. Other less mature sectors, including green hydrogen, clean steel, cement, and clean aviation and shipping, while offering enormous potential, are not yet sufficiently cost-effective to be scaled up without substantial policy support, in particular in a higher-cost-of-capital environment. The implications of this are further discussed in Chapter 5.

The implications of the income- and price-support measures to partly shield households and firms from high energy and other prices can also run counter to longer-term aims of reducing public deficits and transitioning away from fossil fuels and increasing energy security. Similarly, near-term actions by fiscal authorities to provide income support to sections of society hardest hit by rising energy and food prices do not necessarily align with longer-run concerns to contain the size of the public debt. In any case, enhanced perception of limited fiscal space is likely to limit public resources available to promote and deploy clean infrastructure.

Chapter conclusions

Disruptions such as a pandemic or war have the potential to derail efforts on climate policy. In particular, COVID-19 recovery spending and efforts to protect populations from the social and economic consequences of the war against Ukraine are not always aligned with climate policies. Beyond the immediate policy alignments and misalignments highlighted in this chapter, these two crises have laid bare the potential for such disruptions to derail efforts on climate policy and the need to design policies that not only accelerate the transition to net-zero emissions but focus on the resilience of the transition itself when faced with unpredictable disruptions and shocks.

The policy implications of the COVID-19 pandemic and war against Ukraine cannot be seen in isolation from other global events of recent years, going back to the financial crisis of 2008. They are also occurring in the context of global "mega-trends" such as a rapidly changing labour market, ageing societies, digital transformation of economies and, of course, environmental impacts related to climate change, biodiversity loss, degrading ocean health, and the potential for tipping points within these, all of which will come with their own challenges and opportunities.

With this broader perspective, it is clear that climate policy efforts need to be married to efforts to ensure economic resilience in order to remain durable over the long term.

Notes

[1] https://www.oecd.org/coronavirus/en/themes/green-recovery.

[2] Agricultural support that potentially undermines the sector's sustainability average at around USD 338 billion per year in 2018-20, and USD 391 million in 2019-2021 in the 54 OECD and emerging countries covered by the OECD Agriculture Policy Monitoring reports (OECD, 2021[3]; OECD, 2022[22]). OECD and IEA data show that government support for the production and consumption of fossil fuels across 81 major economies totalled USD 351 billion in 2020. More recent OECD/IEA figures indicate fossil fuel support increased markedly in 2021 to over USD 700 billion with further increases expected in 2022 due to the lingering effects of COVID-19 and the war in Ukraine (OECD, 2021[23]; OECD and IEA, 2021[24]).

[3] Environmentally harmful support measures initiated in response to the COVID-19 pandemic are made up primarily of time-limited fossil fuel support and aviation tax changes. These data do not consider recent government support measures in response to the war in Ukraine and the current economic climate of high energy prices and soaring inflation, on which data is still emerging.

[4] https://www.oecd.org/sd-roundtable/papersandpublications/Foot%20on%20the%20Gas_Maintaining%20momentum%20for%20net-zero%20while%20responding%20to%20the%20war%20in%20Ukraine.pdf.

References

Aulie, F. et al. (2022), *Will post-COVID-19 recovery packages accelerate low-carbon innovation?*, OECD, https://www.oecd.org/greengrowth/2022GGGSD-IssueNote2-Will-post-COVID-19-recovery-packages-accelerate-low-carbon-innovation.pdf. [20]

Aulie, F. et al. (Forthcoming 2023), *Did covid-19 accelerate the green transition? An assessment of public investments in low-carbon technologies.*, OECD, https://www.oecd.org/greengrowth/2022GGGSD-IssueNote2-Will-post-COVID-19-recovery-packages-accelerate-low-carbon-innovation.pdf. [4]

Brenton, P., M. Ferrantino and M. Maliszewska (2022), *Reshaping Global Value Chains in Light of COVID-19 : Implications for Trade and Poverty Reduction in Developing Countries*, World Bank, http://hdl.handle.net/10986/37032. [9]

Climate Action Tracker (2022), *Global reaction to energy crisis risks zero carbon transition: Analysis of government responses to Russia's invasion of Ukraine*, https://climateactiontracker.org/publications/global-reaction-to-energy-crisis-risks-zero-carbon-transition/. [14]

Ember (2022), *Coal is not making a comeback: Europe plans limited increase*, https://emberclimate.org/insights/research/coal-is-not-making-a-comeback/. [16]

FAO (2022), *FAO Food Price Index*, https://www.fao.org/worldfoodsituation/foodpricesindex/en/. [11]

Financial Times (2022), *Europe's new dirty energy: The 'unavoidable evil' of wartime fossil fuels*, https://www.ft.com/content/b209933f-df7f-49ae-8f82-edc32ed622a6. [15]

FT Adviser (2022), *Energy bill support package not long-term thinking, advisers say*, https://www.ftadviser.com/your-industry/2022/09/12/energy-bill-support-package-not-longterm-thinking-advisers-say/. [19]

Goldthau, A. and L. Hughes (2020), "Protect global supply chains for low-carbon technologies", *Nature*, Vol. 585/7823, pp. 28-30, https://doi.org/10.1038/d41586-020-02499-8. [10]

IEA (2022), *Global Energy and Climate Model*, https://www.iea.org/reports/global-energy-and-climate-model. [21]

McWilliams, B. et al. (2022), "A grand bargain to steer through the European Union's energy crisis", *Bruegel Policy Contribution* 14, https://www.bruegel.org/sites/default/files/2022-09/PC%2014%202022_0.pdf. [13]

O'Callaghan, B. et al. (2021), *Global Recovery Observatory*, https://recovery.smithschool.ox.ac.uk/tracking/. [2]

OECD (2023), *OECD Economic Outlook, Interim Report March 2023: A Fragile Recovery*, OECD Publishing, Paris, https://doi.org/10.1787/d14d49eb-en. [12]

OECD (2022), *Agricultural Policy Monitoring and Evaluation 2022: Reforming Agricultural Policies for Climate Change Mitigation*, OECD Publishing, Paris, https://doi.org/10.1787/7f4542bf-en. [22]

OECD (2022), "Assessing environmental impact of measures in the OECD Green Recovery Database", *OECD Policy Responses to Coronavirus (COVID-19)*, OECD Publishing, Paris, https://doi.org/10.1787/3f7e2670-en. [1]

OECD (2022), "International trade during the COVID-19 pandemic: Big shifts and uncertainty", *OECD Policy Responses to Coronavirus (COVID-19)*, OECD Publishing, Paris, https://doi.org/10.1787/d1131663-en. [7]

OECD (2022), "Why governments should target support amidst high energy prices", *OECD Policy Responses on the Impacts of the War in Ukraine*, OECD Publishing, Paris, https://doi.org/10.1787/40f44f78-en. [18]

OECD (2021), *Agricultural Policy Monitoring and Evaluation 2021: Addressing the Challenges Facing Food Systems*, OECD Publishing, Paris, https://doi.org/10.1787/2d810e01-en. [3]

OECD (2021), *OECD Companion to the Inventory of Support Measures for Fossil Fuels 2021*, OECD Publishing, Paris, https://doi.org/10.1787/e670c620-en. [23]

OECD (2020), "COVID-19 and the low-carbon transition: Impacts and possible policy responses", *OECD Policy Responses to Coronavirus (COVID-19)*, OECD Publishing, Paris, https://doi.org/10.1787/749738fc-en. [8]

OECD (2020), "Food Supply Chains and COVID-19: Impacts and Policy Lessons", *OECD Policy Responses to Coronavirus (COVID-19)*, OECD Publishing, Paris, https://doi.org/10.1787/71b57aea-en. [6]

OECD and IEA (2021), *Update on recent progress in reform of inefficient fossil-fuel subsidies that encourage wasteful consumption*, http://www.oecd.org/fossil-fuels/publicationsandfurtherreading/OECD-IEA-G20-Fossil-Fuel-Subsidies-Reform-Update-2021.pdf. [24]

Reuters (2022), *U.S. to resume oil, gas drilling on public land despite Biden campaign pledge*, https://www.reuters.com/world/us/us-resume-oil-gas-drilling-public-land-despite-bidencampaign-pledge-2022-04-15/. [17]

Vivid Economics, UNFCCC Race to Zero campaign and the Glasgow Financial Alliance for Net Zero (2021), *Net Zero Financing Roadmaps*, https://www.gfanzero.com/netzerofinancing. [5]

4 Systemic resilience: an approach to future-proofing climate action

This chapter highlights how the confluence of recent overlapping global crises with the profound socio-economic changes necessary to enable the net-zero transition point to the need to pursue systemic resilience, ensuring that systems can anticipate, absorb, recover and adapt to potential future shocks. It defines systemic resilience and how it can be applied to climate policy making, including through the use of strategic foresight to identify and prepare for potential future disruptions.

This chapter draws on contributions to the Horizontal Project carried out under the OECD's New Approaches to Economic Challenges (NAEC) programme and Strategic Foresight Unit.

As depicted in the previous chapters, the risk of climate tipping points highlights the non-linear, systemic nature of climate impacts. However, the climate system is only one of many human and natural systems in a highly interconnected world. The COVID-19 pandemic and war in Ukraine are recent examples of interwoven crises with far-reaching socio-economic consequences, including implications for climate action.

The potential for both climate impacts and the transition to net zero by mid-century to trigger cascading socio-economic effects exemplifies the need to consider important interactions between all manner of natural and human systems. This requires systems thinking, as systemic interactions generate impacts that detailed but isolated knowledge of each system's individual parts cannot predict (Hynes et al., 2022[1]).[1]

This chapter defines systemic resilience and how it can be applied to climate policy, highlighting strategic foresight as a means for governments to stress test and future-proof their climate policies against a wide array of possible disruptions.

What is systemic resilience?

Systemic resilience is the ability of a system to anticipate, absorb, recover and adapt to unforeseen shocks (OECD, 2020[2]). It assumes that shocks are inevitable, their consequences large, and their origins unpredictable. As such, systemic resilience is "risk agnostic": it integrates and builds upon risk management in the sense that it considers not just how to anticipate, avoid and limit damages, but also how a system recovers from any given shock and adapts to the resulting new circumstances (Hynes, Trump and Linkov, 2019[3]). Recovery here refers to the ability of a system to return to its pre-shock state as quickly and efficiently as possible, whereas adaptation refers to the ability of a system to adjust based on its experience of the shock in order to increase its resilience to future shocks. As such, resilience stands apart from risk management in the sense that it considers not just how to anticipate, avoid and limit damages, but also how to bounce back from inevitable disruptions and learn from them, in a sense to "bounce forward".

Hynes et al. (2022[1]) point to two broad means of achieving systemic resilience. Resilience by intervention (i.e. exogenous resilience) refers to the transfer of immense resources by governments, usually as a stop-gap measure to avoid systemic collapse following a major shock. Resilience by design (i.e. endogenous resilience) refers to measures that enhance a system's ability to self-regulate or self-organise, internally reallocating resources so as to absorb, recover and adapt to shocks.

The predominant response to recent systemic crises has largely been exogenous. Both the COVID-19 pandemic and 2007-2008 global financial crisis have had lasting global impacts on a wide variety of socio-economic systems. Both originated from local or firm-level disruptions that quickly cascaded throughout other interlinked systems at considerable cost. The reaction to both also focused primarily on large transfers from governments to ensure that financial and economic systems did not collapse. In the case of the global financial crisis, this involved bank bailouts. In the case of the COVID-19 pandemic, furlough schemes and direct transfers to households and affected businesses were widely used to protect livelihoods.

Such direct intervention by governments, while necessary, is extremely expensive and does little to enhance future systemic resilience. For example, austerity measures implemented in response to the global financial crisis starved health care systems of the funding necessary to prepare for a public health crisis such as a global pandemic (OECD, 2020[2]). More recently, policies taken in response to COVID-19 and the war in Ukraine, discussed in the previous chapter in relation to their impacts on climate policies, also have implications for vulnerability to future shocks. This includes the immense transfers governments had to undertake to avoid economic collapse during COVID 19, which raised debt levels and generally contributed to economic volatility. Non-monetary interventions, including widespread lockdown measures, had similarly disruptive effects, including supply chain bottlenecks and global materials shortages. The war in Ukraine has exacerbated this precarious situation. As before, governments have reacted through transfers to households, and now energy subsidies that threaten not only to further lock in fossil fuel use but also to increase public debt levels (OECD, 2022[4]).

These examples illustrate the need for endogenous resilience, whereby systems are able to themselves reallocate resources to absorb and adapt to shocks, reducing the need for exogenous intervention. For example, a health care system that is resilient by design would have been better able to cope with a surge in new patients due to a novel virus such as COVID-19. This would have limited the need for widespread lockdown measures and the resulting government transfers. Pre-emptive resilience by design thus facilitates more effective resilience by intervention when major shocks occur. This is because the initial need for large-scale intervention is reduced, allowing for more targeted and less costly exogenous measures that can ensure a faster and more efficient recovery.

In addition to needing to consider both exogenous and endogenous resilience, there is a trade-off between resilience and short-term efficiency (Hynes et al., 2022[1]). Currently, economic systems are geared towards extracting maximum value in the short term, with little regard for the underlying structure of the system and its ability to self-organise in the face of shocks. This further limits the resources available for resilience by intervention, for example by discouraging strategic redundancies or safety nets that could ensure the continued functioning of a system during shocks.

An example of this compromise can be seen in the 2021 electricity system collapse in Texas. In early 2021, cold weather and soaring demand resulted in near collapse of the entire electricity grid, at considerable human cost (Jin et al., 2021[5]). Decisions guided solely by economic efficiency left the state's electricity system vulnerable to shocks. For example, Texas's energy grid lacked interconnections with other states, allowing efficient governance of the system without federal oversight, but also reducing its ability to manage demand surges with imports. An additional factor is that Texas's plants were only compensated for power produced, not their capacity to produce electricity. This maximises economic efficiency but reduces resilience and redundancy, as plants are not incentivised to prepare for demand surges or other shocks.

Finally, efficient pricing kept prices low, pushing producers to delay winter weatherisation investments in order to maintain profits. These effects were compounded by inadequate risk assessment, with prior testing of the system's ability to withstand shocks based on approaches that did not include the potential for low probability, high-impact events. They were also largely based on historic climate data without taking into account projections of future climate risks in light of global warming (Jin et al., 2021[5]). While Texas's electricity grid is an outlier (electricity systems in other jurisdictions are resilient by law, mandating capacity reserves to ensure energy security (OECD, 2020[2])), similar trade-offs between efficiency and resilience are ubiquitous throughout socio-economic systems.

In addition to trade-offs with efficiency, resilience measures may compromise other objectives such as sustainability (Keenan et al., 2021[6]). For example, recent measures enacted to enhance economic resilience in the face of crisis could be seen as conflicting with other imperatives such as climate action. Despite promises of a "green recovery", a relatively low proportion of COVID-19 recovery spending (33%) has been oriented to environmental objectives.

Ensuring systemic resilience thus requires careful balancing between endogenous and exogenous measures, between resilience and efficiency, and between resilience and other normatively desirable outcomes such as sustainability. Practically, this implies the following:

- Methods for quantifying resilience so that trade-offs between resilience and efficiency – and sustainability – can be made explicit and managed. This requires novel analytical approaches (Box 4.1).
- Oversight of systems and systemic interactions to minimise the potential for cascading failures, as well as communication and co-ordination across systems components and between different systems. This applies to various components of infrastructure systems as well as broader governance, i.e. of the economy, with siloed decision making on economic sectors in isolation inconducive to broader economic resilience.
- Concerted efforts to ensure sufficient resources and redundancies to manage unexpected shocks (OECD, 2020[59]).

Box 4.1. Methodological approaches to assessing systemic resilience

Assessing systemic resilience and designing measures to enhance it requires a broad approach covering multiple domains, from physical to social (Linkov, Trump and Hynes, 2019[7]). Key to this is the availability of a transparent dataset and a clear and replicable framework or approach to processing this data, as well as predetermined criteria for resilience success or failure. Finally, assessing systemic resilience must take into account the dynamic nature of social systems and their implications for resilience, such as political upheaval, etc. (Linkov, Trump and Hynes, 2019[7]). Although systems thinking and resilience assessment remain nascent concepts, concrete methodologies and approaches for better incorporating systemic resilience within policy making are emerging:

Resilience analytics entail the systematic use of data-driven methods to ensure resilience in interdependent infrastructure systems. Thanks to advances in digital network technologies, infrastructure systems can be replicated as real-time digital counterparts, or digital twins, which can be subjected to stress tests and simulations in order to understand and visualise systems responses to shocks. This results in targeted information on which specific system components are likely to fail and how they can be adapted to ensure overall systems resilience. Shocks can be randomised to account for the risk-agnostic nature of resilience, and the low-probability, high-impact nature of systemic risk. Applied to electricity systems, for example, resilience analytics could assess the application of targeted redundancies such as microgrid configurations, in effect reorienting or containing a part of the system, that could be switched on in the event of a significant disruption (Jin et al., 2021[5]).

The use of digital technologies generally can assist in balancing trade-offs between resilience and efficiency, assisting in the collection and process of data and supporting decision making, e.g. through real-time assessment tools. However, digital technologies also come with their own resilience implications, e.g. reliance on a stable power supply and being vulnerable to cyber-attacks (Argyroudis et al., 2022[8]).

The **resilience matrix** is organised across four domains (physical, informational, cognitive and social) and four phases (prepare, absorb, recover and adapt). To employ the matrix, weights and scores are applied to the systems assessed based on relevant indices and indicators, resulting in average overall resilience scores that can be compared across systems. As such, the matrix provides important information on resilience gaps within and across systems (Linkov, Trump and Hynes, 2019[7]). Along with stress testing, the matrix has been suggested as a useful component of a multi-tiered approach to resilience assessments. Under this approach, the first tier entails the gathering of quick qualitative information to identify scenarios and critical systems functions. In the second, the resilience matrix and stress testing are applied to understand overall systems dynamics. The third and final tier provides targeted information on interconnected systems components (Linkov et al., 2022[9]).

Applying systemic resilience to climate policy

Climate change will invariably lead to systemic disruptions, due to its impacts and the rapid transition to net zero emissions. In addition, climate action itself must be resilient to shocks to avoid catastrophic climate impacts. Resilience thus needs to be integral across climate policy.

Concerning mitigation, key systemic interactions threaten policy ambition. First, the transition to net-zero emissions will face numerous socio-economic challenges and bottlenecks, a reality brought into focus by the consequences of interventions made following COVID-19 and the war in Ukraine. Political upheaval may also distract from climate targets as political parties focus on short-term economic stability over long term sustainable development in order to attract voters. Indeed, the current cost-of-living crisis is already testing government commitment to mitigation efforts, with energy subsidies threatening to lock in fossil fuel consumption (IEA and OECD, 2022[10]; OECD, 2015[11]). Increasing capital costs may further threaten investment needs for renewable energy and other green technologies.

Second, the net-zero transition itself will pose systemic challenges. For example, recent research highlights the considerable risk of stranded fossil fuel assets (Semieniuk et al., 2022[12]). Modelling predicts that the fiscal implications of stranded assets will be potentially dire for countries heavily reliant on fossil fuel production and export (see Chapter 6). Assessing the resilience of socio-economic systems to this shock will require transparent monitoring of assets and clear communication of risks. In addition to emissions reductions measures, policy design should include means to limit the potential economic fallout of stranded assets. Societal upheaval due to concern about social impacts of the transition – whether through employment upheaval or inequality or both – is another transition risk. Here, adequate social safety nets and targeted interventions to ensure worker compensation are tried and tested means of ensuring resilience within labour markets (Chapter 8).

Broader systemic effects should also receive more attention. Indeed, just transition concerns are a subset of broader political volatility. Even if fossil fuel-intensive sectors experience a just and orderly transition, social vulnerabilities exacerbated by cost-of-living crises, social media, etc. may still pose a threat to climate ambition overall.

Concerning adaptation, the threat of cascading impacts necessitates transformational policies. Of particular importance is a system's ability not only to recover, but to adapt to new circumstances. For example, air conditioning alone does not ensure resilience to mounting heatwaves, as it does little to address urban heat island multipliers or badly insulated homes. It may in fact threaten emissions reductions if increasing energy demand cannot be met through renewable sources (OECD, 2021[13]).

A more systemic approach to climate action would serve to mitigate emissions while building resilience to physical impacts. Such an approach can also have important synergies with welfare outcomes, as highlighted by the OECD's *Transport Strategies for Net-zero Systems by Design* (OECD, 2021[14]). For example, systems redesign of urban transport focused on accessibility would increase well-being and also reduce emissions and material and energy use. By design, it would also be more resilient to shocks. Multi-modal travel reduces reliance on the manufacturing of electric vehicles and on the electricity grid to power them. Moreover, reducing distances between places increases resilience to extreme weather events by reducing individuals' exposure radius (e.g. shorter commutes may be less affected by local floods inundating roads). Accessibility to health and other services is also important in the case of shocks such as a public health emergency, conflict or natural disaster (OECD, 2021[14]). The synergies between well-being, mitigation, and resilience further highlight the imperative of systemic approaches to climate action.

Addressing climate change also has systemic implications far beyond mitigation and adaptation. For example, rapid technological change, while entailing its own systemic risks, may prove invaluable in reducing emissions and decarbonising the global economy, as well as building resilience to climate impacts. Here, the science and technology system is of particular importance. For example, the response

– and global resilience – to the COVID-19 crisis owes much to rapid progress in vaccination and digital technologies. In both cases, a long-term commitment to innovation support was crucial. Rapid vaccine development could not have occurred without decades-long investment into the sector. Similarly, digital technologies were mature enough to meet demand during the pandemic. This highlights the need for patient and sustained investment in innovation as a means to ensure societal preparedness in the face of shocks (OECD, 2021[15]).

The climate crisis has implications beyond economic, financial and energy systems. For example, the health system co-benefits of climate action are well documented, such as the role of green spaces in improving climate resilience and public health (Anderson, Patiño Quinchía and Prieto Curiel, 2022[16])). Conversely, biofuel demand can have implications for food prices, with cascading effects (Subramaniam, Masron and Azman, 2019[17]). The climate crisis also has considerable mental health and gender implications that are only slowly being explored in detail (OECD, 2021[18]).

Addressing climate change will considerably impact systems for international co-operation. For example, the lead-up to COP26 in 2021 was strongly affected by concerns over vaccine distribution and technology transfer. Climate clubs and proposed schemes such as the EU's proposed carbon border adjustment mechanism (CBAM) will have impacts on international co-operation beyond the climate sphere (Jakob et al., 2022[19]) (OECD, 2020[20]). Russia's war on Ukraine has further exposed considerable vulnerability in the international co-operative system. As such, failure to reach a co-operative agreement on continued climate action may have cascading effects beyond mitigation and adaptation policy. Ensuring that the international co-operative architecture remains strong is paramount to ensuring the net-zero transition.

Biodiversity and other natural systems are extremely vulnerable to climate impacts. At the same time, synergies between these systems can be effective in addressing the climate crisis. Nature-based solutions (NbS) have received increasing attention as a means to mitigate emissions and adapt to climate impacts, with natural systems often considerably more resilient than those managed by human intervention. (NbS are explored in more detail in Chapter 12.)

Strategic foresight as a means to building systemic resilience

Given the complexity of systems and their interactions, governments can strengthen systemic resilience by stress testing their policy strategies. Strategic foresight offers a way to do this by providing a structured approach to exploring possible future disruptions and their implications.

Strategic foresight entails scanning the horizon for new developments and emerging trends, constructing scenarios about how the future could unfold, and designing forward-looking strategies under a wide range of possible circumstances. In a governance context, it allows decision makers to examine the assumptions underlying their current strategies, anticipate how those strategies might be vulnerable to radical changes in areas outside of their control, and design more robust strategies that are better equipped to withstand potential shocks.

The OECD Strategic Foresight for Successful Net-Zero Transitions Toolkit uses strategic foresight to examine factors that could enhance or limit the ability of countries and organisations to meet their net-zero greenhouse gas emissions ambitions. By applying a five-step strategic foresight process specifically to climate policy making, it provides a methodology and guidance for countries and organisations to stress test their net-zero transition plans (Figure 4.1).

Figure 4.1. Strategic foresight for successful net-zero transitions

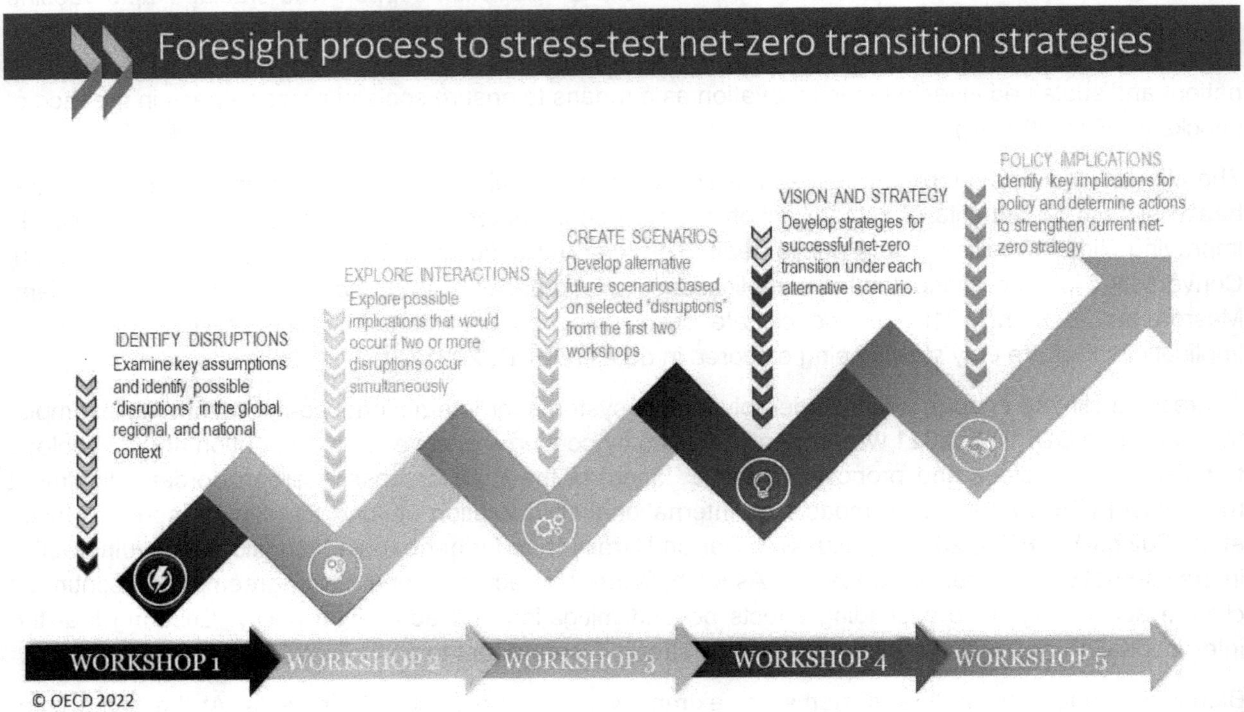

Source: OECD Strategic Foresight Unit.

The toolkit is a highly adaptable model for integrating strategic foresight into long-term planning. It can be applied at multiple levels of government with diverse mandates, and is particularly useful for organisations as an accelerator for horizontal and forward-looking climate policy and strategy development. It can be applied to diverse groups with varying backgrounds. For groups that do not have a traditional climate policy background, the toolkit can introduce a climate lens into long-term planning processes. For more climate focused groups, it provides an opportunity to bring other aspects (e.g. social, geopolitical and technological) into the fold. In all cases, the toolkit is a way to bring forward topics that are insufficiently considered and often treated in separate silos.

A fundamental challenge of net-zero strategies is that, because they are so all encompassing, they are vulnerable to a wide variety of disruptions across sectors. This means that a change in one area could radically alter how net-zero strategies need to be conceived or implemented in several others. To this end, the toolkit provides a way to ensure the robustness of net-zero strategies by testing how they would perform under scenarios in which the world is subjected to various plausible disruptions.

The OECD Strategic Foresight Unit has developed a list of 25 possible disruptions to illustrate how a specific uncertainty in one sector could plausibly occur and lead to surprising implications for net-zero strategies (Figure 4.2).[2]

Figure 4.2. Drivers of change that, if pushed to a plausible extreme, could cause significant system-level changes in the period 2030-2050

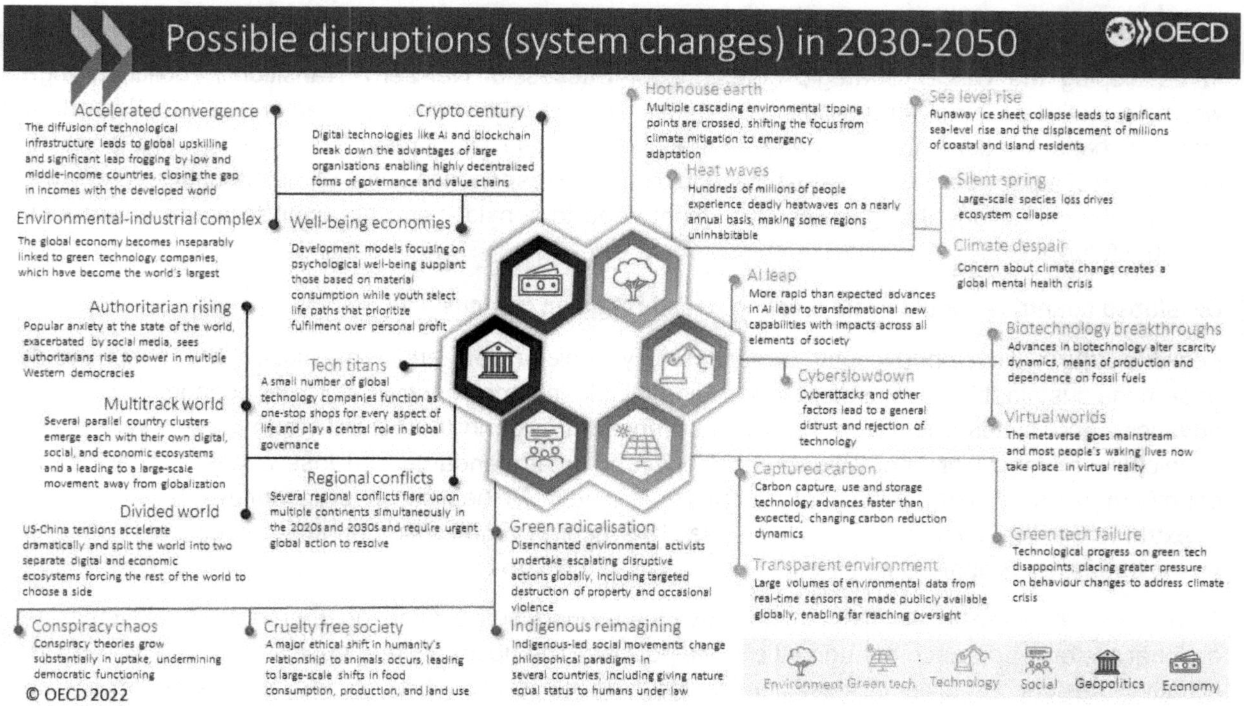

Source: OECD Strategic Foresight Unit.

The disruptions are grouped across six domains: Environment, Green Tech, Technology, Social, Geopolitics and Economy. Each disruption represents a plausible extreme development that could present significant challenges or opportunities. Some of these disruptions are already taking place today: for example, the war in Ukraine exemplifies the threat of regional conflict to net-zero transitions, and emerging evidence on climate tipping points increases the likelihood of reaching a “hot-house Earth” scenario in which multiple cascading tipping points are crossed. This makes foresight all the more necessary in order to build resilience to future possible disruptions.

The disruptions serve as a starting point to raise awareness of potential future shocks. Participants explore how they could occur concurrently and interact, then develop strategies to adapt to, and contingency plan for, various potential futures. These exercises are an important first step in engaging policy makers with long-term resilience plans for the net-zero transition (Figure 4.2).

Preparing for disruptions is necessary due diligence in modern policy making. Successful net-zero transitions depend on the ability to design well-considered and future-ready transition strategies today, with the capacity to continually anticipate, prepare for, and adapt to change over the years and decades ahead. The OECD Strategic Foresight for Successful Net-Zero Transitions Toolkit is one model for governments and organisations to engage in climate-focused foresight work.

Box 4.2. High-level takeaways from piloting the OECD Strategic Foresight for Successful Net-Zero Transitions Toolkit

In developing the OECD Strategic Foresight for Successful Net-Zero Transitions Toolkit through workshops with countries and groups of experts, several takeaways emerged which have important strategic considerations for the net-zero transition. These are presented below in two parts: i) description of a possible future context that could occur in response to some of the disruptions explored, and ii) potential actions that governments might need to consider and act upon to prepare for these possible futures.

Developed countries should avoid creating walled-off green gardens

Possible future: Developed countries successfully achieve net zero domestically, but in ways that undermine sustainable development in low- and middle-income countries. Circular economies boom in advanced economies and green innovations transform cities in the Global North. However, firms in developing countries are not able to meet environmental standards and lose access to developed country markets, while green technology transfer is limited. All the while, poorer countries bear the brunt of extreme weather events and sea-level rise. The result is a green and prosperous Global North and an impoverished Global South struggling to cope with climate catastrophes.

To ensure that net-zero transitions do not leave the Global South behind, governments should integrate a global systems approach throughout climate policies. The upstream and downstream implications for initiatives designed to lower domestic emissions in developed countries should be assessed to ensure that they do not cause undue hardship in developing countries.

Net-zero transitions must be insulated from geopolitical conflict

Possible future: Geopolitical confrontations lead to a breakdown of multilateral co-operation. Separate economic spheres emerge, with little to no trade between major economies, even in critical raw materials, and limited technological interoperability. Markets for green technologies shrink and innovations cannot be shared from one sphere to another. Strategies cannot be co-ordinated globally, and countries and spheres scapegoat each other for collective failures to reduce emissions.

Given the possibility of serious challenges to multilateralism, governments should push for global commitments to preserve co-operation on key areas for net zero (i.e. technology transfer) while preparing safety nets in case of a breakdown of global trade (i.e. sufficient redundancy in or stockpiles of critical inputs and functions). While interconnected economies are preferable, and states should be careful not to encourage protectionism, being prepared for circumstances in which supply chains collapse is appropriate due diligence.

Protecting the information ecosystem from misinformation is crucial

Possible future: Net-zero transition strategies are targeted by misinformation and disinformation campaigns co-ordinated by private actors and countries that export fossil fuels. The quantity and quality of conspiracy content is enabled by next-generation digital technologies such as deepfakes and AI language processors. The result is a nearly complete democratic paralysis, as consensus on most issues becomes impossible without a shared fact base. Polarisation within societies is driven to an extreme where democratic compromise is no longer possible.

Given the possibility that information campaigns could target climate strategies, governments should integrate misinformation and disinformation risk assessments into all major climate initiatives and implementation plans. Governments should make proactive investments in communications plans for climate initiatives to bolster widespread support for sustainable products and behavioural changes.

Urgent and unprecedented behavioural change may be necessary

Possible future: Worsening storm surges and heat waves wreak havoc upon large parts of the global population. Drastic changes in lives and lifestyles are urgently required, including relocation and substantial declines in consumption as a result of the destruction of infrastructure and interruption of supply chains. Governments are forced to mandate strict and unprecedented behavioural changes to manage the climate emergency and have begun to face substantial backlash for these measures to the point of heightened worry of societal breakdown.

To be prepared to take rapid large-scale action to meet climate targets or respond to extreme weather events, governments should explore what can be done to foster legitimacy to act in case large-scale behaviour change policies are needed in the event of future catastrophic events. Buy-in and understanding could be built through tools such as citizens' assemblies and supported through a public narrative focusing on green jobs and the wartime-like mobilisation necessary to address the climate emergency.

Safe and trusted AI development is key

Possible future: Artificial intelligence is deployed with great success in the fight against climate change, leading to breakthroughs in green technologies, better co-ordination of climate policies and a far greater capacity to monitor climate conditions, emissions and weather patterns, as well as numerous other areas relating to climate mitigation, adaptation and finance. The efficiency gains enabled by AI have come with substantial increases in job losses due to automation, invasive surveillance by authoritarian states and incomprehensible behaviours among black box algorithms charged with governing complex social systems.

Given that AI will likely play an important role in facilitating net-zero transitions, governments need to proactively address the social impacts and technical safety risks associated with advanced AI systems. Governments need to ensure that AI safety and controllability mechanisms keep pace with advances in AI systems so that there will be adequate trust and reliability to adopt such systems in key infrastructure and other areas critical to reaching climate goals.

Promote competition, not market concentration

Possible future: Massive government investment in green (and digital) transition benefits ultimately only a few incumbent companies, concentrating immense market and political power. This provokes accusations of profiteering among populations experiencing significant hardship due to climate change. In this scenario, extreme corporate concentration leads to some corporations or individuals exercising nearly complete control over quasi-essential services or infrastructure, giving them incredible leverage to shape public policy to suit their interests at the expense of societal benefit.

To prevent net-zero strategies from creating harmful forms of inequality, governments should promote competitive markets, particularly in sectors highly reliant on government investment, and ensure that returns on public investments are widely distributed to avoid exacerbating inequalities and safeguard public support. In instances where concentrations of power cannot be avoided, transparent processes for engaging and negotiating with the most powerful non-state actors to secure their co-operation throughout the course of just transitions could become a crucial factor in the success of net zero.

Note: This list is not exhaustive: the takeaways above are examples of scenarios that, in the absence of strategic foresight processes, might otherwise be missed in conventional climate policy making.
Source: OECD Strategic Foresight Unit.

Chapter conclusions

The systemic nature of climate risks and risks to climate action require systemic solutions. Systemic resilience entails conceptualising and assessing the ability of specific systems to deal with such risks. A systemic approach should be more widely applied to climate related decision-making processes. This requires stress testing climate policy strategies against potential future disruptions, their interactions, and identifying win-win responses to enhance the resilience of policies themselves. It also requires an awareness and understanding of the interlinkages between climate, other natural and human systems, taking advantage of synergies and minimising trade-offs. The remainder of this report applies this approach to a number of different policy areas, focusing on the resilience of the net-zero transition and on building resilience to climate impacts.

Notes

1 Systems thinking is an approach to problem analysis and decision making in a highly complex world. Rather than dividing complex issues into smaller, more manageable parts, systems thinking attempts to look instead at the whole system, focusing on identifying relationships between systems components, the functioning of the system in question, and interactions with other existing systems. It also specifically accounts for the possibility of non-linear systems behaviour.

2 The 25 disruptions were developed in close consultation with OECD subject matter experts, academics, and members of the OECD's global Government Foresight Community, including through a number of focused expert workshops.

References

Anderson, B., J. Patiño Quinchía and R. Prieto Curiel (2022), "Boosting African cities' resilience to climate change: The role of green spaces", *West African Papers*, No. 37, OECD Publishing, Paris, https://doi.org/10.1787/3303cfb3-en. [16]

Argyroudis, S. et al. (2022), "Digital technologies can enhance climate resilience of critical infrastructure", *Climate Risk Management*, Vol. 35, p. 100387, https://doi.org/10.1016/j.crm.2021.100387. [8]

Hynes, W. et al. (2022), "Systemic resilience in economics", *Nature Physics*, Vol. 18/4, pp. 381-384, https://doi.org/10.1038/s41567-022-01581-4. [1]

Hynes, W., B. Trump and I. Linkov (2019), "Resilience-based Strategies and Policies to Address Systemic Risks", No. SG/NAEC(2019)5, OECD, Paris. [3]

IEA and OECD (2022), *Support for fossil fuels almost doubled in 2021, slowing progress toward international climate goals, according to new analysis from OECD and IEA*, OECD/IEA, https://www.oecd.org/environment/support-for-fossil-fuels-almost-doubled-in-2021-slowing-progress-toward-international-climate-goals-according-to-new-analysis-from-oecd-and-iea.htm. [10]

Jakob, M. et al. (2022), "How trade policy can support the climate agenda", *Science*, Vol. 376/6600, pp. 1401-1403, https://doi.org/10.1126/science.abo4207. [19]

Jin, A. et al. (2021), “Building resilience will require compromise on efficiency”, *Nature Energy 2021 6:11*, Vol. 6/11, pp. 997-999, https://doi.org/10.1038/s41560-021-00913-7. [5]

Keenan, J. et al. (2021), “Exploring the Convergence of Resilience Processes and Sustainable Outcomes in Post-COVID, Post-Glasgow Economies”, *Sustainability*, Vol. 13/23, p. 13415, https://doi.org/10.3390/su132313415. [6]

Linkov, I., B. Trump and W. Hynes (2019), *Resilience-based Strategies and Policies to Address Systemic Risks*. [7]

Linkov, I. et al. (2022), “Resilience stress testing for critical infrastructure”, *International Journal of Disaster Risk Reduction*, Vol. 82, p. 103323, https://doi.org/10.1016/j.ijdrr.2022.103323. [9]

OECD (2022), “Why governments should target support amidst high energy prices”, *OECD Policy Responses on the Impacts of the War in Ukraine*, OECD Publishing, Paris, https://doi.org/10.1787/40f44f78-en. [4]

OECD (2021), *Gender and the Environment: Building Evidence and Policies to Achieve the SDGs*, OECD Publishing, Paris, https://doi.org/10.1787/3d32ca39-en. [18]

OECD (2021), *OECD Science, Technology and Innovation Outlook 2021: Times of Crisis and Opportunity*, OECD Publishing, Paris, https://doi.org/10.1787/75f79015-en. [15]

OECD (2021), “Strengthening adaptation-mitigation linkages for a low-carbon, climate-resilient future”, *OECD Environment Policy Papers*, No. 23, OECD Publishing, Paris, https://doi.org/10.1787/6d79ff6a-en. [13]

OECD (2021), *Transport strategies for net-zero systems by design*, OECD, Paris, https://www.oecd.org/climate-change/well-being-lens/ (accessed on 19 October 2021). [14]

OECD (2020), *A Systemic Resilience Approach to dealing with Covid-19 and future shocks*, New Approaches to Economic Challenges, Paris, https://read.oecd-ilibrary.org/view/?ref=131_131917-kpfefrdfnx&title=A-Systemic-Resilience-Approach-to-dealing-with-Covid-19-and-future-shocks (accessed on 26 July 2022). [2]

OECD (2020), *Climate Policy Leadership in an Interconnected World: What Role for Border Carbon Adjustments?*, OECD Publishing, Paris, https://doi.org/10.1787/8008e7f4-en. [20]

OECD (2015), *OECD Companion to the Inventory of Support Measures for Fossil Fuels 2015*, OECD Publishing, Paris, https://doi.org/10.1787/9789264239616-en. [11]

Semieniuk, G. et al. (2022), “Stranded fossil-fuel assets translate to major losses for investors in advanced economies”, *Nature Climate Change 2022 12:6*, Vol. 12/6, pp. 532-538, https://doi.org/10.1038/s41558-022-01356-y. [12]

Subramaniam, Y., T. Masron and N. Azman (2019), “The impact of biofuels on food security”, *International Economics*, Vol. 160, pp. 72-83, https://doi.org/10.1016/j.inteco.2019.10.003. [17]

Part II Accelerating a resilient net-zero transition

5 A resilience lens on the net-zero transition

Achieving net-zero emissions requires a combined focus on accelerating the transition in the near term, making the transition itself resilient for the longer term, and ensuring that the transition serves to improve broader resilience rather than creating new fragilities. This chapter assesses some of the potential bottlenecks that could slow down or derail the net-zero transition, reinforcing the case for taking a resilience lens to the transition as well as the need to better embrace systems-level thinking beyond individual policy approaches and sectors.

This chapter draws on work carried out under the responsibility of the Environment Policy Committee, the Committee on Agriculture, the Trade Committee, the Public Governance Committee, the International Energy Agency and the Nuclear Energy Agency.

The economy-wide challenge of the net-zero transition

This chapter lays out the challenge of achieving net-zero emissions and sets the scene for subsequent chapters that explore different dimensions of building resilient climate action. It assesses some of the potential bottlenecks that could slow or derail net-zero targets, reinforcing the case for applying a resilience lens to the transition. It also emphasises the importance of a whole-of-government approach to ensure a rapid and resilient net-zero transition, and the need to think beyond individual policy approaches and sectors to better embrace the systems-level thinking described in Part I of this report.

Applying a resilience lens requires a triple focus on accelerating the net-zero transition in the near term, making the transition itself resilient for the longer term, and ensuring that it serves to improve broader resilience rather than creating new fragilities.

The challenge of limiting temperature rise to 1.5°C and achieving global net-zero emissions in 2050 is unprecedented in terms of the scale and pace of transformation required. It implies a significant acceleration of action relative to what has been achieved to date, with radical changes across economies and societies in the near term. Countries' current national commitments and policies, while ambitious, will fall short of meeting the 1.5°C target (Figure 5.1). A dramatically steeper decline in emissions is needed to reach net zero by 2050 and stand a chance of avoiding the climate tipping points described in Part I of this report.

Figure 5.1. Limiting warning to 1.5°C or 2°C requires rapid, deep, and in most cases immediate, emissions reductions

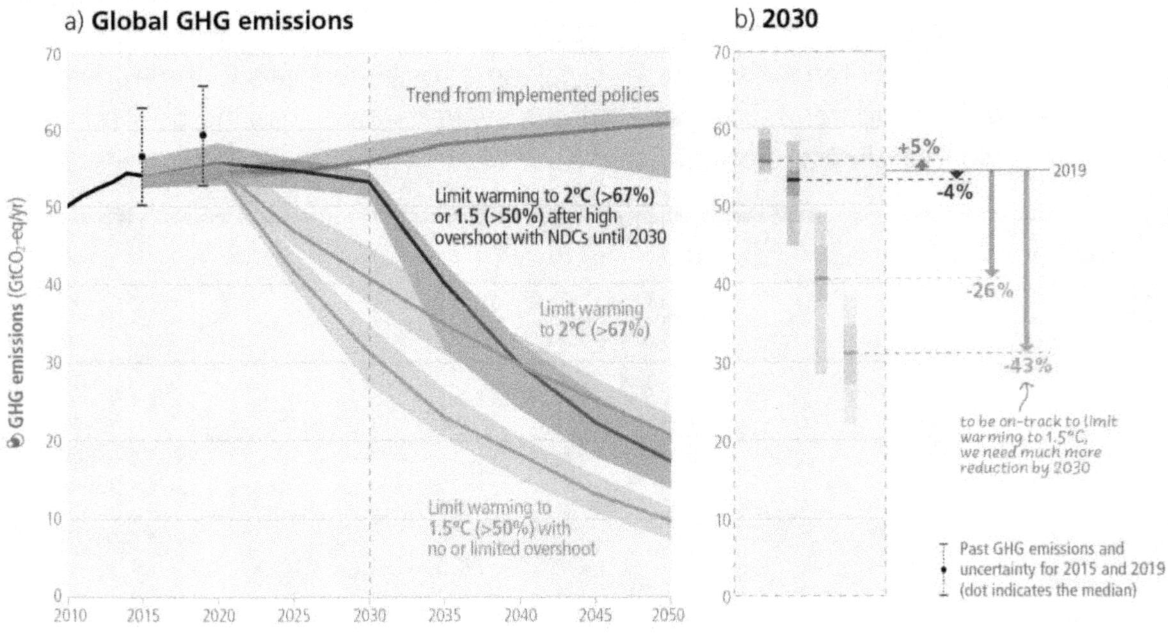

Source: (IPCC, 2023[1])sour

Progress on reducing emissions to date has generally been solid but incremental. Data from the International Programme for Action on Climate (IPAC), carried out under this project, shows that major OECD emitters such as the EU, US and Japan decreased their gross emissions from 2010 to 2019 by 14%, 7% and 5% respectively (Figure 5.2). Nonetheless, these countries remain a considerable distance from their 2030 emissions targets. Additional reductions are required from 2019 to 2030 of 38% (EU), 44% (US) and 34% (Japan).

At the same time, emissions in many emerging economies such as Brazil, China, India and Indonesia have not yet reached their expected peaks. To reach climate targets it is essential that countries reduce energy intensity and decouple greenhouse gas emissions (GHGs) from economic growth and consumption. However, while GHG intensity is declining in both OECD and non-OECD countries, per-capita emissions from energy are increasing in non-OECD countries (Figure 5.3)

Figure 5.2. Accelerated progress is required to stay on track towards 2030 emissions targets

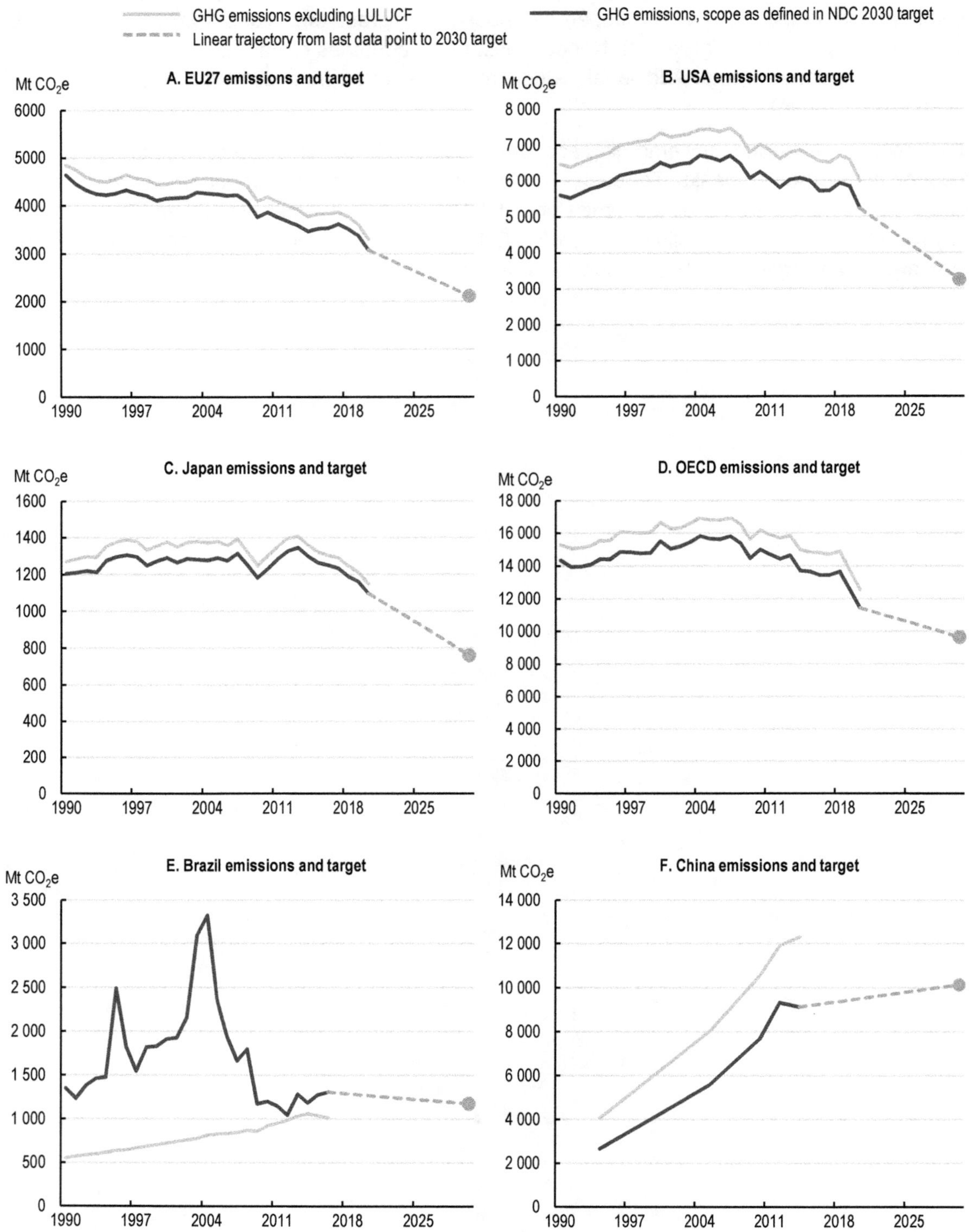

Source: (OECD, 2022[2]).

Figure 5.3. Per-capita emissions have fallen in the OECD but are increasing in non-OECD countries

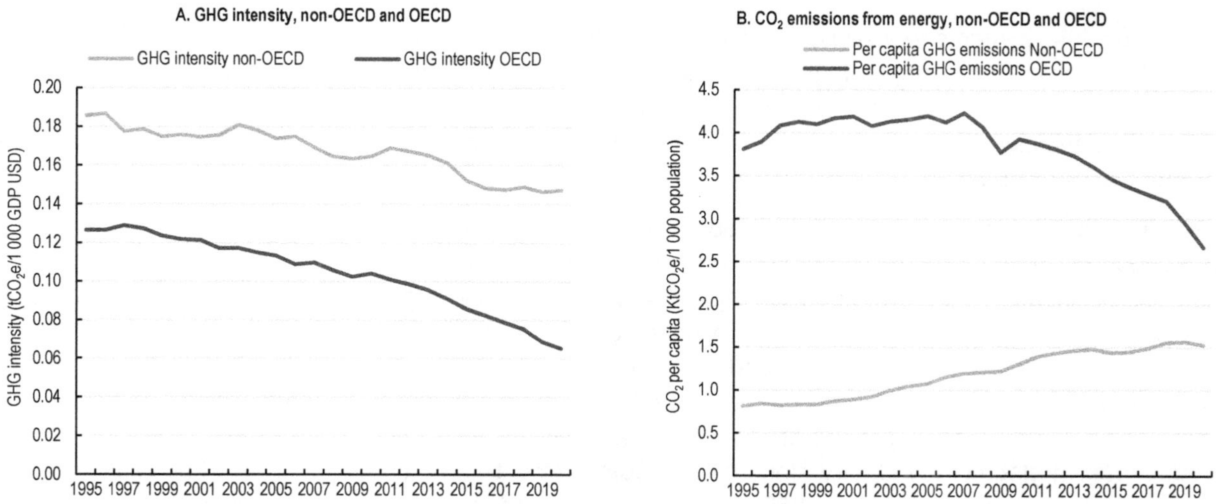

Note: The underlying GDP data used for this chart stems from (OECD, 2023[3]); the underlying CO_2 emissions data stems from (IEA, 2022[4]).
Source: (IEA, 2022[4]).

The figures above illustrate that a resilient net-zero transition necessitates a fair and globally co-ordinated response, with policy approaches tailored to differing national circumstances, and with financial and non-financial support sufficient to fulfil the needs of developing countries. Developing countries are set to account for the bulk of energy generation and consumption – and, on current trajectories, emissions growth – in the coming decades due to economic and population dynamics.

Globally, despite impressive long-term ambition – i.e. 133 countries having adopted net-zero targets by February 2023, covering 83% of emissions – shortfalls in nearer-term climate policy persist. The number and stringency of countries' climate policies has increased since 2010, but progress has been uneven. While most countries covered by IPAC adopted new climate policies between 2015 and 2020, several did not, and others removed or weakened policies. To date, no country has adopted all the major policy types identified by IPAC,[1] clearly showing that a step change in pace is required to achieve climate goals.

Meanwhile, the rapidly changing global circumstances described in Part I of this report, combined with the substantial social and economic implications of the net-zero transition, mean that an accelerated pace will not be enough. Transition strategies must be designed with resilience to disruptions and changing conditions in mind. Efforts also need to be made to ensure that the transition itself does not increase the vulnerability or fragility of systems, whether through technical, social, or economic vulnerabilities.

Potential bottlenecks to the net-zero transition

To ensure a smooth transition that is resilience to changing circumstances, governments need to identify and then anticipate a range of potential bottlenecks to the transition, some of which are described in this section.

Bottlenecks related to stable and secure supply of low-carbon electricity

Net-zero emissions implies substantial changes in the way energy is produced and consumed. As energy is a major source of direct and indirect emissions for most economic sectors, a shift to net-zero emissions implies substantial changes across end-use sectors as well as in energy supply. The shift implies a rapid decline in fossil sources, a rapid rise in low-emissions sources (including some fossil fuels with carbon capture and storage), and a considerable increase in the use of electricity as an energy vector.

A wide-reaching systems reorganisation is necessary to achieve this transition. The shift towards electricity is a key example. For example, in the IEA's Net Zero by 2050 scenario, electricity is projected to account for more than 50% of total energy use in 2050, up from a mere 20% today (IEA, 2023[5]). This implies doubling electricity generation at the same time that the electricity sector undergoes substantial reorganisation as it decarbonises.

A potential bottleneck to the overall transition is therefore a mismatch between rapidly growing electricity demand and the needed stable supply of low-emissions electricity. According to the IEA scenario, global electricity demand will more than double by 2050, even as total energy use declines slightly due to rapid efficiency gains. Demand patterns are projected to change considerably. Geographically, most of the demand growth will be in developing and emerging economies. The main end-use sectors of industry, transport and buildings will all greatly increase their demand for electricity as their contribution to net-zero emissions requires replacing point-of-use solid, gaseous and liquid fuels with electricity and hydrogen produced from electricity. Industry alone will consume almost as much electricity in 2050 (78EJ) as the world's total power demand today (86EJ). Demand for electricity in transport will grow by a factor of 18, with its share of total electricity demand rising from 2% today to more than 20% (IEA, 2021[6]).

Without careful planning, competing new sources of demand for stable low-carbon power might not be met by sufficient supply of clean power. For example, a country with fast-growing traditional sources of electricity demand that also sees an acceleration of electricity demand due to end-uses switching away from fossil fuels, could experience demand crunch at certain times or in certain regions of its electricity grid. An example would be the confluence of increased demand for air conditioning due to rising temperatures, rapid growth of electric vehicle charging, new direct sources of electricity in industry, and a nascent green hydrogen industry requiring continuous electricity supply for electrolysers. By some estimates, hydrogen production capacity is expected to reach 5 000 gigawatts (GW) by 2050, requiring a low-carbon power production of 21 000 terawatt-hour (TWh) purely to produce the hydrogen before considering other demand needs. This implies a total cumulative investment need of USD 11.7 trillion in renewable power, electrolysers and pipeline reconfiguration by 2050 (IRENA, 2022[7]). This confluence of demand sources could lead to a need to continue running emissions-intensive thermal power to meet the peaks and/or a spike in power prices. The latter would result in some demand centres being uneconomic and create affordability concerns for domestic power consumers.

Avoiding this work depends in part on a rapid scale-up in renewables. The IEA's net-zero scenario forecasting very rapid growth in wind and solar in the next five years (IEA, 2022[8]) and further into the future. Renewables generation nearly triples by 2030, and nearly triples again by 2050, with most of the growth led by wind and solar. The investment needs of this growth have been much discussed, though a key additional factor is delivering this investment growth in times of high inflation and rising costs of capital (see below). Another low-carbon source of power is nuclear power in those countries that accept it (Box 5.1).

However, stable zero-carbon power is not just about generation technologies. Stable delivery of power through reinforced and digitised transmission and distribution networks will be essential, along with a strong focus on maintaining power system flexibility. Power systems need to consistently match supply with demand through flexible sources. Weather-dependent renewables such as wind and solar are not flexible power sources unless combined with back-up electricity storage. Traditionally, power systems have four main sources of flexibility – flexible generation, interconnection through grids, managing demand, storing electricity – and thermal power generation has traditionally supplied the lion's share of flexibility (IEA, 2022[9]). As thermal generation phases out in a rapid transition scenario at the same time as more and more parts of the economy come to depend on electricity, it is essential that other forms of flexibility scale up to maintain stable power systems.

The IEA estimates that flexibility needs will increase by a factor of four by 2050 in a net-zero transition with improved power grids, battery storage and demand management becoming key factors. This points to rapid growth in the need for grid-scale power storage, including battery storage, at a time when demand for batteries will be growing strongly from the transport sector, leading to a bottleneck of critical materials for batteries (see below). It also points to a need for greatly reinforced electricity grids, with investment needs tripling by 2030 (IEA, 2022[10]). Increasing digitalisation of power system management has to play a key role in addition to expanded investments in physical transmission capacity, eased by improved permitting processes.

Box 5.1. The role of nuclear power for net-zero transitions

In a special report published in 2018, the IPCC considered 90 pathways consistent with a 1.5°C scenario – i.e. pathways with emissions reductions sufficient to limit average global warming to less than 1.5°C. The IPCC found that, on average, the pathways for the 1.5°C scenario require nuclear energy to reach 1 160 gigawatts of electricity by 2050, up from 394 gigawatts in 2020. This is an ambitious target for nuclear energy, though not beyond reach. It can be achieved through a combination of long-term operations, large-scale new builds and small modular reactors, as shown in Figure 5.4.

The 444 nuclear power reactors in operation worldwide today provide 394 gigawatts of electrical capacity that supplies approximately 10% of the world's electricity. Nuclear energy is the largest source of non-emitting electricity generation in OECD countries and the second largest source worldwide (after hydropower). There are approximately 50 more nuclear reactors under construction to provide an additional 55 gigawatts of capacity and more than 100 additional reactors are planned. Existing nuclear capacity displaces 1.6 gigatonnes of carbon dioxide emissions annually and has displaced 66 gigatonnes of carbon dioxide since 1971 – the equivalent of two years of global emissions (NEA, 2022[11]).

The nuclear sector can support future climate change mitigation efforts in a variety of ways. Existing global installed nuclear capacity is already playing a role, and long-term operation of the existing fleet can continue to make a contribution for decades to come. There is also significant potential for large-scale nuclear new builds to provide non-emitting electricity in existing and embarking nuclear power jurisdictions; in particular, to replace coal. In addition, a wave of near-term and medium-term nuclear innovations have the potential to open up new opportunities with advanced and small modular reactors (SMRs), as well as nuclear hybrid energy systems, reaching into new markets and applications. These innovations include sector coupling combined heat and power (co-generation) for heavy industry and resource extraction, hydrogen and synthetic fuel production, desalination, and off-grid applications.

Figure 5.4. Nuclear power to 2050 in IPCC scenarios

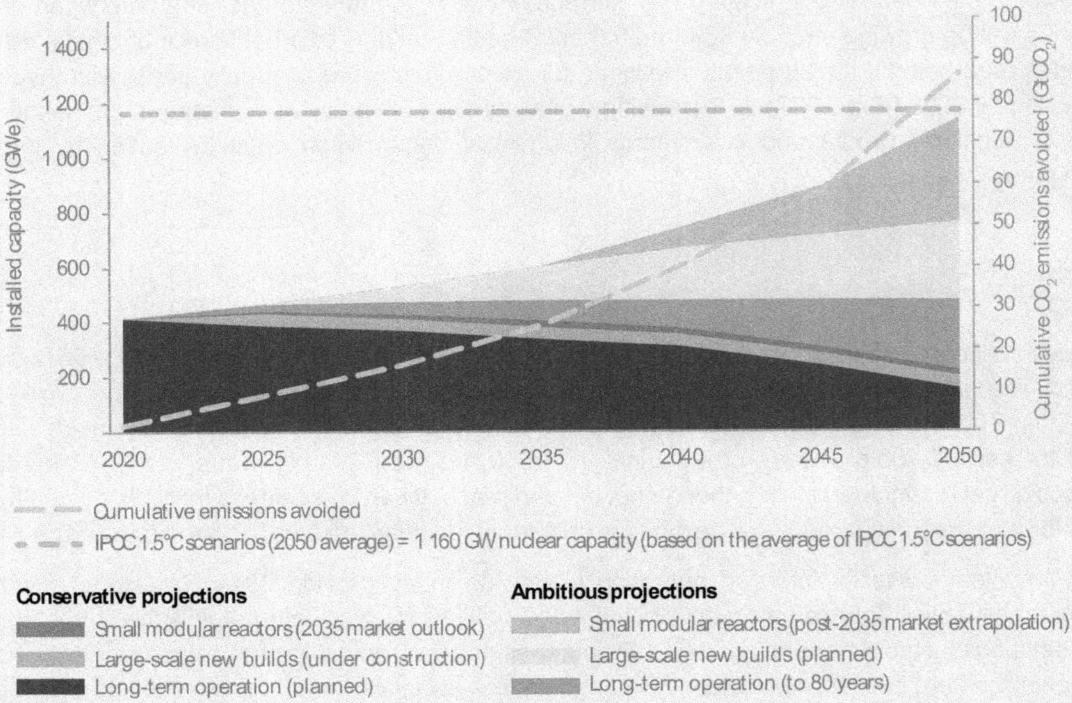

Source: (NEA, 2022[11]).

The potential bottleneck around stable, low-carbon power generation overlaps with other bottlenecks related to the transition. These include resilient supply of critical materials; regulations that allow for the development and commercialisation of new technologies; development and distribution of skills needed given the rapid shifts in technologies and therefore job needs; and the need to massively increase investment flows. These are discussed briefly here and treated in more depth in subsequent chapters.

Bottlenecks related to materials supply for the transition

Technologies needed for the energy transition require more critical minerals and metals per unit of energy than fossil fuel-based energy sources. Several renewable energy technologies as well as batteries for electric vehicles all require significant quantities of materials such as lithium, nickel, cobalt, graphite and rare earth elements. In addition, scaled-up power grids are reliant on copper. The IEA estimates that to reach net zero by 2050, up to six times more minerals would be required for the energy sector than today (IEA, 2021[6]). Even common metals such as steel and aluminium are essential for the construction of renewable energy plants such as wind turbines. Supply issues and rising prices of these materials materially impacted wind turbine production and outlook in 2022, pointing to another potentially important bottleneck for the transition.

While mineral supply chains have responded to increased demand in the past, the sudden increase in demand due to a rapid energy transition could lead to supply shocks, potentially slowing the transition and causing energy security crises. As overall technology costs have fallen over the past decade, the relative proportion of material costs has risen, leaving final products relatively more exposed to price volatility in critical minerals. Without reliable supply chains for key minerals and metals, many of which currently come from high-risk areas, it will not be possible to scale up clean energy technologies quickly enough to meet global climate goals.

Critical minerals, and their use in clean energy supply chains, present several vulnerabilities. First, mineral reserves are often geographically concentrated and, in the case of some minerals, in countries with high political risk. For example, the Democratic Republic of Congo accounts for around 75% of global cobalt production, with the top three lithium producers occupying 90% of the market (IEA, 2023[5]). China is also dominant both for minerals supply (being home to 60% of the world's rare earth elements) but also in particular for processing capacity. Important geographical concentration also currently exists in locations with capacity for transforming minerals into components of clean energy technologies. The dominance of China here is quite striking, as reflected by the regional production of minerals after processing (Figure 5.5).

Figure 5.5. Regional shares of global production of selected critical materials, 2021

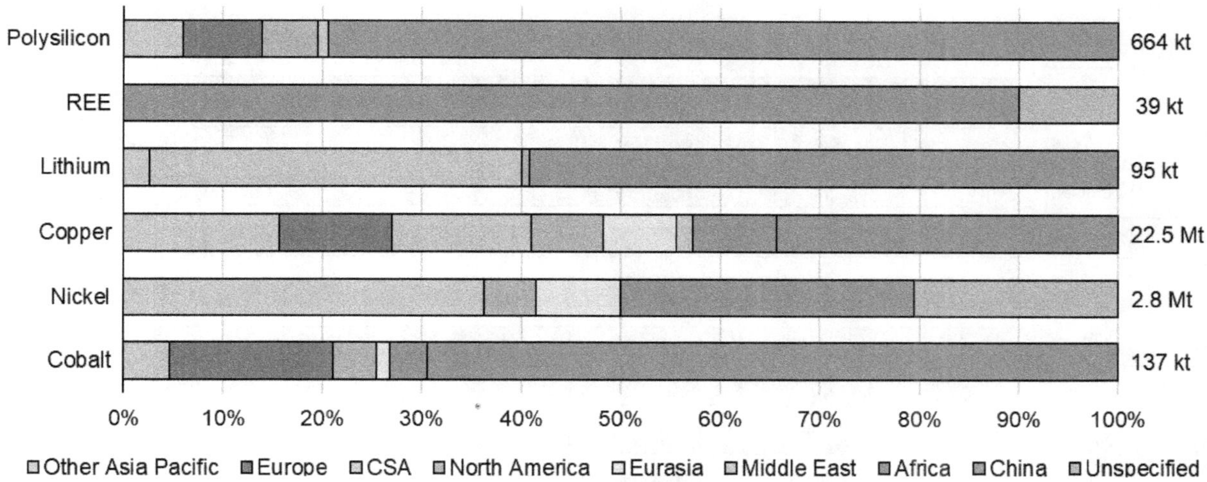

Source: (IEA, 2023[5]).

Geographical concentration can also bring sustainability risks to companies lower down the critical minerals supply chain. Environmental, social and governance (ESG) requirements necessitate scrutiny of supply chains and there are potential reputational risks if mining practices are found to be environmentally or socially damaging. Mines also tend to have long development times, meaning that industry cannot respond quickly to structural shocks requiring ramping up of production. This would be the case if or when a strong political signal is given to accelerate the transition.

Accordingly, policy makers seeking more resilient and sustainable supply chains can ensure that their policies are sending a clear signal that the transition will accelerate. This can trigger new international investments in mineral production and mines that can help overcome long lead-times. Governments can also take steps to diversify sources of supply, whether within their own borders; through new partnerships and agreements; or by providing finance overseas to de-risk new projects. This is even more important given a rise in export restrictions; the OECD's annual database on critical raw materials shows that the global incidence of export restrictions increased more than five-fold in the last decade, with several countries significantly intensifying use of these measures. In recent years, about 10% of the global value of exports of critical raw materials faced at least one export restriction measure (Kowalski and Legendre, 2023[12]).

Another means to improve resilience of mineral supply is through a policy push to encourage greater recycling of minerals, which will help improve the resilience of supply chains to price shocks due to geopolitical events in key countries. Recycling will become especially important as the number of electric vehicle (EV) batteries reaching the end of their useful mobile life jumps considerably – several policy options exist to accelerate recycling in this market (Moïsé and Rubínová, 2023[13]).

Beyond the supply of processed minerals, important geographical concentrations have emerged further down manufacturing supply chains of clean-energy technologies. Here again, the strong role of China is clearly visible, notably in the manufacturing of the main components needed for solar PV installations (Figure 5.6). While this imbalance has not so far slowed the speed of deployment of technologies globally, it does point to potentially important future dependencies as the world moves away from fossil fuels and increasingly relies on renewable energy reliant on these technologies. This highlights the importance of international trade for a resilient transition and the need to diversify supply chains and manufacturing capacity. Recent investment-focused policies, such as the United States' Inflation Reduction Act, aim to accelerate this diversification.

Figure 5.6. Regional shares of manufacturing capacity for selected clean energy technologies and components, 2021

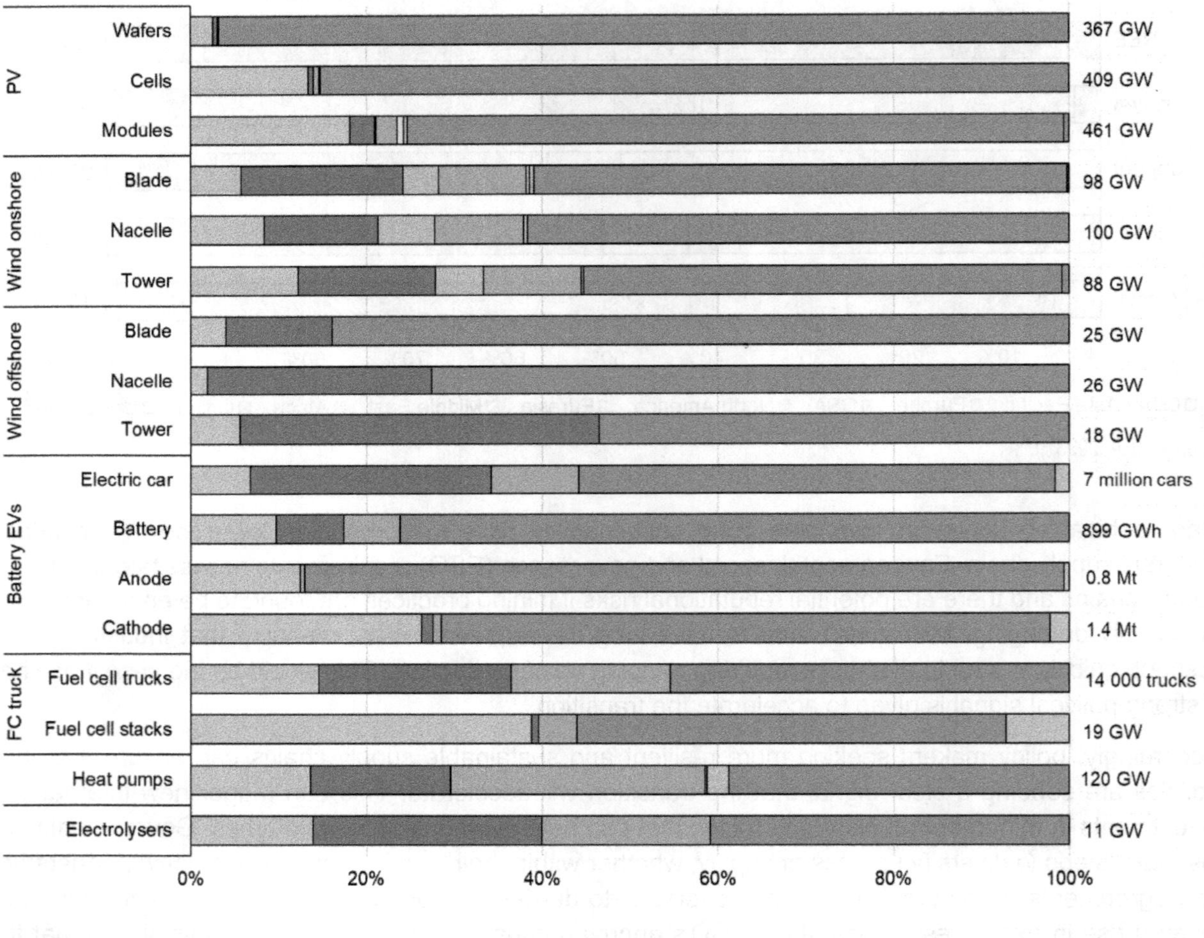

Source: (IEA, 2023[5]).

Bottlenecks related to rising costs of capital

The past decade has seen a boom in renewable energy, with rapid and consistent decreases in the cost of clean-energy technologies. The annual average growth rate in clean energy investment has risen dramatically from 2% from 2015 to 2020 to 12% since 2020. In 2022, clean energy investment is expected to reach USD 1.4 trillion, up from USD 1.1 trillion in 2017, though part of the increased investment is going towards higher costs rather than new energy capacity or energy savings. With overall energy investment growth remaining sluggish (projected 8% increase, with almost half linked to higher costs), clean energy was projected to take up three-quarters of overall energy growth in 2022 (IEA, 2022[10]).

Despite these trends, overall low-carbon investment levels remain below those needed to reach net zero. Investment also remains unevenly distributed across the globe. Investment levels will need to increase even more sharply across all regions if they are to be compatible with climate goals.

Energy system models frequently do not adequately consider the important role of the cost of capital. This risks distorting the outlook for renewable energy. The rapid development of renewable energy over the past decade has taken place at a time of historically low interest rates. Figure 5.7 illustrates how lower base rates have been instrumental in bringing down the levelised cost of electricity generation (LCOE) of offshore wind. Such favourable investment conditions cannot be taken for granted. This raises questions about the possibility of progress towards net-zero emissions stalling in a time of higher financing costs, requiring careful consideration given the trend towards high inflation and tightening monetary policy in many parts of the world since 2022 (OECD, forthcoming, 2023[14]).

Figure 5.7. Trends in cost of debt and equity for offshore wind projects

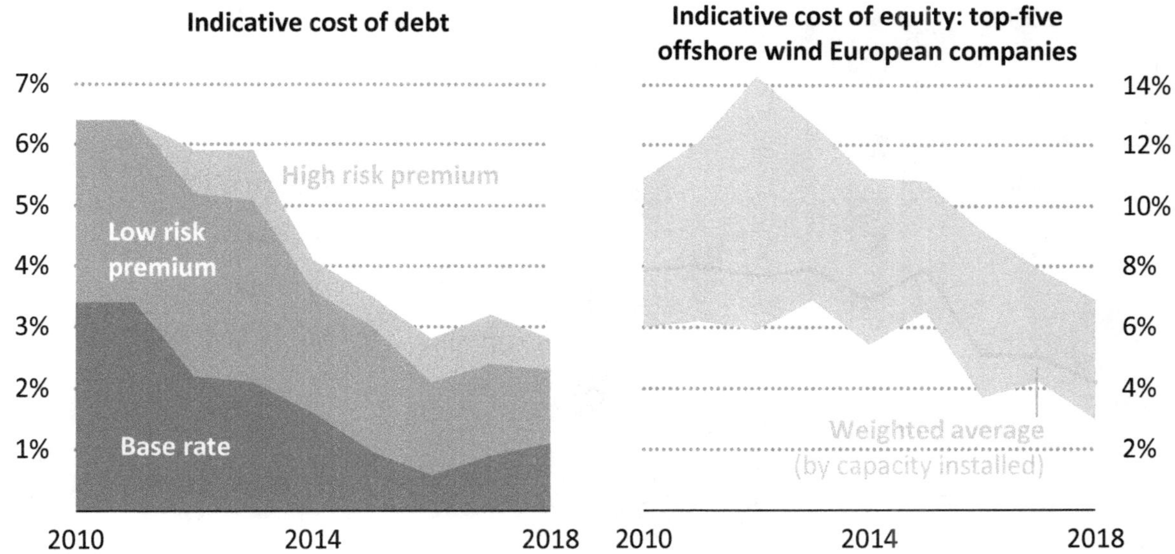

Note: WACC = weighted average cost of capital. LCOE = levelised cost of electricity.
Source: (IEA, 2019[15]).

An important factor affecting investment levels is the financing costs borne by investors, or the minimum required rate of financial return for investing in a company or project. The financing cost of an investment is typically given as the weighted average cost of capital (WACC).[2] In general terms, higher interest rates will result in a higher WACC, potentially strangling investment.

The cost of capital plays a driving role in the net-zero transition in two ways. First, capital costs affect all investments, with higher WACCs representing an obstacle to the net-zero transition insofar as they limit the overall availability of capital for investment of any kind. Second, in addition to this effect on the economy at large, capital costs have a particular effect on low-carbon investments (OECD, forthcoming, 2023[14]). Costing structures differ significantly between different types of investment and play an important role in determining the effect of capital costs. For instance, in the energy sector, fossil-fuel plants require relatively small upfront investments, with the majority of their lifetime costs stemming from fixed operation and maintenance costs (O&M), and variable costs such as fuel, equipment wear and tear, and emissions permits (Figure 5.8). On the other hand, investments in renewable energy technologies require a large amount of upfront capital but have lower lifetime fixed O&M costs and almost no variable costs (Hirth and Steckel, 2016[16]). Due to their capital intensity, financing costs can account for as much as 50% of the levelised cost of electricity (LCOE) of offshore wind projects, as seen in Figure 5.9 (IEA, 2019[15]). Financing costs are estimated at around 25-50% of the LCOE of new solar PV plants, depending on the region in question (IEA, 2022[9]).

Thus, while the costs of all investments increase with higher WACC, they do so unequally. A higher WACC will tend to favour less capital-intensive fossil-fuel investments over low-carbon alternatives. As a result, the cost of renewables will increase more rapidly than fossil fuels as the WACC increases. Estimates suggest that a WACC increase of two percentage points can lead to a 20% increase in the LCOE for wind or solar PV (IEA, 2022[10]). Figure 5.10 illustrates the greater sensitivity of the cost of renewable electricity to capital costs compared to electricity generated from coal or gas.

Figure 5.8. Cost composition of different power generation techniques

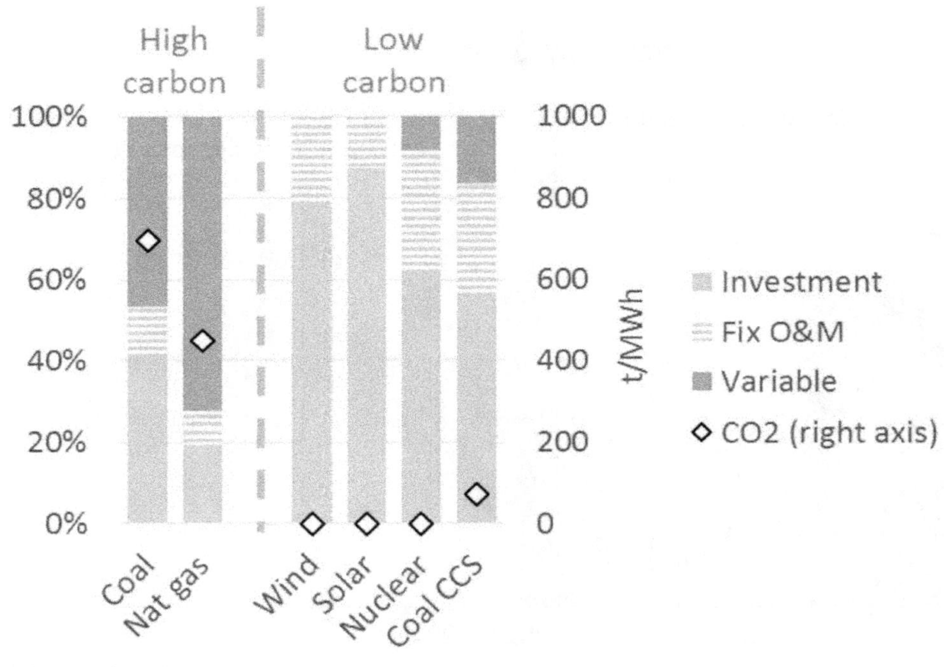

Source: (Hirth and Steckel, 2016[16])

Figure 5.9. Offshore wind: Indicative shares of capital costs by component and levelised costs of electricity for projects completed in 2018

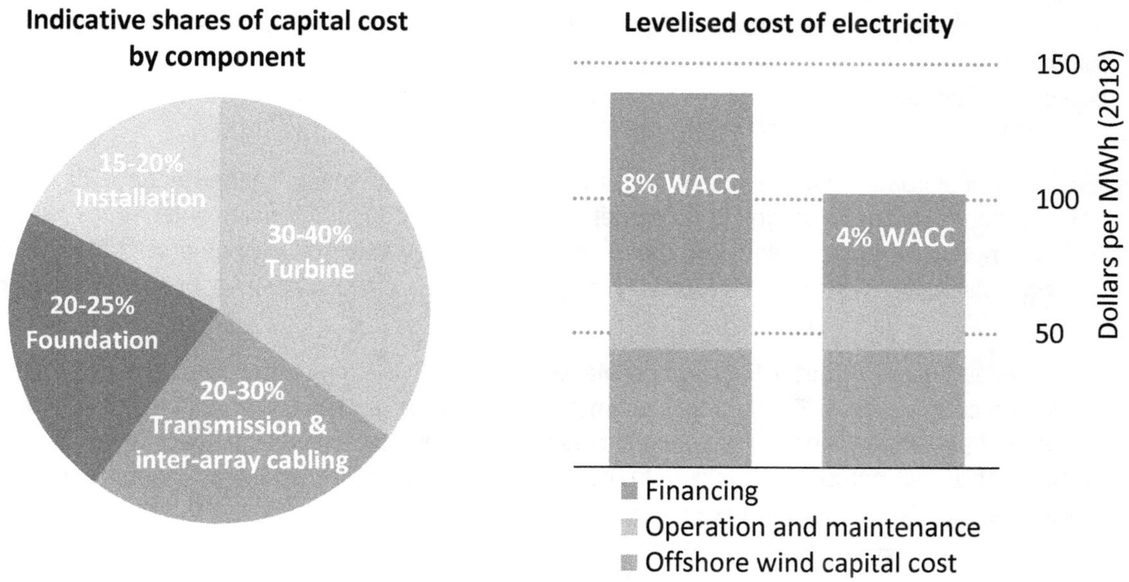

Source: (IEA, 2019[15]).

Figure 5.10. Relative increases in levelised cost of electricity from rising cost of capital

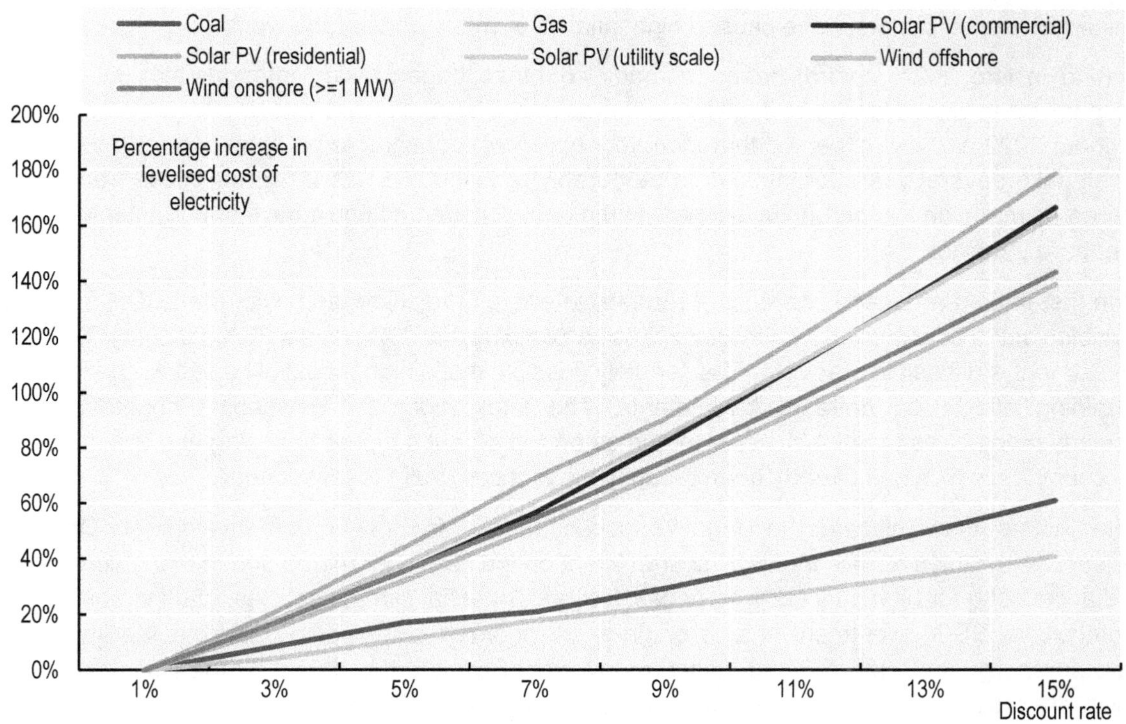

Note: The chart shows the increase in levelised cost of electricity (LCOE) across different technologies as the discount rate increases, relative to the LCOE of each technology when the discount rate is 1%. The discount rate corresponds to the cost of capital in the IEA's LCOE methodology. The results assume a carbon price of 30 USD/ton, a heat price of 37.06 USD/MWh and average coal and gas prices from base year.
Source: (IEA, 2020[17])

Modelling shows that WACCs have a strong bearing on the shares of renewable energy in a cost-optimal energy mix, given renewable technologies' greater sensitivity to capital costs relative to other energy sources. Carbon pricing can attenuate this effect but becomes less impactful as WACCs increase. Moreover, attempts to raise carbon prices to the levels needed to meet net-zero targets have been unfruitful in many major economies to date, even at low costs of capital. This suggests that an even higher carbon price to compensate for high WACCs would be politically unfeasible in many economies (Hirth and Steckel, 2016[16]; Pahle et al., 2022[18]).

Increasing capital costs could also have negative impacts on innovation or other technologies key for net zero. For instance, green hydrogen development, which is both capital-intensive and heavily reliant on vast renewable energy capacity, is doubly exposed to capital-cost volatility (Cordonnier and Saygin, 2022[19]). In this way, rising WACCs could potentially create a vicious cycle, posing a broad threat to net-zero transitions.

Developing countries are particularly vulnerable to rising WACCs. The cost of capital is habitually highest in developing countries; the IEA (2021[20]) estimates that financing costs are up to seven times higher than in Europe and the United States. Research shows that this has acted as a significant barrier to low-carbon investment and the net-zero transition in developing countries, reflected in stagnant clean energy investment levels. The developing country perspective on this issue is explored in more detail in Chapter 10.

Emerging evidence from the current crisis

Investment conditions have been very different in 2022-23 than for much of the past decade. Russia's ongoing war of aggression in Ukraine has had dramatic impacts on global energy and food supply. Global supply chains are still experiencing pressures as a result of the COVID-19 pandemic. These crises, combined with other factors, have caused high inflation in many parts of the world.

Beginning in late 2021, central banks in many countries began hiking interest rates in response to inflationary pressures, leading to higher capital costs.[3] These interest rate increases have continued throughout 2022 and it is expected that monetary policy will continue to be tightened for some time as it will likely take several years for inflation to be durably reduced (OECD, 2022[21]). These trends threaten the progress made on low-carbon investment in the past decade and could have important implications for the net-zero transition.

For the first time in a decade, the cost of renewable energy has increased, with the LCOE from variable renewables set to become 20-30% more expensive compared to 2020 levels (IEA, 2022[10]). The outcome for investment is difficult to predict but it is certainly possible that a higher cost of capital will have significant constraining effects on net-zero investments. The implications for developing countries could be particularly marked, as the global increase comes on top of much higher financing and investment risk in those countries, which has already been recognised as a constraint to investment.

Certain factors may mitigate the negative consequences for low-carbon investment. Despite cost increases, renewables remain the most cost-efficient option for power generation in many countries, even before accounting for high coal and gas prices. Second, national climate policies, and increasing use and expectation for ESG investment criteria or green taxonomies continue to underline the importance of renewable energy investment. Third, concerns over energy security, stoked by the Russian invasion of Ukraine, are driving further interest in renewables, particularly in Europe (IEA, 2022[10]).

If these factors make it difficult to predict how low-carbon technologies will fare relative to the rest of the economy, it is certain that rising interest rates will invariably hamper all investment, including low-carbon. The deep slump in stock markets and sudden need to protect portfolios from inflation has led to upheaval in investment. Portfolio choices previously thought to be relatively safe have performed badly, and riskier assets, in particular, now appear less attractive. High interest rates have reduced the value of future profits, making firms or technologies in early stages of development less desirable (The Economist, 2022[22]). The extent of impacts will depend partly on how long high inflation and interest rates remain. Policy responses from governments will be equally important. Furthermore, even if issues related to the cost of capital are overcome in developed countries, the limited availability of cheap capital for low-carbon investments in developing countries remains a key bottleneck in the global transition to net-zero emissions (OECD, forthcoming, 2023[14]).

Potential solutions

Policy makers should continue to monitor evidence from the current crisis as it emerges. It is important to also prepare responses to minimise collateral damage from the rising costs of capital, thereby protecting low-carbon investment. There are several useful options that policy makers should consider.

Fundamentally, the best way for governments to shield net-zero technologies from the risks associated with rising costs of capital is to put in place strong political commitments to the net-zero transition and maintain the stringency of core climate policies. Political support for the transition at the highest level sends a strong signal to investors and financial institutions about the future role of these technologies (OECD, forthcoming, 2023[14]).

In several major economies, recent government policy intervention has also shown a powerful effect in reducing barriers to investment and stimulating growth. For instance, by expanding clean energy tax credits for both production and investment, and providing for the direct transfer of tax credits to a third party, the US Inflation Reduction Act (IRA) is expected to reduce burdens related to financing clean energy projects. The Act significantly expands loan and loan guarantee authority under the Department of Energy's Innovative Energy Loan Guarantee Program and Energy Infrastructure Reinvestment Financing Program. This authority to support innovative projects that face financing challenges at early stages has been described by a former assistant energy secretary as "a sleeping giant in the law" (Penn, 2022[23]). The support and long-term policy visibility provided by the IRA is expected to have a sizeable positive impact on investment in renewables, with the IEA revising upwards its forecast for capacity growth to 2027 by more than 25% in 2022 compared to 2021 (IEA, 2022[8]).

As a second example, Germany revised its Renewable Energy Sources Act in July 2022 in response to the energy crisis. It sets ambitious new targets for 2030 for the share of renewables in electricity generation and for solar PV and wind capacity. Support policies were also implemented, including regulations to reduce permitting times for onshore wind. And, renewable energy technologies were legally established as a matter of overriding public interest. The impact of these policies on renewable energy is expected to be significant, with the IEA recently revising upwards its five-year forecast for capacity growth by 52% in 2022 compared to 2021 (IEA, 2022[8]).

Policies to reduce investor risk are key to lowering WACCs and, consequently, to keeping renewables above the commercial viability threshold. Finance for utility-scale renewables can be tailored to address specific risks; for instance, by incorporating political risk insurance for uncertainty around project development, partial risk guarantees for revenue risk, or guarantees for non-payment due to delays related to necessary infrastructure (OECD, 2022[24]). Regulation to ensure high-quality and predictable governance can lower risk perception among investors, which can serve to reduce WACCs. Even in countries with strong governance and lower political risks, governments can still act to reduce permitting barriers that add costs to renewables projects in particular (IEA, 2022[8]). It is also important to develop and strengthen financing markets for low-carbon technologies to put downward pressure on financing costs through competition between investors (Egli, Steffen and Schmidt, 2018[25]).

Fiscal support for renewable energy and other key net-zero technologies also still has a role to play. Given renewable energy cost trends over the past decade, some governments have been considering phasing out subsidies for more mature technologies, viewing these as sufficiently competitive. However, the implications of rising costs of capital and the risks of exposing these technologies to the open market suggest that this move may be premature. Fiscal support from governments will be important to ensure the continued economic viability of these technologies in the face of more challenging investment conditions. In addition, government support serves to mitigate perceived investor risk, which also keeps financing costs in check (Pahle et al., 2022[18]).

Central banks can also consider green monetary policies to protect investments essential to the transition. Options include creating dual rates for refinancing, with a lower rate for low-carbon technologies acting as a form of green credit guidance for banks. This has been proposed before, notably as an adjustment to the European Central Bank's system of Targeted Long-Term Refinancing Operations (TLTROs) to incentivise green lending (Voldsgaard, Egli and Pollitt, 2022[26]). Elsewhere, innovative approaches by central banks such as green quantitative easing involving the purchase of green bonds only could contribute to keeping interest rates low for climate-friendly sectors specifically. While this is a promising option, it is largely untested and warrants further research (Pahle et al., 2022[18]).

To ensure that capital continues to go where it is needed, governments also have an important role in supporting the evolution of market products and measurement methodologies to allow investors to better align portfolios with climate objectives, including through improving the use of ESG investing practices. These are discussed further in Chapter 9. Another important option on the financial side relates to reform of multilateral development banks (MDBs). There is growing recognition of the opportunity for MDBs to be changed to better respond to the needs of developing countries faced with the climate crisis, including an explicit call for reform in the Sharm el-Sheikh Implementation Plan. Expanding both the scope and the volume of MDBs' financing can improve developing countries' access to capital at low cost, thereby alleviating some of the described effects of this bottleneck (Songwe, Stern and Bhattacharya, 2022[27]). Possible options to address the shortfall of affordable finance in developing countries are addressed in further detail in Chapter 10.

Bottlenecks related to innovation and technology commercialisation, including for hard-to-abate sectors

Some of the technologies necessary to reach net-zero emissions already exist but their cost needs to be reduced so that they can become fully competitive with carbon-based alternatives and be deployed rapidly and at scale (IPCC, 2022[28]). This said, climate targets cannot be achieved by only deploying existing mature technologies, such as power from wind and solar PV. Other technologies such as green hydrogen are still in their infancy and need to be further developed. According to the IEA's Net-Zero Emissions by 2050 Scenario, half of the global reductions in energy-related CO_2 emissions through 2050 will have to come from technologies that are currently at the demonstration or prototype phase.

In heavy industry and long-distance transport, the share of emissions reductions from technologies that are still under development today is even higher. For example, the decarbonisation of the manufacturing industry requires not only the adoption of technologies that are close to the market, such as a massive increase in renewable electricity generation to enable the electrification of low-temperature heat processes, but the deployment of many technologies that are still far from maturity, notably bio-based products and green hydrogen (Anderson et al., 2021[29]). However, the production of green hydrogen is still about three times more expensive than grey hydrogen (made out of natural gas through steam reforming) even under the most favourable conditions. Major cost reductions – and the rapid deployment that they would induce – crucially depend on massive improvements in the cost of electrolysers through research and development, and large-scale demonstration projects. Even within technologies that are considered mature such as renewable energy there is room for breakthrough innovations; for example, in geothermal or concentrated solar power. All of these require regulations that do not create barriers to entry for these technologies, but rather, allow for their deployment and then, scaling.

Insufficient pace of technological innovation is therefore a clear bottleneck for a rapid transition, especially as low-carbon innovation rates were actually slowing until 2020. Proactive policies to drive innovation are therefore essential, as explored further in Chapter 7.

Bottlenecks related to skills transitions

The transformation needed for the energy transition implies substantial shifts in employment between firms and between sectors as some traditional jobs become obsolete in time, particularly in the fossil-fuel industry. While there is likely to be a net increase in jobs globally, some sectors, firms and communities will suffer significant negative impacts, which is why a proactive approach by governments to ensure a fair and equitable transition to net zero is essential. Such policies can include reskilling and retraining, but to be effective it is necessary to understand which skills are currently lacking in particular regions and sectors in order to have a better visibility of where potential skills bottlenecks lie.

Potential skills gaps and shortages are already recognised in a number of sectors important for the net-zero transition, such as renewable energy, energy and resource efficiency, renovation of buildings, construction, environmental services and manufacturing (OECD, 2020[30]). However, data is not yet comprehensive. Understanding the types of skills that are lacking and the extent to which the lack of appropriately trained workers is a potential bottleneck for the transition in different countries is an important focus area for future work. In addition, better data will inform governments of the best strategies for scaling up reskilling programmes both to complement workers' skill sets and to maximise transferability of skills from existing industries (including fossil-fuel based) to those essential for the net-zero transition. This is discussed further in Chapter 8

Bottlenecks related to agriculture and land use

The net-zero transition debate often focuses on energy and industry despite the important role of agriculture and the essential role of land use, land-use change and natural ecosystems for overall net-zero transition. The agriculture, forestry and other land-use (AFOLU) sector account for around 22% of global GHG emissions, of which around 11% is from agriculture (IPCC, 2022[31]), highlighting its importance for mitigation efforts.

Policies to ensure rapid and sustained reductions in direct emissions from agriculture (particularly nitrous oxide and methane) and CO_2 emissions from land use, land-use change and forestry (LULUCF) are integral to the transition (Henderson et al., 2021[32]). Moreover, net-zero transition scenarios often rely heavily on CO_2 removals via enhanced carbon sequestration in soils and biomass in the AFOLU sector. Strong policy action is needed to take advantage of these important sources of mitigation, including actions to address bottlenecks for the uptake of mitigation practices.

The significant amount of agricultural support with strong potential to harm the environment and distort markets and trade can be an obstacle to the transition, and should be phased out. These include market price support, output-based transfers and unconstrained payments to variable inputs, which are known for their potential to increase pressures on natural resources and to raise national GHG emissions. Even though the global effect of removing market price support is uncertain, these measures potentially contribute to higher national GHG emissions. These types of support are also potentially most production- and trade-distorting; are inefficient tools for transferring income to farmers; and tend to be inequitable as they are not targeted to producers with low incomes. Unconditional support to high emission intensity products should also be avoided as well as subsidies to fossil fuel and fertiliser consumption (OECD, 2022[33]). Instead, budgetary support should be oriented towards investments in innovation to foster emissions saving, sustainable productivity growth, and new mitigation technologies. Such investments would benefit from renewed partnerships between the public and private sectors to maximise synergies on research and development (OECD, 2022[33]).

Climate policies in AFOLU will pose different challenges depending on the costs they impose on producers, the sources of mitigation they target, and their impacts on food production and rural livelihoods. Policy packages that align productivity and mitigation will minimise trade-offs between climate objectives, and producer and consumer welfare. This includes most practices that augment soil carbon stocks in agriculture as well as land-sparing productivity improvements, whereby productivity on existing agricultural land is intensified in a sustainable way in order to "spare" remaining land for nature. The effectiveness of these measures will also depend on policies to protect and ensure the permanence of carbon stocks in agricultural soils and forests (OECD, 2019[34]; Henderson et al., 2022[35]).

Furthermore, the net-zero transition will require stronger policy actions to stimulate afforestation and deep cuts to agricultural emissions that will certainly entail trade-offs between mitigation; competition for land with food production and bioeconomy feedstocks; and producer livelihood objectives (Henderson et al., 2021[32]). These trade-offs need to be managed with well-designed policy packages that can stimulate emission reductions and soften the impacts on food consumers and producers, including through the provision of appropriate social safety nets (OECD, 2019[34]; Henderson et al., 2021[32]).

Investment in accurate and affordable measurement, reporting and verification (MRV) procedures and technologies is also critical, particularly for policies that depend on providing incentives for precise emission reductions (e.g. carbon-pricing policies). While MRV is important for policies in all sectors, it is particularly challenging in the AFOLU sector, given the wide geographical distribution of producers and the diffuse nature of emission and mitigation sources. Important progress is being made in this area but further R&D is needed to improve the accuracy and scalability of MRV approaches for important mitigation sources such as soil carbon sequestration and contracting solutions to address the issues of non-permanence (to be sure that gains are not quickly erased by a change in agricultural practices) and lower transaction costs, and to provide greater assurance of additionality (where actions are being awarded carbon credits) (OECD, 2019[34]; Henderson et al., 2022[35]). Policy packages will also need to address additional farm-level barriers to adoption such as access to credit, behavioural barriers and technical knowledge gaps to stimulate widespread adoption of low-emission practices (Wreford, Ignaciuk and Gruère, 2017[36]).

The role of government in a rapid and resilient transition

Governments have a wide range of policy instruments at their disposal to accelerate the transition towards net zero. These are well known and have been extensively analysed, including by the OECD, the IPCC and others. They include price-based measures including different forms of carbon pricing; non-priced-based measures including subsidies and tax incentives; regulatory policies; technology deployment incentives; R&D investment; de-risking policies and so on. Public governance tools such as green budgeting, infrastructure-planning procedures and public procurement are vital for realising climate objectives and must be fully aligned with them in order to drive the needed public and private investment.

The process of selecting, designing and implementing appropriate policy mixes is complex and highly specific to country and local contexts. To help governments with this, the OECD has developed a framework for designing and implementing decarbonisation strategies while considering broader economic and social issues (D'Arcangelo et al., 2022[37]). The methodological framework consists of a series of steps to design country-specific decarbonisation strategies and monitor efforts, organised in two main stages: i) a 'diagnostic' stage to identify priority areas; ii) an 'action' stage to devise and evaluate concrete policy interventions, including a strong focus on ensuring fairness of policies by assessing distributional effects and focusing on public communication. Other OECD work is focusing specifically on the role and effectiveness of individual policies, notably the OECD's new Inclusive Forum on Climate Mitigation Approaches. That work is not repeated here; instead, this section reviews progress on reforming public governance for climate objectives and focuses on the important role that "centres of government" can play in developing genuinely whole-of-government approaches to climate change.

Progress on reforming public governance for the net-zero transition

Ramping up public governance tools is critical to achieving the ambitious changes needed for climate and environmental action. Revamping these tools to deliver on these changes also helps reinforce trust in climate action by strengthening the climate governance framework and demonstrating commitment. OECD countries are steadily making progress in using public governance tools to align with environmental objectives but there is room for growth (Figure 5.11). For example, OECD countries and the European Union increasingly require consideration of potential environmental impacts when designing regulations (Figure 5.11, Panel C). In general, policy makers have been provided with methodological information about how and what to include when assessing potential environmental impacts of rules. Engaging all relevant stakeholders, including trade unions, through social dialogue and public consultation can help ensure that regulations are appropriate, effective and efficient. It will also contribute to better acceptance of and compliance with sometimes burdensome regulatory measures among all stakeholders.

Budgets can be powerful instruments for aligning policies with national and global climate and environmental commitments. "Green budgeting", the use of budgetary policy-making tools to give policy makers a clearer understanding of the environmental and climate impacts of budgeting choices, and help them achieve climate and environmental goals, is becoming more common across OECD countries (OECD, 2021[38]). The OECD composite indicator on green budgeting practices notes that, in 2021, 14 out of 38 OECD countries (37%) reported practising green budgeting (Figure 5.11, Panel A) (OECD, 2022[39]). More and more regional and subnational governments are also launching green budgeting exercises (OECD, 2022[40]).

Despite its growing use, green budgeting still raises challenges for OECD countries when it comes to implementation. The OECD is working with Members on this topic through the OECD Paris Collaborative on Green Budgeting, a platform for countries to share best practices and build resources on how green budgeting can inform public expenditure decisions. Established in 2017, it aims to design new, innovative tools to assess and drive improvements in the alignment of national expenditure and revenue processes with climate and other environmental goals. This is a crucial step in achieving a central objective of the Paris Agreement on climate change, the Aichi Biodiversity Targets and the United Nations' Sustainable Development Goals: aligning national policy frameworks and financial flows on a pathway towards low greenhouse gas emissions and environmentally sustainable development.

Figure 5.11. Governing green: key indicators

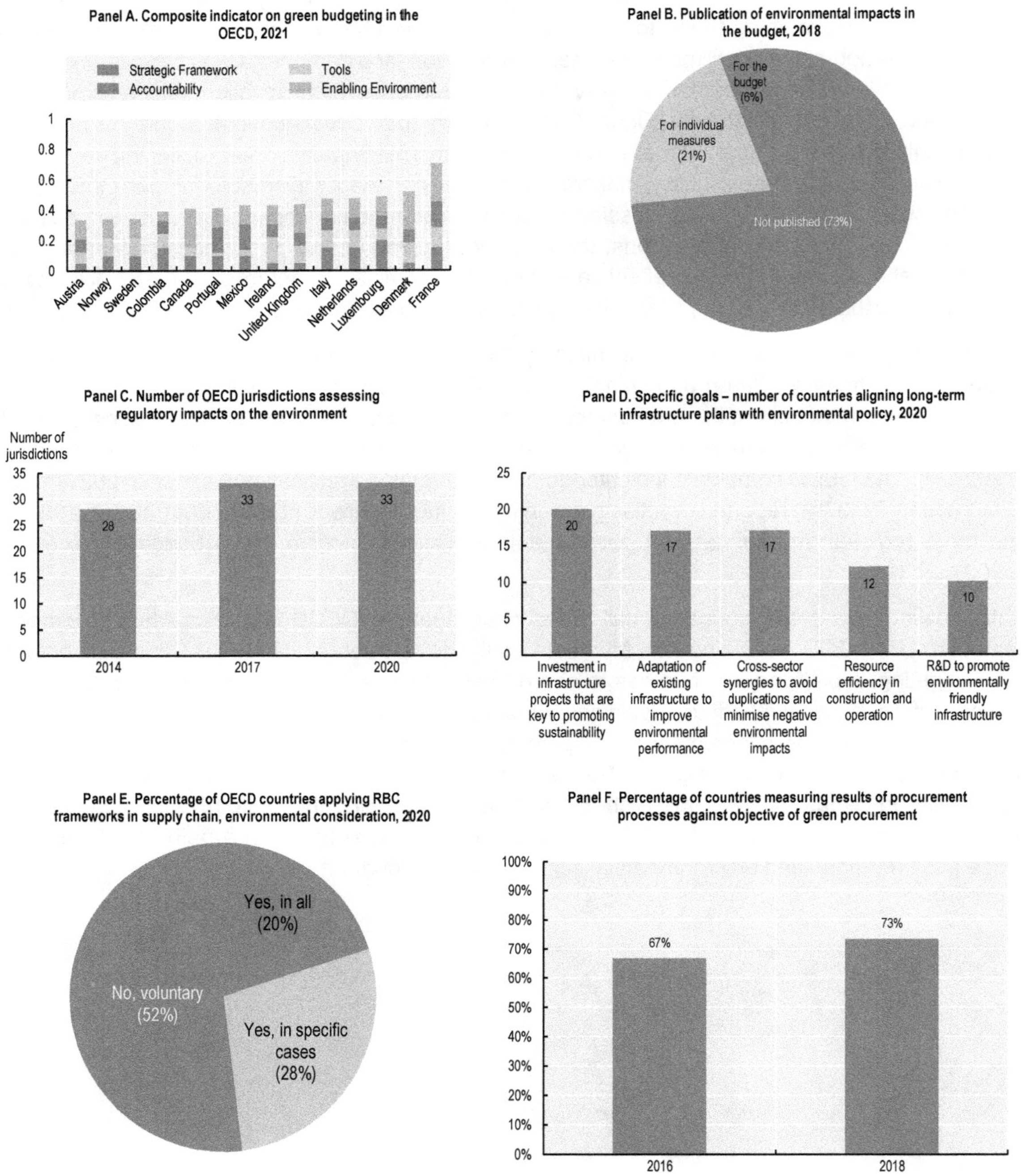

Source: (OECD, forthcoming[41]), OECD and EC (2020), Joint Survey on Emerging Green Budgeting Practices; OECD (2018), OECD Budget Practices and Procedures Survey; OECD Indicators of Regulatory Policy and Governance surveys 2014, 2017 and 2021; OECD (2020), Survey on the Governance of Infrastructure; OECD (2020), Survey on Leveraging Responsible Business Conduct through Public Procurement; OECD (2018), Survey on the Implementation of the 2015 OECD Recommendations on Public Procurement.

Countries are also gradually developing responsible public procurement frameworks that account for environmental considerations alongside social considerations to ensure that public investments work for people, planet and society along global supply chains (Figure 5.11, Panels E and F).

Linking major infrastructure decisions and plans with climate and environmental objectives is critical to shaping the net-zero transition. Governments face challenges to tie infrastructure planning to climate objectives. This includes putting in place criteria for selecting infrastructure projects in line with these objectives and delivering, operating, maintaining, upgrading or retiring infrastructure assets in ways that accelerate the reduction of carbon emissions. Governments should develop long-term strategic infrastructure plans that align with commitments on environmental protection and climate-change mitigation. Further, countries can mobilise greater amounts of private financing for sustainable quality infrastructure by adapting regulatory frameworks, strengthening procurement systems and adopting infrastructure certifications.

Innovative governance approaches can help ensure the effectiveness of green policies. Mission-oriented innovation and anticipatory governance mechanisms can be used to inform climate and environmental decision-making and policies, further discussed in Chapter 7. Strategic foresight, as examined in Part I of this report is an important tool and is being used in several places including the European Environment Agency, Germany, Ireland, the Netherlands, and the UK. Behavioural insights (BI) can also help governments to better design and implement green policies through approaches that consider behavioural barriers and biases. Canada's Privy Council's Impact and Innovation Unit is using BI in a survey to measure and promote acceptability and uptake in climate action and green policies among Canadians.[4]

Centres of government at the heart of whole-of-government approaches

The systemic, long-term, and cross-border nature of climate change represents a complex challenge for traditional governance practices – calling for an increase in government co-ordination. Misalignment of strategic objectives often results from the complex interaction between different administrative and political variables, relating to conflicting sectoral interests, contextual political priorities, and poorly designed co-ordination mechanisms (OECD, forthcoming 2023[42]).

Bolder climate action requires a shift towards more integrated, evidence-based and co-operative policy action to ensure political buy-in, avoid political inertia, and reconcile short- and long-term objectives and needs. Preliminary OECD evidence provides an overview of the institutional set-ups used by governments to steer, co-ordinate, and deliver on climate policy (OECD, forthcoming 2023[42]). These set-ups are generally fragmented, as they need to engage actors and institutions across public administrations. Efforts to tackle this fragmentation through institutional levers include: dedicated ministry of the environments; superministries; dedicated units or leadership at the centre of government (CoG); and line ministries with no overarching co-ordinating or steering body.

Uniquely placed to align the machinery of government around strategic priorities, centres of government play an essential role in the prioritisation of high-level policy objectives, and the co-ordination of the design and implementation of policy responses across government, such as those needed to deliver on climate. CoGs increasingly play a direct or indirect climate-related role, whether through the articulation of policy priorities or their monitoring or co-ordination of the head of government's agenda in climate-related events. Nine of the 38 OECD Members have explicitly tasked the CoG with responsibilities linked to climate resilience (OECD, forthcoming 2023[43]). While still a minority of OECD countries, there is an upward trend in this regard. For most of these countries, this shift has occurred in the past two years, a clear sign of the perceived need for increased levels of co-ordination and coherence to deliver on national and international commitments. CoG's role in this policy area can be broken down into two key functions: (i) steer and co-ordinate environmental and climate action at the domestic level and/or monitor the implementation of a national climate strategy and; (ii) co-ordinate government position for international environment- and climate- related commitments and negotiations.

Policy makers and regulators should also proactively consider how to strategically increase interactions among wider public sector institutions in order to co-ordinate and harmonise climate-relevant actions across sectors and borders. Some countries have already identified synergies among sectors that can be captured through sector coupling as well as co-benefits to decarbonisation that extend beyond the sector in question (such as the improvement in air quality that accompanies climate mitigation efforts). Some regulators have also looked beyond national borders to benefit from cross-border co-operation. This is the case in Europe, for example, through the Body of European Regulators for Electronic Communications (BEREC) working groups focusing on promoting sustainability among European e-communications regulators. Further examples of this kind of cross-sectoral co-ordination and collaboration may be helpful in strengthening such practices.

Leading by example: A greener and more resilient public sector

To promote climate action, governments need to lead by example, taking assertive measures to transform government institutions, policies and operations to face environmental challenges. To effectively act on these issues, governments need to have detailed information on the environmental impacts of their work across agencies, levels of government and types of operations.

Governments can also lead by example through green procurement; strengthening responsible supply chain requirements on their suppliers; and encouraging suppliers to implement responsible business conduct (RBC) standards if they want to conduct business with the public sector. With public procurement accounting on average for 12% of GDP in OECD countries and 20-30% of GDP in developing economies (OECD, 2020[44]), green procurement is an effective strategic policy tool for promoting sustainability, inclusiveness, and resilience (for a discussion of the role of the private sector and RBC in enabling a resilient net-zero transition see Chapter 9). Countries are gradually developing responsible public procurement frameworks that account for environmental considerations, including for global supply chains (Figure 5.11, Panel E) (OECD, forthcoming[45]).

Some countries have already put in place whole-of-government strategies to make their operations greener and support the achievement of their domestic and international commitments on climate and environmental targets. For instance, Canada has put in place the Greening Government Strategy to support the governments' commitment for net-zero emissions by 2050, including an interim target of a 40% emissions reduction by 2025 for federal facilities and conventional fleet. In the United States, the federal government is directed to align its management of federal procurement and real property with a 100% clean energy economy by 2035 and net-zero emissions no later than 2050 (Executive Office of the President, 2021[46]).

Subnational governance: The role of cities and regions

Subnational governments play an important role in climate action and support the urgently needed transformation to achieve a climate-resilient and net-zero emissions pathway. It is estimated that 50-80% of adaptation and mitigation actions already are or will be implemented at the regional and local levels (Regions4SD, 2016[47]). Many cities and regions have adopted climate targets and actions that are more ambitious than those of their national governments (OECD, 2019[48]). Subnational governments can mainstream climate action into their spatial planning, infrastructure, local economic and fiscal policies through climate strategies that are locally tailored to be in line with national objectives (OECD, 2019[49]). They are also responsible for most public spending and investment with impacts on the climate and environment (OECD, 2021[50]). At the same time, cities account for more than 70% of global energy-related CO_2 emissions and two-thirds of energy demand (IEA, 2016[51]). These shares are expected to increase significantly over the coming decades if there is no significant climate action.

Acting alone, cities' full potential in the response to climate change remains untapped. Local governments are estimated to have direct power to cut up to one-third of GHG emissions in their cities but the remaining two-thirds of urban emission reductions depend either on national and state governments or on co-ordination across levels of government (Coalition for Urban Transitions, 2019[52]).

This hinders systemic and impactful action because national governments often do not sufficiently consider geographical disparities across regions and cities. There is huge variation in emissions per capita as well as in the challenges to transitioning to net zero across regions within the same country (OECD, 2021[50]). Moreover, GHG emissions data in regions and cities are still lacking or are not reported in a comparable manner due to a range of financial, regulatory and capacity challenges. Because of the lack of comprehensive GHG emission monitoring and reporting frameworks at the local and regional levels, subnational governments are unable to demonstrate to national policy makers that they are significantly contributing to achieving national targets.

To overcome these challenges, a "territorial" approach to climate action can deliver better understanding of domestic GHG emissions, local challenges and local exposure to climate risks by sector and geographic area. This will allow national and subnational governments to tailor relevant, placed-based policies. In this process, national governments have a crucial role in supporting local governments in their place-based actions to drive the net zero transition. For example, cities and regions play an essential role in decarbonising buildings. Buildings and construction are an indispensable component of transition to a zero-carbon society as they account for nearly 40% of energy-related global CO_2 emissions, with up to as much as 70% in large cities like Paris, New York or Tokyo. Not only do cities and regions own an important share of public buildings but they are responsible for land use and building code enforcement. They are familiar with the local building stock and are in close contact with citizens and local businesses. Cities and regions are fundamental to OECD work on an effective multilevel governance approach to decarbonising buildings (OECD, 2022[53]).

Applying systems thinking to the net-zero transition

Part I of this report identified the importance of systems thinking in improving economic resilience while taking action on climate change. Such thinking is also important in the design and delivery of government net-zero strategies. Systems thinking acknowledges that challenges occur within complex systems, recognises these interconnections and interdependencies and seeks to address the system as a whole rather than its parts. Some countries, such as the United Kingdom, have made strides in leveraging systems thinking to promote strategic coherence across policy sectors for climate resilient development (OECD, forthcoming 2023[54]).

The need for systems thinking stems from the recognition that patterns of behaviour are a product of the system they are embedded in rather than independent of it. This means changes in systems' design and structure are needed to bring about the significant behavioural change (OECD, 2022[55]) required for a resilient net-zero transition. The IPCC calls for such "transformative" change to reverse current behavioural patterns, for example, in the transport sector in order to meet climate mitigation goals (IPCC, 2022[28]). Lasting behavioural change will also be essential to ensuring the transition remains durable in the long run. This is exemplified particularly well in the rapid rebound of global emissions following their decline during the first wave of COVID-19 lockdowns.

Current policy practices rarely focus on improving the overarching design or structure of a system. Rather, they address specific system parts. For example, in the transport sector, climate policy efforts often focus on replacing emitting technologies (combustion engines) with low-carbon alternatives (electric vehicles). But emissions from the transport sector continue to grow because the overall design of transport systems and the mental models these designs are based on remain unchanged. A transportation system focused on private passenger vehicles maximises individuals' mobility but undervalues people's proximity to places they access. This encourages urban sprawl and the demand for private vehicles, and reduces the use of shared and active modes of transport. Focusing on individual components within this system does little to address the unsustainable design of the system itself. As a result, urban sprawl and reduced shared or active modes of transportation will further increase demand for private vehicles, obstructing mitigation efforts. (OECD, 2021[56]).

A systemic approach would: i) envision the objectives of a system and the patterns of behaviour a well-functioning system would result in, and challenge the mental models prevailing in the current system; ii) aim to understand why the current system is not achieving these goals or behavioural patterns; and iii) develop policies to redesign the system to better achieve its goals and foster desirable patterns of behaviour.

In the case of the transport system, its objective is to provide individuals with access to places, minimising the effort individuals need to make to do so. This is informed by a combination of each individual's mobility and their proximity to the places they would like to access. However, the current transport system focuses almost exclusively on the former, enhancing mobility through private vehicle use. Policies to rebalance the system towards accessibility rather than just mobility include street redesign, spatial planning, and enhanced use of shared modes of transportation. This, in turn, would reduce demand for private vehicles, making it easier to replace the existing vehicle fleet with low-carbon alternatives. Such systems redesign can also harness important other benefits, such as increasing well-being (OECD, 2021[56]).

The OECD recently applied a systemic approach to transport systems redesign in Ireland. The analysis shows how this approach can tap into immense potential for emissions reductions through lasting behavioural change while enhancing well-being and ensuring a just transition (OECD, 2022[55]). Policies included road space reallocation, the mainstreaming of on-demand shared services, and communication strategies that shed light on the benefits of a transition towards sustainable transport systems and the consequences of inaction. While such policies are already often part of current policy efforts, they need to be scaled up considerably in order to take advantage of their transformative potential.

Box 5.2. Systems thinking in the UK's Net Zero Strategy Directorate

The UK government has set a bold and ambitious target to reach net-zero carbon emissions by 2050. The Net Zero Strategy Directorate in the Department for Business, Energy and Industrial Strategy (BEIS) uses a systems approach to visualise how different parts of the net-zero system are interconnected. This helps identify where to make changes in the system to achieve government priorities. The directorate can then use this insight to support delivery modelling, policy development, and the reporting or understanding of net zero.

In particular, the directorate has made use of systems maps to build its understanding and Sankey diagrams to show anticipated changes to the energy system over time. The directorate is also building and developing a systems interrogation tool for land use and heat and building systems to help inform decisions by policy makers.

Joining up air quality and climate-change policies

Climate change and air quality were historically seen as separate issues, even though greenhouse gases and air pollutants are co-emitted. A systems approach appeared to be an effective way to join up these two areas and build a shared understanding of how to simultaneously tackle both issues. There are many past examples of where actions have been taken to combat one of these issues with a knock-on effect on the other. For example, diesel cars were incentivised to tackle greenhouse gas emission but had unintended consequences on air quality.

A soft systems methodology was used to convene experts and facilitate knowledge exchange between stakeholders holding responsibility for different parts of the system. The Air Quality Expert Group subsequently wrote up a report to summarise the findings of this workshop. This publicly available report shares key findings and highlights potential risks associated with different policies. For example, the report summarises the risks and hazards of potential climate policies (for example, the risk of bioenergy to air quality) which helps stakeholders consider how these could be mitigated.

Source: (OECD, forthcoming 2023[42]).

Chapter conclusions

Achieving net-zero emissions requires a combined focus on accelerating the transition in the near term, making the transition itself resilient for the longer term, and ensuring that the transition serves to improve broader resilience rather than creating new fragilities. To do this, governments need to get the policy basics right, implementing nationally appropriate policy mixes that consider the full range of policy options, both price- and non-price-based.

Implementing ambitious climate policies alone is not enough, however. As this chapter has shown, the net-zero transition is vulnerable to various bottlenecks, including materials shortages, supply-chain vulnerabilities, skills gaps, rising costs of capital, and obstacles to scaling up clean energy supply. A whole-of-government approach is needed to raise awareness of such potential disruptions and develop strategies to anticipate and overcome them.

Notes

[1] Policies covered under the Climate Actions Policy Measurement Framework https://www.oecd.org/climate-action/ipac/.

[2] The WACC is calculated as a weighted average between the cost of equity and the cost of debt, where the former is the financial return expected by shareholders on equity and the latter is the interest rate secured from lenders by a company.

[3] In October 2022, the European Central Bank announced its third consecutive major interest rate increase. There were further interest rate increases in November from the U.S. Federal Reserve, the Bank of England, the Reserve Bank of Australia, the Reserve Bank of New Zealand, Norway's Norges Bank and Sweden's Riksbank. These hikes brought the total in 2022 from G10 central banks to 2 400 basis points. Central banks in many other countries, including Mexico, South Korea, Israel, South Africa, Indonesia, Thailand, Malaysia and the Philippines, also raised interest rates in November 2022. At time of writing, interest rate hikes have been continuing, with the U.S. Federal Reserve, Bank of England and European Central Bank all increasing their key interest rates in early 2023, along with other central banks.

[4] https://impact.canada.ca/en/behavioural-science/parca.

References

Anderson, B. et al. (2021), “Policies for a climate-neutral industry: Lessons from the Netherlands”, *OECD Science, Technology and Industry Policy Papers*, No. 108, OECD Publishing, Paris, https://doi.org/10.1787/a3a1f953-en. [29]

Coalition for Urban Transitions (2019), *Climate Emergency, Urban Opportunity: How National Government Can Secure Economic Prosperity and Avert Climate Catastrophe by Transforming Cities*, https://urbantransitions.global/en/publication/climate-emergency-urban-opportunity/. [52]

Cordonnier, J. and D. Saygin (2022), “Green hydrogen opportunities for emerging and developing economies: Identifying success factors for market development and building enabling conditions”, *OECD Environment Working Papers*, No. 205, OECD Publishing, Paris, https://doi.org/10.1787/53ad9f22-en. [19]

D'Arcangelo, F. et al. (2022), “A framework to decarbonise the economy”, *OECD Economic Policy Papers*, No. 31, OECD Publishing, Paris, https://doi.org/10.1787/4e4d973d-en. [37]

Egli, F., B. Steffen and T. Schmidt (2018), “A dynamic analysis of financing conditions for renewable energy technologies”, *Nature Energy*, Vol. 3/12, pp. 1084-1092, https://doi.org/10.1038/s41560-018-0277-y. [25]

Executive Office of the President (2021), *Executive Order 14008 Tackling the Climate Crisis at Home and Abroad*. [46]

Henderson, B. et al. (2021), “Policy strategies and challenges for climate change mitigation in the Agriculture, Forestry and Other Land Use (AFOLU) sector”, *OECD Food, Agriculture and Fisheries Papers*, No. 149, OECD Publishing, Paris, https://doi.org/10.1787/47b3493b-en. [32]

Henderson, B. et al. (2022), “Soil carbon sequestration by agriculture: Policy options”, *OECD Food, Agriculture and Fisheries Papers*, No. 174, OECD Publishing, Paris, https://doi.org/10.1787/63ef3841-en. [35]

Hirth, L. and J. Steckel (2016), “The role of capital costs in decarbonizing the electricity sector”, *Environmental Research Letters*, Vol. 11/11, p. 114010, https://doi.org/10.1088/1748-9326/11/11/114010. [16]

IEA (2023), *Energy Technology Perspectives 2023*. [5]

IEA (2022), *Greenhouse Gas Emissions from Energy*. [4]

IEA (2022), *Renewables 2022*. [8]

IEA (2022), *World Energy Investment 2022*, IEA, https://www.iea.org/reports/world-energy-investment-2022. [10]

IEA (2022), *World Energy Outlook 2022*, IEA, https://www.iea.org/reports/world-energy-outlook-2022. [9]

IEA (2021), *Financing Clean Energy Transitions in Emerging and Developing Economies*, https://www.iea.org/reports/financing-clean-energy-transitions-in-emerging-and-developing-economies. [20]

IEA (2021), *Net Zero by 2050.* [6]

IEA (2020), *Levelised Cost of Electricity Calculator*, https://www.iea.org/data-and-statistics/data-tools/levelised-cost-of-electricity-calculator. [17]

IEA (2019), *Offshore Wind Outlook 2019*, IEA, https://www.iea.org/reports/offshore-wind-outlook-2019. [15]

IEA (2016), *Energy Technology Perspectives 2016*, OECD Publishing, Paris, https://doi.org/10.1787/energy_tech-2016-en. [51]

IPCC (2022), *Climate Change 2022: Mitigation of Climate Change. Contribution of Working Group III to the Sixth Assessment Report of the Intergovernmental Panel on Climate Change*, https://doi.org/10.1017/9781009157926. [28]

IRENA (2022), *Geopolitics of the Energy Transformation: The Hydrogen Factor*, https://www.irena.org/publications/2022/Jan/Geopolitics-of-the-Energy-Transformation-Hydrogen (accessed on 24 March 2022). [7]

Kowalski, P. and C. Legendre (2023), "Raw materials critical for the green transition: Production, international trade and export restrictions", *OECD Trade Policy Papers*, No. 269, OECD Publishing, Paris, https://doi.org/10.1787/c6bb598b-en. [12]

Lee, H. and J. Romero (eds.) (2023), *Summary for Policymakers*, IPCC. [1]

Moïsé, E. and S. Rubínová (2023), "Trade policies to promote the circular economy: A case study of lithium-ion batteries", *OECD Trade and Environment Working Papers*, No. 2023/01, OECD Publishing, Paris, https://doi.org/10.1787/d75a7f46-en. [13]

NEA (2022), *Meeting Climate Change Targets: The Role of Nuclear Energy*, OECD Publishing, https://www.oecd-nea.org/jcms/pl_69396/meeting-climate-change-targets-the-role-of-nuclear-energy?details=true. [11]

OECD (2023), "Labour Force Statistics: Population and vital statistics", *OECD Employment and Labour Market Statistics* (database), https://doi.org/10.1787/data-00287-en (accessed on 3 February 2023). [3]

OECD (2022), *Agricultural Policy Monitoring and Evaluation 2022: Reforming Agricultural Policies for Climate Change Mitigation*, OECD Publishing, Paris, https://doi.org/10.1787/7f4542bf-en. [33]

OECD (2022), *Aligning Regional and Local Budgets with Green Objectives: Subnational Green Budgeting Practices and Guidelines*,, OECD Publishing, Paris, https://doi.org/10.1787/93b4036f-en. [40]

OECD (2022), *Composite Indicator on Green Budgeting in the OECD.* [39]

OECD (2022), *Decarbonising Buildings in Cities and Regions*, OECD Urban Studies, OECD Publishing, Paris, https://doi.org/10.1787/a48ce566-en. [53]

OECD (2022), "OECD blended finance guidance for clean energy", *OECD Environment Policy Papers*, No. 31, OECD Publishing, Paris, https://doi.org/10.1787/596e2436-en. [24]

OECD (2022), *OECD Economic Outlook, Volume 2022 Issue 2*, OECD Publishing, Paris, https://doi.org/10.1787/f6da2159-en. [21]

OECD (2022), *Redesigning Ireland's Transport for Net Zero: Towards Systems that Work for People and the Planet*, OECD Publishing, Paris, https://doi.org/10.1787/b798a4c1-en. [55]

OECD (2022), *The Climate Action Monitor 2022: Helping Countries Advance Towards Net Zero*, OECD Publishing, Paris, https://doi.org/10.1787/43730392-en. [2]

OECD (2021), *Green Budgeting in OECD Countries*, OECD Publishing, Paris, https://doi.org/10.1787/acf5d047-en. [38]

OECD (2021), *OECD Regional Outlook 2021: Addressing COVID-19 and Moving to Net Zero Greenhouse Gas Emissions*, OECD Publishing, Paris, https://doi.org/10.1787/17017efe-en. [50]

OECD (2021), *Transport Strategies for Net-Zero Systems by Design*, OECD Publishing, Paris, https://doi.org/10.1787/0a20f779-en. [56]

OECD (2020), *Integrating Responsible Business Conduct in Public Procurement*, https://www.oecd-ilibrary.org/docserver/02682b01-en.pdf?expires=1673259936&id=id&accname=ocid84004878&checksum=B8A94B660ACFD34FBFFA031A4EDA0698. [44]

OECD (2020), *Making the green recovery work for jobs, income and growth*, OECD Policy Responses to Coronavirus (COVID-19). [30]

OECD (2019), ""An integrated approach to the Paris climate Agreement: The role of regions and cities"", *OECD Regional Development Working Papers* 2019/13, https://doi.org/10.1787/96b5676d-en. [48]

OECD (2019), *Enhancing Climate Change Mitigation through Agriculture*, OECD Publishing, Paris, https://doi.org/10.1787/e9a79226-en. [34]

OECD (2019), "Financing climate objectives in cities and regions to deliver sustainable and inclusive growth", *OECD Environment Policy Papers*, No. 17, OECD Publishing, Paris, https://doi.org/10.1787/ee3ce00b-en. [49]

OECD (forthcoming), *Composite Indicator on Green Budgeting in the OECD*. [41]

OECD (forthcoming), *Policy brief: Economic benefits for governments to ensure the integration of RBC standards throughout supply chains in public procurement activities*. [45]

OECD (forthcoming 2023), *Strenghtening decision-making processes to deliver on climate commitments: Review of current government practices*. [43]

OECD (forthcoming 2023), *Strengthening decision-making processes for climate resilience: review of current government practices*. [42]

OECD (forthcoming 2023), *Strengthening decision-making processes for climate resilience: Review of current government practices*. [54]

OECD (forthcoming, 2023), *The role of the cost of capital in clean energy transitions*. [14]

Pahle, M. et al. (2022), "Safeguarding the energy transition against political backlash to carbon markets", *Nature Energy*, Vol. 7/3, pp. 290-296, https://doi.org/10.1038/s41560-022-00984-0. [18]

Penn, I. (2022), *Expansion of Clean Energy Loans Is 'Sleeping Giant' of Climate Bill*, https://www.nytimes.com/2022/08/22/business/energy-environment/biden-climate-bill-energy-loans.html. [23]

Regions4SD (2016), *RegionsAdapt 2016: An assessment of risks and actions*, Regions for Sustainable Development, https://www.regions4.org/publications/regionsadapt-2016-report-an-assessment-of-risks-and-actions. [47]

Shukla, P. et al. (eds.) (2022), *Summary for Policymakers*, Cambridge University Press, https://doi.org/10.1017/9781009157926.001. [31]

Songwe, V., N. Stern and A. Bhattacharya (2022), *Finance for climate action: Scaling up investment for climate and development*. [27]

The Economist (2022), *Rising interest rates and inflation have upended investing*, https://www.economist.com/briefing/2022/12/08/rising-interest-rates-and-inflation-have-upended-investing. [22]

Voldsgaard, A., F. Egli and H. Pollitt (2022), "Can we avoid green collateral damage from rising interest rates?", *UCL IIPP Blog*, https://medium.com/iipp-blog/can-we-avoid-green-collateral-damage-from-rising-interest-rates-1259ea94c9ea (accessed on 15 December 2022). [26]

Wreford, A., A. Ignaciuk and G. Gruère (2017), "Overcoming barriers to the adoption of climate-friendly practices in agriculture", *OECD Food, Agriculture and Fisheries Papers*, No. 101, OECD Publishing, Paris, https://doi.org/10.1787/97767de8-en. [36]

6 Public finance implications of the net-zero transition

Given the scale of investment needed to achieve carbon-neutrality, ensuring the fiscal feasibility of net-zero strategies will be important for making them resilient to future economic disruptions. This chapter presents the results of new modelling carried out by the OECD on the public finance resilience of net-zero emissions scenarios. It shows how these implications vary across regions and considers the need for alternative public revenue streams in order to account for tax-base erosion in the long-term.

This chapter draws on contributions to the horizontal project carried out under the responsibility of the Environment Policy Committee and the Committee on Fiscal Affairs.

Achieving net-zero emissions will considerably alter economic structures, requiring vast investments in new technologies and implying a shift of activities across and within economic sectors. This in turn will entail substantial investment needs, with public resources expected to play a key role in driving the transition (IEA, 2021[1]). The disruptive events of the COVID-19 pandemic and Russia's large-scale war of aggression in Ukraine highlight the importance of economic resilience when faced with shocks. Government responses to COVID-19 and the war in Ukraine have required substantial public spending, only part of which has been oriented towards green priorities, as highlighted in Chapter 3. It is clear that the large fiscal deficits incurred by recovery and energy-price support spending cannot be sustained in the long run.

It is imperative that climate policy design considers not only the ability to achieve the rapid emissions reductions needed to reach net zero, but the implications of different policy approaches for public finances over the longer term. Given the scale of investment needed to achieve carbon-neutrality, ensuring the fiscal feasibility of net-zero strategies will be important for making them resilient to future economic disruptions.

Achieving net-zero emissions will require a broad policy mix (D'Arcangelo et al., 2022[2]). This includes market-based policies such as carbon taxes, emissions trading schemes and subsidies to enhance the development and deployment of low-carbon technologies, as well as non-price-based instruments such as regulations and standards. These climate policy measures have different fiscal implications. Carbon prices, whether as a carbon tax or emissions trading scheme, generate government revenues. On the other hand, subsidies imply government spending or, if in the form of tax credits, foregone revenue. Removing or decreasing subsidies would thus result in reduced government expenditures or increasing tax revenues. Regulations and standards, while playing a potentially important role in steering the net-zero transition, have no direct fiscal implications.

In addition to direct fiscal implications, all climate policy measures have indirect fiscal effects as they shift economic structures and activities (phasing out of power generated from fossil fuels; increase in renewable energy sources; changes in demand for construction and transport services, etc.). These changes have indirect effects on public revenues and expenditures related to changes in economic activity in the corresponding sectors – for example, labour tax revenues – which can be both positive and negative for public finances.

In addition, many governments derive a substantial part of their tax revenues from excise duties on fossil fuels such as diesel for transport. A transition towards net-zero emissions will see consumption patterns shift away from fossil fuels in favour of low-carbon alternatives, leading to a loss in fiscal revenues from fuel excise duties, regardless of whether climate policies are price-based or otherwise. Such erosion of the tax base can have a considerable effect on public finances in the long run, warranting the more detailed analysis presented below.

This chapter reviews recent evidence on the public finance implications of the net-zero transition, taking into consideration differences across policy instruments and in regional contexts.

Public finance resilience in the net-zero transition across policy instruments and regions

For this report, new modelling was undertaken assess the fiscal implications of net-zero transitions. The modelling framework considered the impact on public finances of reaching net-zero emissions globally by mid-century (Box 6.1). A Net-Zero Ambition Scenario was compared to a baseline scenario reflecting countries' current policies and those already legislated to be implemented in the future. The Net-Zero Ambition Scenario models a broad, regionally differentiated climate policy mix combining carbon pricing, removal of fossil fuel support, regulations in the power sector, and policies to stimulate investment in low carbon technologies by firms and households (e.g. building refurbishments and subsidies for electric vehicles). Regional differences are based on the structure of different economies, not least their energy sector composition, but do not necessarily reflect the preferences and political constraints specific to the corresponding region. In other words, instruments are assumed to be implemented such that regional targets are reached without excluding specific instruments in specific regions for political considerations.

Box 6.1. Modelling policy instruments in a global net-zero emissions scenario in ENV-Linkages

The ENV-Linkages model

The ENV-Linkages model is global recursive-dynamic computable general equilibrium model that describes economic activities in different sectors and regions and how they interact. It is based on the GTAP 10 database (van der Mensbrugghe, 2019[3]) and GTAP-Power satellite account (Chepeliev, 2020[4]). The model links economic activity to environmental pressures, including greenhouse gas emissions, air pollutants and materials. CO_2 emissions from combustion of energy are directly linked to the use of different fuels using constant coefficients, while process CO_2 emissions (for example in cement production) are linked to production levels in sectors where they are generated. The baseline scenario is carefully calibrated to offer a credible projection of economic activity by 2050 without ambitious climate action but including the impact of existing and stated policies. The baseline calibration includes technological progress through various productivity parameters (e.g. autonomous energy efficiency improvements and labour productivity improvements) as well as shifts in the structure of the economy towards the services sectors. Particular attention is given to the calibration of the energy sector, including power generation and energy demand, based on information from the IEA World Energy Outlook (IEA, 2022[5]).

The Net-Zero Ambition Scenario

The paper presents a Net-Zero Emissions Ambition Scenario which reflects the ambition to achieve net-zero CO_2 emissions globally by mid-century, i.e. where carbon emissions do not exceed carbon sequestration. Specifically, all countries that have announced a commitment to achieve net-zero emissions by 2050 meet their target while all other countries achieve net-zero emissions by 2060. This Net-Zero Ambition Scenario is compared to a baseline scenario which reflects policies currently in place or legislated to be implemented. Both scenarios are presented with a 2050 time horizon. To achieve these emission reductions, ENV-Linkages has been tailored to model a broad policy package that combines various pricing and non-pricing policy instruments. Overall, the policy package targets all sources of CO_2 emissions, including fossil fuel combustion as well as process and fugitive emissions.

Fiscal implications of the Net-Zero Ambition Scenario

Governments have a wide array of policy instruments they can use to achieve emission reductions. This paper focuses on six key policies to decarbonise the economy, which were chosen because (i) they reach all key sources of carbon emissions, and (ii) they contain some of the most widely used instruments available to governments. The instruments considered are:

- Carbon pricing
- Fossil fuel support removal
- Regulations in the power sector to enforce a switch away from fossil fuels
- Regulations to stimulate investments to decarbonise building and transport emissions

- Policies to stimulate firms' energy efficiency improvement
- Subsidies to reduce and decarbonise energy consumption by households.

Each regional policy mix is determined by first calibrating regulations and subsidies based on available data on mitigation potential and investments based on information from the IEA's Net Zero Emissions Scenario (2021[1]); then adding energy efficiency policies and fossil fuel support removal; and finally, adjusting the level of carbon pricing to match emission targets.

In addition to analysing the effects on carbon pricing revenues, the ENV-Linkages model can identify direct and indirect effects of changes in economic activity on net revenues from taxes and subsidies on: (a) production and consumption of fossil fuels, (ii) production, (iii) consumption, (iv) production factors such as labour and capital, (v) income including transfers to households and (vi) imports and exports.

The economic impact of reaching net zero

Under the baseline scenario, which reflects policies currently in place or legislated to be implemented, global CO_2 emissions are projected to increase to 40 Gt in 2050, a 13% increase compared to 2019 levels. Such emissions increases would result in approximately 3.5°C of warming by the end of the century (Figure 6.1).

Global emissions in the baseline results calibrated here differ from some other commonly referred to scenarios, such as the IEA STEPS scenario, due to diverging macroeconomic assumptions such as on GDP growth trajectories, as well as diverging assumptions about the potential for energy efficiency improvements, particularly in industrial sectors. The reason for these diverging assumptions is partly a difference in policy assumptions (existing legislated policies versus those that have been announced) and results in a less optimistic outlook, appropriate for a conservative estimation of public finance risks. The baseline is nevertheless in line with the lower end of IPCC baselines. Global emissions in this baseline are considerably higher than some other commonly referred to scenarios, such as the IEA STEPS.

Figure 6.1. The baseline scenario projects a continued increase in CO_2 emissions expected to exceed 2°C by 2050 and could lead to 2.8-4.6°C in 2100

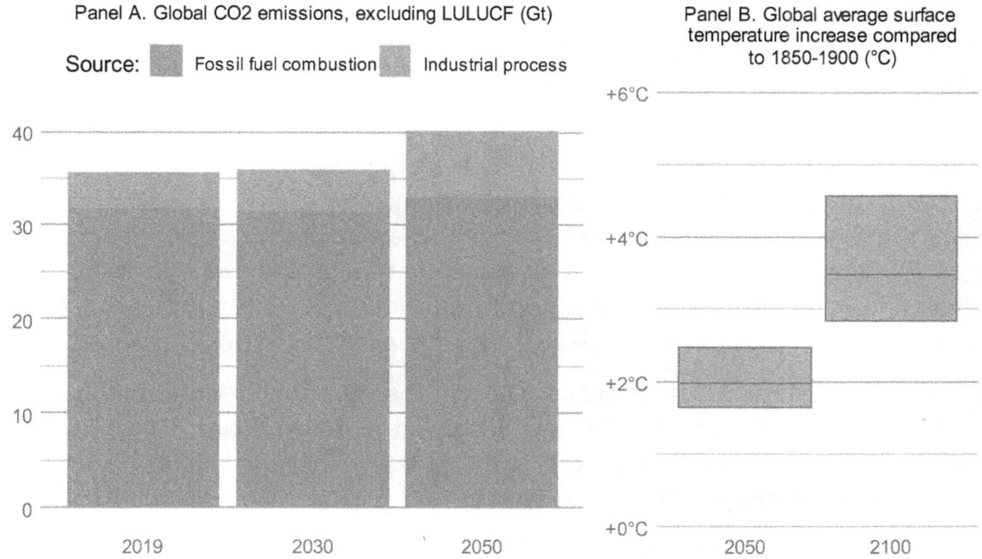

Note: LULUCF stands for 'Land use, land-use change and forestry'. Error bars in Panel B represent the 5th and 95th percentiles of the climate sensitivity in 2100.
Source: OECD ENV-Linkages model (Panel A) and MAGICC 7 based on OECD ENV-Linkages model emissions (Panel B).

The Net-Zero Ambition Scenario, however, reduces global CO_2 emissions by more than two-thirds compared to 2019 levels, to 11 Gt by 2050. A further 5 Gt is sequestered through afforestation and other land-use sequestrations, and negative emissions technologies in 2050 according to existing estimates. As such, net-global CO_2 emissions reach 6 Gt in 2050, a trajectory to reach net-zero before 2060. Under this scenario global average temperatures would peak just above 1.5°C in the second half of the century.

Figure 6.2. Gross and net CO_2 emissions steadily decline in the Net-Zero Ambition Scenario

Emissions and sequestration of CO_2 in the Net-Zero Ambition Scenario (Gt CO_2)

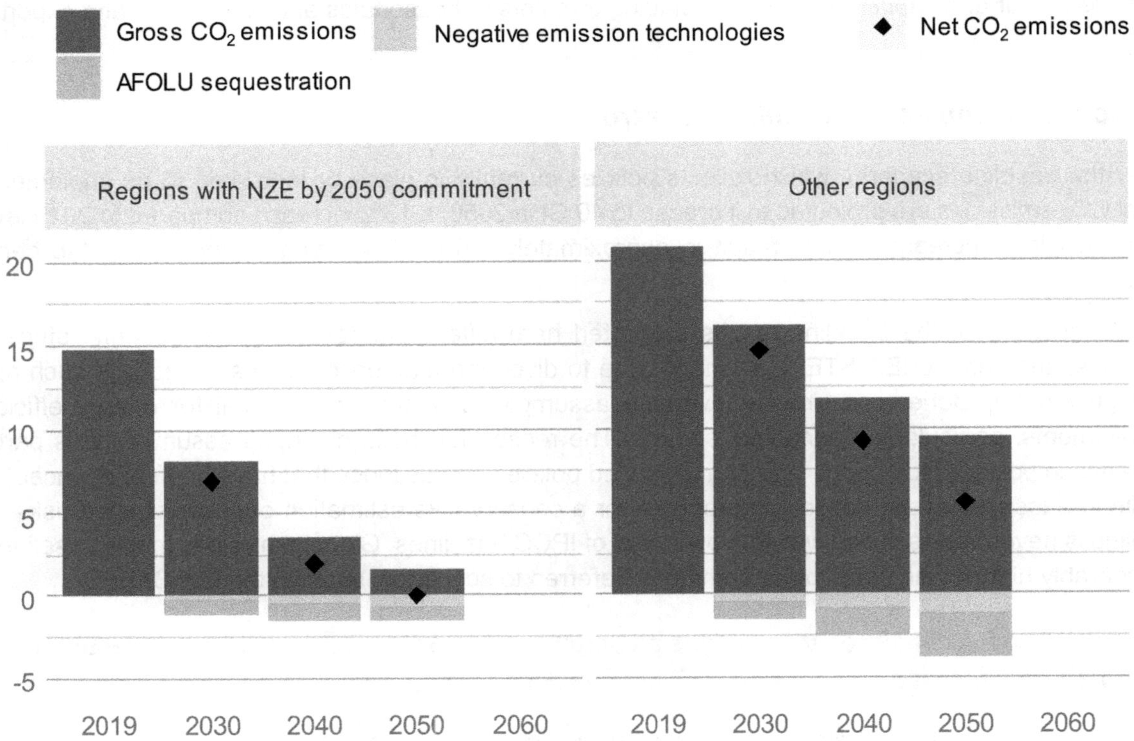

Note: The modelling exercise only considers years up to 2050.
Source: OECD ENV-Linkages model and IMAGE dataset (Van Vuuren et al.2021).

Overall, the Net-Zero Ambition Scenario results in a strong shift away from fossil-fuel-intensive sectors, reducing the energy intensity of the global economy, with most emissions reductions resulting from the decarbonisation of the energy system. Under the model's assumptions, this considerable restructuring of the global economy also results in a moderate slowdown of economic growth. Globally, GDP in 2050 is 5.6% lower than under the baseline scenario, with most of these reductions occurring after 2030. This corresponds to a 0.3 percentage point change in growth rate over the 2019-2050 period.

The results of the Net-Zero Ambition Scenario highlight the insufficient ambition of countries' current Nationally Determined Contributions (NDCs) and legislated climate policies. They also underline the considerable inertia of the economic system with many emissions already tied up in long-lasting durable goods across economic sectors (which become stranded assets under the Net-Zero Ambition Scenario).

Macroeconomic impacts differ by region. This reflects a number of factors, including the regional gap between baseline emissions and sequestration potential; the policy mix employed by each country to reduce emissions; and countries' overall economic structure. It is also assumed that investors are aware of policy signals and invest accordingly, implying a least-cost transition to net zero, where increased policy ambition leads to an immediate reaction among investors towards climate-friendly investments.

To avoid overly optimistic projections of the consequences of the net-zero transition, the Net-Zero Ambition Scenario assumes limited levels of negative-emissions technologies such as direct air capture and bioenergy with carbon capture and storage (BECCS). Energy efficiency breakthroughs in hard-to-abate sectors are also assumed to be limited. Likewise, the Net-Zero Ambition Scenario assumes limited behavioural changes beyond those due to by fiscal incentives and regulations. This results in higher macroeconomic costs compared to scenarios assuming more rapid development of these technologies. Nonetheless, a less optimistic scenario is better suited to the evaluation of potential downside risks for public finances. The Net-Zero Ambition Scenario allows for significant increases in investments, however these do not in themselves lead to a Keynesian boost to economic growth. Further analysis can be done to identify how specific policy instruments in the Net-Zero Ambition Scenario's policy package can be designed to enhance growth and prevent the negative indirect effects on public revenues found in the current analysis.

These results should be interpreted in the context of benefits of climate policies on avoided climate damages and potential co-benefits such as reduced air pollution. As depicted in Chapter 2, these benefits are considerable given the increased possibility of climate system tipping points being triggered. In addition, projected higher economic costs after 2030 highlight the importance of accelerating technological innovation for a resilient and sustained transition. If this innovation is achieved along with the economic co benefits of climate action and avoided damages, GDP effects compared to baseline are likely to be far more positive, especially in the long run.

Government revenue effects of the net-zero transition across policy instruments and regions

Overall, public revenues and expenditures increase in the baseline scenario due to rising GDP. Net public revenues from climate-related taxation (i.e. carbon prices and fossil fuel production and consumption taxes (excise duties)) remain limited in both 2030 and 2050 as increases in carbon price revenue are balanced out by decreasing revenues from fossil fuel production and consumption taxation as energy efficiency gains erode the fiscal base.

Under the Net-Zero Ambition Scenario, global net public revenues decrease moderately in 2050, by -1.8% of baseline GDP. This reflects a trade-off between revenue-generating or expenditure-decreasing policy instruments such as carbon pricing and the removal of fossil fuel support, and the decrease in public revenues due to additional subsidies and tax-base erosion of other taxes, not least in energy-related taxation.

In the Net- Zero Ambition Scenario, the global average carbon price in 2050 increases from USD 22 per tonne of CO_2 in the baseline scenario to USD 88 – with prices ranging from USD 0 to USD 714 depending on the region. Overall, although mitigation ambition erodes the fiscal base of carbon pricing over time as emissions decrease, the increase in carbon price levels and resulting revenues more than compensates for this, with revenues from carbon pricing increasing from 0.5% of baseline GDP in the baseline scenario to 0.9% of baseline GDP in the Net-Zero Ambition Scenario. This is the outcome of three main drivers illustrated in Figure 6.3: carbon prices increase significantly (second column) but at the same time CO_2 emissions decrease compared to the baseline, both due to carbon pricing (third column) and other instruments (fourth column). However, only about half of the resulting revenues can be recycled to finance other policies, due in part to the indirect effects of carbon pricing on other tax bases (fifth column). This indicates that base-erosion in excise duties remains an important challenge despite the revenue generation potential of carbon pricing and fossil fuel subsidy reform.

Figure 6.3. Reduction in CO_2 emissions and erosion of other tax bases partially offsets revenue increases from carbon pricing

Carbon pricing revenues in 2050 (% of baseline GDP)

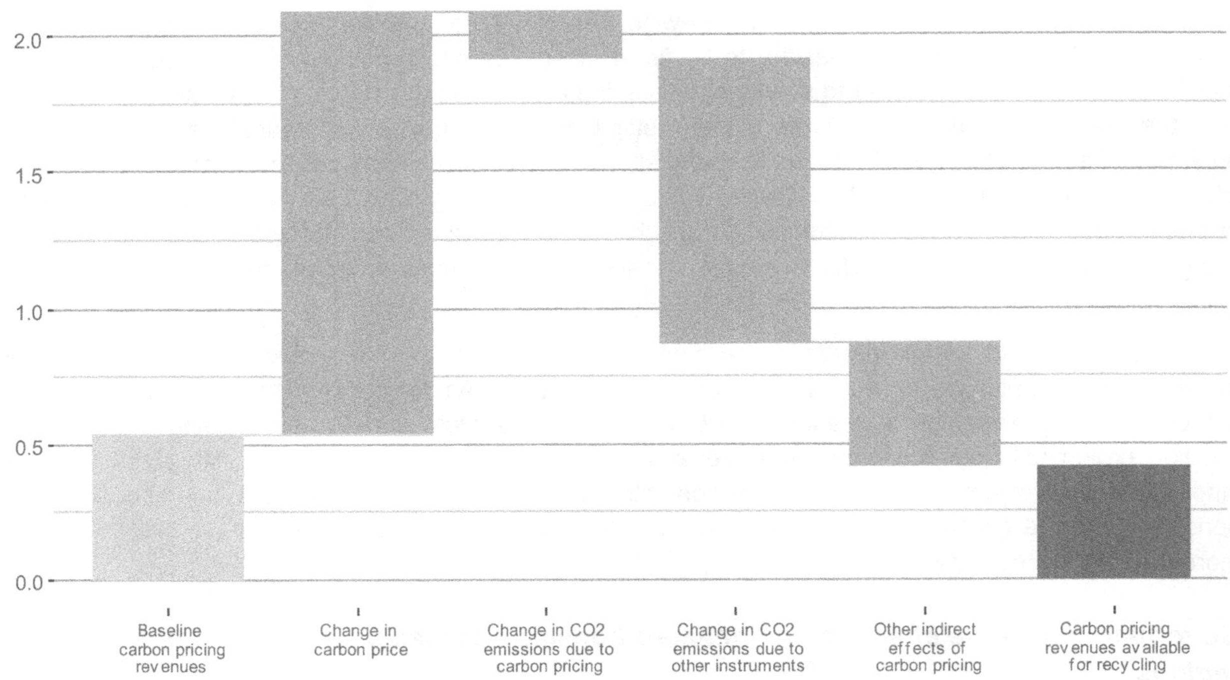

Source: OECD ENV-Linkages model.

Among policy instruments considered, the largest effects on public finances are the direct effects of carbon pricing (net additional revenues) and household subsidies (net additional expenditure), and to a lesser extent, fossil fuel subsidies removal (net additional revenues), as shown in Figure 6.4. However, all instruments entail large indirect effects that reduce net public revenues (e.g. through changes to fossil fuel production and consumption and changes in the broader fiscal base due to economic restructuring).

Indirect effects generally result from a shift of economic activity towards sectors that are on average less heavily taxed, leading to a net decrease in tax revenue (Figure 6.4), particularly concerning revenues from income and production factor taxation. When the net tax rate is negative (which is the case, on average, at the global level), meaning countries earn less in income tax revenues than they expend in transfers to households, a reduction in income leads to an overall decrease in net income tax expenditures. As such, the decrease in income under the Net-Zero Ambition Scenario results in a decrease in transfer expenditure as transfers are linked to income levels, implying an overall gain in public revenues from income taxation for almost all policy instruments.

In addition to income taxation, relative changes between economic sectors also play a large role in determining revenues from production factors, depending on how countries choose to tax different sectors. In some regions, less heavily taxed (or more heavily subsidised) sectors benefit more from the net-zero transition, implying a decrease in public revenues from production factors. In other regions the opposite is true, and more heavily taxed (or less heavily subsidised) sectors benefit, implying public revenues from production factor taxation increase. At the global level and for almost all policy instruments, these changes in production result in a decrease in net revenues from production factors and production.

Figure 6.4. Most indirect effects of policy instruments lead to a decrease in net public revenues, while direct effects of carbon pricing and fossil fuel support removal represent additional revenues

Effect of individual policy instruments on net public revenues in 2050, by fiscal base (% of GDP)

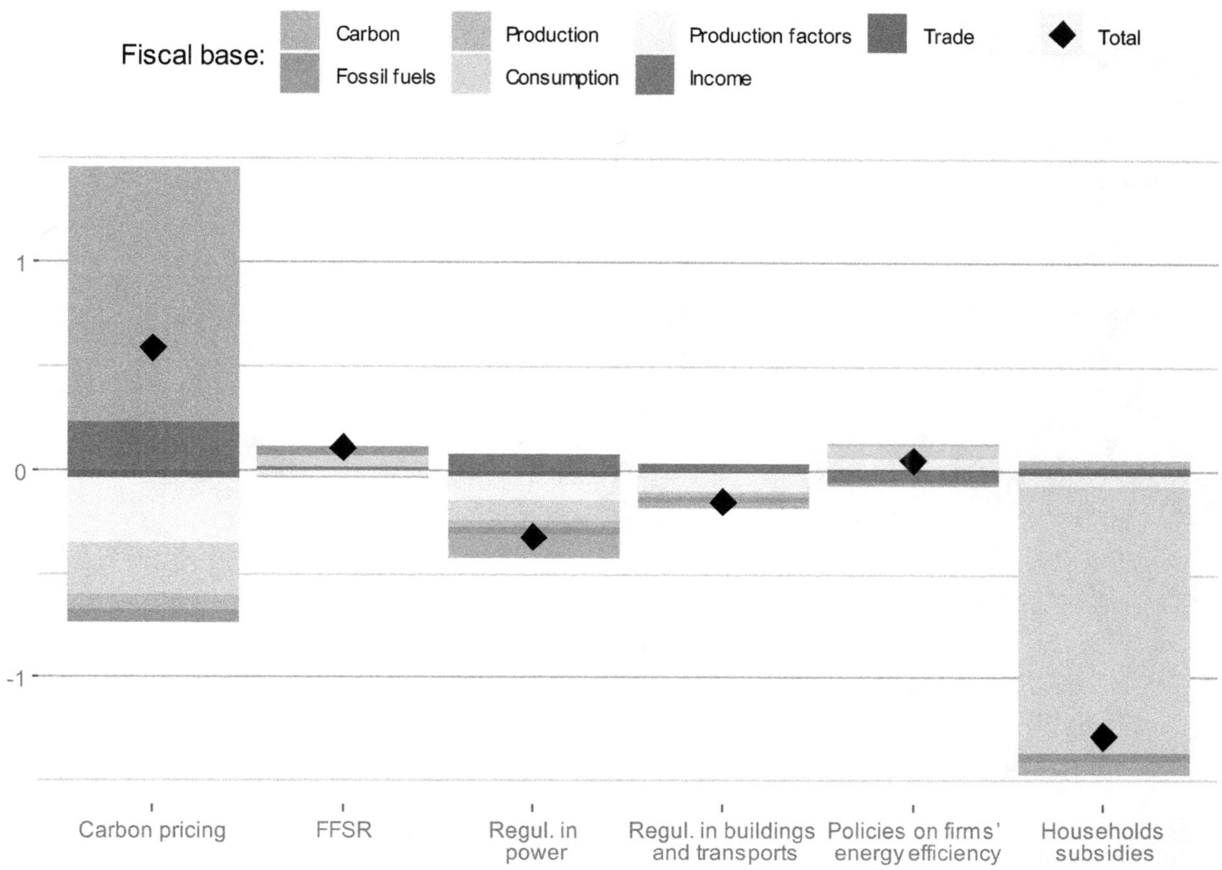

Note: Each category corresponds to a scenario where only the policy instrument mentioned is implemented. FFSR stands for "fossil fuel subsidy removal".
Source: OECD ENV-Linkages model.

Although the net global fiscal effects of reaching net-zero are limited, there are significant regional differences, with regional net public revenue changes in the Net-Zero Ambition Scenario ranging from - 0.7% to - 3.4% of baseline GDP, depending on the policy mix employed and the regional economic characteristics (Figure 6.5). These differences are driven in particular by differences in the effect of carbon pricing and fossil fuel subsidy removal on net revenues across regions.

Figure 6.5. Changes in net public revenues in the Net-Zero Ambition Scenario range from -0.7% to 3.4% of baseline GDP in 2050 depending on the region

Changes in net public revenues in Net-Zero Ambition Scenario compared to baseline in 2050 (% of baseline GDP)

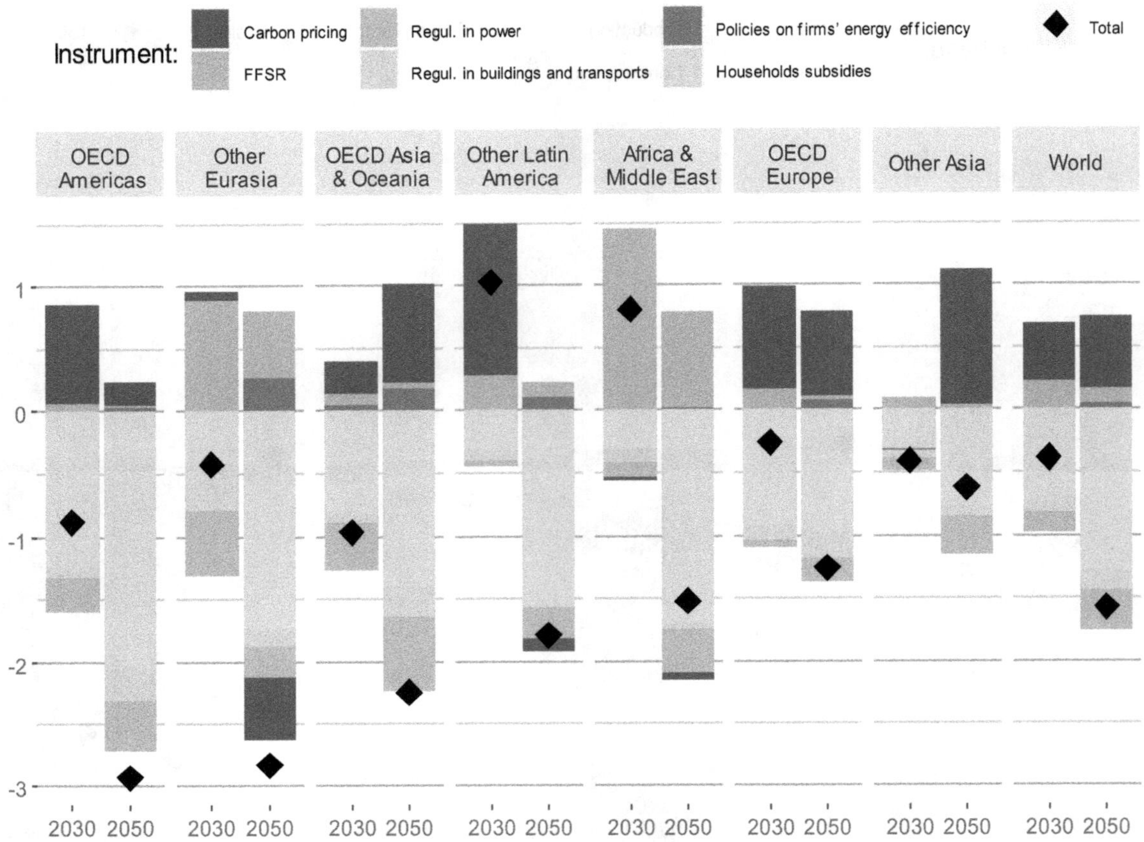

Note: The black diamonds correspond to the full Net-Zero Ambition Scenario, which implements the policy instruments all together. It differs from the sum of the effects of individual policy instruments depicted in the bars due to interactions between the different policy instruments.
Source: OECD ENV-Linkages model.

Carbon pricing leads to a net increase in public revenues for almost all regions. In the group of non-OECD Latin American countries, these direct effects even result in an increase in total net public revenues by 2030 due to a large increase in carbon pricing revenues necessary to achieve the NDC target. More generally, the extent of the impact of carbon pricing depends on the importance of carbon pricing for meeting regional mitigation targets as well as the influence of other indirect effects. For regions with high sequestration potential, such as in the group of non-OECD Latin American countries, only minimal carbon price increases are needed between 2030 and 2050 to reach net zero. As a result, revenues generated through carbon pricing also remain minimal. GDP losses due to economic restructuring in order to meet net zero, as projected for the Other Eurasia region, also lead to minimal net public revenue gains from carbon pricing (and even a decrease by 2050) because other factors balance out the large revenue gains from carbon pricing, such as lower income taxation, fuel consumption taxes, and production.

The total net effect on regional public finances is a result of the trade-off between (it) these direct effects, mostly revenue-generating, (ii) the direct cost of financing households' net-zero transition through subsidies, and (iii) the indirect effects of all instruments, mostly leading to a decrease in net public revenues as explained above. Countries that rely heavily on fossil fuel production (Other Eurasia, Africa & Middle East) are particularly at risk in the long run, as climate mitigation threatens both revenues from fossil fuel consumption taxes and trade taxes. The removal of fossil fuel support can provide revenue gains by 2030, somewhat lessening the fiscal deficit incurred in the long term and could even lead to a net increase in total public revenues for countries in Africa and Middle East where regulations in the power, transport and buildings sectors contribute negatively to net public revenues through indirect effects as previously discussed. As mentioned above, if policy measures are designed specifically to be growth enhancing, the outcome for public revenues would be more favourable than modelled here.

Considering the results presented, countries can benefit from improved awareness of the possible implications of their chosen policy mix on public finances. Past experiences show that public budgets are able to address such shifts in economic structure through creating new tax revenue streams (e.g. value added tax). Similarly, net-zero transition strategies should also consider fiscal strategy, for example introducing new tax bases to counter-balance the effects of base erosion.

In addition to managing the fiscal effects of restructuring across economic sectors and activities, addressing undesirable distributional outcomes will also be paramount to making sure that the transition is fair and equitable, an important prerequisite for a resilient transition. Factoring in the possible need for additional government expenditure (alongside climate-related expenditures) to protect low-income households is essential for sound fiscal policy going forward, in particular concerning recent shocks such as COVID-19 and the war in Ukraine. These distributional impacts are discussed in more detail in Chapter 8.

Overall, the modelling results show that the net-zero transition is feasible from an economic and fiscal standpoint. Governments have considerable leeway in carefully designing policies to match their economic and energy context while simultaneously considering other policy implications such as the effect of decarbonisation on public finances. Here the analysis highlights the importance of tailoring policy packages and support measures to national contexts, with fiscal effects differing substantially depending on economic structure and the climate policy mix employed.

The role of environmentally related taxes and carbon pricing for ensuring public finance resilience

Whereas the modelling analysis informing the previous section highlights the implications of net zero based on a stylised representation of aggregated sectors and regions, in practice many countries already have considerable experience with implementing carbon pricing policies. Drawing on the OECD's Effective Carbon Rates work (OECD, 2021[6]; OECD, 2022[7]) and related analyses, this section considers how carbon pricing is implemented in practice, showing significant heterogeneity in countries' effective carbon rate profiles. Considering carbon pricing practice and elasticities, the section highlights key implications for fiscal policy in the short- to medium-term. Finally, the section considers how these effects will play out in the long term, further highlighting the considerable risk of base-erosion in certain sectors as economies decarbonise, and policy measures to overcome this.

The principal interactions between tax policy and the transition to net-zero greenhouse gas emissions are twofold. First, progressive taxation is part of the policy toolkit to reduce greenhouse gas emissions and ensure a just transition. Second, as described in the modelling work above, the low-carbon transition induces the decline of carbon-intensive tax bases, creating a need for fiscal policy adaptation where revenues related to the consumption and production of fossil fuels (e.g. excise duties and royalties) are significant. Both dimensions are critical to maintain a stable, resilient transition towards net-zero emissions.

Taxes and similar instruments, e.g. fees or emissions trading systems, can encourage emissions reductions in various ways. They can be used to price carbon, and tax incentives can also be used to steer investment choices towards low- and zero-carbon choices. While the principal objective may be to create incentives to expedite the transition to net zero, as highlighted in the previous section, tax policy choices have budgetary impacts that should be considered when designing climate policy. In particular, policy makers need to anticipate the tax base erosion caused by declining carbon-based fuel use.

Carbon-intensive tax bases are set to erode and ultimately disappear as the transition to net zero progresses. This creates revenue challenges in fossil-fuel producing countries and in countries where taxes on carbon-based energy are a significant source of revenue. Some of these challenges may be relatively easy to address if preparations to shift to alternative tax bases start early, e.g. in the case of distance-based charges in transport instead of fuel taxes. But where alternative revenue sources are scarce, e.g. in countries heavily reliant on fossil-fuel extraction revenue, structural transformations need to be envisaged to ensure economic prosperity and fiscal capacity.

In addition to implications for public finances, climate-related tax policy can also play a key role in shaping the distributional impact of broad climate policy packages. There is a significant literature in this context on how the use of revenues from carbon pricing can shape distributional outcomes, helping support vulnerable households but also improving public support for climate policy. This is discussed in detail in Chapter 8.

Why price carbon, and how?

By increasing the price of carbon-intensive fuels, carbon prices provide incentives to reduce their use and encourage a shift to cleaner fuels. Unlike energy efficiency standards and other regulations, prices leave households and businesses a wide range of choices on how to cut emissions.[1] This greater flexibility lowers the costs of cutting emissions, in particular where mitigation costs differ widely across emitters. Regulations tend to have a narrower focus and allow for a limited set of solutions, which in general drives up abatement costs. The compliance costs incurred with regulations are typically less visible than with carbon prices, but they too are real and abatement costs per tonne of CO_2 tend to be higher.[2] Pricing also creates ongoing mitigation incentives contrary to most regulations, where once the standard set by a regulation is met, there is no additional incentive to continue the abatement effort and innovate.

Carbon prices take three broad forms: carbon taxes and the price of permits in emissions trading systems on one hand,[3] and fuel excise taxes on the other. The primary objective of carbon taxes and emissions trading systems is to reduce greenhouse gas emissions, but they also have important revenue implications, as described in the previous section.[4] Excise taxes on energy use exist for a variety of reasons, including environmental ones, but their current structure remains heavily influenced by revenue-raising objectives and considerations related to political economy. The base for fuel excise taxes usually is the volume or weight of the fuel that they apply to. Since the carbon content of each fuel is proportional to such tax bases, fuel excise tax rates can be seen as a form of carbon pricing just like carbon taxes.

In addition to carbon prices, governments also subsidise or support fossil fuel production and consumption. This incentivises fossil fuel use, increasing emissions, and so has important implications for climate policy. In addition, fossil fuel subsidies also imply government expenditure and so have fiscal implications. As such, they play an important role in determining the overall implications of price-based climate policies on public budgets.

To the extent that carbon prices achieve their primary goal of reducing greenhouse gas emissions, the base to which they apply erodes (this is "base erosion that we want"). However, the use of carbon-based fuels is so widespread across most countries that, even with alternatives increasingly becoming available at declining costs, moving away from fossil fuels will take time. With a broad base and gradual erosion, the revenues that would be raised if carbon prices drive the low-carbon transition therefore are significant and can be expected to remain so over the next one to two decades, as shown in the modelling results above.

While fuel excise taxes can usefully be thought of as implying a carbon price, they are often not optimally designed from a carbon pricing perspective. Rates differ across fuels and users, often including generous exemptions to certain activities, meaning that excise taxes do not apply a uniform price across all emissions. Reforming excise taxes so that they reflect the carbon content of fuel and broaden their base (e.g. by getting rid of exemptions).[5] could improve the environmental and climate performance of energy excise taxation (which includes fuel and electricity excise taxes). If ambitious in scope, such reforms could raise considerable revenues as they generally increase both the rates applied across fuels and expand the base to which these rates apply. This is part of what has also been termed "environmental fiscal reform" which aims to internalise external environmental costs.

The cost of carbon-based energy and other sources of greenhouse gas emissions is set to increase due to increasingly stringent policy efforts to transition to net-zero emissions. This raises concerns about differential impacts on different types of households, which may clash with equity objectives, for example when lower-income households are affected disproportionally. Here the revenue-raising potential of carbon pricing approaches may offer a key tool to help alleviate distributional concerns and maintain support for climate policies.

How have carbon prices evolved? Recent trends

The OECD tracks countries' use of carbon taxes and emissions trading systems as well as their deployment of excise taxes on energy use.[6] The sum of carbon taxes, tradeable emission permit prices and excise taxes on fuels is called the effective carbon rate (ECR). Accounting for forms of fossil fuel support that reduce pre-tax prices of fossil fuels produces the net effective carbon rate. Recent OECD data show that several countries have significantly increased their use of carbon pricing, primarily through emissions trading systems, with increasing coverage and price levels (OECD, 2022[7]).

In 2021, more than 40% of GHG emissions faced a positive net effective carbon rate, up from 32% in 2018. This increase is the result of the introduction or extension of explicit carbon pricing mechanisms in several countries, including Canada, China and Germany. Average carbon prices from emissions trading systems and carbon taxes more than doubled to reach EUR 4.3 per tonne of CO_2e over the same period. This average hides very large and rising differences between countries. Not all countries focus on carbon pricing as part of their climate mitigation policies, but carbon prices increased in 47 of the 71 countries covered in the report in 2021.

Prices continued to rise in those countries that already implemented high net carbon prices in 2018. In these countries, changes were mostly driven by the rise of carbon taxes and permit prices in emissions trading systems. In contrast, increases in net carbon prices were generally less common in countries where prices were relatively low in 2018.

Net carbon prices often remain low outside of the transport and building sectors but inter-country heterogeneity is large. Where emissions from industry and electricity are priced, this is usually through emissions trading systems or carbon taxes. While many emissions remain unpriced, some emitters now face substantial carbon prices, especially in Europe. Nevertheless, the highest net effective carbon rates tend to result from relatively high fuel taxes (excise taxes) in the road sector.

Increasing effective carbon prices could raise substantial revenues while cutting emissions. Revenues from carbon pricing can play an important role during the net-zero transition where there will be substantial adjustment costs. Countries could raise an amount equivalent to approximately 2.2% of GDP on average if they were to introduce a carbon price floor of EUR 20 per tonne of CO_2 – a mid-range estimate of carbon prices required by 2030 to drive the transition to net zero, but here too differences across countries are large, as is discussed below. These results align with those of the modelling exercise detailed previously, underscoring the revenue-raising potential of carbon pricing but also the large country differences as conditioned by the effect of the transition on different economic structures.

The effects of carbon prices on emissions and government revenues

Designing optimal carbon pricing policies requires understanding how businesses and consumers will respond to them in practice. A recent OECD paper carried out for the Net Zero+ project estimates the responsiveness of CO_2 emissions from fossil fuel use to effective carbon rates (D'Arcangelo et al., 2022[8]). The estimated responsiveness levels enable simulations of the effects of changes in effective carbon rates both on emissions and on the revenues from carbon pricing.[7]

The simulated carbon price floors capture two options available to policy makers: increasing effective carbon rates for emissions already priced or broadening the emission base to which effective carbon rates apply. For emissions already priced, the policy scenarios consider price floors between EUR 0 and EUR 175 per tonne of CO_2; for unpriced emissions the floors vary from EUR 0 to EU 60 per tonne of CO_2.[8]

The simulations highlight the key importance of a broad policy mix for reaching net-zero emissions, with carbon pricing alone unlikely to be enough to meet net-zero objectives. This supports the Net-Zero Ambition Scenario modelling results presented in the previous section. Indeed, the simulations show that, given the moderate estimated responsiveness of emissions to carbon pricing, meeting net-zero targets would require a substantially higher price floor than those considered in the simulations. Combining the price floor of EUR 175 on already priced emissions and of EUR 60 on unpriced emissions is estimated to reduce total emissions from fossil fuel use by around 29% compared with the 2018 level (Figure 6.6, right panel). Sixty percent of this decline would come from emissions already priced in 2018.

Complementing carbon pricing with policies that increase the emission responsiveness to carbon pricing (e.g. related to green innovation) can also ease the substitution of clean energy sources for fossil fuels, thus reducing emission abatement costs (e.g. with new technologies) and making carbon pricing more effective. For instance, policy simulations show that an emission responsiveness twice as large as the baseline estimate combined with an effective carbon rate (ECR) floor of EUR 40 on priced and unpriced emissions would result in the same emissions reduction as baseline responsiveness estimates combined with an ECR floor of EUR 175 on priced emissions and EUR 60 on unpriced emissions.

Carbon-related government revenues (including fuel excise-tax related revenues) would increase almost four-fold compared with 2018 levels, with the base broadening price floor of EUR 60 increasing revenues by about 2.5 times. Across the range in the carbon pricing floors considered, more than half of the revenue increase would come from pricing previously unpriced emissions (Figure 6.6, left panel). The rate of the increase in revenues declines as the ECR floor rises, as higher ECRs progressively erode the emissions base. However, for the range of ECR floors considered this "base erosion effect" is always smaller than the "price increase effect" so total revenues continue rising with price floor levels. This aligns with the modelling results depicted previously, showing that carbon pricing can generate government revenues even while their revenue base (emissions) decrease in the long term.

Figure 6.6. Aggregate effects of an effective carbon rate floor on emissions and revenues

CO_2 emissions from fossil- fuel use and revenues changes, indexed to 100 in 2018

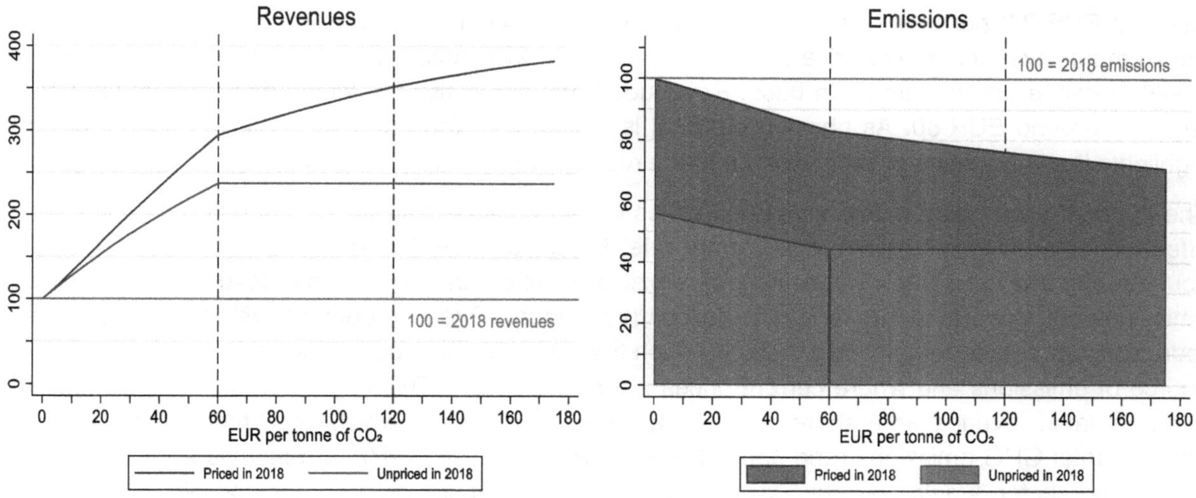

Note: Simulations of a global ECR floor by EUR 5 increments. The maximum ECR floor for emissions unpriced in 2018 is EUR 60 per tonne of CO_2. Beyond EUR 60, the price floor on emissions already priced in 2018 keeps on rising until EUR 175, while that for unpriced emissions in 2018 remains at EUR 60. Semi-elasticities are allowed to differ by sector. An ECR floor of 0 corresponds to 2018 policies.
Source: OECD.

Carbon pricing effects on different sectors, fuels and countries

The effects of price floors on emissions and revenues differ across sectors, fuels and countries because of differences in current price levels and in the price-sensitivity of emissions. In sectors other than the road and off-road transport sector (where the base is broad to begin with), broadening the emissions base would result in substantial emission reductions.

Price increases triggered by the price floors are largest in the industry and electricity sectors since ECRs tend to be low for these sectors, particularly in high-emitting countries including China and the United States. Combined with the price-responsiveness observed in these sectors, this contributes to these two sectors also displaying the largest emissions reductions. Despite the large contraction of the emissions base, carbon-related revenues from these sectors would increase for all ranges of ECR floors considered.

The simulated increase in road sector carbon prices is markedly smaller than in industry and electricity as rates are generally already high, with an emission-weighted average of nearly EUR 90 per tonne of CO_2 in the road sector against around EUR 3 in industry and electricity sectors. Already high effective carbon rates (ECRs) in the road sector imply that there would be almost no effects on emissions up to a EUR 40 price floor. As such, other measures beyond carbon pricing may be needed to incentivise substantial emissions reductions in transport.

The agriculture and fisheries sector is responsive to changing ECRs, and the analysis suggests that increasing ECRs in these activities would be effective in reducing CO_2 emissions due to fossil fuel use. However, this must be considered in the context of reforming existing subsidies, both for fossil fuels and other support measures, which are considerable in these sectors. In addition, fuel use is not the largest emissions source in agriculture – greenhouse gas emissions there are mainly due to livestock emitting methane and agricultural soil treatment causing nitrous oxide emissions. Overall impact on total emission reduction and revenues would therefore likely be relatively small.

Simulations distinguishing between fuels underline the importance of pricing emissions from coal and other solid fossil fuels used to reduce global CO_2 emissions. This is because of coal's high responsiveness to carbon pricing and its low current price in most countries (including China and the United States, where a lot of coal is used in electricity generation and industry). In 2018, the average effective carbon rate of coal was just EUR 2.2 per tonne of CO_2. Increasing prices on coal emissions would initially generate large government revenues at low price floor levels, but high price responsiveness means that higher prices would quickly erode the emission base. Revenues from coal emissions would decline from carbon price levels of around EUR 80. As phasing out coal is essential to the net-zero transition, this result further highlights the importance of fiscal planning for a resilient transition.

The effect of price floors differs across countries in part because low carbon price floors do not strongly affect countries with a high average current rate. Moreover, both the share of unpriced emissions in a country and the sectoral composition of emissions determine the country-level responsiveness of emissions and government revenues to carbon price floors. Overall, countries with the largest emission reductions and revenue gains are those in which the electricity and industry sectors are the predominant source of emissions and where current prices are relatively low. This might not necessarily mean large carbon-related revenue as a share of GDP, however. Countries in which fossil fuels account for a low share of total GHG emissions (and hence have a low intensity in GDP), for example because of a large agricultural sector, would not attain large carbon-related revenues as a percentage of GDP despite the steep increase in the average effective carbon rate. In these countries, the emission base to which ECR applies is small, relative the size of the economy, and hence they would raise less carbon-related revenues as a share of GDP than other countries. This further underlines the modelling results presented earlier in the chapter and again highlights the need to consider contextual factors when assessing the public finance implications of carbon pricing.

Beyond carbon pricing: the public finance implications of other policy instruments

Given that carbon pricing alone will not suffice to reach climate neutrality goals, governments seeking to accelerate a resilient transition need to deploy a suite of policies as part of a comprehensive decarbonisation strategy including tax incentives for clean technologies, standards and regulations, and complementary policies to facilitate the structural changes along the transition (D'Arcangelo et al., 2022[2]; Blanchard, Gollier and Tirole, 2022[9]).

Tax incentives can encourage specific consumption, production and investment choices by reducing the tax burden associated with these choices. Tax incentives can be channelled through the corporate or the personal income tax system, for example, to encourage the use and production of, or investment in low or zero-carbon technologies. They can be seen as a subsidy delivered through preferential tax treatment instead of through direct government outlays.

In the corporate income taxation context, tax incentives are frequently granted for specific types of investment and take different forms (Celani, Dressler and Wermelinger, 2022[10]). By providing a favourable deviation from a country's general tax treatment, tax incentives reduce or postpone the tax liability of an investor, which can encourage investment under certain circumstances. Tax incentives can take the form of investment allowances and credits, accelerated depreciation, reduced tax rates, and tax exemptions, among others. Tax incentives are costly as they imply potentially considerable foregone government revenue, i.e. tax revenue that authorities do not collect because business receives preferential tax treatment on investments that it would have made in absence of the incentive (e.g. see modelling results on subsidies and their indirect effects discussed previously). There also are administrative costs, which can be considerable as determining eligibility and compliance is complex.

Tax incentives can complement or substitute carbon pricing as part of the needed broader policy mix. They can play a key role in supporting innovation and deploying new technology, but regulations and technology support are also needed to stimulate learning-by-doing to help overcome capital market imperfections, unlock network externalities and overcome path dependencies (for a more detailed discussion on innovation see Chapter 7). While a combination of instruments allows better alignment of climate change mitigation policies with the different policy concerns, political economy constraints can lead to deviations from ideal approaches – the imperative is to act in the way best suited for a country at a given moment in time.

A key example of tax incentives in practice is the recent United States' Inflation Reduction Act (IRA), signed into law on 16 August 2022. The IRA relies on tax incentives to incentivise the uptake of clean technologies, both at the corporate and the personal tax level, and does not introduce new carbon pricing mechanisms (with the exception of a methane charge in oil and gas extraction). The Act contains two main spending areas: energy and climate (estimated cost of USD 386 billion from 2022-2031) and health care (USD 98 billion). On the revenue side, savings on health spending and new sources of revenue including a 15% minimum corporate income tax amount to USD 790 billion.[9] Approximately two-thirds of the energy and climate spending will take the form of tax incentives, amounting to around 0.05% to 0.18% of GDP depending on the year, but analysis suggests the IRA is expected to be revenue positive overall, reducing the deficit by around 0.2% in 2031.[10] Emissions reductions are expected to be significant, cutting CO_2 emissions by 30% by 2050 compared to a no additional policy action scenario. The IRA is estimated to lead to a modest GDP increase of 0.1% in 2031, and a more significant increase of 0.6% in 2050 and 2.7% in 2100, illustrating the benefits of climate action – and the high costs of inaction.

Early analysis of the likely effects of the IRA shows that a climate policy mix not oriented around carbon pricing can still be effective at reducing emissions without unnecessarily burdening public finances. However, the risk of base-erosion also persists when emissions are reduced predominantly through tax incentives rather than pricing as demand shifts from fossil fuels to cleaner alternatives. In general, designing effective tax incentives is difficult as they risk distorting the allocation of resources in an economy by providing preferential treatment to certain groups. But when used to address market failures, as in the case of green incentives, they improve efficiency. While there is evidence that tax incentives can encourage investment (Maffini, Xing and Devereux, 2019[11]), not all incentives create additional investment, i.e. investment attracted exclusively by the incentive, and risk being at least partly redundant, i.e. are granted to investment that would have also taken place without the incentive, highlighting the importance to consider the "additionality" of considered tax incentives.[11]

The risk of base erosion along the net-zero transition and how to address it

Environment-related tax revenue is substantial across OECD countries and regions. The largest component of this comes from energy taxes (notably transport fuels and electricity), followed by transport taxes (mostly on road transport vehicles) (Table 6.1). There are large differences across OECD regions in how much revenue is raised from energy taxes, with European countries raising more revenue mostly because of higher road transport fuel tax rates. In general, however, revenues as a share of GDP have declined over the past two decades, a consequence of changes in the tax base (e.g. improving fuel economy), tax rates (not always increased in line with inflation), and the weight of transport sector in countries' GDP.

Table 6.1. Environment-related tax revenue in the OECD, % of GDP

2000, 2010 and 2020

	Energy	Transport	Pollution	Resources
		2000		
OECD	1.31	0.45	0.05	0.02
OECD America	0.73	0.29	0.01	0.01
OECD Asia Oceania	1.19	0.69	0.01	0.01

	Energy	Transport	Pollution	Resources
OECD Europe	1.93	0.52	0.10	0.03
		2010		
OECD	1.16	0.42	0.05	0.02
OECD America	0.47	0.25	0.01	0.01
OECD Asia Oceania	1.22	0.57	0.01	0.01
OECD Europe	1.84	0.54	0.10	0.02
		2020		
OECD	0.97	0.34	0.02	0.01
OECD America	0.51	0.21	0.01	0.01
OECD Asia Oceania	0.49	0.28	0.01	0
OECD Europe	1.65	0.51	0.04	0.02

Source: OECD PINE database: https://www.compareyourcountry.org/environmental-taxes/en/3/185+186+2006+2007/default/2000

The data depicted in Table 6.1 suggest that, from a public finance point of view, the transition to net zero creates the need to address the erosion of the fossil fuel tax base, predominantly in the road transport sector, and more so in European countries than in other regions even though fuel tax and vehicle tax revenue is significant everywhere. As discussed above, carbon tax revenue can compensate part or even most of the declining fuel tax revenue in the medium term. The revenue potential could exceed 2% of global GDP with a carbon price floor of EUR 120/tCO_2 (see previous section) and the UK Office for Budget Responsibility (OBR, 2021) estimates the revenues lost from base erosion at circa 1.6% of GDP in 2050, compared to revenues gained from carbon pricing (0.5-1.7% of GDP).

Over the longer term, however, as fossil fuel use declines, carbon tax revenue will also decline, and other options need to be considered. This involves assessing whether and when the declining revenue needs to be compensated, a matter informed by the scarcity of public revenue (as seen in the modelling results depicted previously) and the economic and political economy characteristics of alternative revenue-raising options. One option is to raise revenue not from transport energy but more directly from transport activity itself, e.g. through distance-based charges.

Base erosion in the transport sector: the need for distance-based charges

A key example of the base-erosion risks posed by climate policies lies in the transport sector. Governments have three options for dealing with declining revenues in the sector: choose not to replace the declining fuel tax revenue, look to tax bases outside of the transport sector, or consider tax policy reform within transport. This section discusses the latter option, specifically looking at the potential for distance-base charges as a mobility management and revenue-raising instrument.

In addition to climate policies, other trends including technological advancements and changes in transport use have the potential to erode fossil fuel tax bases in the transport sector. For instance, ongoing improvements in the fuel efficiency of traditional car technologies tend to reduce the demand for fuel. Furthermore, battery electric vehicles and plug-in hybrids are increasingly penetrating the car fleet, reducing the demand for fossil fuels. Systemic transformations in the transport sector may also impact tax revenues as consumer preferences shift away from private vehicles to public transportation or other shared modes of transport.

Fossil fuels are not the only tax base in road transport. Governments typically collect tax revenues from three tax bases: energy use, vehicle stock and road use. Taxes on vehicles reflect a variety of influences beyond the need to raise revenue. Geographic, industrial, social, energy, transport, urban and environmental policy considerations have all had an influence on the level and structure of taxation. Many taxes on vehicles were instituted in a time when cars were considered luxury items, but broadening car ownership has reduced the progressivity of those taxes. Taxes at the point of purchase and recurrent taxes are based on various characteristics, including polluting emissions, weight, engine power, number of axles, age, fuel efficiency, equipment, suspension, cylinder capacity, number of seats, type of fuel or electric propulsion.

The three tax bases in road transport interact and the technological trend towards fuel-efficient and electric vehicles will affect each of the bases differently. The evolution of tax bases in road transport remains uncertain: for example in relation to the speed at which fuel-efficiency increases and alternative technologies will penetrate the vehicle fleet. An OECD analysis for Slovenia (OECD/ITF, 2019[12]), where 14.6% of total tax revenue collected in 2016 came from excise duties and carbon taxes levied on diesel and gasoline used in road transport, developed scenarios for declining fuel tax revenues. The study aligned with the International Energy Agency's 2°C Scenario for Europe, assuming that alternative fuel technologies account for 25% of passenger car purchases in 2030 and 62% in 2050 – compared to a 2% share in 2017. Under this assumption and with no policy responses, the tax revenue loss from reduced fossil fuel use in private cars would be substantial in the coming decades. Total tax revenues from fuel used in passenger cars in Slovenia in 2050 would be 56% lower than in 2017. The EU proposal for a ban on petrol and diesel vehicle sales by 2035 could exacerbate the impact on revenues. For trucks, the decline in fossil fuel use would likely be less important over the horizon considered because of slower take-up of alternative technologies.

As the fuel tax base erosion will be gradual, given the time it takes for new technologies to enter the fleet, a gradual reform of the tax system is possible but should start soon. Tax reform implementation takes time and requires preparation and discussion with stakeholders, especially when new types of taxes are considered, e.g. distance-based charges that could replace declining fuel tax revenue. To stabilise revenues from the sector, a new mix of taxing distances driven, vehicles and fuel or, more generally, transport energy will be needed.

In the short to medium term, increasing fuel or carbon taxes and regular adjustments of nominal rates to inflation can effectively continue to raise revenue. However, the politics around recent energy price increases, and previously the "yellow vest' protest movement in France, highlight that such policies may be untenable from a political economy perspective without carefully designed distributional policies. As the fleet penetration of electric vehicles gathers momentum, the revenue potential from fuel taxes will be increasingly limited especially in the passenger car segment of the market. In some countries, fuel tax competition and distributional considerations will also constrain the scope for continued rate increases (Dechezleprêtre et al., 2022[13]).

Over the longer run, revenues can be sustained by gradually increasing fuel or carbon taxes that cover the external costs closely related with fossil fuel use in vehicles and by phasing-in distance-based charges for cars to reflect external costs closely related with driving. Such a tax system would gradually shift revenues to an alternative and likely more stable tax base, namely road use, while further reducing distortions. An efficient distance-based system for passenger cars would set as a base the number of kilometres driven (not annual vignettes). Distance-based charges could be complemented by congestion charges where necessary, keeping in mind that political support may require that the revenues from such local systems also accrue locally. Vehicle taxes may also be part of the tax reform package. An advantage of vehicle taxes is their relatively low administrative burden. However, if the idea would be to cover the shortfall in revenues from fuel excise over time, vehicle taxes would need to increase substantially over time and gradually cover alternative fuel vehicles too. In addition to the political feasibility and equity concerns over such a policy, their limited ability in managing external costs from driving reduces their appeal from a transport and broader mobility perspective.

Careful design and tailored communication are essential for the success of comprehensive tax reform in the road sector, given the involvement of numerous stakeholders. To gain support for tax reform it is necessary to develop a good understanding of the potential negative consequences (e.g. how changes in tax liability from reform distribute along income and spatial dimensions) and to design appropriate policy responses (including improving access to public transport, for example).

Chapter conclusions

The transition to net-zero emissions will have a substantial effect on countries' public finances. Different policy approaches can increase or decrease public revenues in the net-zero transition, meaning that aggregate global effects mask stark country differences. Governments should carefully consider how their intended climate policy mix affects government revenues. Large revenue gains, as can generally be expected from a carbon pricing-centred mitigation policy approach, could create fiscal space, and this is potentially important given that public funds are scarce in many countries. Creating fiscal space improves economies' resilience to risk in an era where exposure to catastrophic risk (e.g. from climate change, disease, cyberattacks or war) is rising. Revenues can also be recycled and may be integral to balancing out distributional concerns of carbon pricing and generating public support (Chapter 8).

Non-market-based policy instruments such as subsidies or tax incentives generally imply foregone government revenues, but the example of the Inflation Reduction Act (IRA) suggests they can be designed effectively in tandem with tax increases and expenditure savings to minimise the overall fiscal burden. Importantly, although tax incentives still result in a negative impact on public finances, the budgetary costs take the form of foregone revenue, which tends to be less salient than budgetary outlays or tax increases and can thus improve the political feasibility of tax incentives vis-à-vis other policies.

The indirect effects of climate policy instruments on public finances and their interactions with domestic economic structures mean that climate policy mixes need to be carefully designed for each context. Tax reforms that replace highly distortive taxes with less distortive climate-related taxes (i.e. environmental fiscal reform) may be possible in p The indirect effects of climate policy instruments on public finances and their interactions with domestic economic structures mean that climate policy mixes need to be carefully designed for each context. Tax reforms that replace highly distortive taxes with less distortive climate-related taxes (i.e. environmental fiscal reform) may be possible in principle, but tax policy approaches to climate change and the spending of any revenue that they generate will need to be carefully aligned with the spending needs associated with the transition to net zero, the distributional concerns this raises and the imperative of securing public support for it in principle, but tax policy approaches to climate change and the spending of any revenue that they generate will need to be carefully aligned with the spending needs associated with the transition to net zero, the distributional concerns this raises and the imperative of securing public support for it.

Notes

[1] The same logic holds for carbon emissions which are not due to fuel use, such as industrial process emissions. Carbon pricing on those can encourage a switch to cleaner technology alternatives as well.

[2] See, e.g. the abatement cost estimates in (OECD, 2013[14]), where it is worth noting that these estimates are derived in a static microeconomic framework that does not allow for learning effects, among others.

[3] The similarities and differences between these approaches in terms of incentives created are discussed in (Flues and van Dender, 2020[15]), noting that specific policy design features drive performance, and that the differences between both forms of pricing tend to be smaller in practice than in the polar textbook cases.

[4] For emissions trading systems, even with free allocations, the behavioural incentive to decrease emissions created at the margin remains. Investment incentives, however, can be weakened by free permit allocation depending on the allocation rule, see (Flues and van Dender, 2017[16]).

[5] The recent EU Energy Tax Directive (ETD) revision proposal, for example, goes in that direction.

[6] Carbon taxes here are meant as all taxes on greenhouse gases and not CO_2 only.

[7] Responsiveness was measured by the semi-elasticity of CO_2 emissions to effective carbon rates, which measures by what percentage CO_2 emissions vary when effective carbon rates increase by EUR 1 per tonne of CO_2.

[8] EUR 0 represents maintaining the status quo.

[9] Estimated Budgetary Effects of H.R. 5376, the Inflation Reduction Act of 2022 (cbo.gov); What's In the Inflation Reduction Act? | Committee for a Responsible Federal Budget (crfb.org).

[10] assessing-the-macroeconomic-consequences-of-the-inflation-reduction-act-of-2022.pdf (moodysanalytics.com)

[11] The IMF, OECD, United Nations and World Bank (citation) summarise international evidence suggesting that tax incentives are often found to be redundant and that taxation is only one of many factors that determine investors' decisions of where to invest – and not the most important factor in developing economies. Without well-functioning infrastructure, macroeconomic stability and a stable rule of law, tax incentives are unlikely to attract (additional) investment. The effectiveness of tax incentives, however, is sector- and incentive-specific and deserves careful monitoring and analysis.

References

Blanchard, O., C. Gollier and J. Tirole (2022), *The Portfolio of Economic Policies Needed to Fight Climate Change*, https://www.piie.com/sites/default/files/2022-11/wp22-18.pdf. [9]

Celani, A., L. Dressler and M. Wermelinger (2022), "Building an Investment Tax Incentives database: Methodology and initial findings for 36 developing countries", *OECD Working Papers on International Investment*, No. 2022/01, OECD Publishing, Paris, https://doi.org/10.1787/62e075a9-en. [10]

Chepeliev, M. (2020), "GTAP- Power Database: Version 10", *Journal of Global Economic Analysis*, Vol. 5/2, pp. 110-137, https://doi.org/10.21642/jgea.050203af. [4]

D'Arcangelo, F. et al. (2022), "A framework to decarbonise the economy", *OECD Economic Policy Papers*, No. 31, OECD Publishing, Paris, https://doi.org/10.1787/4e4d973d-en. [2]

D'Arcangelo, F. et al. (2022), "Estimating the CO2 emission and revenue effects of carbon pricing: new evidence from a large cross-country dataset", *Working Party No. 1 on Macroeconomic and Structural Policy Analysis*, No. ECO/CPE/WP1(2022)7, OECD, Paris. [8]

Dechezleprêtre, A. et al. (2022), “Fighting climate change: International attitudes toward climate policies”, *OECD Economics Department Working Papers*, No. 1714, OECD Publishing, Paris, https://doi.org/10.1787/3406f29a-en. [13]

Flues, F. and K. van Dender (2020), “Carbon pricing design: Effectiveness, efficiency and feasibility: An investment perspective”, *OECD Taxation Working Papers*, No. 48, OECD Publishing, Paris, https://doi.org/10.1787/91ad6a1e-en. [15]

Flues, F. and K. van Dender (2017), “Permit allocation rules and investment incentives in emissions trading systems”, *OECD Taxation Working Papers*, No. 33, OECD Publishing, Paris, https://doi.org/10.1787/c3acf05e-en. [16]

IEA (2022), *World Energy Outlook 2022*. [5]

IEA (2021), *World Energy Outlook 2021*. [1]

Maffini, G., J. Xing and M. Devereux (2019), “The Impact of Investment Incentives: Evidence from UK Corporation Tax Returns”, *American Economic Journal: Economic Policy*, Vol. 11/3, pp. 361-389, https://doi.org/10.1257/pol.20170254. [11]

OECD (2022), *Pricing Greenhouse Gas Emissions: Turning Climate Targets into Climate Action*, OECD Series on Carbon Pricing and Energy Taxation, OECD Publishing, Paris, https://doi.org/10.1787/e9778969-en. [7]

OECD (2021), *Effective Carbon Rates 2021: Pricing Carbon Emissions through Taxes and Emissions Trading*, OECD Series on Carbon Pricing and Energy Taxation, OECD Publishing, Paris, https://doi.org/10.1787/0e8e24f5-en. [6]

OECD (2013), *Effective Carbon Prices*, OECD Publishing, Paris, https://doi.org/10.1787/9789264196964-en. [14]

OECD/ITF (2019), *Tax Revenue Implications of Decarbonising Road Transport: Scenarios for Slovenia*, OECD Publishing, Paris, https://doi.org/10.1787/87b39a2f-en. [12]

van der Mensbrugghe, D. (2019), *The Environmental Impact and Sustainability Applied General Equilibrium (ENVISAGE) Model. Version 10.01*, Center for Global Trade Analysis, Purdue University, https://mygeohub.org/groups/gtap/envisage-docs. [3]

7 The importance of innovation for a resilient net-zero transition

Innovation is essential to the net zero transition. This chapter considers the need for innovation to ensure a successful and resilient transition, reviewing recent policy trends and suggesting ways to enhance government efforts to support technological development. To fully harness innovation potentials, governments will need to do more than just redirect their science, technology and innovation policies, shifting instead towards a mission-oriented approach to both technology development and deployment to ensure efforts are streamlined across policy areas.

This chapter draws on contributions to the horizontal project carried out under the responsibility of the Committee for Industry, Innovation and Entrepreneurship and the Committee for Scientific and Technological Policy.

Some of the carbon-free technologies necessary to reach net-zero emissions already exist, but are still too expensive to be fully competitive with carbon-based alternatives and deployed rapidly and at scale (IPCC, 2022[1]). However, climate targets cannot be achieved by only deploying existing technologies, e.g. mature forms of renewable energy such as wind and solar. Other technologies such as green hydrogen are still in their infancy and need to be further developed and have their costs reduced to allow rapid scale-up. According to the International Energy Agency's (IEA) Net-Zero Emissions by 2050 Scenario, half of the global reductions in energy-related CO_2 emissions through 2050 will have to come from technologies that are currently at the demonstration or prototype phase (IEA, 2021[2]). Even within technologies sectors that are for the most part considered mature, such as renewable energy, there is room for breakthrough innovation, for example in geothermal or concentrated solar power (IEA, 2017[3]; IRENA, 2018[4]).

In heavy industry and long-distance transport, the share of emissions reductions from technologies still under development today is even higher. For example, decarbonisation of the manufacturing industry requires not only the adoption of technologies that are close to the market such as a massive increase in renewable electricity generation to enable the electrification of low-temperature heat processes, but also the deployment of many technologies that are still far from maturity, notably bio-based products and green hydrogen (Anderson et al., 2021[5]).

Alongside low-carbon technologies, climate neutrality will rest on innovation in other domains, in particular digital technologies and recycling. The digital transformation could be a key enabler for reaching climate goals, thanks to technologies such as smart meters, sensors, artificial intelligence (AI), the Internet of Things (IoT) and blockchain, and to digitally-induced changes in business models and consumption (OECD, 2020[6]; OECD, 2019[7]). Improved recycling technologies can also contribute to decarbonisation by reducing the need for fossil-based feedstock in the chemical industry or primary steel in the metal industry. Mechanical or chemical recycling can transform existing products into new feedstock, thereby closing the materials chain, but many options need further technological development and cost reductions to be deployed widely.

This chapter considers the need for innovation to ensure a successful and resilient transition, reviewing recent policy trends and suggesting ways to enhance government efforts to support technological development.

Tracking low-carbon innovation: recent trends

The current pace of low-carbon innovation is not in line with the carbon neutrality challenge. Climate related innovation as measured by patent filings has decreased as a share of inventions in all technology areas over the past decade (Figure 7.1). Following a period of strong growth between 2004 and 2011, innovation efforts in climate-related technologies have declined recently as a share of total patenting, from 12.6% of global patents in 2011 to 9.0% in 2020. Between 2005-2011, the number of climate-related inventions patented globally grew at an average annual rate of 16.3%, while innovation in all technologies only grew at 6.2% per year on average.

Climate innovation efforts started to decline around 2012, however, despite the ambitious climate objectives and signing of the Paris Agreement in 2015. Since 2012, climate related inventions patented globally increased at an average rate of 0.3% per year (with over 5% decreases in 2014 and 2015) while overall innovation continued to grow at an average pace of 4.6% per year. Importantly, the decrease in low-carbon patenting affects nearly all technologies with the exception of energy storage (batteries) and can be observed across nearly all major innovating countries around the world, except Denmark.

Figure 7.1. Global low-carbon patenting efforts have recently declined

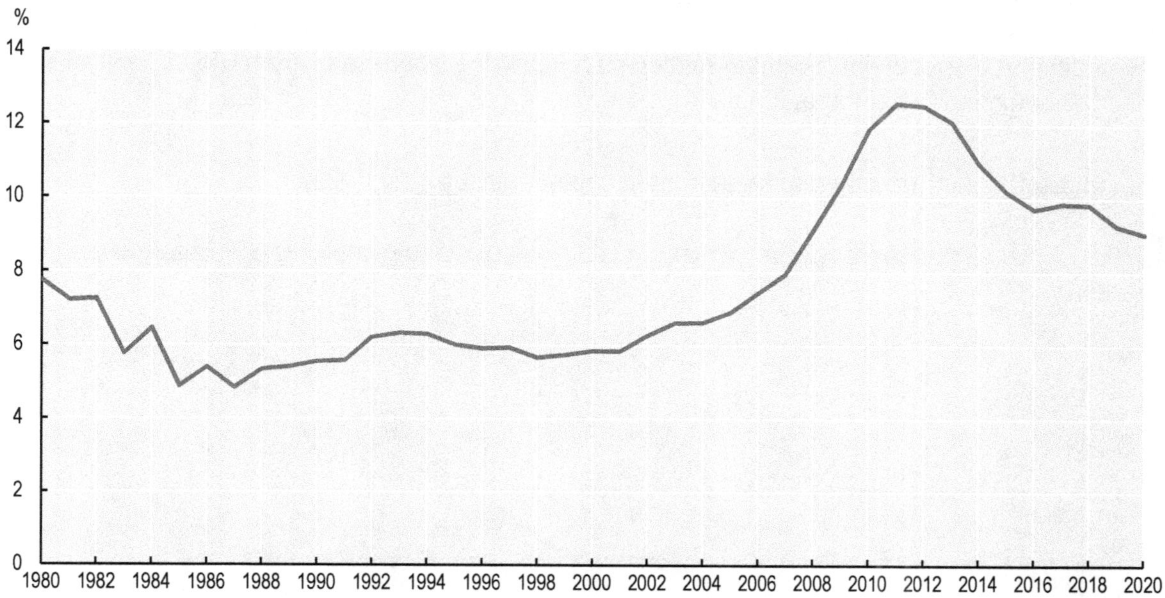

Note: Data refer to families of patent applications filed under the Patent Cooperation Treaty (PCT), by earliest filing date.
Source: OECD, STI Micro-data Lab: Intellectual Property Database, http://oe.cd/ipstats, November 2022.

In contrast with frontier innovation efforts as measured by patent filings, deployment of existing technologies seems to be on the rise, as suggested by the growth of trademark filings for climate-related goods and services observed over the last two decades (Figure 7.2). This proportion has tripled in the US and in Japan (from 1% to 3%) and has nearly quadrupled in Europe (from 2% to 8%). As for patents, a decrease was observed around 2012-2014, but the trend has picked up again in the most recent available years. This suggests that while firms have reduced research and development (R&D) efforts toward climate-related technologies, diffusion and commercialisation efforts have continued to increase.

Figure 7.2. Trademark filings in climate-related goods and services, 1995-2018

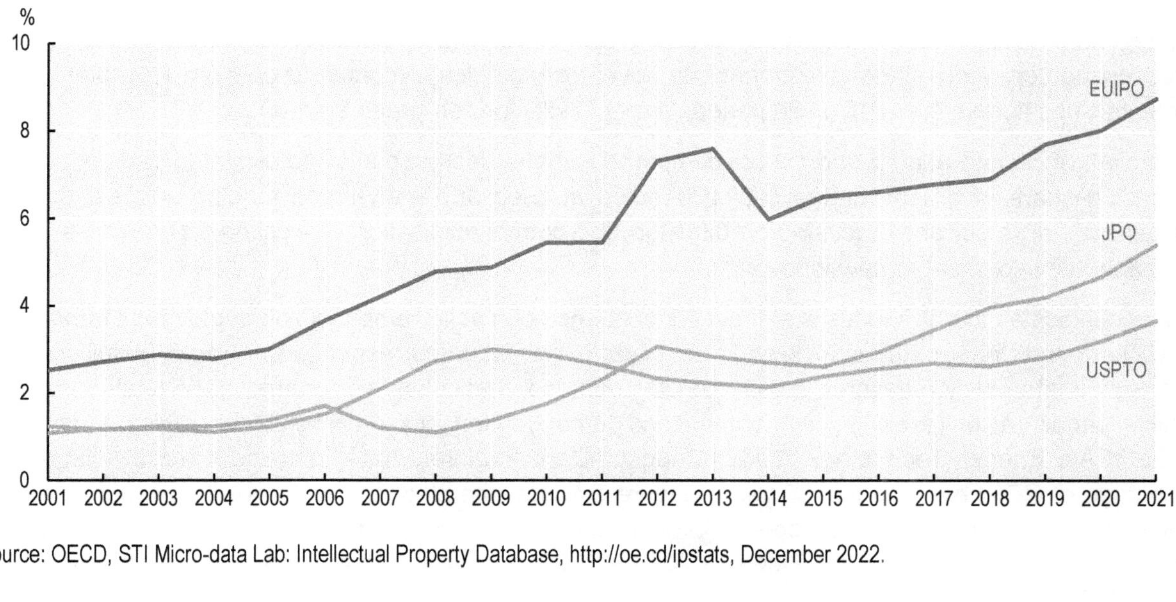

Source: OECD, STI Micro-data Lab: Intellectual Property Database, http://oe.cd/ipstats, December 2022.

Data on venture capital investment in green start-ups confirms the focus of investors on the deployment of relatively mature technologies, as opposed to the development of exploratory solutions. A new database of clean-tech start-ups developed by the OECD shows that there has been a large increase in global venture capital (VC) investment in climate-related start-ups in the last decade, from USD 3.1 billion in 2010 to USD 18.6 billion in 2020 (Figure 7.3).

Figure 7.3. Global venture capital investment in green start-ups, 2010-2020

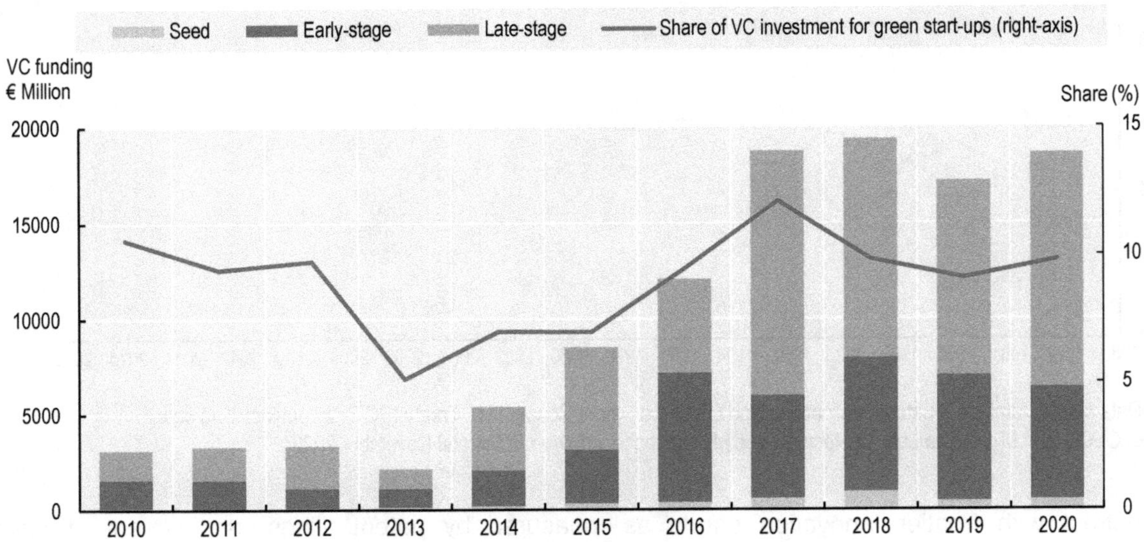

Note: Clean-tech start-ups are identified using information on their sector of operation (e.g. renewable energy) and on the textual description of their activity using natural language processing (NLP) methods, based on a climate change- related vocabulary.
Source: Bioret, Dechezleprêtre and Sarapatkova, forthcoming.

However, after a peak in 2018, global VC investment in green start-ups has decreased in the last two years. The share of total VC funding going to climate-related start-ups has remained fairly stable. This suggests that growth in VC funding for clean-tech start-ups partly reflects the global growth in VC funding across all sectors of the economy. Importantly, the sharp increase in green VC observed since 2017 is to a large extent driven by large and late-stage funding rounds of more than USD 250 million, which accounts for more than 50% of total funding between 2016 and 2019. The share of VC directed at seed funding (representing very early-stage investment into novel technologies) amounts to only 3.5% of total VC for green start-ups across the 2010-2020 period, against 7.8% for non-green start-ups.

The growth of climate-related trademarks compared with the decrease in climate-related patents and the decreasing share of green venture capital directed at seed and early-stage funding suggest that the business sector is currently focusing on diffusion and commercialisation of existing technologies rather than on the development of new innovations.

Evidence indicates that this focus is a direct consequence of a policy emphasis on deployment rather than on R&D support. Indeed, the slowdown in low-carbon innovation corresponds to a recent levelling-off of concrete climate policy measures across OECD countries, particularly so for innovation-related policies. Public expenditures on research, development and demonstration for low-carbon technologies, as reported by the IEA's Energy Technology RD&D Budgets Data Explorer, have remained broadly flat (as a percentage of GDP) over the last 30 years (Figure 7.4), despite pledges by Mission Innovation, a global initiative of 22 countries and the European Commission, to double clean energy research and development funding between 2016 and 2021. Between 2016 and 2019, total public expenditures on energy RD&D across all IEA Member countries increased by less than 20% to EUR 19 billion.

There is heterogeneity across countries in terms of public R&D budgets devoted to low-carbon innovation. Eighteen OECD countries devoted more than 3% of their national R&D budgets to R&D in low-carbon technologies in 2022 (or in the latest available year), the maximum being 8.9% in France (due to large nuclear R&D), 8.0% in Belgium and 7.1% in Finland.

Figure 7.4. Low-carbon public RD&D expenditures in GDP across IEA countries, 1974-2020

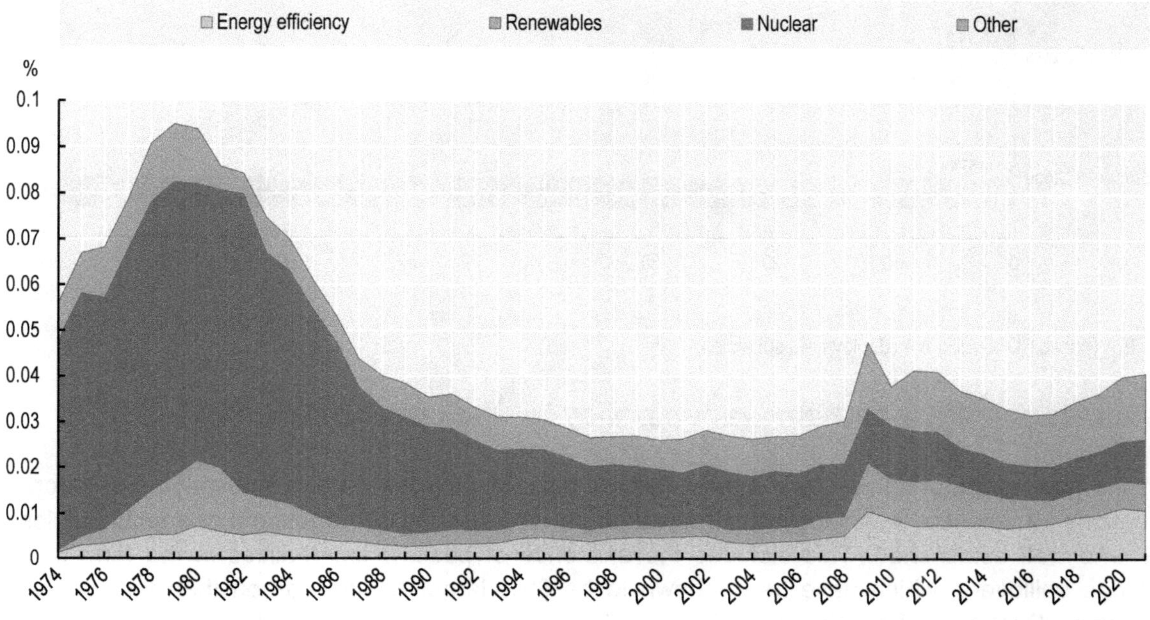

Note: The "Other" category includes carbon capture and storage, hydrogen and fuel cells, other power and storage technologies, and other cross-cutting technologies and research. See https://www.iea.org/data-and-statistics/data-product/energy-technology-rd-and-d-budget-database-2.
Source: IEA Energy Technology RD&D Budgets database, December 2022.

The contrast with support for deployment and adoption is striking. For example, European countries spent EUR 458 million in 2018 to support R&D activities in wind and solar power. The cost to society implied by subsidies for the deployment of wind and solar technologies that same year represented EUR 78 400 million – 150 times more than public R&D expenditures (Figure 7.5). The ratio is smaller in the US and in Japan, but across these three major economic players the emphasis is clearly on support for deployment.

Figure 7.5. Public RD&D vs deployment support in renewable energy, 2018

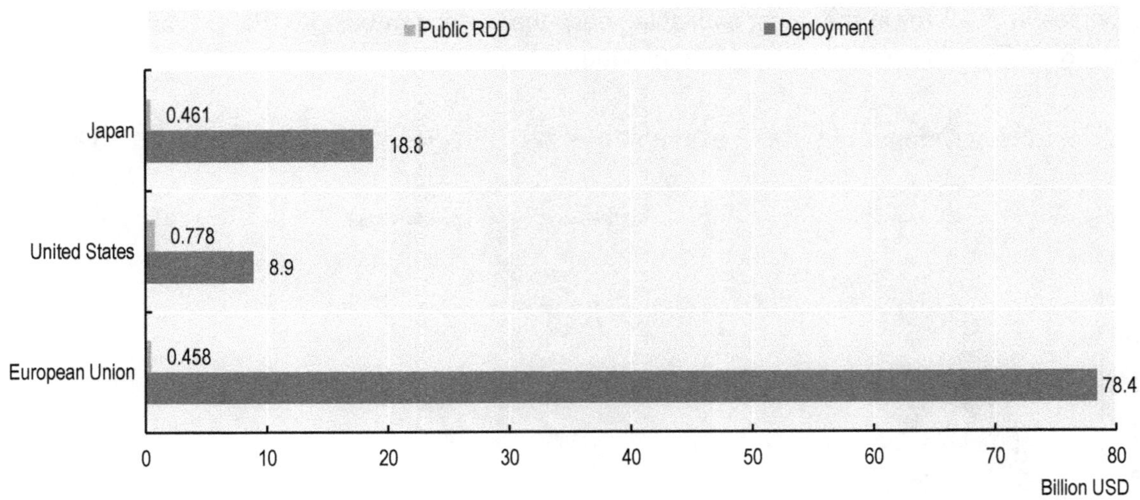

Source: IEA (public RD&D); IRENA (deployment subsidies).

Science, technology and innovation policy for the net-zero transition

Given the wide range of barriers and market failures discouraging low-carbon innovation, the theoretical justifications for science, technology and innovation policies specifically targeting these technologies are sound and well established. This includes the existence of positive externalities in the form of large knowledge spillovers, which have been shown to be 60% larger for low-carbon than for high-carbon technologies (Dechezleprêtre, Martin and Mohnen, 2014[8]), but also learning-by-doing, which occurs when costs to manufacturers or users fall as cumulative output increases (Rubin et al., 2015[9]). For example, production costs in renewable energy typically fall by around 15% each time the cumulative installed capacity doubles, with higher learning rates in earlier stages of deployment (Grubb et al., 2021[10]). The presence of learning-by-doing provides a strong justification for deployment subsidies. In the renewable electricity domain, these subsidies have taken the form of feed-in tariffs and auctions, which have been instrumental in inducing the massive cost reductions observed in the last couple of decades (Nemet, 2019[11]).

Imperfections in the market for capital such as risk aversion and asymmetric information also limit the amount of private capital available for low-carbon R&D. Firms developing clean innovations seem to face particularly high financial constraints, as shown by Howell (2017[12]). Another major market failure is related to the traditional problem of environmental externalities. Because carbon pollution (and the damages it generates) is not priced by the market, the market for technologies that reduce emissions will be limited because the lack of economic incentives imply low financial returns. This in turn reduces incentives to develop such technologies.

Beyond market failures, a number of factors create inertia in economic systems and therefore impede innovation. These include systemic barriers to change and innovation; barriers to competition; lack of co-operation within innovation systems; and prevailing norms and habits; as well as technology lock-in and path dependence (Aghion, 2019[13]). Government failures including preference for incumbents, lack of policy predictability and stability, and regulatory barriers may also act as barriers to low-carbon innovation. In particular, climate policy uncertainty is associated with significant decreases in investment, particularly in pollution-intensive sectors that are most exposed to climate policies and among capital-intensive companies (Berestycki et al., 2022[14]).

Science, technology and innovation (STI) policies are critical for climate action because technological progress – which originates from investments in R&D activities but also from learning-by-doing and knowledge spillovers – reduces the investment costs of emissions-reduction policies. This is demonstrated by sharp declines in the costs of batteries and solar, which have both experienced a 90% reduction over the past decade, as shown in Figure 7.6. As a result, many carbon-free technologies (especially renewable energy) are already cheaper than fossil fuels.

A consequence of the cost reductions brought about by technological progress is that STI policies reduce the social and economic cost of reaching climate objectives (Acemoglu et al., 2016[15]). Indeed, by reducing the costs of low-carbon technologies, innovation policies can increase the responsiveness of emissions to carbon prices (D'Arcangelo et al., 2022[16]). Including effective STI policies in the climate policy mix reduces the carbon price levels needed to reach a given climate target. STI policies can therefore partially substitute for low carbon prices (although not fully). As such, suboptimal carbon prices, as are in place today, support the case for even stronger STI policies.

Figure 7.6. Declining renewable energy and battery costs since 2010

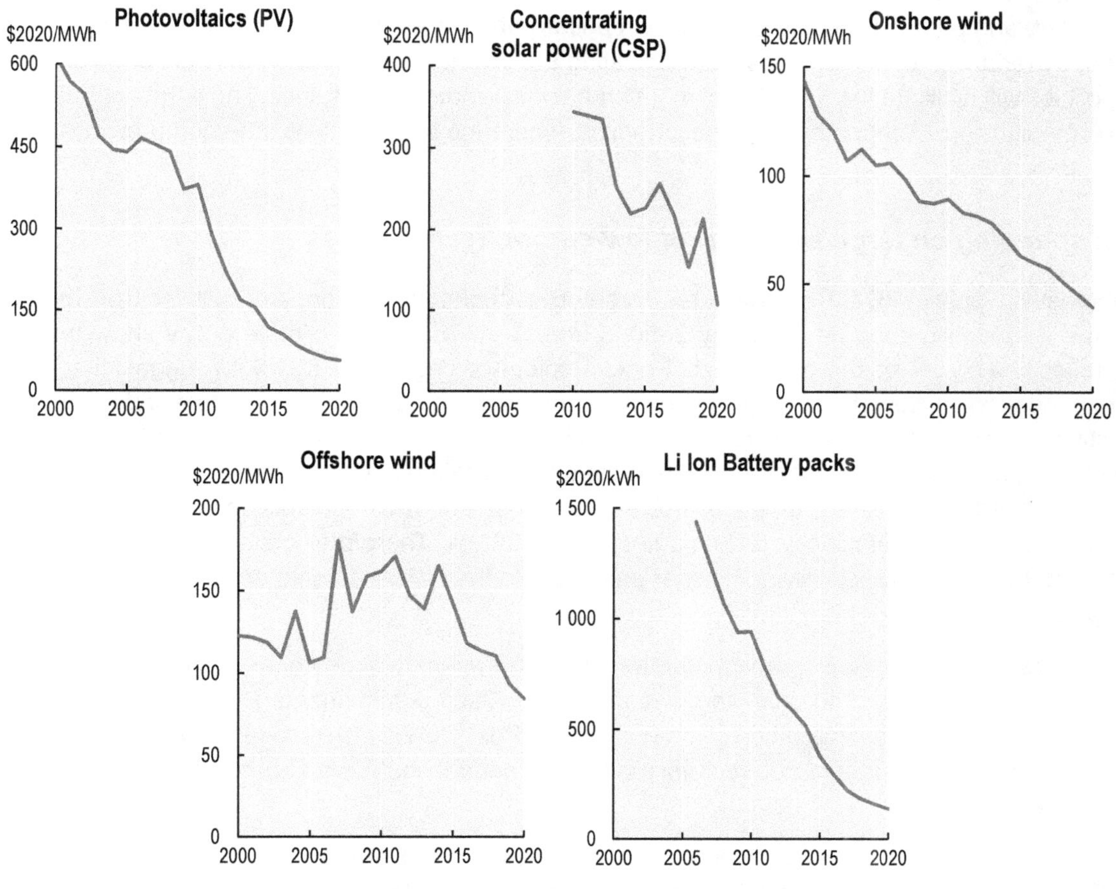

Note: The lines indicate average unit cost in each year. For batteries, costs shown are for 1 kWh of battery storage capacity; for renewables, costs are LCOE, which includes installation, capital, operations, and maintenance costs per MWh of electricity produced.
Source: (IRENA, 2021[76]) (IPCC, 2022[25]).

There is also an important political argument for including STI policies in the overall climate policy mix. A nationally representative population survey recently implemented across 20 OECD and non-OECD countries shows that subsidies to low-carbon technologies are systematically the most favoured climate policy compared to carbon pricing, bans or regulations. Similarly, support for a carbon tax is largest if its revenues are used to fund green infrastructure or to subsidise low-carbon technologies (Dechezleprêtre et al., 2022[17]). From a public acceptability point of view, STI climate policies thus appear to be a highly attractive option.

Policy options to drive innovation

Given the significant reallocations implied by the low-carbon transition (between activities, sectors, firms, workers, and technologies), the focus of climate policy is gradually shifting to transition costs and how to mitigate them. Bringing about the necessary cost reductions to make carbon-free technologies competitive with high-carbon options should therefore be a primary objective of climate policy. This would also help to accelerate the diffusion of available technologies, which is critical to reaching medium term carbon-emissions reductions.

For these reasons, innovation and industrial policies – focussed on both development and deployment of low-carbon technologies – should constitute a cornerstone of strategies to reach carbon neutrality. Given the large range of barriers and market failures discouraging low-carbon innovation, the theoretical justifications for these policies are sound and well established. Innovation and industrial policies can also complement, and partially substitute for, carbon prices, which are often difficult to implement politically. In addition, by reducing technology costs and boosting the growth of new carbon-efficient firms and sectors, such policies will facilitate the adoption of more ambitious climate policies, including – through international technology diffusion – among emerging economies, where the bulk of future emission growth is projected to take place.

Boost spending on targeted RD&D of low-carbon technologies

An increase in public RD&D expenditures targeted at technologies that are still far from market but necessary to reach carbon neutrality by 2050 is urgent. All models of climate policy show that optimal policy relies heavily on research subsidies. For example, Acemoglu et al. (2016[15]) suggest that 90% of all R&D expenditures in clean technologies should be funded by government for a couple of decades until the productivity of clean technologies catches up with that of dirty technologies. Critical areas such as electrification, hydrogen, bioenergy and carbon capture, utilisation and storage (CCUS) today receive only around one-third of the level of public R&D funding of the more established low-carbon electricity generation and energy efficiency technologies (IEA, 2021[2]). Therefore, governments should consider rebalancing their STI policies, giving greater emphasis to the RD&D stages, particularly for technologies that are not mature yet.

This increase should be gradual, though, for the research system to experiment with multiple search paths and technologies and adapt to changing circumstances. Such commitments should provide a long-term and stable perspective as for other climate policies. Post-COVID-19 recovery programmes can help increase public RD&D budgets but such increases will need to be sustained in the long run rather than one-off increases.

Importantly, specific R&D support instruments are required. Governments can financially support the innovation activities of firms through direct and targeted instruments (e.g. research grants) or via horizontal and untargeted instruments (R&D tax credits). Empirical evidence suggests that R&D tax credits have positive effects on firms' innovative activity, with the effect on experimental development about twice as large as the effect on basic and applied research, and heterogeneous effects across types of firms (OECD, 2020[18]) (Bloom, Van Reenen and Williams, 2019[19]). R&D grants also have positive effects on firms' innovative activity but the effect seems concentrated on small firms that are likely to be more financially constrained and focused on incremental innovations to meet short-term market demands (Bronzini and Piselli, 2016[20]; Bronzini and Iachini, 2014[21]). For clean technologies specifically, Howell (2017[12]) shows that firms that received a grant from the US Department of Energy's Small Business Innovation Research programme increased patenting, survival rate and the probability of subsequently receiving venture capital among recipients, with stronger effects for firms that were more financially constrained. No study has examined the impact of R&D tax credits specifically on clean technology innovation.

Scale up funding for large-scale projects at the demonstration phase

A critical part of the climate innovation policy package is to close the funding gap for large-scale demonstration projects in order to help breakthrough innovators escape the "valley of death" of clean technology venturing (between research and commercialisation). The amount of funding which needs to be made available for demonstration support on technologies that still have a low technology readiness level is very significant, particularly in the industry sector: for example, a single 100 MW electrolyser for green hydrogen production costs between EUR 50-75 million; the production of green hydrogen is still about three times more expensive than grey hydrogen (made out of natural gas through steam reforming) even under the most favourable conditions. Major cost reductions – and the rapid deployment that they would induce – crucially depend on massive improvements in the cost of electrolysers through research and development and large-scale demonstration projects.

Despite this, the amount of public funding available for demonstration projects appears to be small. For example, the European Union recently introduced a new Innovation Fund as a funding mechanism for the demonstration of innovative low-carbon technologies. The first call for large-scale projects attracted 311 applications for a total amount requested of EUR 21.7 billion, while only around EUR 1 billion is available. By comparison, a typical carbon capture and storage (CCS), demonstration projects currently cost around USD 1 billion, take five years or more to build, and have a market value of around one-tenth of their cost. The IEA recommends that USD 90 billion be mobilised as soon as possible to complete a portfolio of demonstration projects before 2030 in electrification of end-uses, CCUS, hydrogen and sustainable bioenergy (IEA, 2021[2]).

Fischer, Newell & Preonas (2017[22]) model the US energy system and determine the optimal distribution of public spending between R&D support and deployment under various scenarios. They find that the optimal ratio of deployment spending to R&D spending does not exceed one for wind energy in almost all scenarios. With extreme assumptions on the magnitude of learning-by-doing, this ratio goes to 6.5. The ratio of public spending on deployment to R&D exceeds one for solar energy but not by much. The ratio reaches 10-to-1 under the "high learning-by-doing" scenario. This is far from the ratios observed in Figure 7.5. Support for early-stage deployment of clean technologies should continue, as it is justified by barriers and market failures at this stage (e.g. learning spillovers, technology and market risks, second-mover advantage), but additional efforts should primarily be focused on RD&D.

Target public-good technologies for the long term

As regards what sorts of technologies should be priority for funding, governments should focus their support on technologies that are central to any decarbonisation pathway and have a strong public- good component (and are therefore less likely to be provided by the market). The goal is to avoid providing public support for research that the private sector would otherwise do on their own. This could include projects supporting long-term research needs where the payoff occurs further into the future (such as hydrogen), as well as infrastructure that has a public- good dimension (including transportation networks and storage for carbon, smart grids, and infrastructure for electric vehicles). In the IEA's Net Zero Emissions scenario, electrification, CCUS, hydrogen and sustainable bioenergy account for nearly half of the cumulative emissions reductions to 2050. Just three technologies are critical in enabling around 15% of the cumulative emissions reductions between 2030 and 2050: advanced high-energy density batteries, hydrogen electrolysers and direct air capture (DAC). These technologies should be the focus of government support.

Support a diverse technology portfolio, research collaboration, and technology diffusion

In general, there is a need to adopt a portfolio approach in order to diversify industrial and technology risks. Given the technological uncertainty inherent to the transition to a net-zero economy, countries should aim to support an array of technologies while still focusing on national technological strength. A focus on particular production process should be avoided in order to prevent lock-in and give all green technologies a fair chance.

Barriers to external funding should be reduced to help high-risk companies raise funds. Favourable tax schemes, low-interest or subsidised loans for young firms, and a greater mobilisation of government venture capital toward the green transition can help (Hepburn, Pless and Popp, 2018[23]).

Collaboration in low-carbon innovation should be strengthened, both nationally and internationally. There is ample room for improvement in collaborative R&D between firms, between firms and public research institutions, and between countries to capitalise on complementary skills and resources at the domestic and international levels. Strengthening international co-operation and technology transfer will be particularly important to accelerate the development and diffusion of low-carbon technologies. Co-ordinated action can accelerate innovation, enhance economies of scale, strengthen incentives for investment, and foster a level playing field where needed. Sharing experiences between countries and industries can reduce individual risks and accelerate progress towards viable solutions. Measures and commitments to deployment can accelerate economies of scale and corresponding cost reductions. International co-ordination of R&D funding across different technologies and stages of innovation will be critical to developing the next generation of clean technologies. A relevant model is the International Thermonuclear Experimental Reactor (ITER) nuclear fusion project, funded by the EU, India, Japan, China, the Russian Federation, Korea and the US.

Beyond STI policies: broad policy packages that include stable carbon pricing

Low-carbon innovation policies need to be embedded in a broader package. Although innovation and industrial policies should play a greater role in carbon neutrality strategies, they are insufficient on their own and need to be part of broader packages of climate policies. Although technology policy can help facilitate the creation of new environmentally friendly technologies, it provides little incentive to adopt these technologies unless R&D activities manage to make clean technologies competitive with high-carbon alternatives on economic grounds. Until then, incentives for adoption need to be provided by demand-side policies, which can make low-carbon options more attractive economically. However, demand-side policy cannot supplant the need for technology policy, given the presence of barriers and market failures at the R&D and demonstration stages.

In particular, carbon pricing is necessary to encourage the adoption of clean technologies that are closer to market and thus “redirect” innovation toward low-carbon activities. There is ample empirical evidence that by encouraging the diffusion of low-carbon technologies, carbon pricing affects innovation activity further up the technology supply chain, favouring R&D in clean technologies and discouraging it in conventional (polluting) technologies. For example, Figure 7.7 shows that the introduction of the European carbon market (EU ETS) led to a large and rapid increase in low-carbon innovation (as measured by patent filings) among regulated companies, compared to a carefully selected control group of unregulated but similar firms.

Figure 7.7. The relationship between carbon pricing and innovation

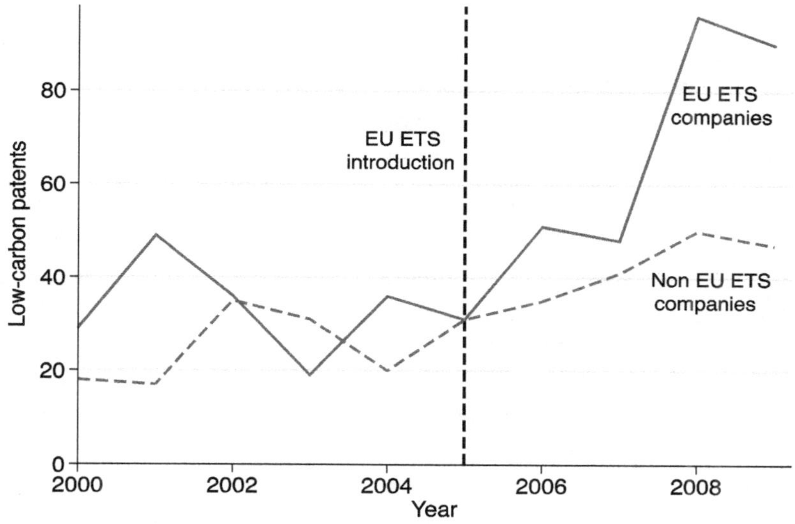

Note: Around 3000 companies regulated under the EU ETS are included in the sample. "Non-EU ETS companies" are a group of 3000 European companies that are not regulated under the EU ETS but operate in the same country and the same economic sector and are comparable in size and innovation capacity to companies regulated under the EU ETS.
Source: (Calel and Dechezleprêtre, 2016[83]).

Carbon prices can serve as a necessary backstop against possible rebound effects following efficiency improvements brought about by technological progress. They can also provide a useful source of revenue that can be earmarked for technology support policy. The current limited take-up of carbon pricing reduces incentives to develop and adopt new low-carbon technologies. In 2018 (the last year for which comprehensive data is available), 60% of carbon emissions among 44 OECD and G20 countries were not priced at all, and only 10% were priced at or above EUR 60/tonne CO_2 (OECD, 2021[24]).

Commitments to raising carbon prices in the future and clear carbon prices trajectories can already spur innovation even if current carbon prices are low. Carbon Contracts-for-Difference (CCfD), an experimental mechanism announced in Germany in 2022, may decrease uncertainty thanks to forward-contracts on the price of abated greenhouse gases. The Dutch carbon levy, a top-up on the EU ETS with an explicit carbon price trajectory, is another example of how policy instruments can reduce carbon price uncertainty for investors (Anderson et al., 2021[5]).

The importance of standardisation and mission-oriented policies

Standard-setting is also necessary to reduce uncertainty and support the deployment of particular technologies. For green hydrogen, this includes standardisation of guarantees of origin, hydrogen purity, the design of liquefaction/conversion and regasification/reconversion facilities, equipment specifications and blending hydrogen into the gas grid. Another example is standardisation of plugs for electric cars across vehicles and charging stations. Such standards are best set at the international level and call for international co-ordination of national standards in the context of standard-setting organisations (Vollebergh and van der Werf, 2014[25]). Co-ordination on standards across countries could help to overcome barriers to first deployment created by international competition. Standards can also be helpful in restricting or phasing out particularly undesirable high-emitting activities or technologies (D'Arcangelo et al., 2022[26]).

Beyond carbon pricing and climate-related standards, the low-carbon transition will involve a massive structural transformation that will require the alignment of policy frameworks beyond innovation and climate policies. Competition and entrepreneurship policies play a critical role in encouraging business dynamism, the creation of new innovative firms and the reallocation of resources toward the most resource-efficient firms. Government venture capital may serve as a resource to help entrepreneurs finance projects with high social value. Education and skills policies are necessary to make sure that the transformation can rely on the right set of skills and research. For example, it has been shown that green investment made through the American Recovery and Reinvestment Act adopted after the Global Financial Crisis was more effective in geographic areas where green skills were more prevalent (Popp et al., 2020[27]).

An efficient and cost-effective shift to a low-carbon economy requires the engagement of many parts of government beyond those traditionally mobilised in the development of climate-change policies. Developing such a package requires the development of mission-oriented strategies across all countries committed to carbon neutrality. Mission-oriented innovation approaches, which are increasingly adopted by countries to address a wide variety of societal challenges, can help to promote systemic change because of their integrated nature (Larrue, 2021[28]). They are expected to improve co-ordination over traditional innovation policies through the collective development of a strategic agenda, the setting of a dedicated governance structure, and the implementation of a tailor-made and integrated policy mix. However, recent analysis shows that, despite displaying some systemic features, existing net-zero missions remain for the most part focused on support to research and innovation, led by STI authorities and drawing almost exclusively on STI funds (Larrue, 2022[29]). To realise their transformative potential, missions for net-zero need to move beyond this "STI only trap".

Chapter conclusions

Innovation has an essential role in the net-zero transition yet current trends show that innovation in low carbon technologies is lagging. Governments should strengthen their science, technology and innovation (STI) policies with a focus on innovation. The scale and scope of the transformation needed will also require efforts beyond traditional STI policies, in education, labour markets, and infrastructure development, and extending beyond the remit of traditional climate policy making. Enhancing innovation efforts in this way will crucially depend on adequate forms of finance and investment (see Chapter 8).

The need to build systemic resilience into the net-zero transition further strengthens the call for a broad approach to supporting innovation. The mission-oriented approach outlined above offers clear synergies and follows many of the recommendations made throughout this report on needing to work across government institutions and systems components, taking interlinkages between systems into account and stress-testing mission-oriented strategies against future disruptions.

References

Acemoglu, D. et al. (2016), "Transition to Clean Technology", *Journal of Political Economy*, Vol. 124/1, pp. 52-104, https://doi.org/10.1086/684511. [15]

Aghion, P. (2019), "Path dependence, innovation and the economics of climate change", in *Handbook on Green Growth*, Edward Elgar Publishing, https://doi.org/10.4337/9781788110686.00011. [13]

Anderson, B. et al. (2021), "Policies for a climate-neutral industry: Lessons from the Netherlands", *OECD Science, Technology and Industry Policy Papers*, No. 108, OECD Publishing, Paris, https://doi.org/10.1787/a3a1f953-en. [5]

Berestycki, C. et al. (2022), “Measuring and assessing the effects of climate policy uncertainty”, *OECD Economics Department Working Papers*, No. 1724, OECD Publishing, Paris, https://doi.org/10.1787/34483d83-en. [14]

Bloom, N., J. Van Reenen and H. Williams (2019), “A Toolkit of Policies to Promote Innovation”, *Journal of Economic Perspectives*, Vol. 33/3, pp. 163-184, https://doi.org/10.1257/jep.33.3.163. [19]

Bronzini, R. and E. Iachini (2014), “Are Incentives for R&D Effective? Evidence from a Regression Discontinuity Approach”, *American Economic Journal: Economic Policy*, Vol. 6/4, pp. 100-134, https://doi.org/10.1257/pol.6.4.100. [21]

Bronzini, R. and P. Piselli (2016), “The impact of R&D subsidies on firm innovation”, *Research Policy*, Vol. 45/2, pp. 442-457, https://doi.org/10.1016/j.respol.2015.10.008. [20]

D’Arcangelo, F. et al. (2022), “A framework to decarbonise the economy”, *OECD Economic Policy Papers*, No. 31, OECD Publishing, Paris, https://doi.org/10.1787/4e4d973d-en. [26]

D’Arcangelo, F. et al. (2022), “Estimating the CO2 emission and revenue effects of carbon pricing: New evidence from a large cross-country dataset”, *OECD Economics Department Working Papers*, No. 1732, OECD Publishing, Paris, https://doi.org/10.1787/39aa16d4-en. [16]

Dechezleprêtre, A. et al. (2022), “Fighting climate change: International attitudes toward climate policies”, *OECD Economics Department Working Papers*, No. 1714, OECD Publishing, Paris, https://doi.org/10.1787/3406f29a-en. [17]

Dechezleprêtre, A., R. Martin and M. Mohnen (2014), “Knowledge spillovers from clean and dirty technologies”, *CEP Discussion Papers*, No. CEPDP1300, LSE, London, http://eprints.lse.ac.uk/60501/ (accessed on 19 December 2018). [8]

Fischer, C., L. Preonas and R. Newell (2017), “Environmental and Technology Policy Options in the Electricity Sector: Are We Deploying Too Many?”, *Journal of the Association of Environmental and Resource Economists*, Vol. 4/4, pp. 959-984, https://doi.org/10.1086/692507. [22]

Grubb, M. et al. (2021), “Induced innovation in energy technologies and systems: a review of evidence and potential implications for CO2 mitigation”, *Environmental Research Letters*, Vol. 16/4, p. 043007, https://doi.org/10.1088/1748-9326/abde07. [10]

Hepburn, C., J. Pless and D. Popp (2018), “Policy Brief—Encouraging Innovation that Protects Environmental Systems: Five Policy Proposals”, *Review of Environmental Economics and Policy*, Vol. 12/1, pp. 154-169, https://doi.org/10.1093/reep/rex024. [23]

Howell, S. (2017), “Financing Innovation: Evidence from R&D Grants”, *American Economic Review*, Vol. 107/4, pp. 1136-1164, https://doi.org/10.1257/aer.20150808. [12]

IEA (2021), *Net Zero by 2050: A Roadmap for the Global Energy Sector*, OECD Publishing, Paris, https://doi.org/10.1787/c8328405-en. [2]

IEA (2017), *World Energy Outlook 2017*, OECD Publishing, Paris/IEA, Paris, https://doi.org/10.1787/weo-2017-en. [3]

IPCC (2022), *Climate Change 2022: Mitigation of Climate Change. Contribution of Working Group III to the Sixth Assessment Report of the Intergovernmental Panel on Climate Change*, https://doi.org/10.1017/9781009157926. [1]

IRENA (2018), *Innovation prioirities to transform the energy system*, https://www.sciencedirect.com/science/article/pii/S0964339798806344 (accessed on 19 December 2018). [4]

Larrue, P. (2022), *Do mission-oriented policies for net zero deliver on their many promises?*, OECD Green Growth and Sustainable Development Forum 2022 Issue note, https://www.oecd.org/greengrowth/2022GGSD-IssueNote1-mission-oriented-policies.pdf. [29]

Larrue, P. (2021), "The design and implementation of mission-oriented innovation policies: A new systemic policy approach to address societal challenges", *OECD Science, Technology and Industry Policy Papers*, No. 100, OECD Publishing, Paris, https://doi.org/10.1787/3f6c76a4-en. [28]

Nemet, G. (2019), *How Solar Energy Became Cheap: A Model for Low-Carbon Innovation*, Routledge, https://doi.org/ISBN 9780367136598. [11]

OECD (2021), *Effective Carbon Rates 2021: Pricing Carbon Emissions through Taxes and Emissions Trading*, OECD Series on Carbon Pricing and Energy Taxation, OECD Publishing, Paris, https://doi.org/10.1787/0e8e24f5-en. [24]

OECD (2020), *The Digitalisation of Science, Technology and Innovation: Key Developments and Policies*, OECD Publishing, Paris, https://doi.org/10.1787/b9e4a2c0-en. [6]

OECD (2020), "The effects of R&D tax incentives and their role in the innovation policy mix: Findings from the OECD microBeRD project, 2016-19", *OECD Science, Technology and Industry Policy Papers*, No. 92, OECD Publishing, Paris, https://doi.org/10.1787/65234003-en. [18]

OECD (2019), *Artificial Intelligence in Society*, OECD Publishing, Paris, https://doi.org/10.1787/eedfee77-en. [7]

Popp, D. et al. (2020), *The Employment Impact of Green Fiscal Push: Evidence from the American Recovery Act*, National Bureau of Economic Research, Cambridge, MA, https://doi.org/10.3386/w27321. [27]

Rubin, E. et al. (2015), "A review of learning rates for electricity supply technologies", *Energy Policy*, Vol. 86, pp. 198-218, https://doi.org/10.1016/j.enpol.2015.06.011. [9]

Vollebergh, H. and E. van der Werf (2014), "The Role of Standards in Eco-innovation: Lessons for Policymakers", *Review of Environmental Economics and Policy*, Vol. 8/2, pp. 230-248, https://doi.org/10.1093/reep/reu004. [25]

8 An effective, fair and equitable transition

The transition to net-zero emissions can only be successful and resilient in the long term with strong public support and widespread opportunities for people and firms. This chapter illustrates how governments can maintain a net-zero transition that balances environmental effectiveness with fairness and equitability and how these characteristics contribute to a transition that is ultimately more resilient, focusing on how to enhance public support for climate policies, manage the economic burden of policies across households and regions, and how to address the labour market implications of the net-zero transition.

This chapter draws on contributions to the horizontal project carried out under the responsibility of the Economic Policy Committee, Public Governance Committee, Environment Policy Committee, and Employment, Labour and Social Affairs Committee.

The transition to net-zero emissions will require transformative changes and necessarily entail significant economic and social impacts. The transition can only be successful and resilient in the long term with strong public support and widespread opportunities for people and firms. Proactive policies are required to ensure that the social and economic implications of net-zero measures are addressed. Nevertheless, even with tailored policy intervention, impacts will not be distributed evenly. As a whole, the net-zero transition is for the benefit of all, insofar as its goal is to mitigate climate change. Still, in relative terms, while the net-zero transition may leave some better off economically, some sectors, workers, and households will be negatively affected relative to business-as-usual.

How these potential impacts are measured is important. First, the net-zero transition involves a policy agenda for the medium term, and systemic shifts in the future may temper immediate impacts. In this way, losses and gains stemming from climate policies can be temporary. Second and more fundamentally, any attempt to quantify and address impacts from the transition must also account for the counterfactual. While the status quo can appear to be a natural starting point for assessment, any losses should be compared to the cost of inaction in the face of major economic and social impacts from climate change or, vice versa, the benefits of mitigation that provide the very rationale for policies for the net-zero transition (Tovar Reaños and Lynch, 2022[1]). Thus, choosing the appropriate baseline is a crucial consideration for policy makers.

Public opinion is a key factor in the ability of governments to enact effective climate policies. Conversely, public opinion can pose a considerable barrier if the impacts of climate policies result in widespread opposition. It is crucial that governments are seen as legitimate, credible actors in this space, a key challenge at a time of declining trust in public institutions and increasing discontent with democracy. Effective communication with the public on the modalities and impacts of climate policies as well as strengthened governance standards, are important to forge long-term consensus for resilient climate action.

Distributional impacts of the transition can be observed in a wide range of dimensions, including income and wealth, jobs and employment, and housing. They can be both direct and indirect. Impacts must be carefully managed in order to maintain public support for climate policies and protect the broader well-being of populations. However, impacts of the transition are highly heterogeneous in their distribution across groups and regions and influenced by myriad country-specific factors. Analysing and addressing these impacts represents another key challenge for policy makers.

The net-zero transition will require transformative changes to economic structures, resulting in major shifts in production and employment patterns, the nature of jobs, and skills needs. These changes will take place in parallel with other ongoing megatrends such as digitalisation, demographic change, and globalisation. Here again, adjustment costs across populations will not be uniformly distributed. As far as possible, countries will need to anticipate complex labour market implications and alleviate them where necessary.

This chapter illustrates how governments can maintain a net-zero transition that balances environmental effectiveness with fairness and equitability, and how these characteristics contribute to a transition that is ultimately more resilient. By focusing on effectiveness, fairness and equitability, this chapter takes a broad approach to the concept of a just transition.

An informed public strengthens climate policy resilience

Ensuring the resilience of the net-zero transition requires building and maintaining public support for climate policies. In particular, it is essential for governments to address inequalities and possible economic hardships the introduction of such policies may cause. Failure to do so risks virulent political backlash becoming an obstacle to the transition, as exemplified by the *gilets jaunes* protests in France and *Estallido Social* riots in Chile. Current cost-of-living and energy crises have highlighted the importance of these issues and placed them at the top of countries' policy agendas.

At the same time, these crises, if managed carefully, may also present an opportunity to introduce climate policies. For instance, a carbon tax may face less opposition from consumers who have already had to adjust to higher prices for energy and other goods, provided it is introduced in a timely manner once inflation has begun to decrease. In addition, policies need not occur in isolation and can be managed as part of a package, for example by redistributing revenues generated by environmental taxes. Furthermore, high current prices for fossil fuels may encourage public support for renewable energy sources, which are the lowest-cost energy sources in many countries.

A recent OECD survey of 40 000 people across 20 high- and middle-income countries provides insight into the factors that induce public support for climate policies as well as the conditions that might lead individuals to change their own behaviour (Dechezleprêtre et al., 2022[2]). Three policies in particular formed the core focus of the survey: a carbon tax with cash transfers, a green infrastructure programme, and a ban on combustion-engine cars. The survey found that many respondents view the three policies as environmentally effective but regressive and against their own financial interest (Figure 8.1). In both high- and middle-income countries, a majority of respondents agreed that the three policies would reduce GHG emissions and air pollution. In contrast, few respondents believed that the policies would have positive impacts on the economy and employment, although this share was somewhat higher in middle-income countries. In terms of perceived distributional effects, the three policies were mostly considered regressive except in India, Indonesia and China, where they were viewed as more progressive. Respondents also expressed pessimism about expected financial impacts on their own households, although again with significantly different results in India, Indonesia and China. In both high- and middle-income countries, the most support was expressed for the green infrastructure programme, followed by the ban on combustion-engine cars, with carbon taxes receiving the least support.

The survey found that while certain socio-economic and lifestyle characteristics were correlated with support for climate policies – especially access to public transport – they were weak predictors of respondents' attitudes to climate policies. Far more important were respondents' perceptions of policy effectiveness and of distributional impacts. By some distance, the most impactful beliefs were that one's own household would lose as a result of a given policy (explained 14.6% of variation in responses), that the policy would reduce GHG emissions (14%), that the policy would reduce pollution (10%) and that low-income earners would lose because of the policy (8.3%). Notably, these perceptions had a much greater impact on support for a given policy than beliefs about a policy's economic effects or perceptions about climate change and its consequences overall.

Figure 8.1. International attitudes toward climate policies: survey respondents' perceived characteristics of selected policies

Share of respondents who agreed with statements.

	Green Infrastructure Program			Carbon Tax w. Cash Transfers			Ban on Combustion-Engine Cars		
	High Income	Indonesia India China	Ohter Middle Income	High Income	Indonesia India China	Ohter Middle Income	High Income	Indonesia India China	Ohter Middle Income
Effects of Main Climate Policies									
Reduce air pollution	76	84	82	68	84	77	79	85	83
Reduce GHG emissions/Reduce CO_2 emissions from cars				64	80	71	73	80	77
Make electricity production greener	70	80	77						
Encourage insulation of buildings				64	72	67			
Increase the use of public transport/Encourage less driving	60	77	67	51	75	64			
Positive effect on economy and employment	37	45	45	31	41	41	35	41	39
Costless way to fight climate change	30	39	38	27	37	34	39	38	37
Distributional Impats of Main Climate Policies									
Believes the following groups would gain									
Own household	23	62	40	20	58	28	15	51	24
Those living in rural areas	25	62	41	21	58	32	16	51	24
Low-income earners	21	57	40	22	57	31	12	51	24
The middle class	22	54	43	21	51	31	15	47	26
High-income earners	39	52	50	33	45	37	40	50	47
Perceived Fairness and Support									
Support main climate policies	57	81	76	37	73	50	43	72	60
Main climate policies are fair	51	77	67	35	67	47	39	68	53

Source: (Dechezleprêtre et al., 2022[2]).

The survey highlights that the public reacts to the specific modalities of policies. Sources of funding are expected to be progressive. For instance, stronger support was expressed for policies funded by higher taxes on highest-income households than for those funded by reductions in social or military spending, additional public debt, or increases in sales taxes. Equally, the use of revenue generated is expected either to address distributional concerns or further contribute to environmental objectives. For instance, the survey demonstrates that at face value, carbon taxes are extremely unpopular. However, if carbon tax revenue is used to fund environmental infrastructure, subsidise low-carbon technology, or reduce income taxes, carbon taxes generate approximately 70% higher support in high-income countries (for a level of support around 55%) and 25% higher support in middle-income countries (70%). The same is true of carbon taxes with transfers to the poorest or the most constrained households. However, carbon taxes with revenues used to reduce corporate taxes or with equal transfers garner less support.

An experimental part of the survey observed that while showing participants an informational video on climate impacts had only a weak positive effect on policy support, the effects of showing a video about the design and consequences of the three main climate policies were much stronger (Figure 8.2). Effects were strongest on participants who watched both videos. Importantly, all three treatments had large positive effects on respondents' perceptions of the fairness of the policies, and alleviated concerns about the policies' distributional impacts. In addition, the effects of the video treatment were observed on support for policies outside of the three policies featured in the Climate Policies video. However, these effects were limited to policies that are closely related, for example carbon taxes, a tax on fossil fuels, and a tax on flying.

Figure 8.2. International attitudes toward climate policies: effects of video exposure treatment on public support

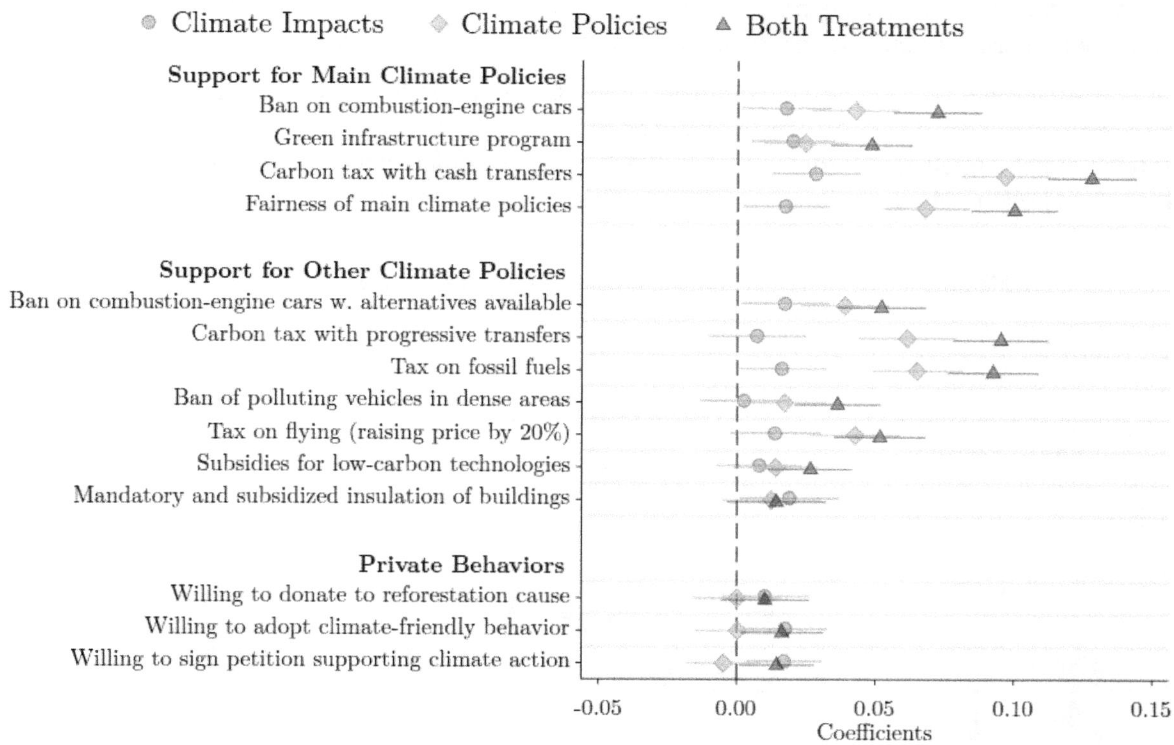

Source: (Dechezleprêtre et al., 2022[2]).

The OECD survey on public attitudes toward climate policies clearly demonstrates that providing accurate and easily accessible information on policies to the public is critical to foster policy support and thus ensure a resilient transition. It is clear that the public wants to know how policies work and who can benefit from them, and how those who may lose out can be compensated. It is also important to explain the workings of policies individually, as the extent to which respondents extrapolate information about one policy's effect on another is limited. If explained in a manner that addresses the three key concerns (environmental effectiveness, effects on one's own household and effects on low-income households), explanations of policies can be very effective in improving support for climate policies. By contrast, information on the dangers of climate change alone without a corresponding explanation of the policies that can help has only limited impacts on policy support.

The survey results highlight the importance of ensuring a just transition. Concerns for individual economic hardship are important predictors of support for climate policy, meaning that assessing distributional impacts of policies is essential. In addition to policy design itself, another important factor is trust in the government itself.

Credible climate policies enhance trust in government

As mentioned above, governments face the challenge of forging long-term consensus on urgent climate and other environmental measures against a backdrop of declining trust in public institutions and increasing discontent with democracy. Findings from the 2021 *OECD Survey on Drivers of Trust in Public Institutions* (Trust Survey) (OECD, 2022[3]) shed light on the nexus of climate action and trust in public institutions. The Trust Survey incorporates questions on the reliability of government, including whether people consider their government prepared to deal with systemic shocks such as natural disasters or the spread of contagious diseases. It shows how investing in public governance to deliver more effective policies to fight climate change may pay off in securing more credibility and trust in government. It also demonstrates how measuring people's trust in climate policies can help inform decision making and strengthen public support and acceptability for green reforms (OECD, 2022[4]).

Public perceptions of government competence are illustrated in Figure 8.3. On average, only 35.5% of people are confident that countries will succeed in reducing their country's contribution to climate change by reducing greenhouse gas emissions. People may not be confident that public institutions are competent and reliable enough to deliver climate policies effectively, and for long enough, to generate benefits.

Figure 8.3. Attitudes towards government priorities on climate change and their competence to act

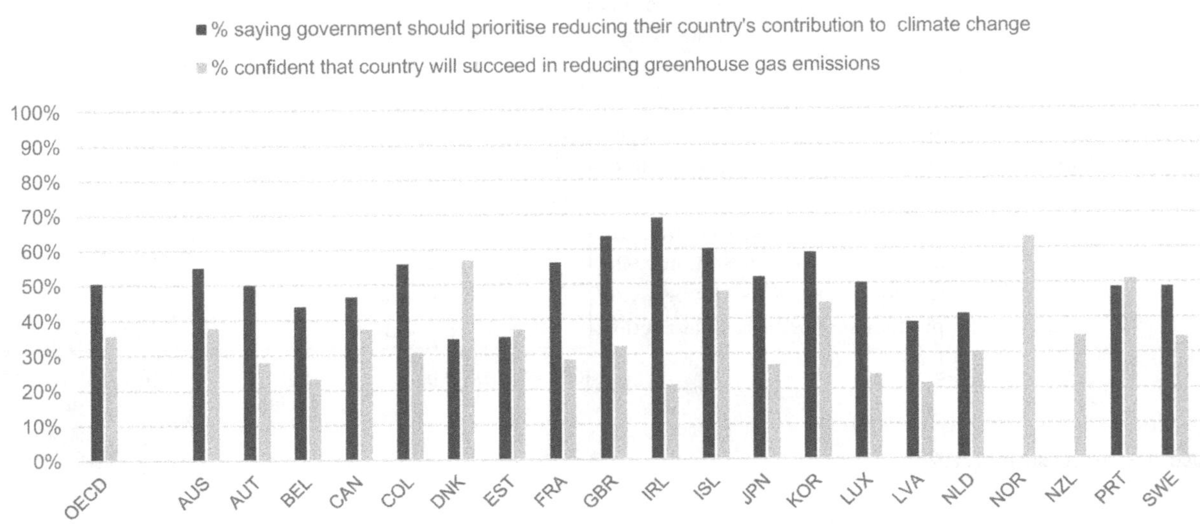

Note: Figure presents the average share of respondents to the questions "On reducing your country contribution to climate change, do you think the government should be prioritising a lot more, more, about the same, less, or a lot less?". The "more" share in the figure is the aggregation of the responses "a lot more" and "more". Respondents were asked "How confident are you that your country will succeed in reducing greenhouse gas emissions in the next 10 years?" The "confident" share is the aggregation of response choices "somewhat confident" and "very confident". "OECD" presents the unweighted average of responses across countries. Finland, Mexico, New Zealand and Norway are excluded (or partially excluded) from this figure as comparable data were not available. For more detailed information on the survey questionnaire and processes in specific countries, please find the survey method document at http://oe.cd/trust.
Source: (OECD, 2022[3]).

Cross-nationally, high levels of confidence in a government's ability to commit to addressing climate change are positively correlated with trust in government. Analysis from the OECD Trust Survey finds that people's confidence that the country will reduce greenhouse gas emissions has a statistically significant, positive relationship with trust in national government and, to a lesser extent, local government and civil service. In other words, investing in public governance to deliver more effective policies to fight climate change may pay off in securing more credibility and trust in government. This relationship holds within countries, too: those who are confident that their government can credibly commit to reducing greenhouse gas emissions are more likely to trust their government (Figure 8.4).

Figure 8.4. Countries perceived as more competent in the fight against climate change benefit from higher levels of trust in government

Share of respondents that are confident that their country will succeed in reducing greenhouse gas emissions over the next 10 years (x-axis) and the share who trust their national government (y-axis), 2021

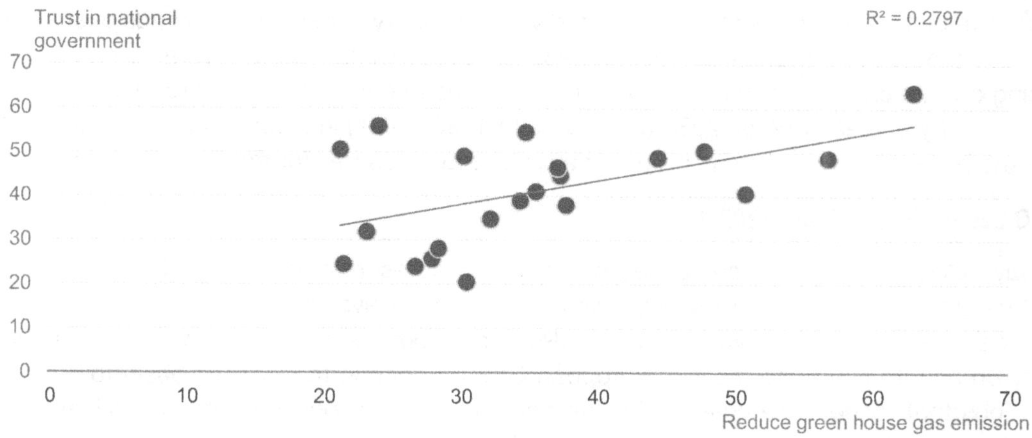

Note: This scatterplot presents the share of "trust" responses to the question "On a scale of 0 to 10, where 0 is not at all and 10 is completely, how much do you trust each of the following? The national government", equal to the values of responses 6-10 on the response scale, on the y-axis. The x-axis presents the share of "confident" responses to the question "How confident are you that [country] will succeed in reducing greenhouse gas emissions in the next 10 years?". The "confident" response is the aggregation of responses "somewhat confident" and "completely confident". "OECD" presents the unweighted average of responses across countries. Finland is excluded as the results on confidence were not available, and Mexico is excluded due to lack of data on both questions. New Zealand here shows trust in civil service as respondents were not asked about trust in the national government (note that trust in civil service on average tends to be higher than trust in national government). For more detailed information please find the survey method document at http://oe.cd/trust.
Source: (OECD, 2022[3]).

Some challenges require more than a reliable and responsive national government – they require the involvement of other actors and partners, and importantly international co-operation. Yet there is still relatively low public support for global co-operation to target such challenges: only around half of respondents call on governments to work together to address climate change. When asked about how to co-operate globally, the most popular response, "joining forces with other governments internationally", was selected by 43.4% of respondents, on average cross-nationally. The next three most commonly selected answer choices – "engaging citizens on global issues"; "strengthening co-ordination across government offices", and "strengthening the country's role in international institutions" – were selected by fewer than one in three respondents.

As the risks associated with climate change become ever more urgent – and as costs increase for diffuse, long-term payoffs – governments must do better in communicating to the public the benefits of co-operation to tackle these challenges. These kinds of issues can only be resolved through global co-operation.

Citizen participation and public integrity

Ensuring stakeholder participation, citizen dialogue and integrity and transparency in climate and environmental governance is crucial to secure public trust and buy-in for green policies. The scale of the transformation required to act on climate and other environmental issues call on governments to revamp stakeholder dialogue and citizen participation. In the past years, France, Germany, Ireland, Luxembourg and Spain have initiated deliberative processes addressing climate-related issues aiming to secure legitimacy of climate-related policies (Box 8.1)

Box 8.1. Examples of deliberative processes addressing climate-related issues

Citizens' Convention on Climate in France (2019-2020)

The Citizens' Convention on Climate was a deliberative process that brought together 150 citizens representative of the French population, selected via civic lottery, for seven weekends over six months. It was designed to give citizens an opportunity to propose informed policy recommendations for addressing climate change, to define a range of measures to enable France to reduce its greenhouse gas emissions by at least 40% by 2030 (compared to 1990 levels) in a socially just and equitable way. After extensive deliberation, citizens prepared a list of 149 measures for the French government.

Besaya Citizens' Jury in Spain (2021)

The Besaya Citizens' Jury was comprised of a broadly representative group of 35 everyday citizens selected by civic lottery from ten municipalities in Spain's Besaya region. Citizens met online and in person for six weekends. They were asked to develop recommendations for the Regional Ministry of Economy on how to make the most of European Green Funds in the Besaya basin to create and/or maintain jobs that respect the criteria of a fair and inclusive ecological transition. Citizens identified three strategic priorities and 26 specific recommendations for action.

The Klima-Biergerrot (Citizens' Assembly on the Climate) in Luxembourg (2022)

Between January and July 2022, the Klima-Biergerrot brought together a representative sample of 100 people living or working in Luxembourg to discuss the country's current commitments on climate change and develop possible additional measures or proposals. The outputs will be presented and debated at the Luxembourg Parliament and are likely to influence the new version of the Integrated National Energy and Climate Plan (NECP).

Source: Besayaeuropa.es. 2021. Besaya delibera en Europa. Available at : https ://besayaeuropa.es/ ; Convention Citoyenne pour le Climat. 2021. Site officiel de la Convention Citoyenne pour le Climat. Available at: https://www.conventioncitoyennepourleclimat.fr/; https://www.klima-biergerrot.lu/en.

Governments should pay particular attention to strengthening integrity standards in public institutions involved in the design and implementation of climate and environmental policies. The appointment of climate advisory bodies and environmental expert groups should include transparency and integrity safeguards to ensure the legitimacy of their advice. To allow for public scrutiny, information on a group's structure, mandate, composition and selection criteria must be made available to the public. Such groups also need rules of procedure, including terms of appointment, standards of conduct, and, most importantly, procedures for preventing and managing conflicts of interest (OECD, 2022[5]). To ensure greater transparency around climate-related policies, governments can consider several policy options including strengthened lobbying disclosure requirements and expanding corporate political spending disclosures to allow for increased scrutiny of involvement in climate policies.

OECD evidence shows that the development of public communication campaigns can encourage greater support for and compliance with climate policy across diversified segments of the public and help sustain these attitudes over the long term. The OECD International Report on Public Communication (OECD, 2021[6]) outlines five key principles for effective public communication, namely (i) empowering the public communication function through mandates and strategies that support policy objectives and open government; (ii) institutionalising and professionalising communication; (iii) transitioning towards a more informed communication function; (iv) leveraging digital technologies and data responsibly; and (v) strengthening the strategic use of public communication to counter mis- and disinformation.

The COVID-19 pandemic response has served as an accelerator and testing ground for public communication practices that can achieve these objectives at scale (Alfonsi et al., 2022[7]). Leveraging recent innovations in the field, government communicators can test messaging and deliver highly tailored information to diverse groups in society in support of climate policy. Communication channels and social listening offer a continuous understanding of public discourse and attitudes around those policies, and can help adjust information and messaging based on public feedback.

Some countries are taking steps to revamp public communication to inform and engage with the public, while preventing and reacting to the spread of mis- and dis-information. Scotland's Turning the Tide campaign and the EU Council's Taking the Lead on Climate Change campaign provide good examples. Governments can support the timely and effective sharing of information, data and policy options to address disinformation around environmental pressures, notably climate change. Agreeing on common data standards to monitor climate change, proactively publishing unrestricted access data on climate change for analysis and re-use; and identifying the provenance of both trusted and untrusted data sources are among actions governments can take to fight dis- and mis-information on climate change (OECD, 2022[5]).

Distributional impacts of climate policy

The distributional impacts of climate policies have an important bearing on maintaining public support for climate policies, but are also fundamental from a well-being and inequalities perspective. The OECD Well-being Framework identifies work and job quality, health, income and wealth, and safety as the four key dimensions of people's well-being. Policy responses that share the impacts of the transition as equitably as possible are thus important for supporting populations' broader well-being as well as building public support for the transition (OECD, 2021[8]). The transformative changes required to reach net-zero emissions will have profound effects on labour markets and skills needs, with implications for the work and job-quality dimension of populations' well-being.

Price-based measures taken by governments, such as carbon taxes, may raise energy costs. The risk that this presents to well-being and inequalities has been particularly showcased by the current energy crisis. Domestic fuels are both necessities and a main source of household-level emissions. When energy prices go up, the lowest-income households may be ill-equipped to draw on savings or to cut back on other expenditures (OECD, 2022[9]; Sologon et al., 2022[10]; Immervoll et al., 2023[11]). Thus, even if the incidence of increased prices is broadly similar across income groups or is progressive (impacting wealthier groups more heavily), energy affordability can remain a concern and vulnerable households may find it difficult to maintain minimum levels of energy use and comfort. Similarly, if segments of the elderly population are required to limit energy consumption for heating and cooling, their health and well-being may be put at risk. Higher taxes on road transport fuels may affect rural residents more than urban dwellers since the former tend to rely more on private cars and have limited access to viable public transport alternatives (OECD, 2021[8]).

This is supported by a recent study for EU countries on the prospective reform of the EU's Energy Tax Directive and the introduction of an emissions-trading system for the road transport and household sectors (Gore, 2022[12]). The direct impact of these reforms is regressive, with lower-income households seeing a greater welfare reduction. However, impacts differ strongly by characteristics other than household income. Impacts are much smaller for urban households compared to rural households, owner-occupiers are more strongly affected than renters, and women-headed households, single-parent households and households with one older person are generally less affected. These examples illustrate the heterogeneity of impacts across households and the potential for climate policies to have regressive impacts, increase inequality, and worsen key aspects of material deprivation and social exclusion.

A key aspect of heterogeneity between households is their response to carbon pricing. Some parts of the population are better able than others to adjust their behaviour in a way that reduces their economic burden from climate-change mitigation. For some households, adjustments may be impossible, e.g. because they spend most or all of their income on necessities and are unable to cover the short-term costs of reducing their carbon footprint (e.g. by insulating their home or moving closer to their workplace to reduce commuting). Since rebalancing consumption and resource use is the very purpose of carbon pricing, these behavioural dimensions must be reflected in assessments of how the resulting burdens are shared.

Tax and fiscal policy can influence the incidence of price increases by providing preferential tax rates for selected groups of energy users or by introducing accompanying fiscal measures (transfers) when prices rise because of climate policies or other factors. The downside of preferential tax rates is that incentives to cut emissions are blunted for eligible groups. In addition, preferential rates are an implicit form of spending as they forego possible revenue. Direct spending through transfers, on the other hand, can mute adverse impacts on selected groups while preserving abatement incentives (OECD, forthcoming 2023[13]) (OECD, 2022[9]; Immervoll et al., 2023[11]).

While transfers are a superior alternative to price-based measures in principle, implementing them may require innovations in transfer mechanisms. In response to recent energy price increases, governments have typically resorted to broad-based price support measures to shield households and businesses, in part due to the complexity of implementing more targeted measures (OECD, 2022[14]). Existing social and fiscal systems may lack the necessary sophistication to address the highly heterogeneous impact of energy price increases across households (Kalkuhl et al., 2022[15]).

The discussion above indicates the need for careful distributional analysis by governments as they prepare and accelerate necessary climate change mitigation while simultaneously managing impacts on well-being. Two recent OECD country studies reaffirm the importance of these distributional analyses when introducing pricing measures and demonstrate how they could be done (Immervoll et al., 2023[11]) (OECD, 2022[16]). The studies demonstrate that the heterogeneous incidence of carbon taxes requires careful analysis, with effects varying significantly across income deciles and regions but likely also across other socio-demographic categories.

The overall burden of a carbon tax on households' budgets depends on three factors: their reliance on different fuels for heating and transportation ("direct" effect); their consumption of other goods that give rise to carbon emissions during the production process ("indirect" effect); and their behavioural responses to the price changes that occur. The magnitude of indirect effects can be greater than that of direct effects (Immervoll et al., 2023[11]). This emphasises the need for governments assess not only of households' fuel consumption profiles but their entire consumption bundles. In addition, behavioural adjustments in response to price signals reduce effective tax burdens and are important determinants of distributional impacts. The responsiveness to price changes differs across goods and households according to households' propensity and ability to rebalance consumption towards less carbon-intensive (and less costly) products.

Beyond the distributional effects on households' living costs, there are geographical dimensions of carbon pricing, with variations between rural and urban areas and diversified versus single-industry urban centres focused on heavy industry (OECD, 2022[16]). This emphasises the need for governments to consider the regional effects of climate policies and consider geographically targeted support to counteract adverse distributional outcomes.

Both studies indicate that detailed analysis of distributional impacts can provide governments with important information on how best to use revenues generated by carbon taxes to alleviate distributional concerns. Revenues generated by carbon taxes are substantial. Channelling them back to households allows governments considerable scope to cushion losses and shape the distributional profile as part of a broader policy package, with both studies providing examples of how targeted revenue recycling can result in progressive outcomes.

Similar studies could be carried out wherever climate policies are being proposed and introduced. This can be important for balancing social and environmental objectives, and for ensuring that broader concerns related to well-being are addressed. It can also allow for transparent communication with the public in order to enhance support. Note though that both examples depicted exclusively study the incidence of carbon tax proposals whereas net-zero will require a far broader policy mix.

Lastly, it is important to note that housing represents another important area where the impacts of the transition will not naturally be distributed equally across populations. Housing accounts for a quarter of carbon emissions in OECD countries, making it an essential component of plans to reach net zero. Investments in "green" housing to improve energy efficiency and help mitigate the effects of extreme weather conditions on households are likely to sustain employment in the construction sector. However, these investments are not affordable for all. Housing prices have increased over the past decades, and households are dedicating a larger share of their budget to housing costs than they used to (OECD, 2021[17]). OECD countries can introduce subsidies to building regeneration among other climate policy measures targeting housing. Housing support can also affect the reallocation of individuals across regions. To the extent that residential mobility is linked to labour mobility, restrictive housing policies can delay the transition to net zero by increasing the incidence of long-term unemployment (OECD, 2020[18]; Causa, Abendschein and Cavalleri, 2021[19]). These factors merit serious consideration in government analyses to facilitate the net-zero transition and ensure that its impacts are fairly distributed

Labour market implications: jobs and skills

The pace of the net-zero transition and the ambition of policies needed to achieve it will transform economic structures, changing production and employment patterns, with considerable labour market implications. The costs of adjusting to these employment shifts will be unevenly distributed across society, leaving some better and some worse off, potentially exacerbating the distributional concerns highlighted above. This exemplifies the challenges faced by governments to ensure that these labour market shifts are not to the detriment of a fair and equitable transition.

Labour market effects of the net-zero transition

Employment effects

The transition to a low-carbon and resource-efficient economy will have a significant impact on jobs. First, in broad terms it will entail a drastic reduction in jobs in firms or "brown" sectors with a high greenhouse gas (GHG) footprint. It will simultaneously increase jobs directly linked to emissions-saving "green" technologies (e.g. renewables). In reality, the picture is more complex. Defining which job is green is challenging, and they may or may not substitute for existing jobs in emissions-intensive firms or sectors; some green products and services may be entirely new (e.g. direct air capture of CO_2). Each new green job can also foster the creation of other non-green jobs locally (Vona, Marin and Consoli, 2019[20]).

In addition to changing the allocation of available jobs across sectors, the transition to a net-zero economy will also entail a transformation in the nature of jobs, with the tasks workers are required to perform and the skills they need to do so changing. For example, the manufacture of combustion-engine vehicles requires a different set of tasks and skills to that of an electric vehicle. Adding further complexity, these shifts will occur in an already rapidly changing job market, with the nature of jobs already changing due to digital transformation, for example.

Beyond the immediate effect of the transition on production and consumption patterns, it will also have indirect effects on the inputs for production. For example, higher energy prices are associated with increasing demand for capital and decreasing demand for labour as the input mix to produce a specific good changes. This elasticity of labour to energy prices, however, varies significantly across studies (Vona, 2021[21]). The extent to which workers are able to switch between sectors and occupations according to these new production and consumption patterns influences the overall effect of the transition on employment and wages. The incidence and pervasiveness of unemployment, in turn, introduces income effects that produce further changes in the demand for labour. Extensive empirical evidence suggests that in most OECD countries, labour market adjustments are not immediate due to rigidities in the labour market such as shortages in the supply of certain occupational or skill profiles or wage-setting rigidities.

The impacts of climate change itself (e.g. extreme weather events, rises in temperatures and sea levels) will also affect labour markets. For example, there may be a reallocation of production and labour away from areas most affected by climate impacts (e.g. from coastal regions prone to increasing storms or sea-level rise). Climate impacts may also affect the productivity of certain sectors such as the farming or forestry sector, shifting labour to other, more productive sectors (i.e. renewable energy construction).

Lastly, other megatrends running in parallel to the net-zero transition, e.g. digitalisation, population ageing and (de)globalisation, also have complex labour market implications. The way these changes in the structure of the economy and society interact with each other can impact the pace of convergence to net zero, and the effect of the transition on jobs, income, and health as a consequence.

Box 8.2. Challenges in defining "green" jobs

The net-zero transition implies a reallocation away from jobs that are downsizing because of climate change and decarbonising efforts, all while acknowledging that not all jobs created and filled as a consequence of climate change and mitigation policies will necessarily be fully low-emission. The current definitions of "brown" and "green" jobs, however, usually encompass the outcomes of decarbonisation efforts only.

Several attempts have been made to produce a narrower definition, across national and international policy organisations. Table 8.1 introduces one possible way to classify these definitional approaches (OECD, forthcoming[22]). Jobs that are in growing demand due to climate policies have often been labelled as "green". This simple definition, however, risks inflating the number of "green jobs" insofar as some jobs are in-demand because of the transition but achieve no environmental gains ("grey jobs") or because of competing but contemporaneous drivers of job growth. Other approaches hinge instead on the identification of certain features of the job that are "green" (i.e. energy-efficient, emission-efficient, or non-polluting), including production processes, the output itself, or – when these cannot be easily identified in relation to the job – the tasks performed while on the job.

Table 8.1. Different approaches for defining "green" jobs

Approach	Definition
Policy-driven	A job that is in demand because of the implementation of climate change policies
Process-based	A job in an establishment that uses green production processes and practices
Output-based	A job in an establishment that produces green goods and services, i.e. that generate little harm to the environment while produced or consumed
Task-based	A job that is intensive in green tasks

Source: Elaboration on OECD Skills Outlook (forthcoming[22]).

Net employment effects

The net-zero transition will reduce labour demand in some sectors while increasing it in others. Given the distributional implications of labour market effects and their importance in ensuring that the transition is fair, equitable, and widely supported, quantifying the overall impact of the transition on employment is especially important. Studies that model the introduction of climate mitigation policies predict – under a number of simplifying assumptions – that the net labour market impact will likely be modest in the long run. While certain green sectors will grow at a rapid pace, labour should shift from emissions-intensive to less emissions-intensive sectors in the long run. This will have large impacts on specific sectors but a small aggregate impact on unemployment overall (Chateau, Bibas and Lanzi, 2018[23]). Other estimates suggest that reaching net zero by 2050 could create 30 million jobs globally by 2030 compared to 8 million jobs lost (International Energy Agency, 2021[24]).[1]

The same limited impact of the net-zero transition on employment is found in partial equilibrium analyses but conclusions can change depending on time scales and level of aggregation at which the analysis is performed (OECD, 2021[25]). At the microeconomic level and in the short run, stringent environmental regulations are found to reduce employment in energy- and pollution-intensive industries but effects are small and do not seem to persist in the long run (Dechezleprêtre and Sato, 2017[26]) (Ferris, Shadbegian and Wolverton, 2014[27]).

Inference from past evidence, however, should not be cause for complacency. Past policy changes and reduction efforts have been gradual and their impact on employment may not be a good guide to the impact of much larger or more rapid changes. The same modelling exercises above, furthermore, show that large and sudden changes in climate policy can produce large employment losses (Chateau, Bibas and Lanzi, 2018[23]). The extent and pace of employment adjustment is also affected by a number of labour market policies and by the extent to which policies can alleviate the regressive impacts of climate change on households' income. This exemplifies the need for careful labour market policy planning and design to accompany climate policies, ensuring that the net-labour market effects remain minimal, and the negative distributional outcomes of labour market shifts are addressed.

Beyond aggregate impacts – projected changes within the labour market as a result of the transition

A manageable net aggregate employment impact of climate change and climate policy can still imply substantial labour market changes across sectors, with a considerable number of workers needing to change jobs and entailing considerable distributional implications. Such reallocation of workers can take different forms:

- **Sectoral transitions**. Workers in emissions-intensive sectors or industries or ones that are especially exposed to climate change may need to move to other sectors or industries. Such shifts can have further indirect effects on other sectors that are not necessarily emissions-intensive or vulnerable to climate impacts via input-output linkages.
- **Occupational transitions**. Some particular occupational profiles may progressively lose employment if they are typical of emissions-intensive industries or those vulnerable to climate impacts. One such example are coal miners, who are decreasing in number with the progressive phasing out of coal use for energy production.
- **Regional transitions**. The geographic impact of this transformation may be highly uneven, considering the geographical concentration of certain emissions-intensive activities (e.g. mining) or those more exposed to climate impacts. Other regions, conversely, can benefit disproportionately from the creation of "green" jobs, e.g. regions with considerable renewable energy potential.

- **Employer churning**. Lastly, employment may shift within sectors and regions but also across firms as emissions-intensive firms are substituted by firms producing comparable products but without the associated emissions or resource use. Indeed, technology adoption is uneven across firms, even within narrowly defined sectors of production. Thus, workers may need to seek employment in "greener" firms.

Lastly, the likelihood of these transitions (as well as those from and into unemployment) are affected by the alignment of skills and knowledge between workers and the requirements in jobs that emerge from the green transition, as developed further below.

The importance of skills for enabling the net-zero transition

As the skills required for jobs adversely impacted by climate change and climate policies are usually not completely transferrable to new jobs in low-carbon sectors and industries, workers in transition may have to adapt their skills set to fulfil the requirements of the destination job. Skills gaps and shortages are already recognised as a major bottleneck in a number of sectors such as renewable energy, energy and resource efficiency, renovation of buildings, construction, environmental services and manufacturing (OECD, 2020[28]).

Understanding which skills are or will be in stronger demand, however, is not straightforward. The urgency of the transition imposes new challenges, and past evidence may not be informative for the future, considering the scale and scope of the net-zero transition. Limited evidence exists on the type of skills that are most complementary to (or substitute for) "green" technologies and production processes. Similarly, evidence that the net-zero transition is skills-biased (i.e. production requires high- rather than low-level skills) is still limited (Marin and Vona, 2019[29]). Some evidence points to most job creation and reallocation being concentrated among mid-skill occupations.

The limited existing evidence concludes that the net-zero transition requires both technical skills that are specific to green industries but also transversal skills such as management skills, skills in innovation and change management and communication skills (OECD, 2014[30]) (Vona et al., 2018[31]). Many if not most of the skills in demand for the net-zero transition therefore do not seem specific to "green" jobs only. There may be some skills that are more frequently relied upon as a consequence of climate change and climate change policies, but these may also be present in other jobs.

Uneven distribution of labour market effects across populations

The labour market impact of the climate transition will likely be unequal. Many workers will benefit from new job opportunities and potential earnings growth in expanding industries. Others working in shrinking emissions-intensive industries, risk unemployment and may need to reskill. Job displacements often entail some form of adjustment costs, including long-term earnings losses (Walker, 2013[32]) (McKibbin et al., 2009[33]).

The distributional impact of labour market shifts disproportionately affects low-skilled workers who face above-average adjustment costs, as lower levels of education and competencies are crucial barriers to reskilling and job mobility. Generally, low-skilled workers tend to participate in training less than high-skilled workers, and display lower motivation to train (OECD, 2019[34]). This may be especially constraining if the climate transition imposes a disproportionate burden of training on the low-skilled, as for instance in the case of a skills-biased transition (with "brown" industries characterised by relatively low-educated workforce whereas "green" industries require higher-level skills).

Beyond skills levels, research has consistently shown that older workers tend to experience greater adjustment costs following job displacement, including because of the higher cost of reskilling. Furthermore, existing evidence shows that when older workers are displaced, they are likely to be out of work longer, and, if they find a new job, replace less of their former wages than their younger counterparts

(OECD, 2018[35]). Older people are also more exposed to the consequences of climate change itself, which will occur in parallel to the shifts initiated by the net-zero transition. Excess heat-related mortality and health risks related to pollution increases with age. Older people's decreased mobility and changes in physiology and often more limited access to resources limit their adaptive capacity in case of climate change.

The labour market impacts of the net-zero transition are also unevenly felt by different genders. Some of the most carbon-intensive industries (e.g. mining) employ disproportionately more men than women. Female employment in occupations related to science, technology, engineering and mathematics (STEM) is low as is female entrepreneurship. Labour demand in both of these areas is projected to increase along the transition. In addition, although in general better represented in the renewable energy sector than in the traditional energy sector, they mostly hold non-STEM positions (OECD, 2020[36]). A gender-sensitive transition strives to understand how business and policy makers can bring women into green jobs. Furthermore, women's empowerment and leadership in the energy sector could help accelerate the transition to a low-carbon economy by promoting clean energy and more efficient energy use as well as help to tackle energy poverty (OECD, 2021[37]).

As mentioned already, employment in emissions- or pollution-intensive industries is often geographically concentrated. Indeed, within-country regional variation in emissions is larger than between countries (OECD, 2021[38]). As such, labour market shifts may have important regional and local implications and may exacerbate regional inequalities. For example, the high-tech and knowledge-intensive nature of many "green" jobs may further marginalise rural and industrial areas in favour of de-industrialised urban centres.

The same holds true for the impact of climate change itself, either in the form of extreme weather events or because of the regional specialisation in activities that are sensitive to climate changes (e.g. tourism, agriculture, energy production) (OECD, 2020[39]). Moreover, insofar as climate change affects disproportionally the productivity of sectors that are prevalent in rural areas (e.g. agriculture, fisheries) while high-tech and knowledge-intensive employment concentrates in urban areas, the urban-rural divide may be exacerbated (Hsiang et al., 2017[40]). Rural households are also more affected by rising fuel costs because they are more car-dependent (Joyce et al., 2022[41]), but less so by air pollution and rising temperatures (OECD, 2021[42]).

Other megatrends and the net-zero transition

The transition to net zero needs to be managed alongside other megatrends such as the digital transformation of production and population ageing. These changes themselves come with important labour market implications, interacting with the net-zero transition in ways that affect the overall pace and scope of the transition, both negatively and positively.

The digital transformation

For both the net-zero and digital transitions, technology adoption and innovation foster the reallocation of labour away from some occupations and sectors; stimulate the creation of new jobs and professional profiles; and change the task composition and skill requirements of (some) jobs. Digitalisation will enable savings generated by firms that automate parts of production or adopt artificial intelligence technologies to be reinvested in "green" technologies, thus expanding employment in "green" jobs. At the same time, increasing automation is a clear challenge for labour markets and may be accelerated if many "green" jobs are automatable. In this case, the coexistence of both structural changes can raise unemployment and exacerbate voters' resistance to climate policies.

Demographic change

Demographic change poses a significant challenge to the net-zero transition. Ageing and lower fertility are projected to shrink the size of the working-age population and thereby labour force. Older workers, moreover, are less likely to engage in reskilling activities, including those that enable their reallocation towards "greener" jobs. Lastly, several studies show that, currently, older adults are less inclined to sacrifice part of their income on behalf of a clean environment than younger adults (Stokes, Wike and Carle, 2015[43]). While increasing awareness of the climate crisis among younger adults now may mean that they may have different attitudes when they grow older, the demographic shifts towards ageing populations is nevertheless an important factor.

Resilient labour markets: What can governments do?

Carefully designed policies can enhance the adaptive capacity of labour markets and protect those most adversely impacted without wasting public resources, all while preserving or strengthening the economic incentives to achieve net zero by 2050. In line with the OECD Jobs Strategy (OECD, 2018[44]), the structural adjustment pressures resulting from the net-zero transition should reconcile employment flexibility and security by securing workers' employability and income rather than their jobs, and fostering resilient and adaptable labour markets.

Regulatory framework and labour market institutions

A well-functioning labour market is a prerequisite for a successful net-zero transition. Workers – and in particular those in emissions- or pollution-intensive jobs – should be able to shift across jobs without long periods of unemployment in order to meet rising demand in low-carbon sectors. Similarly, opportunities for the unemployed can only be created if employers have the right incentives to hire, create new ventures or possibly relocate their business elsewhere.

The efficiency of this process of reallocation is largely determined by the functioning and regulation of financial, housing and product markets, including through policies that affect entry and exit of firms. Labour market regulation can enable the development and diffusion of new "green" technologies if they do not unduly prevent firms that lead in the development of green technologies from growing and gaining market shares. Labour regulation should also be supportive of the creation of new firms, considering that business start-ups account for a large share of new technologies, in particular breakthrough innovations.

A key role in determining the rate of reallocation away from emissions-intensive firms or sectors is played by employment protection provisions (EPL). A balanced approach to employment protection does not prevent job reallocation by excessively increasing termination costs for the firm but still protects workers from unfair hiring or firing practices and the destruction of viable worker-firm matches (OECD, 2018[44]). By preventing excessive turnover, job protection can ease resistance to change in the workforce. It can support the adoption of new technologies and innovation, and engagement in training, which in turn can accelerate the restructuring of production where needed. It is also important that the quality of green jobs is emphasised so that the net-zero transition is not perceived as transitioning workers towards low-quality jobs.

At the same time, workers' protection should not hamper the reallocation of workers away from emissions- or pollution-intensive activities when these are downsizing because of climate policies. A balanced approach to EPL should be reflected in the system of benefits and transfers that protects workers in case of job losses. Relatively generous unemployment benefits can co-exist with less stringent dismissal regulation and at the same time mitigate voter resistance to climate policies among displaced workers.

Other labour market institutions can support the mobility of workers between firms by removing barriers to and strengthening incentives for job mobility. Over-restrictive occupational licenses, for instance, by imposing too-high standards of competence to practice for pay would unnecessarily limit labour mobility by impeding workers seeking to adjust to the net-zero transition. Other provisions can enhance labour mobility by reducing labour market concentration and monopsony power. Policies that directly limit concentration or counteract uneven employer power in the employment relationship include an expansion of the scope of action of antitrust authorities; the investigation of mergers and no-poaching agreements; and a renewed effort to legislate these phenomena. It would also include strengthening collective bargaining (Araki et al., 2022[45]). Lastly, removing obstacles to geographical mobility can also expand workers' options. First-order tools in this sense are housing policies such as rental regulation, land-use and planning reforms, taxation on housing purchases, and investments in social housing (OECD, 2021[46]). Public investment programmes, and improvements in healthcare and transport policies in a region (Causa, Abendschein and Cavalleri, 2021[19]) should also be considered.

Well-functioning collective bargaining institutions, particularly when associated with high coverage, can also accelerate the net-zero transition. Collective bargaining can foster innovation in the workplace and skills development and skills use. Moreover, OECD work on displaced workers highlights the significant role that collective bargaining, in particular, at the sectoral level, can play in helping displaced workers back into good jobs (OECD, 2018[35]). Lastly, by contributing to improved working conditions and remunerations, collective bargaining can ease the risk of political backlash, and accelerate the convergence towards net zero. As sectors differ in their needs and preparedness to tackle the green transition, sector-specific approaches to collective bargaining are reasonable and relevant. However, the uneven cost of climate policies across sectors can also generate sector-specific resistance to change and demands for specific support. A cross-sectoral approach to social dialogue at the national level can help design equitable measures of government support for the transition of the most affected workers and negotiate new regulations.

Green active labour-market policies

Jobless individuals who are marginally attached to the labour market often face barriers that prevent them from finding suitable jobs or discourage them from actively seeking work. Active labour market policies or programmes (ALMPs) ensure that workers and firms can adapt quickly to changes brought about by the net-zero transition. However, current active labour market programmes do not generally have a specific focus on green jobs or skills, whether that means supporting the retraining of workers into "greener" jobs or the absorption of unemployed individuals into "green" jobs. This may be beginning to change. In several EU Member States, public employment services (PES) have been involved in identifying green jobs and greening occupations and establishing corresponding occupational profiles. The experience of these countries shows that close co-operation with other partners – including social partners – is important as it can lead to an easier identification of prospective job opportunities and transferable skills (European Commission, 2021[47]).

Active labour market policies can also be used to support workers who have lost their jobs due to the transition, i.e. workers in emissions-intensive industries. While supporting these vulnerable workers is an essential component of ensuring a fair and equitable transition, defining who fits into this "vulnerable" category is difficult. While some industries and occupations can clearly be considered emissions-intensive, or "brown", others may be more difficult to place, and different employers in the same sector may use technologies of different emissions intensity. Moreover, the downsizing of an emissions-intensive company may have regional spillovers, calling into question whether workers in satellite activities that are potentially less emissions-intensive should also receive assistance. Lastly, not all workers in emissions-intensive activities need the same level of assistance if their skills set is transferrable or already in demand on the labour market.

Lastly, the structural transformation of the labour market imposed by the net-zero transition strengthens the need to co-ordinate ALMPs with well-designed tax-and-benefit systems. These decrease displacement costs by providing income support during the period of unemployment and effective re-employment services.

Upskilling and reskilling for the net-zero transition

Labour market policies for a successful net-zero transition should ensure that workers are equipped with the right skills to thrive in the transforming labour market. Upskilling and reskilling can be strengthened to ensure a smooth transition of workers across jobs (within the same firm or outside) or to adapt their current job to the needs of the climate transition. In the short run, government-supported training programmes for individuals and firms can help reduce skill shortages.

Targeted training programmes are more effective than broad training programmes. However, strategies, policies and initiatives that focus explicitly on green skills and employment are still rare (Cedefop, 2019[48]).[2] Countries need high-quality labour-market information systems that track emerging skills needs. Countries also need that information to be shared with labour market actors, policy makers, and training and education providers. OECD (Forthcoming[49]) describes effective strategies to leverage information on skills needed in a low-carbon economy into relevant policy actions.

Training policies in the net-zero transition can be more effective if they include reaching out to potential learners and guiding them in their choice of training course and potential new jobs. They should also call for a recognition of individuals' existing skills and the development of a high-quality market for training providers. In the longer term, new skills required by the net-zero transition will affect the design of curricula in initial education. This can reduce skills imbalances and poor school-to-work transitions.

Vocational education and training (VET) is particularly well-placed to support the net-zero transition. Because of its close link to the world of work, VET develops and delivers curricula that match market needs and promote work-based learning. The skills acquired through vocational training are also well-suited to activities such as tooling up, and developing prototypes and testing, all of which are needed to develop and diffuse the radically different products and processes a net-zero transition entails and make incremental improvements to existing ones. VET systems must be able to anticipate new skills needs and adapt curricula quickly enough to avert significant skill mismatches.

Lastly, educational institutions should provide the foundational knowledge and skills to identify and resolve environmental challenges, and shape attitudes and behaviours that lead to individual and collective action. PISA 2018 reveals that most countries already deploy curricula that include climate change and global warming but that this does not translate into uniform acquisition of environmental sustainability competences. Family, society, and education institutions complement curricula in developing these competencies. Schools in particular can influence students' educational and professional aspirations, particularly in STEM disciplines (Borgonovi et al., 2022[50]).

Social protection

Beyond direct labour market policies, social protection is a crucial building block of governments' strategies to promote necessary adjustments for the net-zero transition. It is needed to prevent or cushion any damaging disruptions of people's livelihoods the transition and climate change may produce. Social protection can cushion or prevent income losses, ease short-term credit constraints, and financially help those who are hardest hit to invest in adaptation strategies. And, by making the green transformation more inclusive, especially, as an opportunity to escape poverty, social protection can help ease voter resistance to mitigation efforts.

Past lessons on the generosity and transitory nature of unemployment benefits show that benefit systems should be moderately generous and achieve as high a coverage as possible. Generosity, conditional on the rigorous enforcement of mutual obligations, can enhance the success of active labour market strategies by encouraging job search. Conversely, benefit replacement rates for the unemployed that are too high can translate into relatively strong downward wage rigidities; that is, a resistance to wage cuts, especially among low-wage workers (OECD, 2012[51]). This can discourage employment, in particular among workers with low educational attainment or limited employment experience.

Chapter conclusions

Achieving net zero by 2050 requires important changes across society and the economy. A resilient fair and equitable transition requires strong and widespread public support for ambitious action and fairness in how it impacts different groups. This is a key challenge for governments, with multiple angles: introducing policies that make credible progress towards environmental objectives; ensuring trust in government itself; addressing and communicating on the distributional effects of climate policies; and assessing and acting on important labour market shifts. Moreover, the impacts of climate policies on populations are widespread and complex, intersecting with other megatrends, including digitalisation and demographic change as well as the impacts of climate change themselves. Reasonably flexible employment and social policies based on careful analysis will play an important role in facilitating the low-carbon transition and maintaining strong public support for climate action.

Impacts on different populations can be limited if sufficient investment is made to ensure resilience to climate impacts. Financing accelerated action in the near term can help ensure an orderly transition, which may help keep adjustment costs and distributional impacts down for different populations. In this way, ensuring alignment of finance with net-zero goals and embedding resilience to climate impacts will be important for ensuring that the transition itself is fair, equitable, and resilient.

Notes

---

1 All these estimates account for differences between "green' and "brown" industries in capital-labour intensities and in intensity in labour of different occupational profiles.

2 There are, of course, examples of training programmes that target green skills. The French public employment service (Pôle Emploi), for example, monitors green developments and directs clients into green job opportunities.

References

Alfonsi, C. et al. (2022), "Public communication trends after COVID-19: Innovative practices across the OECD and in four Southeast Asian countries", *OECD Working Papers on Public Governance*, No. 55, OECD Publishing, Paris, https://doi.org/10.1787/cb4de393-en. [7]

Araki, S. et al. (2022), "Monopsony and concentration in labour markets", in *OECD Employment Outlook 2022*, OECD Publishing. [45]

Borgonovi, F. et al. (2022), "Young people's environmental sustainability competence: Emotional, cognitive, behavioural, and attitudinal dimensions in EU and OECD countries", *OECD Social, Employment and Migration Working Papers*, No. 274, OECD Publishing, Paris, https://doi.org/10.1787/1097a78c-en. [50]

Causa, O., M. Abendschein and M. Cavalleri (2021), "The laws of attraction: Economic drivers of inter-regional migration, housing costs and the role of policies", *OECD Economics Department Working Papers*, No. 1679, OECD Publishing, Paris, https://doi.org/10.1787/da8e368a-en. [19]

CEDEFOP (2019), *Skills for green jobs: 2018 European synthesis report*, Luxembourg: Publications Office. Cedefop reference series; No 109., http://data.europa.eu/doi/10.2801/750438. [52]

Cedefop (2019), *Skills for green jobs: 2018 update*, Luxembourg: Publications Office, https://doi.org/10.2801/036464. [48]

Chateau, J., R. Bibas and E. Lanzi (2018), "Impacts of Green Growth Policies on Labour Markets and Wage Income Distribution: A General Equilibrium Application to Climate and Energy Policies", *OECD Environment Working Papers*, No. 137, OECD Publishing, Paris, https://doi.org/10.1787/ea3696f4-en. [23]

Dechezleprêtre, A. et al. (2022), "Fighting climate change: International attitudes toward climate policies", *OECD Economics Department Working Papers*, No. 1714, OECD Publishing, Paris, https://doi.org/10.1787/3406f29a-en. [2]

Dechezleprêtre, A. and M. Sato (2017), "The Impacts of Environmental Regulations on Competitiveness", *Review of Environmental Economics and Policy*, Vol. 11/2, pp. 183-206, https://doi.org/10.1093/reep/rex013. [26]

European Commission (2021), *Greening of the labour market – impacts for the Public Employment Services*. [47]

Ferris, A., R. Shadbegian and A. Wolverton (2014), "The Effect of Environmental Regulation on Power Sector Employment: Phase I of the Title IV SO₂ Trading Program", *Journal of the Association of Environmental and Resource Economists*, Vol. 1/4, pp. 521-553, https://doi.org/10.1086/679301. [27]

Gore, T. (2022), *Can Polluter Pays policies in the buildings and transport sectors be progressive? Assessing the distributional impacts on households of the proposed reform of the Energy Taxation Directive and extension of the Emissions Trading Scheme*. [12]

Hsiang, S. et al. (2017), "Estimating economic damage from climate change in the United States", *Science*, Vol. 356/6345, pp. 1362-1369, https://doi.org/10.1126/SCIENCE.AAL4369/SUPPL_FILE/AAL4369_HSIANG_SM.PDF. [40]

Immervoll, H. et al. (2023), "Who pays for higher carbon prices? Illustration for Lithuania and a research agenda", *OECD Social, Employment and Migration Working Papers*. [11]

International Energy Agency (2021), "World Energy Outlook 2021". [24]

Joyce, R. et al. (2022), *The cost of living crunch*, Institute for Fiscal Studies, https://ifs.org.uk/publications/15905. [41]

Kalkuhl, M. et al. (2022), *Effects of the energy price crisis on households in Germany: Socio-political challenges and policy options*. [15]

Marin, G. and F. Vona (2019), "Climate policies and skill-biased employment dynamics: Evidence from EU countries", *Journal of Environmental Economics and Management*, Vol. 98, https://doi.org/10.1016/j.jeem.2019.102253. [29]

McKibbin, W. et al. (2009), "Consequences of alternative US cap-and-trade policies: Controlling both emissions and costs", *CAMA Working Papers*. [33]

OECD (2022), *Building Trust and Reinforcing Democracy: Preparing the Ground for Government Action*, OECD Public Governance Reviews, OECD Publishing, Paris, https://doi.org/10.1787/76972a4a-en. [5]

OECD (2022), *Building Trust to Reinforce Democracy: Main Findings from the 2021 OECD Survey on Drivers of Trust in Public Institutions*, OECD Publishing, Paris, https://doi.org/10.1787/b407f99c-en. [4]

OECD (2022), *Building Trust to Reinforce Democracy: Main Findings from the 2021 OECD Survey on Drivers of Trust in Public Institutions*, Building Trust in Public Institutions, OECD Publishing, Paris, https://doi.org/10.1787/b407f99c-en. [3]

OECD (2022), *Coping with the cost-of-living crisis: Income support for working-age individuals and their families*, OECD, https://www.oecd.org/social/Income-support-for-working-age-individuals-and-their-families.pdf. [9]

OECD (2022), *OECD Economic Surveys: United Kingdom 2022*, OECD Publishing, Paris, https://doi.org/10.1787/7c0f1268-en. [16]

OECD (2022), "Why governments should target support amidst high energy prices", *OECD Policy Responses on the Impacts of the War in Ukraine*, OECD Publishing, Paris, https://doi.org/10.1787/40f44f78-en. [14]

OECD (2021), *Assessing the Economic Impacts of Environmental Policies: Evidence from a Decade of OECD Research*, OECD Publishing, Paris, https://doi.org/10.1787/bf2fb156-en. [25]

OECD (2021), *Brick by Brick: Building Better Housing Policies*, OECD Publishing, Paris, https://doi.org/10.1787/b453b043-en. [46]

OECD (2021), *Building for a better tomorrow: Policies to make housing more affordable*, Employment, Labour and Social Affairs Policy Briefs, OECD Publishing. [17]

OECD (2021), *Gender and the Environment: Building Evidence and Policies to Achieve the SDGs*, OECD Publishing, Paris, https://doi.org/10.1787/3d32ca39-en. [37]

OECD (2021), *OECD Regional Outlook 2021: Addressing COVID-19 and Moving to Net Zero Greenhouse Gas Emissions*, OECD Publishing, Paris, https://doi.org/10.1787/17017efe-en. [38]

OECD (2021), *OECD Report on Public Communication: The Global Context and the Way Forward*, OECD Publishing, Paris, https://doi.org/10.1787/22f8031c-en. [6]

OECD (2021), "The inequalities-environment nexus: Towards a people-centred green transition", *OECD Green Growth Papers*, No. 2021/01, OECD Publishing, Paris, https://doi.org/10.1787/ca9d8479-en. [8]

OECD (2021), "The inequalities-environment nexus: Towards a people-centred green transition", *OECD Green Growth Papers*, No. 2021/01, OECD Publishing, Paris, https://doi.org/10.1787/ca9d8479-en. [42]

OECD (2020), *Greening energy and ensuring a just transition for men and women*, 2020 Global Forum on Environment: Mainstreaming Gender and Empowering Women for Environmental Sustainability. [36]

OECD (2020), *Housing Amid Covid-19: Policy Responses and Challenges*, OECD Policy Responses to Coronavirus (COVID-19). [18]

OECD (2020), *Job Creation and Local Economic Development 2020: Rebuilding Better*, OECD Publishing, Paris, https://doi.org/10.1787/b02b2f39-en. [39]

OECD (2020), *Making the green recovery work for jobs, income and growth*, OECD Policy Responses to Coronavirus (COVID-19). [28]

OECD (2019), *Getting Skills Right: Future-Ready Adult Learning Systems*, Getting Skills Right, OECD Publishing, Paris, https://doi.org/10.1787/9789264311756-en. [34]

OECD (2018), "Back to work: Lessons from nine country case studies of policies to assist displaced workers", in *OECD Employment Outlook 2018*, OECD Publishing, Paris, https://doi.org/10.1787/empl_outlook-2018-8-en. [35]

OECD (2018), *Good Jobs for All in a Changing World of Work: The OECD Jobs Strategy*, OECD Publishing, Paris, https://doi.org/10.1787/9789264308817-en. [44]

OECD (2014), *Job Creation and Local Economic Development*, OECD Publishing, Paris, https://doi.org/10.1787/9789264215009-en. [30]

OECD (2012), "What Green Growth Means for Workers and Labour Market Policies: An Initial Assessment", in *OECD Employment Outlook 2012*, OECD Publishing, Paris, https://doi.org/10.1787/empl_outlook-2012-5-en. [51]

OECD (forthcoming 2023), *Climate and fiscal policy working paper.* [13]

OECD (forthcoming), *OECD Skills Outlook 2023: Skills and the environment*, OECD Publishing. [22]

OECD (Forthcoming), *The climate transition and the labour market: A conceptual framework*. [49]

Sologon, D. et al. (2022), *Welfare and Distributional Impact of Soaring Prices in Europe*, IZA Discussion Paper Series. [10]

Stokes, B., R. Wike and J. Carle (2015), *Global Concern about Climate Change, Broad Support for Limiting Emissions*, Pew Research Center. [43]

Tovar Reaños, M. and M. Lynch (2022), "The benefits of action on implementing carbon taxation in Ireland: a demand system approach", *Journal of Environmental Planning and Management*, pp. 1-25, https://doi.org/10.1080/09640568.2021.2006157. [1]

Vona, F. (2021), "Managing the distributional effects of environmental and climate policies: The narrow path for a triple dividend", *OECD Environment Working Papers*, No. 188, OECD Publishing, Paris, https://doi.org/10.1787/361126bd-en. [21]

Vona, F., G. Marin and D. Consoli (2019), "Measures, drivers and effects of green employment: evidence from US local labor markets, 2006–2014", *Journal of Economic Geography*, Vol. 19/5, pp. 1021-1048, https://doi.org/10.1093/JEG/LBY038. [20]

Vona, F. et al. (2018), "Environmental regulation and green skills: An empirical exploration", *Journal of the Association of Environmental and Resource Economists*, Vol. 5/4, pp. 713-753, https://doi.org/10.1086/698859/ASSET/IMAGES/LARGE/FG3.JPEG. [31]

Walker, W. (2013), "The transitional costs of sectoral reallocation: Evidence from the Clean Air Act and the workforce", *Source: The Quarterly Journal of Economics*, Vol. 128/4, pp. 1787-1836, https://doi.org/10.2307/26372537. [32]

9 Aligning finance flows and private sector action with a resilient net-zero transition

Public finances alone are not enough to meet transition needs. Aligning investment and financial markets and getting private sector buy-in is critical but current commitments too often lack credibility. This chapter looks at how government policies can harness and redirect key public and private finance flows including by strengthening financial market practices through focusing on environmental, social and governance (ESG) rating and investment approaches, and strengthening metrics used to track financial sector progress can better support finance flows aligned with the transition. Finally, the chapter addresses the role of the private sector in ensuring the resilience of net-zero commitments and their transition pathways.

This chapter draws on contributions to the horizontal project carried out under the responsibility of the Investment Committee including the Working Party for Responsible Business Conduct and the Environment Policy Committee.

Article 2.1(c) of the Paris Agreement calls for "making finance flows consistent with a pathway towards low greenhouse gas (GHG) emissions and climate-resilient development" (UNFCCC, 2016[1]). It recognises the critical role of finance in enabling large-scale emissions reductions and adaptation to climate impacts. Tracking financial sector progress in aligning finance flows with these objectives and addressing opportunities to further scale aligned finance is key to ensuring the immediate and longer-term resilience of the net-zero transition.

Although financial markets are beginning to integrate climate transition risks and opportunities into investment decision making, constraints remain to the efficient and scaled mobilisation of finance into net-zero aligned activities. This chapter looks at how strengthening market practices by focusing on environmental, social and governance (ESG) rating and investment approaches, and strengthening metrics used to track financial sector progress, can better support scaled and aligned climate finance flows in accelerating the transition.

In addition, this chapter focuses on how government policies can harness and redirect key public and private finance flows in such a way that they do not increase the vulnerability or fragility of systems or undermine net-zero goals but, rather, accelerate a resilient net-zero transition. Two important examples are used to exemplify how and where these policy actions can take hold. First, an examination of Foreign Direct Investment (FDI) and specific recommendations of the OECD FDI Qualities Policy Toolkit.[1] Second, an examination of how investment treaties promote long-term lock-in of emissions-intensive investment, potentially disincentivising governments' implementation of ambitious climate policy.

Lastly, this chapter addresses the role of the private sector in ensuring the resilience of net-zero commitments and their transition pathways. First, by ensuring commitments are being implemented with integrity, avoiding greenwashing (United Nations, 2022[2]) and safeguarding against adverse impacts across other areas of business operations or responsibilities. Second, by strengthening the resilience of global supply chains critical for the net-zero transition.

Measuring climate alignment of finance flows through real-economy investments

Climate "alignment", or the consistency of finance with climate policy goals, entails scaling up finance for activities aligned with the Paris Agreement. This includes financing activities and economic sectors transitioning towards low greenhouse gas (GHG) emissions while also building resilience to the impacts of climate change. This can be done through market practices that enable the reallocation of capital towards greener alternatives; discourage capital flows to GHG-intensive projects; and embed environmental integrity to ensure the resilience of these efforts.

The climate alignment of financial stocks and flows can be measured by looking at the subsequent alignment of real-economy investments and activities. OECD analysis shows that very low volumes of real-economy investment are, in fact, aligned with climate mitigation objectives (Box 9.1). Moreover, climate-alignment assessments of financial assets based on a number of different methodologies have all found a high degree of misalignment of financial stock with the Paris Agreement temperature goal (Noels and Jachnik, 2022[3])

Despite these initial results, tracking progress on alignment with the level of detail needed to effectively assess the impact of decarbonisation incentives remains difficult. This is due to the lack of granular climate performance data and reference points, comparable and transparent methodologies, and credible metrics (OECD, 2021[4]). Moreover, the inconsistencies and gaps in the methodologies used to assess the climate alignment of finance can allow for greenwashing and threaten the environmental integrity of efforts to channel finance into climate-aligned activities. For example, a partial coverage of asset classes could result in decisions to move emissions-intensive assets from listed to unlisted companies where the latter are currently less scrutinised by climate-alignment assessment methodologies. These circumstances could result in, on aggregate, emissions not being reduced though disclosure is improved (Noels and Jachnik, 2022[3]).

Box 9.1. Measuring the alignment of real-economy investments with climate mitigation policy goals

Initial assessments of the alignment of real-economy investments with climate mitigation policy goals conducted by the OECD demonstrated that investments can only be considered aligned with climate mitigation policy objectives in very limited cases.

Between 2019 and 2021, the OECD Research Collaborative on Tracking Finance for Climate Action conducted three country-sector pilot studies, covering the building sector in the United Kingdom (Jachnik and Dobrinevski, 2021[5]), the transport sector in Latvia (Dobrinevski and Jachnik, 2020[6]), and the manufacturing sector in Norway (Dobrinevski and Jachnik, 2020[7]). The results indicated that in all cases only very limited volumes of investments could be considered as aligned. For example, the results of the United Kingdom building sector pilot study showed that less than 1% of new construction investments between 2010 and 2019 could be considered consistent with net-zero objectives (Jachnik and Dobrinevski, 2021[5]).

The outcomes of the pilot assessments were significantly influenced by the availability of comprehensive and/or granular data on investments, financing, GHG emissions, and the level of detail required by alignment reference points used. While emissions and decarbonisation efforts are best analysed at the financial asset level, reference points (including climate mitigation scenarios) are typically provided at a higher level of aggregation (e.g. at the sector or country level).

Moreover, the studies revealed challenges in exposing the direct links between real-economy investments, and financing sources and financial intermediaries. While real-economy investments can be traced more closely than financial stocks to climate objectives, decisions relating to capital allocation in the financial system – as directed by market practices including ESG ratings and related investment approaches – strongly influence real-economy progress on climate action.

Figure 9.1. Investments in newly built residential buildings, by Energy Performance Certificate band, 2010-2019 (GBP billions)

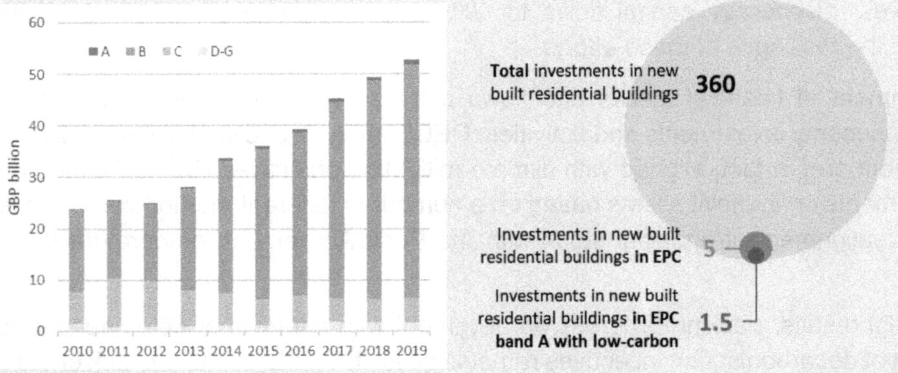

Source: (Jachnik and Dobrinevski, 2021[5])

Strengthening financial market practices

Financial institutions committing to net zero is becoming mainstream, whether they are asset owners or multinational banks, including under the umbrella of coalitions.[2] A number of initiatives set out guidance on metrics and information to be reported by investors and financial institutions in relation to their low-emissions transition and net-zero strategies. These include, among others, the Financial Stability Board (FSB)-affiliated Taskforce for Climate-related Financial Disclosures (TCFD) to establish disclosure guidance; and the International Financial Reporting Standards (IFRS) International Sustainability Standards Board (ISSB) to create reporting standards.

Yet, investment decisions are still hampered by different uncertainties, notably relating to national climate policies (e.g. support schemes, carbon pricing) and new or unproven technologies which will increasingly be relied upon to further reduce GHG emissions. Additionally, in practice, many net-zero initiatives take the form of coalitions or frameworks, which, while putting forward overall guidance, do not provide a concrete methodological approach for tracking progress (Noels and Jachnik, 2022[3]). Even among initiatives providing tracking methodologies, there is significant variation in alignment assessment results due to differences in perspectives (and a lack of consensus on a range of methodological dimensions). For example, some methodology providers find absolute emissions metrics to be more relevant whereas others prefer an “economic intensity contraction” approach (where GHG emissions are divided by economic output) as it is more closely linked to decoupling. This means the same financial asset could be deemed climate-aligned by some assessments but not by others (Noels and Jachnik, 2022[3]).

There is also evidence that financial market participants hesitate to provide transition financing for companies on the basis of insufficient clarity on how to assess credible corporate alignment with a pathway in line with the Paris Agreement temperature goal (OECD, 2022[8]). This highlights the need to continue to further develop indicators, metrics, and methodologies to assess climate alignment of assets to better inform financial market participants and policy (Noels and Jachnik, 2022[3]). These challenges are further addressed below in the context of ESG investing.

Within industries, some GHG-intensive firms that are acknowledging stranded assets and making progress on their transition plans are showing an improved enterprise value (OECD, 2021[4]; OECD, 2021[9]). This firm-level progress is vital for financial institutions whose own net-zero targets will rely on GHG reductions by their borrowers or portfolio assets. Fully capturing such real-economy progress and managing portfolio risks in assessments of climate alignment will require comprehensive coverage of financial assets and asset classes as well as further approaches at the portfolio level (Noels and Jachnik, 2022[3]).

Alignment of ESG rating and investing approaches with the net-zero transition

ESG investing refers to the process of incorporating environmental, social and governance (ESG) factors into asset allocation and risk decisions so as to generate sustainable, long-term financial returns. ESG investing has become a leading form of sustainable finance due to its perceived potential to deliver financial returns, align with societal values, and contribute to sustainability, including climate-related objectives.

Driven by market participants showing greater awareness of the impacts of physical and climate-transition risks on financial stability and market efficiency, ESG rating providers and investment funds are increasingly integrating metrics aligned with environmental impact, climate risk mitigation, and strategies to scale use of renewable energy and climate-related innovation. In this way, ESG rating and investing approaches can help to align finance flows with net-zero objectives and accelerate the transition. They could also strengthen the resilience of the transition itself by ensuring that finance flows are evaluated not only with respect to climate, but also with respect to their interlinked governance and social implications. This will be important where adverse outcomes related to corporate governance, people and communities could undermine progress made on climate.

There has been important progress in developing ESG rating and investing approaches, particularly with respect to the environmental pillar (Box 9.2). However, to better harness these methodologies as tools to accelerate net-zero transitions, it will be important that they focus less on rewarding disclosure practices and more on rewarding alignment of issuer activities with climate objectives. This will provide markets with the information needed to better align their investments with ESG criteria and thereby climate objectives.

Box 9.2. The environmental pillar of ESG progress and opportunities for reform

ESG rating providers appear to give greater weight to the existence of climate-related corporate policies, targets and objectives than actual climate metrics, namely a corporation's reductions in greenhouse gas emissions and emissions intensity over time and increased investment in climate mitigation, adaptation and renewable energy.

OECD analysis finds that high environmental pillar scores do not always mean that a firm has reduced its greenhouse gas emissions and emissions intensity over time or increased use of and investment in renewable energy. Rather, it is the firm's disclosure of climate risks and opportunities that is prioritised. This makes the environmental pillar a less useful tool for assessing or indicating a company's current level of short-term reduction in greenhouse gas emissions and emissions intensity, and investment in environmental R&D and renewable energy.

While the E pillar of ESG ratings can be an important tool to ensure capital is allocated to investments that support an accelerated transition to net zero, to fully realise this potential the above shortcomings need to be addressed by both government policies and good practices.

Source: (Boffo, Marshall and Patalano, 2020[10]) (OECD, 2022[11])

Further, in harnessing the role of ESG investing in a resilient transition, reform efforts need to take into account ESG investing in emerging markets and developing economies, and not just the developed world. This is critical as carbon emissions in developing countries have not yet peaked (see Chapter 5) and these economies will need significant and increasing financing to reduce emissions and adapt to climate impacts.

However, emerging economies can often be at a disadvantage due to lower ESG scores and low investment allocations from ESG funds, as highlighted by a recent International Monetary Fund (IMF) study (IMF, 2022[12]). Addressing issues of higher cost of capital; strengthening enabling environments for investments; supporting the development and deepening of financial systems; and carrying out risk-based due diligence aligned with OECD recommendations can support the financial sector and businesses in responsibly engaging in developing countries and higher-risk sectors and supply chains.

Metrics to support tracking financial sector progress against net-zero commitments

To ensure that market practices (including ESG investing) and related climate policies encourage climate-aligned finance flows, it is necessary to track the progress financial institutions and investors towards their net-zero commitments. One of the main obstacles to this is the current lack of comparable and quality metrics.

For example, interim emissions reductions targets (e.g. for 2030) are often set at disparate target years and values in contradiction with emerging good practices (such as using harmonised interim target years or science-backed scenarios). In addition, as interim targets are not required to be set along linear trajectories from the base year to the target year, they can range widely across financial institutions in terms of their level of ambition. This raises obvious questions about how such targets are established and precisely what "progress" means across various non-linear pathways, creating a number of uncertainties.

For example, is a financial institution that is advancing in a linear manner toward a modest interim target making more or less progress than a peer that is falling short of a much more ambitious interim target, particularly if the latter has achieved greater reduction of gross emissions during this period? How does one evaluate the ambition and credibility of a target based on known technologies such as the production of electric cars versus unproven or nascent innovations such as hydrogen fuel? To what extent does a pathway depend on GHG emissions reductions versus carbon offsets (and do such offsets align with environmental integrity)? Indeed, corporate-related financial assets are more often found to be misaligned with climate goals when assessment methodologies explicitly exclude the use of offsets (Noels and Jachnik, 2022[3]).

Clarity on these dimensions is important in ensuring consistency and comparability across measurements and the assessment of progress towards commitments. A range of complementary metrics will be needed to provide a more nuanced and comprehensive view of the contribution of finance to reaching climate policy goals (Noels and Jachnik, 2022[3]). Aside from GHG performance metrics, non-GHG-based metrics relating to production plans, capital expenditure and technology-based metrics can usefully inform progress towards climate policy goals. Such metrics should cover different temporal perspectives (backward-looking, current and forward-looking). Moreover, more methodological developments for financial asset classes other than corporate equity (i.e. real estate and sovereign bonds) are needed to cover all portfolio segments of financial institutions (Noels and Jachnik, 2022[3]).

Achieving progress in the short-, medium- (through interim targets) and long-term (net-zero targets) suggests that financial intermediaries need to make fundamental changes to their portfolios and lending policies, and strategic and operational changes to incorporate climate transition at many levels within organisations. To this end, the G20 Sustainable Finance Working Group's 2022 Sustainable Finance Report includes a recommendation that governments and international organisations and networks could consider measures to enhance the accountability and comparability of financial sector net-zero commitments in a manner consistent with their mandates and objectives (G20 SFWG, 2022[13]).

Progress on harnessing key finance flows

Drawing on two specific examples, this section focuses on: (i) harnessing Foreign Direct Investment (FDI) and specific recommendations of the OECD FDI Qualities Policy Toolkit; and (ii) the operation of investment treaties as an important part of the public policy framework governing finance flows. Both FDI and the finance flows associated with investment treaties represent substantial shifts in capital that need to be increasingly directed towards a resilient net-zero transition.

Accelerating the transition to net zero through foreign direct investment

FDI can play a critical role in promoting sustainable development. For the host country, it can support growth and innovation, generate quality jobs, raise living standards and improve environmental sustainability. It can accelerate the net-zero transition through: (i) direct investment in technologies, services and infrastructure; and (ii) "FDI spillovers" or the added positive impact of FDI by multinational enterprises with access to innovative low-carbon technologies and operating procedures that could boost environmental performance.

FDI can contribute to environmental and climate objectives, particularly when coming from jurisdictions with more stringent environmental regulation – FDI accounted for 30% of global new investments in renewable energy in 2020. However, foreign investors can also worsen environmental outcomes; for example, by offshoring highly polluting activities to countries with less stringent regulations or inducing a race to the bottom with respect to environmental standards as countries compete to attract FDI. The latter, in particular, can inhibit the resilience of the net-zero transition.

Uncertainty and unpredictability are barriers to green or climate-aligned FDI. Green investors, like all investors, seek a stable, predictable, and transparent investment environment in which to identify bankable projects. Efforts to mobilise green investment to support an accelerated and resilient net-zero transition will fail to meet these criteria unless governments ensure a regulatory environment that provides investors with fair treatment and confidence in the rule of law, notwithstanding disruptions or shocks.

The OECD FDI Qualities Policy Toolkit (OECD, 2022[14]) outlines specific enabling conditions and policies to attract investment contributing to reducing GHG emissions, and relating to (i) governance, (ii) regulation, and (iii) targeted support measures.

Governance

Setting a clear, long-term net-zero transition trajectory linked to the national vision for growth and development is critical. This allows investors to understand transition risks and attracts foreign investment that contributes to the country's climate agenda. Transparency and predictability, which are critical for investment decisions in general, matter even more when considering returns on investments with long time horizons.

A strategic framework for addressing climate change should integrate climate objectives across sector strategies and plans; translate national-level emissions targets into science-based targets at the sector level; include key performance indicators to measure outputs and outcomes and establish procedures to collaborate effectively with other relevant public agencies and stakeholders – including the private sector. Clearly delineating the role of private investors, both domestic and foreign, in achieving climate objectives can help tailor investment promotion efforts to target investors.

Measuring and tracking the impact of FDI on carbon emissions, and its potential contribution to decarbonisation can also help identify appropriate policy responses. Collection and production of timely and internationally comparable data on FDI by sector is important for monitoring its contribution to decarbonisation.

Regulation

The OECD Policy Framework for Investment (PFI) (OECD, 2015[15]) and its chapter on Green Growth provide insights on global good practices for creating a regulatory framework conducive to green investment; reiterating the governance recommendations referred to above. More specifically, the OECD FDI Regulatory Restrictiveness Index suggests that some sectors critical to decarbonisation efforts remain partly off-limits to foreign investors in many countries – notably, transport, electricity generation and distribution, and construction. Removing discriminatory restrictions on FDI in these sectors would open up opportunities for climate-aligned FDI and associated spillovers such as knowledge transfer and technology deployment. Services typically associated with lower carbon emissions and in some cases those that are crucial for energy-saving technologies (e.g. digital services) are also often restricted from foreign participation. This stops FDI from contributing to the net-zero transition.

Regulatory reform to address this, as well as environmental regulations and standards that reinforce climate goals more broadly, can help level the playing field for foreign investments in climate-friendly technologies, services and infrastructure. Countries should regularly assess whether their technology and performance standards are in line with long-term climate goals.

Targeted support measures

Policies conducive to FDI will not automatically result in a substantial increase in green or climate-aligned FDI. In addition to general climate policies that internalise the cost of emissions, targeted financial and technical support, and information sharing can help address market failures that reduce the competitiveness of climate-aligned investments.

In particular, investment promotion agencies (IPAs) are key players in bridging information gaps that may otherwise hinder the realisation of foreign investments and their potential sustainable development impacts. The primary role of IPAs is to create awareness of existing investment opportunities, attract investors, and facilitate their establishment and expansion in the economy, including by linking them to potential local partners. Most IPAs prioritise certain types of investments over others. The prioritisation approaches and tools adopted by IPAs should reflect the national investment promotion strategy and the climate considerations embedded therein. Since few economies can offer an attractive environment for all low-carbon technologies and all segments of their value chains, IPAs should review and identify specific economic activities where they see potential to develop and scale low-carbon activities. They should also design targeted investment promotion packages combining a variety of tools that range from intelligence gathering (e.g. market studies) and sector-specific events (inward and outward missions) to proactive investor engagement (one-to-one meetings, email/phone campaigns, enquiry handling).

Achieving a role for investment treaties in climate-aligned finance

Investment treaties are an important part of the public policy framework governing finance flows but remain largely unregulated when it comes to alignment with climate objectives, specifically Article 2.1(c) of the Paris Agreement (Novik and Gaukrodger, 2022[16]). In its April 2022 report, Working Group III of the IPCC expressed concern that much of international governance still promotes fossil fuels and highlighted the role of investment treaties and investor-state dispute settlement.

Investment treaties (including investment chapters and provisions in trade agreements as well as stand-alone investment treaties) are entered into by governments to protect and encourage foreign investment. They provide treaty-covered investors with protection from financially adverse impacts of government action (i.e. policy action that may financially injure projects funded by an investor) in host countries. Government actions that are covered include policy action that could result in discrimination, uncompensated expropriation of property, a failure to provide "fair and equitable treatment", or limitations on rights to transfer capital. In this way, investment treaties can de-risk foreign investment, acting as a form of political risk insurance, and in instances where compensation claims can be made via investor-state dispute settlement (ISDS) – a process of ad-hoc international arbitration.

In the context of the transition to net zero, policy efforts to curb demand and limit supply of fossil fuels will have financial impacts on investors, likely impacting fossil fuel projects funded by foreign investment and covered by an investment treaty. In such a scenario, i.e. where a government revokes licenses or permits to restrict the development of fossil fuels in its territory or detrimentally affects fossil fuel projects funded by a treaty-protected foreign investor, foreign investors can claim against the government in ISDS for damages, including loss of profits.

While there have been few government policies creating stranded fossil fuel assets to date, some of the first non-discriminatory OECD government policies directed at gradual exits from coal have generated major claims in ISDS (Braun, 2021[17]) or agreements to pay billions of Euros, reportedly, in exchange for release from ISDS claims (Reuters, 2020[18]). This is an important consideration when looking to bolster the resilience of the global net-zero transition. The implementation of net-zero commitments by governments may be deterred by the threat of ISDS litigation or awards, with the issuing of such awards potentially diverting crucial public finance flows from climate mitigation, particularly in the global south.

Investor-state dispute settlements have the highest average claim for payment and highest average number of binding awards requiring payment of any legal system in the world (Gaukrodger, 2022[19]). Between June 2017 and May 2020, the mean amount claimed in ISDS cases was USD 1.1 billion. The mean amount awarded to a successful claimant has recently risen since from June 2017 by more than 184% to USD 315.5 million (Hodgson, Kryvoi and Hrcka, 2021[20]).

Fossil fuel coverage and claims are often at issue. As of May 2022, at least 231 ISDS cases were a result of investments in fossil fuels – constituting close to 20% of the total known number of cases (Tienhaara et al., 2022[21]). Seven of the ten largest ISDS damages awards against governments under investment treaties have involved fossil fuel investor claimants, each for over USD 1 billion and all in the last 15 years (UNCTAD, 2022[22]). Law firms are advising investors who are likely to be adversely affected financially by government action pursuant to their climate-change commitments, such as the phase-down of coal and other fossil fuels, to engage in corporate structuring to maximise access to ISDS.

There is limited evidence of governments considering the alignment of their investment treaties with the Paris Agreement or global climate-accountability mechanisms such as the Task Force for Climate-related Financial Disclosures (TCFD) and the Glasgow Financial Alliance for Net Zero (GFANZ). Given widespread government commitments to net zero, and, in particular, to ending support for coal and all fossil fuels abroad, it is important that they prioritise such alignments. This should include analysing the substantial finance flows associated with fossil fuels that are currently supported by investment treaties, particularly in light of the insurance-like characteristics of the support provided to treaty-covered investment.

There is growing recognition of investor-state dispute settlements as potential deterrents to ambitious government policy on climate change and the need to rethink investment treaty policies and frameworks. Strong public-private collaboration on a range of conceptual and operational issues will be important for such change. Well-designed investment treaties can contribute to climate-aligned finance and investment, prevent fossil fuel lock-in, drive action towards net-zero emissions and better support the resilience of the transition.

Private sector-led action towards resilience and integrity

Businesses play a key role in scaling climate ambition and implementing net-zero transition, channelling policy commitments and related finance and investment into aligned activities across the real economy. Net-zero commitments are growing among companies and financial institutions. More than one-third of the world's largest publicly traded companies have set net-zero targets (Science Based Targets, 2021[23]; Net-Zero Tracker, 2022[24]).

The private sector also has an important role in ensuring the resilience of these commitments and their transition pathways. First, by ensuring commitments are being implemented with integrity without greenwashing (United Nations, 2022[2]) and safeguarding against adverse impacts across other areas of businesses' operations or responsibilities. Second, by strengthening the resilience of global supply chains that are critical for the net-zero transition. In examining how businesses can drive progress in these areas, this section draws on the OECD responsible business conduct (RBC) framework to support these efforts.

Implementing net-zero commitments with integrity

The proliferation of sustainability standards over the past 30 years has created a crowded and sometimes confusing landscape for business and policy makers alike. A broad range of net-zero guides, coalitions, frameworks, methodologies, benchmarks and standards have emerged to support the private sector in setting GHG emissions-reduction targets; measuring, cutting and disclosing their GHG emissions; and aligning their activities with net-zero transition pathways. While this has led to an increase in net-zero pledges, there has been growing concern about their credibility.

Preliminary OECD analysis and external assessments, notably the recent report of the UN High Level Expert Group on the Net-Zero Emissions Commitments of Non-State Entities (UN HLEG) (United Nations, 2022[2]), reveal considerable variation in how voluntary private sector climate commitments materialise in practice. They also raise concerns about the quality of commitments with regard to the credibility and transparency of their methodological approaches.

This has led to significant concerns over greenwashing, with businesses committing to net zero while simultaneously investing in fossil fuels; engaging in environmentally destructive activities such as deforestation; purchasing questionable carbon credits rather than reducing emissions throughout their value chains; and lobbying in such a way that goes against climate objectives. The UN HLEG report identifies the lack of a level playing field as an important underlying barrier to implementing net zero with credibility (United Nations, 2022[2]).

In addressing these challenges, lessons can be drawn from the OECD Guidelines for Multinational Enterprises (MNEs) on Responsible Business Conduct (RBC) and the OECD Due Diligence Guidance (together forming the "RBC Framework") on supporting a resilient net-zero transition through the credible implementation of net-zero commitments by businesses (Box 9.3).

Box 9.3. The OECD Responsible Business Conduct Framework

RBC sets out an expectation that all businesses – regardless of their legal status, size, ownership or sector – avoid and address negative impacts of their operations while contributing to sustainable development in the countries where they operate. This expectation is enshrined in the OECD Guidelines for MNEs and related OECD due diligence guidance.

OECD Guidelines for MNEs

The OECD Guidelines for Multinational Enterprises (the "MNE Guidelines") consist of government-backed recommendations to multinational enterprises ("MNEs") operating in or from Adhering countries. The MNE Guidelines are currently the only authoritative, government-backed instrument on RBC operating at the international level. The recommendations cover all areas of business responsibility: disclosure, human rights, employment and industrial relations, consumer interests, bribery and corruption, science and technology, competition, taxation and the environment. The MNE Guidelines include the expectation that businesses carry out risk-based due diligence to identify, prevent and mitigate actual and potential adverse impacts related to each of these areas and account for how these impacts are addressed.

A number of provisions across different Chapters of the Guidelines intersect with climate mitigation and adaptation considerations for business. For example, and in the context of mitigation specifically, the Environment Chapter provides that enterprises should have an environmental management system in place, which includes establishing "measurable objectives and, where appropriate, targets for improved environmental performance and resource utilisation". This expectation also includes periodically reviewing the continuing relevance of these objectives and that where appropriate, "targets should be consistent with relevant national policies and international environmental commitments".

The Environment Chapter also provides that businesses should "continually seek to improve corporate environmental performance at the level of the enterprise and, where appropriate, of its supply chain" and references a number of activities including: the "development and provision of products or services that […] reduce greenhouse gas emissions"; "promoting higher levels of awareness among customers of the environmental implications of using the products and services of the enterprise, including, by providing accurate information on their products (for example, on greenhouse gas emissions […]"; and "exploring and assessing ways of improving the environmental performance of the enterprise over the longer term; for instance, by developing strategies for emission reduction".

Importantly, a number of the expectations related to climate-change responsibilities extend beyond the Environment Chapter and are embedded in chapters on General Policies, Disclosure, Science and Technology, Human Rights, Competition and Consumer Interests.

Targeted update to the MNE Guidelines

The Working Party on Responsible Business Conduct is considering options to ensure that the MNE Guidelines and their implementation remain fit for purpose. Pursuant to this, in 2021, the Working Party initiated a Stocktaking of the MNE Guidelines to help identify key issues for a potential targeted update. The Stocktaking Report identified climate change as a priority issue and text on climate change has been added to a proposed updated draft of the MNE Guidelines. The public consultation on the draft ended in February 2023, with the outcome of the targeted update expected to be issued later this year.

OECD Due Diligence Guidance for RBC

To help businesses (including financial institutions and investors) implement the MNE Guidelines, the OECD developed the Due Diligence Guidance for RBC as well as specific sector guidance. These provide concrete recommendations on how businesses can identify, prevent and mitigate actual and potential adverse impacts of their operations (including in their supply chains, business relationships and investments) on people and the planet while contributing to sustainable development.

The core measures for implementing RBC due diligence are outlined below (Figure 9.2). These six steps together with detailed practical actions and examples for implementing them are described in more detail in the OECD Due Diligence Guidance.

Figure 9.2. The due diligence process

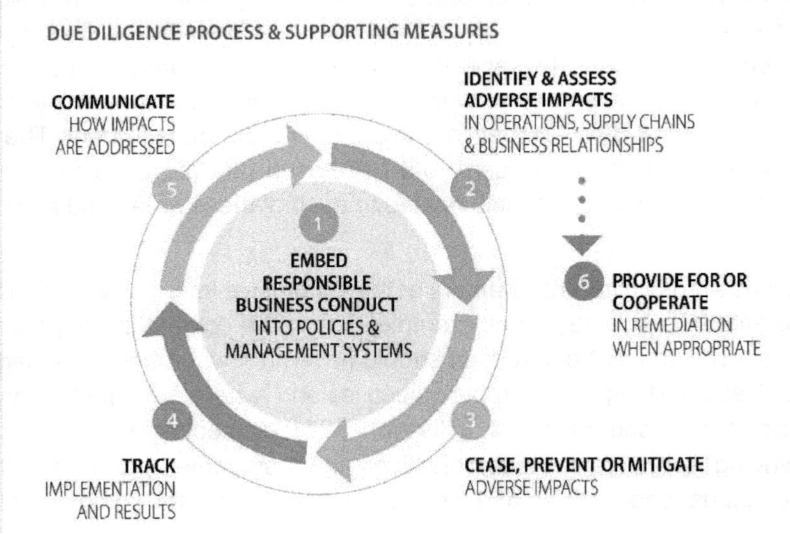

Source: (OECD, 2011[25]); (OECD, 2018[26]); (OECD, 2018[27]); (OECD, 2017[28]); (OECD, 2017[29]); (OECD, 2016[30]); (OECD/FAO, 2016[31]).

RBC expectations relevant to the net-zero transition include businesses having a responsibility to i) reduce GHG emissions and the adverse climate-related impacts of their operations on people and the planet; and ii) strengthen the climate resilience of companies, including across supply chains, to address and adapt to the impacts of climate change (this extends to addressing impacts on workers, local communities and the natural environment) (OECD, 2021[32]).

The comprehensive nature of the RBC framework means that in implementing net-zero commitments (and the expectations referred to above), businesses are also required to take into account the interlinkages with other areas of business responsibility including those extending to disclosure, science and technology, human rights, workers, competition and consumer interests (OECD, 2021[32]). In this way, the MNE Guidelines offer a framework to support businesses in avoiding or mitigating adverse impacts stemming from the implementation of net-zero commitments and their transition pathways, thereby strengthening the credibility and consequently the resilience of net-zero transitions globally.

Building the resilience of supply chains critical to the transition

The comprehensive approach of the RBC framework also provides guidance for businesses, trade unions, and governments in strengthening the resilience of global supply chains more broadly (OECD, 2021[33]). This is relevant to not only building robust supply chains in response to the impacts of climate change but ensuring that supply chains critical to the net-zero transition can bounce back from global shocks and disruptions (including, but also going beyond, those related to climate impacts).

The debate on how to build long-term resilience in supply chains, including how to diversify supply chains while remaining unwaveringly committed to open and rules-based trade, is at the forefront of policy discussions following the COVID-19 pandemic and has been amplified most recently by Russia's unprovoked war against Ukraine (see also Chapter 3).

This is especially evident in the context of sourcing critical raw materials needed for the transition to renewable energy. As mentioned in Chapter 5, achieving the climate mitigation objectives of the Paris Agreement would mean quadrupling minerals supply for clean energy by 2040 (IEA, 2021[34]). To diversify sourcing of these materials, sourcing from conflict-affected or high-risk areas will be unavoidable. The production of critical minerals is highly concentrated in a few countries, including areas where RBC-related risks are prevalent (Figure 9.3) (Katz, 2021[35]). For example, it is estimated that nearly 50% or more of current volumes of cobalt, copper and are found in areas with significant governance challenges (IEA, 2021[34]). Recent estimates also suggest that more than half of the world's resources of energy-transition minerals and metals are located on or near the lands of Indigenous peoples, whose rights and claims over their lands and natural resources require specific processes for extracting companies and related government authorities (Owen et al., 2022[36])

Figure 9.3. Public reports of RBC-related risks by mineral supply chain and by region (2017-2019)

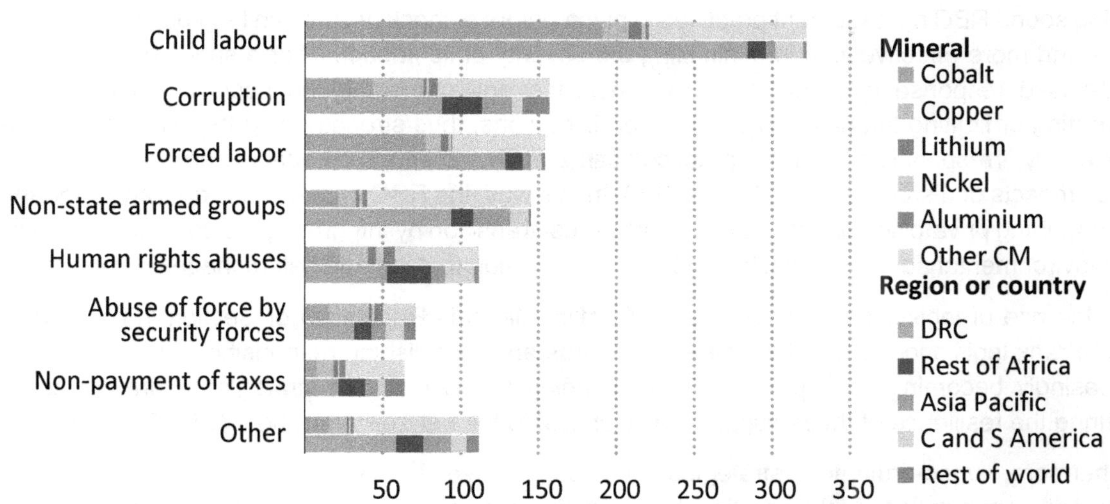

Source: (IEA, 2022[37]).

Incidences of RBC-related adverse impacts can erode public support for mining projects and increase scrutiny from downstream industries, investors and civil society. This potentially leads to short-term production disruptions and local and international resistance to mining investments. This may, in turn, limit the supply of critical minerals and metals, jeopardising the resilience of the net-zero transition. Failure to properly manage these risks may also expose governments and companies to regulatory, ethical and reputational criticism.

RBC standards play an important role in supporting the responsible operation of minerals supply chains. By providing guidance on how to mitigate adverse risks and impacts, including in a way that is necessary to attract needed investment, the OECD Due Diligence Guidance for Responsible Supply Chains of Minerals from Conflict-Affected and High-Risk Areas (the Minerals Guidance) and the OECD Due Diligence Guidance for Meaningful Stakeholder Engagement in the Extractive Sector can help businesses and governments strengthen the durability of critical minerals supply chains through RBC. This, in turn, supports the resilience of the net-zero transition, given its reliance on energy-transition minerals and metals (Box 9.4).

Box 9.4. Shared standards on RBC in promoting responsible supply of critical raw materials

Shared standards and practices on RBC are essential to promote trust, facilitate trade and ensure the sustainable supply of goods (see also Box 10.1). These elements are all critical to building the resilience and durability of supply chains, and their ability to bounce back from global shocks and disruptions.

An inability to identify and mitigate environmental and social harms can make it difficult to obtain – and maintain – a social licence to operate; exacerbating community tensions and leading to community pressure, adverse publicity and regulatory challenges. There have been numerous cases in recent years where local opposition has stopped or slowed new minerals developments; for example, high-profile lithium projects in Bolivia and Serbia (IEA, 2022[37]).

Specific supply chain incidents may also give rise to short-term supply disruptions with implications for supply chains and prices. For example, safety failures can harm workers and lead to long-term interruptions to operations. In addition, corruption in the mining sector and a volatile business climate appear to be associated with periodic shut-downs and shake-downs of mine sites producing energy transition minerals – which all can be better identified and mitigated when robust RBC due diligence is conducted.

Having sound RBC management practices in place before a shock occurs can help businesses respond faster and more effectively, thus minimising the severity of its impact. After a shock has occurred, an RBC-based response can contribute to minimising environmental and social impacts while also preventing or limiting the cascading effects of disruptions, thus strengthening the entire supply chain. Conversely, irresponsible business practices can amplify the knock-on effects and environmental and social impacts of disruptions (OECD, 2021[33]). In this way, the RBC framework is also an important tool for supporting private sector action aligned with a just transition by integrating the consideration of social and environmental adverse impacts into business decision making and risk management processes.

With the rise of legislation such as the EU Conflict Minerals Regulation or Section 1502 of the U.S. Dodd-Frank legislation, observing shared standards and establishing responsible sources of supply is increasingly becoming an imperative for companies and a factor of strategic security of supply in ensuring the resilience of these supply chains critical to the net-zero transition. (OECD, 2021[33])

Furthermore, unco-ordinated strategies and competitive behaviours (i.e. strategic stockpiling, commodity speculation, fuel price rises) among key actors, including governments, engaged in the global race to supply and procure minerals could inadvertently derail the net-zero transition and impede the scaled development of clean technologies needed to meet global climate goals. Promoting a level playing field and strengthening policy efforts aimed at all tiers of the value chain – from mining to end-use products – based on RBC standards can create a common baseline and help foster an orderly and fair transition toward net zero (OECD, 2021[33]).

Source: OECD, IEA.

Chapter conclusions

An accelerated and resilient net-zero transition necessitates the climate alignment of finance flows. Strengthening market practices is critical in enabling these efforts and safeguarding the resilience of the transition by ensuring investments result in long-term net-zero-aligned action in the real economy. Although there is progress, market practices require further reform in driving these efforts. This includes improving global collaboration, interoperability and comparability across ESG investing approaches; strengthening the availability and use of reliable, comparable, and high-quality metrics and data to assess physical and transition climate risks and opportunities; and harnessing ESG approaches to focus more on the alignment of real-economy investments with climate objectives.

In addition, government policies can work to harness and redirect key public and private finance flows to accelerate the net-zero transition and ensure they do not increase the vulnerability or fragility of systems, undermining the resilience of the transition itself. Scaling and directing Foreign Direct Investment (FDI) to align with net-zero objectives, as recommended by the OECD FDI Qualities Policy Toolkit[3], is a key example. Exploring how investment treaties potentially threaten the resilience of the net-zero transition or support the climate alignment of finance flows, is a second.

More broadly, businesses are a critical conduit for realising emissions reductions and adaptation through their direct operations and across their supply chains. Private sector net-zero commitments need to be implemented with integrity. This means not only avoiding greenwashing but taking into account "just transition" priorities across all areas of business operations. The OECD Responsible Business Conduct (RBC) framework guides governments and businesses in implementing these responsibilities, including on supply-chain due diligence to improve supply-chain resilience (especially in the context of climate impacts). OECD Due Diligence Guidance can also play a key role in the responsible and sustainable sourcing of critical raw materials required for the transition to renewable energy.

Notes

1 The OECD FDI Qualities Policy Toolkit offers a framework for governments to leverage the catalytic role of foreign direct investment in financing the SDGs and supporting an inclusive and sustainable recovery and future growth.

2 For example, the UN-convened Asset Owners Net Zero Alliance and the Net Zero Asset Managers both launched in 2019, the UN's Environmental Programme's Financial Initiative's (UNEP FI) Net Zero Banking Alliance launched in 2021, and the Glasgow Financial Alliance for Net Zero (GFANZ) launched at COP26 in 2021, bringing together existing and new net-zero finance initiatives, representing 450 financial firms with a total and estimated USD 130 trillion in assets under management.

3 The OECD FDI Qualities Policy Toolkit offers a framework for governments to leverage the catalytic role of foreign direct investment in financing the SDGs, and supporting an inclusive and sustainable recovery and future growth.

References

Boffo, R., C. Marshall and R. Patalano (2020), *ESG Investing: Environmental Pillar Scoring and Reporting*, http://www.oecd.org/finance/esg-investing-environmental-pillar-scoring-and-reporting.pdf. [10]

Braun, S. (2021), *Multi-billion euro lawsuits derail climate action*, Deutsche Welle, https://www.dw.com/en/energy-charter-treaty-ect-coal-fossil-fuels-climate-environment-uniper-rwe/a-57221166. [17]

Dobrinevski, A. and R. Jachnik (2020), "Exploring options to measure the climate consistency of real economy investments : The manufacturing industries of Norway", *OECD Environment Working Papers*, No. 159, OECD Publishing, Paris, https://doi.org/10.1787/1012bd81-en. [7]

Dobrinevski, A. and R. Jachnik (2020), "Exploring options to measure the climate consistency of real economy investments: The transport sector in Latvia", *OECD Environment Working Papers*, No. 163, OECD Publishing, Paris, https://doi.org/10.1787/48d53aac-en. [6]

G20 SFWG (2022), *2022 G20 Sustainable Finance Report, Sustainable Finance Working Group*, https://g20sfwg.org/wp-content/uploads/2022/10/2022-G20-Sustainable-Finance-Report-2.pdf. [13]

Gaukrodger, D. (2022), "Investment treaties and climate change: The alignment of finance flows under the Paris Agreement", https://www.oecd.org/investment/investment-policy/oecd-background-investment-treaties-finance-flow-alignment.pdf. [19]

Hodgson, M., Y. Kryvoi and D. Hrcka (2021), "2021 Empirical Study: Costs, Damages and Duration in Investor-State Arbitration", https://www.biicl.org/documents/136_isds-costs-damages-duration_june_2021.pdf. [20]

IEA (2022), *Why is ESG so important to critical mineral supplies, and what can we do about it?*, https://www.iea.org/commentaries/why-is-esg-so-important-to-critical-mineral-supplies-and-what-can-we-do-about-it. [37]

IEA (2021), *The Role of Critical Minerals in Clean Energy Transitions*, https://iea.blob.core.windows.net/assets/ffd2a83b-8c30-4e9d-980a-52b6d9a86fdc/TheRoleofCriticalMineralsinCleanEnergyTransitions.pdf. [34]

IMF (2022), *Scaling up Climate Finance in Emerging market and developing economies*. [12]

Jachnik, R. and A. Dobrinevski (2021), "Measuring the alignment of real economy investments with climate mitigation objectives: The United Kingdom's buildings sector", *OECD Environment Working Papers*, No. 172, OECD Publishing, Paris, https://doi.org/10.1787/8eccb72a-en. [5]

Katz, B. (2021), *Making global value chains for critical minerals more resilient through diversification and due diligence*. [35]

Net-Zero Tracker (2022), *Net-Zero Stocktake 2022: Assessing the status and trends of net zero target setting*, https://zerotracker.net/insights/pr-net-zero-stocktake-2022. [24]

Noels, J. and R. Jachnik (2022), *Assessing the climate consistency of finance: taking stock of methodologies and assessing their links to climate mitigation policy objectives*, OECD, https://one.oecd.org/official-document/ENV/EPOC/WPCID(2022)12/REV1/en. [3]

Novik, A. and D. Gaukrodger (2022), *Investment Treaties and Climate Change: Paris Agreement and Net Zero Alignment - agenda*, https://www.oecd.org/investment/investment-policy/draft-agenda-oecd-investment-treaties-climate-change-conference.pdf. [16]

OECD (2022), "ESG ratings and climate transition: An assessment of the alignment of E pillar scores and metrics", *OECD Business and Finance Policy Papers*, No. 06, OECD Publishing, Paris, https://doi.org/10.1787/2fa21143-en. [11]

OECD (2022), *FDI Qualities Policy Toolkit*. [14]

OECD (2022), *OECD Guidance on Transition Finance: Ensuring Credibility of Corporate Climate Transition Plans*, Green Finance and Investment, OECD Publishing, Paris, https://doi.org/10.1787/7c68a1ee-en. [8]

OECD (2021), *Building more resilient and sustainable global value chains through responsible*. [33]

OECD (2021), *ESG Investing and Climate Transition: Market Practices, Issues and Policy Considerations*, https://www.oecd.org/finance/ESG-investing-and-climate-transition-Market-practices-issues-and-policy-considerations.pdf. [4]

OECD (2021), *Financial Markets and Climate Transition: Opportunities, Challenges and Policy Implications*, https://www.oecd.org/finance/Financial-Markets-and-Climate-Transition-Opportunities-Challenges-and-Policy-Implications.pdf. [9]

OECD (2021), *The role of OECD instruments on responsible business conduct in progressing*. [32]

OECD (2018), *OECD Due Diligence Guidance for Responsible Business Conduct*. [26]

OECD (2018), *OECD Due Diligence Guidance for Responsible Supply Chains in the Garment and Footwear Sector*, OECD Publishing, Paris, https://doi.org/10.1787/9789264290587-en. [27]

OECD (2017), *OECD Due Diligence Guidance for Meaningful Stakeholder Engagement in the Extractive Sector*, OECD Publishing, Paris, https://doi.org/10.1787/9789264252462-en. [28]

OECD (2017), *Responsible business conduct for institutional investors: Key considerations for due diligence under the OECD Guidelines for Multinational Enterprises*. [29]

OECD (2016), *OECD Due Diligence Guidance for Responsible Supply Chains of Minerals from Conflict-Affected and High-Risk Areas: Third Edition*, OECD Publishing, Paris, https://doi.org/10.1787/9789264252479-en. [30]

OECD (2015), *Policy Framework for Investment, 2015 Edition*, OECD Publishing, Paris, https://doi.org/10.1787/9789264208667-en. [15]

OECD (2011), *OECD Guidelines for Multinational Enterprises, 2011 Edition*, OECD Publishing, Paris, https://doi.org/10.1787/9789264115415-en. [25]

OECD/FAO (2016), *OECD-FAO Guidance for Responsible Agricultural Supply Chains*, OECD Publishing, Paris, https://doi.org/10.1787/9789264251052-en. [31]

Owen, J. et al. (2022), "Energy transition minerals and their intersection with land-connected peoples", *Nature Sustainability*, https://doi.org/10.1038/s41893-022-00994-6. [36]

Reuters (2020), *German government approves lignite compensation contract*, https://www.reuters.com/business/finance/german-government-approves-lignite-compensation-contract-2020-12-16/. [18]

Science Based Targets (2021), *The Net Zero Standard*, https://sciencebasedtargets.org/net-zero#:~:text=The%20SBTi's%20Corporate%20Net%2DZero,rise%20to%201.5%C2%B0C. [23]

Tienhaara, K. et al. (2022), "Investor-state disputes threaten the global green energy transition", *Science*, Vol. 376/6594, pp. 701-703, https://doi.org/10.1126/science.abo4637. [21]

UNCTAD (2022), "Investment dispute navigator", https://investmentpolicy.unctad.org/investment-dispute-settlement. [22]

UNFCCC (2016), *Decision 1/CP.21 - Report of the Conference of the Parties on its twenty-first session, held in Paris from 30 November to 13 December 2015*, https://unfccc.int/resource/docs/2015/cop21/eng/10a01.pdf#page=2. [1]

United Nations (2022), *Integrity Matters: Net Zero Commitments by Businesses, Financial Institutions, Cities and Regions.* [2]

10 Interlinkages between the net-zero transition and development

Climate change is a global problem requiring globally coordinated responses, meaning that development cooperation has a key role to play in supporting design of policies that align development priorities with climate objectives. This chapter draws on OECD work on aligning development and energy transitions, and greening developing countries' financial systems. It uses these sectoral examples to provide insights into: (i) how a global response to climate action is inherent to resilient climate policy making today, and (ii) the role of development co-operation in supporting aligned transitions towards net zero and countries' development objectives.

This chapter draws on contributions to the Horizontal Project carried out under the responsibility of the Development Assistance Committee.

Achieving the Paris Agreement goals requires a transition towards net-zero emissions globally, with the types and speed of climate action by countries depending on their national circumstances and capabilities. This necessitates a globally co-ordinated response, with policy approaches tailored to differing national circumstances, and financial and non-financial support to developing countries. Due to economic and population dynamics, developing countries are set to account for the bulk of energy generation and consumption – and, on current trajectories, emissions growth – in the coming decades. They will need strong development co-operation providers to enable their net-zero transitions (IEA, 2021[1]).[1]

Given the scale of the climate emergency described in Part I of this report, the development process is now inextricably interwoven with policy responses to climate change. This is apparent in the need to adapt and build resilience to the increasingly severe impacts of climate challenge to which large numbers of people are particularly vulnerable (discussed further in Part III). It is also true as developing countries consider how to accelerate their development process while implementing progress towards net-zero emissions in their national context.

The momentum of development transitions can be leveraged to progress in tandem with transformative action on climate.

This chapter draws on OECD work on aligning development and energy transitions, and greening developing countries' financial systems. It provides insights into: (i) how a global response to climate action is inherent to resilient climate policy making today, and (ii) the role of development co-operation in supporting aligned transitions towards net zero and countries' development objectives.

The role of development co-operation in climate-aligned development

Important synergies or points of alignment exist between development objectives and a resilient net-zero transition, particularly in the longer term. Given the limited resources and financing challenges of developing countries, and the need to avoid redundancies and contradictions in development and climate efforts, understanding the relationship between climate and development is critical (OECD, Forthcoming[2]).

Developing countries' heightened vulnerability to climate change impacts poses broad risks across socio-economic systems. This makes climate adaptation objectives essential and inseparable from the development process. Economic development is a driving force for reshaping sectors and systems, and allows governments to align socio-economic systems with the transition to net zero.

Recent global events have also demonstrated the interconnected nature of development and climate priorities, and the need to consider both in safeguarding the resilience of local and global action towards net zero. For example, amidst the enduring effects of the COVID-19 pandemic and Russia's war of Ukraine, limited fiscal space, volatile market frameworks and significant tightening of monetary policy in response to inflationary shocks may lead developing countries to favour fossil fuel-based technologies (see also Chapter 3). Even in cases where renewable energy is increasingly cheaper than fossil fuel alternatives, financial constraints and the need to universally provide affordable and reliable energy services represent formidable challenges for developing countries (Taskin, 2022[3]). Development co-operation has a crucial and evolving role to play in this process (IEA, 2021[1]). It should provide general support for energy transitions in partner countries and specific support via multilateral and bilateral development banks (OECD, 2021[4]).

IEA analysis finds that policy support, capacity building and direct financing is needed to promote market maturity and lower risks to private capital to increase willingness to invest in net-zero technologies and related projects in developing countries. Development co-operation needs to use all levers of support –

provision of financial resources, capacity building and policy support (OECD, 2019[5]; World Bank, 2020[6]), and has a particular role in supporting just energy transitions in developing countries.

The two sector-focused examples below illustrate how development co-operation can act as a conduit for aligned development and the net-zero transition, and work towards embedding resilience in the net zero transitions.

Aligning climate and development priorities to drive the net-zero transition: the energy sector in developing countries

Meeting developing countries' rising energy demands is important for delivering development priorities, enabling growth and reducing poverty (Stern, 2011[7]; Shahbaz et al., 2018[8]; Burke, Stern and Bruns, 2018[9]). Sustainable Development Goal (SDG) 7 sets the objective of universal access to modern energy services for all and establishes targets to be attained by 2030 for energy access, renewable energies and energy efficiency.

Developing countries generally focus on three main priorities when developing their energy systems:

- **Modern energy services** such as electricity and clean cooking play a crucial role in decreasing poverty, achieving better health and education, and reducing inequalities. Today, 733 million people lack access to electricity and 2.4 billion people lack access to clean cooking appliances and fuels (IEA, IRENA, UNSD, World Bank, WHO, 2022[10]). Even before Russia's invasion of Ukraine, the world was off track to reach universal access to energy by 2030. The ensuing global energy crisis is now expected to increase the number of people living without electricity by nearly 20 million in 2022, mostly driven by an increase in unserved populations in sub-Saharan Africa (IEA, 2022[11]). Insufficient access to finance is a key barrier to progress on energy access: in countries with the largest access deficits, the level of finance is only around one third of required volumes to reach SDG 7 (Sustainable Energy for All, 2021[12]).
- **Energy affordability** is a priority for developing countries in order to meet growing demand and safeguard and build on past development gains. Developing countries collectively make up almost two-thirds of the global population today and will drive global population growth over the coming decades. This population growth, combined with the energy access challenge, rapid urbanisation, growth in industrial activity and increasing demands for a better quality of life translate into developing countries representing the largest sources of global energy demand growth (IEA, 2021[1]).
- **Energy security**. Disruptions in energy supply and systems have the potential to limit economic and societal development. This leads to countries taking a long-term and short-term approach to energy security by addressing energy supply investments in line with development needs and strengthening the ability of the energy system to react to sudden changes in the supply-demand balance (Taskin, 2022[3]).

Developing countries' net-zero transitions must reflect and respond to all three priorities in order to maintain progress in the face of development objectives interlinked with global shocks or disruptions.

Moreover, while all developing countries recognise the universal provision of affordable and reliable energy services as crucial to their development, the specific relevance attached to this priority differs depending on individual countries' development stage. For example, some developing countries may give higher priority to reliability and security, given their economic dependence on hard-to-decarbonise industries like steel and cement. For others, particularly some on the African continent, affordability is the absolute priority, which requires advances on energy and material efficiency to help curtail demand growth (IEA, 2022[13]).

Further, developing countries' existing energy mixes vary widely depending on their level of development, available resources, and policy choices. Some developing countries are among the largest energy consumers globally, while others are major energy suppliers. Some are leading the deployment of clean energy technologies while others are just beginning to strengthen policies for clean energy promotion. Figure 10.1 provides an overview of selected indicators highlighting the different starting points of developing countries in their energy transitions. This demonstrates the importance of taking into account varying developing country contexts when pursuing policy approaches that support development (particularly in the context of energy) transitions and transitions to net zero.

Figure 10.1. Selected indicators relevant for energy transitions

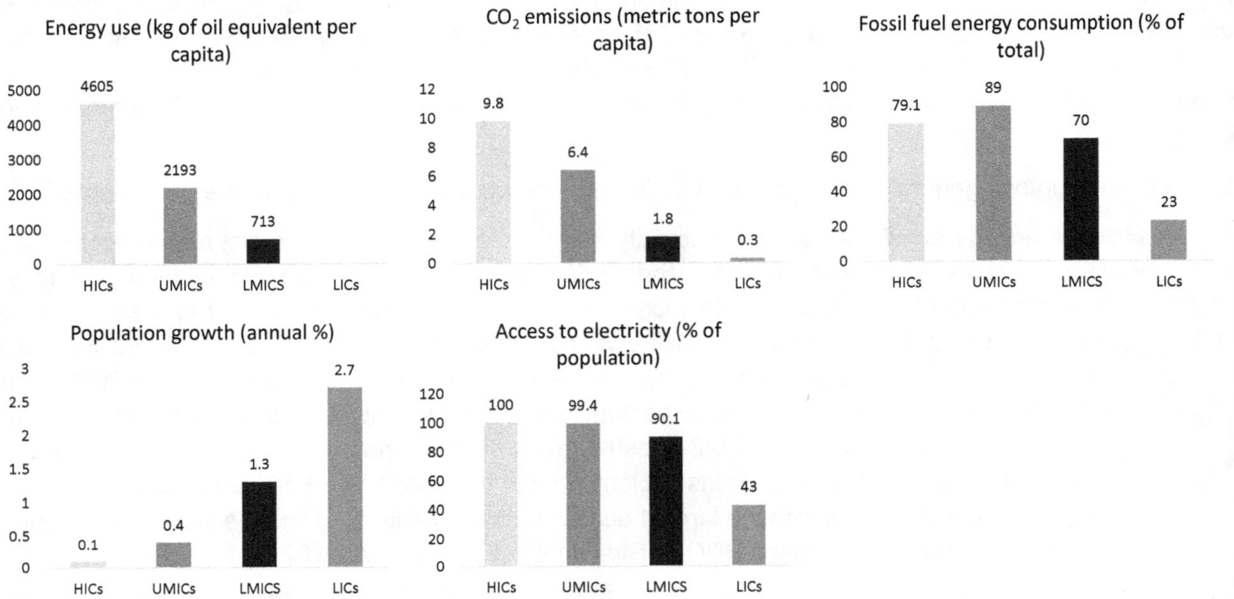

Note: HICs = High-income countries; UMICS = Upper middle-income countries; LMICs = Lower middle-income countries; LICs = Low-income countries. No data available for energy use for LICs.
Source: (World Bank, 2022[14]).

Development finance for the energy sector

Large shares of bilateral and multilateral development finance have supported the energy sector in the last decades, reflecting the importance of energy for development and developing countries' expressed priorities. From the 1980s until the mid-1990s, the share of multilateral development finance for energy oscillated between 15% and 20% of total multilateral finance while bilateral development finance for energy was in the range of 5% to 10% of total bilateral support (Taskin, 2022[3]).

Support to the energy sector usually targets three main areas: i) energy policy, ii) energy distribution and iii) energy supply (see also Chapter 5). All three have a key role to play in net-zero transitions (Figure 10.2). Since 2016-2020, support to renewable energy supply has been the major focus of both bilateral and multilateral institutions, followed by energy distribution and energy policy (Taskin, 2022[3]). A large part (74%) of bilateral official development assistance (ODA) for energy policy has a mitigation objective.

Figure 10.2. Bilateral and multilateral support to energy sub-sectors

Official Development Finance (ODF), in shares, 2016-2020

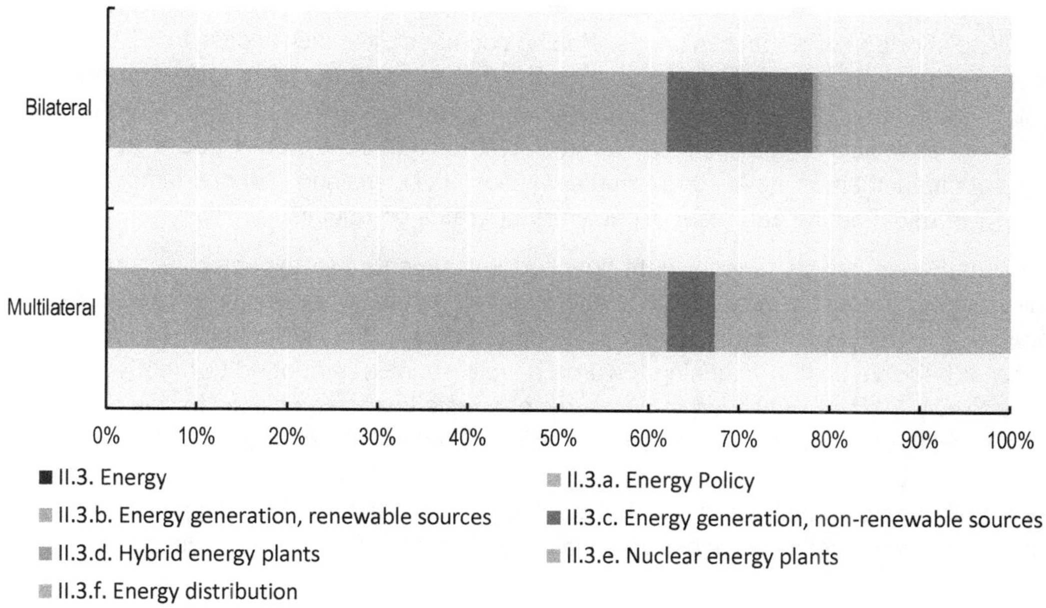

Source: (Taskin, 2022[3]) based on (OECD, 2022[15]).

Support to strengthen energy policy for the transition is particularly important given the wide-ranging and often system-level challenges many developing countries face in pursuing ambitious sustainable energy policies. This includes establishing policy frameworks that enable commercial capital to be mobilised for the transition (OECD, 2022[16]).

The three key target areas for development finance directed to the energy sector of developing countries also demonstrate the overlap between development and net-zero transition priorities for this sector and how development co-operation can be utilised in harnessing synergies between both transitions. Specific challenges and opportunities for this process are addressed below.

Policy and financing challenges for developing country energy transitions

A surge in clean energy investment in developing countries to USD 1 trillion annually in 2030 can help address the emissions growth projected for developing countries while strengthening developing countries' development prospects (IEA, 2021[1]).[2] Renewable energy power production has a low levelised cost of energy (LCOE) in an increasing number of developing countries (IEA, 2021[1]; IRENA, 2022[17]; IEA, 2021[18]).[3] Relatedly, clean energy investment in developing countries is a cost-effective way to reduce emissions on a global basis. Around 35% of the emissions reductions that occur in developing countries over the next decade are estimated to have negative abatement costs, meaning they would reduce emissions and save money (IEA, 2021[1]).

Two interlinked challenges need to be addressed to increase investment:

- First, developing countries have constrained access to finance to drive the transition due in part to underdeveloped domestic financial sectors.
- Second, developing countries often have limited capacities, including to develop ambitious Nationally Determined Contributions (NDCs) and sector-level decarbonisation plans, both of which

involve developing sustainable energy policies and regulations, and integrating these into NDCs and long-term low-emissions strategies (LTSs).

Developing countries lack access to capital

While there is no shortage of global capital, developing countries often lack access to it. This makes upfront investment in, for example, renewable energy difficult. While renewable energy power production is overall cheaper, it is more capital-intensive than fossil-fuel alternatives (IEA, 2021[1]; IRENA, 2022[17]; IEA, 2021[18]). This is especially challenging as the cost of capital is consistently and significantly higher in developing countries than in developed countries (Box 10.1), making it more difficult for developing countries to raise debt finance and meet expected return rates on equity.

This is particularly relevant as private, debt-financed investments are expected to play a major role in funding the net-zero transition. While today's energy investments in developing countries rely heavily on public finance (in particular, through state-owned enterprises), the International Energy Agency (IEA) forecasts that a decisive shift in financing towards private sources is needed to meet energy needs and reach net zero (IEA, 2021[1]). However, the amounts of private finance mobilised for the net-zero transition in developing countries are below expectations (OECD, 2022[16]). Instead, most private climate finance currently mobilised by developed countries targets projects in middle-income countries with relatively conducive enabling environments and low-risk profiles (OECD, 2022[16]). Development co-operation must go beyond transaction-level approaches such as blended finance and increase support for greening financial systems.

Box 10.1. Challenges associated with the cost of capital in developing countries

Developing countries are among the most vulnerable to the impacts of climate change and require large amounts of finance to green their economies and invest in adaptation actions. However, mobilising climate finance for developing countries has been a challenge, and capital flows have consistently fallen short of the level needed. Heightened macroeconomic risks, underdeveloped or shallow financial sectors, and challenges associated with investing in projects such as an absence of strong contract enforcement and other arrangements that support predictable revenues or subsidies that continue to favour investment in unsustainable technologies lead to higher economy-wide costs of capital in developing countries. Hence, their insufficient access to finance. More specifically, the IEA outlines that nominal financing costs in developing countries are up to seven times higher than in Europe or the United States (IEA, 2021[1]). This is particularly significant given the capital intensity of low-carbon investments, as described above.

These challenging conditions can result in a "climate investment trap" severely limiting low-carbon investments in developing countries. In the face of high weighted average costs of capital (WACCs), investors are frequently deterred from investing in low-carbon assets and technologies in developing markets, leading to insufficient mitigation efforts. This potentially results in worse climate and economic impacts in developing countries, which may reinforce domestic risks and hinder development of financial markets, feeding back into high WACCs in a vicious circle (Ameli et al., 2021[19]).

In the face of these challenges, investment has remained limited in developing countries (Figure 10.3). While clean energy investment worldwide has risen significantly since the signing of the Paris Agreement, it remains broadly at 2015 levels in developing countries (with the exception of China) (IEA, 2022[20]). This growing gap will need to be addressed for a global net-zero transition.

Figure 10.3. Trends in annual clean energy investment by region

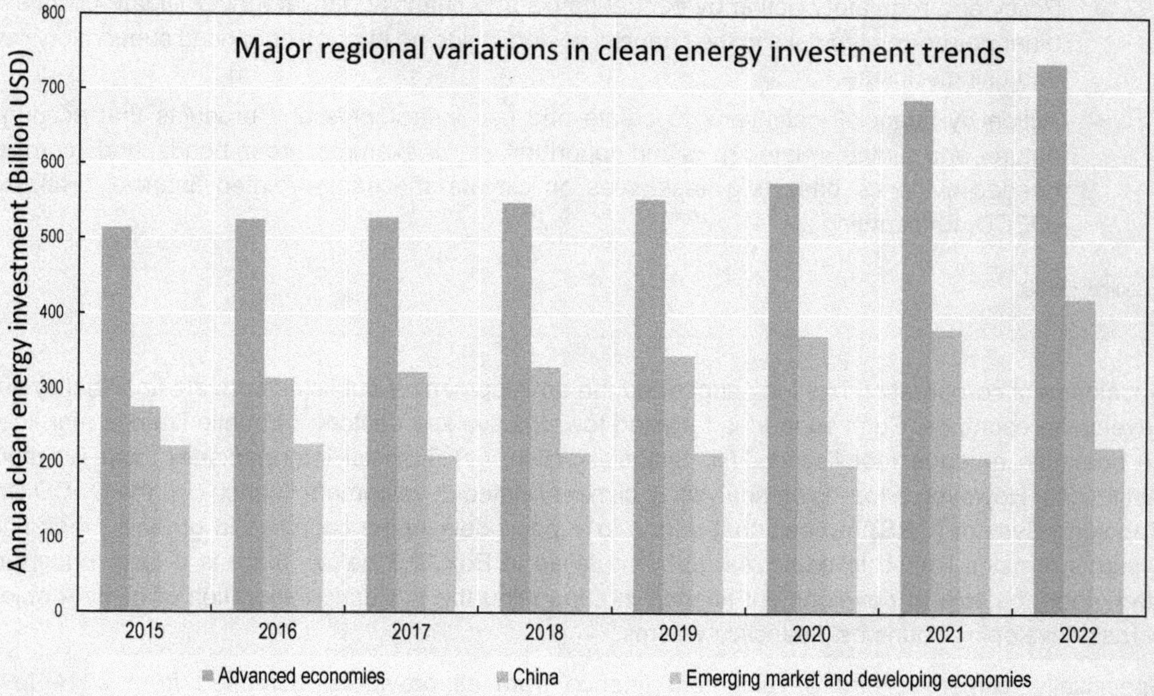

Source: Figure based on (IEA, 2022[20]). (OECD, forthcoming, 2023[21]).

Greening developing countries' financial systems

Greening the financial systems of developing countries is critical to aligning development and climate objectives – including and beyond the energy sector – and enabling a resilient global transition to net zero.

The Sharm el Sheikh Implementation Plan for the first time expressly referenced the need to transform the "financial system and its structures and processes, engaging governments, central banks, commercial banks, institutional investors and other financial actors" (UNFCCC, 2022[22]) in order to operationalise Article 2.1 (c) of the Paris Agreement and deliver on the investment required to reach net zero emissions. The strategic use of development finance to green developing countries' financial systems will be key to supporting progress on this commitment (OECD, 2019[23]).

Box 10.2. Defining "green" financial systems

This section, based on the OECD Creditor Reporting System (CRS), defines green financial systems as: *systems of public and private finance that integrate nature and climate-related externalities and allocate and intermediate financial resources on true cost and risk-effective pricing.*

Existing approaches to green financial systems include:

- Policy and regulatory action by governments to establish financial sectors that integrate nature and carbon externalities into financial decision-making, including through carbon markets and pricing, energy tax and subsidy reform, and emission trading systems.

- Public financial management and budgetary processes that seek alignment with environmental objectives.
- Policy and regulatory action by central banks and financial regulators to mitigate climate- and other nature-related risks to the financial sector, including through enhanced supervisory review and risk disclosure.
- Action by financial institutions to create and use instruments and products that account for nature- and climate-related risks and opportunities (for example, green bonds, and improve the needed evidence base, e.g. taskforces on climate-and nature-related financial disclosures) (OECD, forthcoming[24])

Source: OECD.

Development co-operation has long supported the development of public and private financial systems in developing countries. Such support is targeted towards five key sectors: (i) public finance management, (ii) domestic revenue mobilisation, (iii) financial policy, (iv) financial intermediaries, and (v) monetary institutions. However, a top-down analysis of climate-related development finance (via the OECD Creditor Reporting System (CRS)) reveals that efforts to support developing countries in greening their financial systems remains limited to date.[4] As further detailed in Box 10.3 below, there is a clear opportunity to strengthen the role of development finance in supporting the systemic integration of climate objectives across developing countries' financial systems.

Specifically, climate-related development finance from all providers increased from 2014 to 2020, amounting to USD 98 billion in 2020 (OECD, 2022[25]). In contrast to climate-related development finance overall, there is no identifiable pattern in climate-related support to financial systems for the 2014-2020 period (See Figure 10.4 on support from bilateral donors and multilateral funds, and Figure 10.5 on support provided by MDBs). This is noteworthy given countries' 2015 commitment to align all financing flows with the global mitigation and adaptation goals as expressed in the Paris Agreement, Article 2.1(c), (UNFCCC, 2015[26]; UNFCCC, 2015[26])), and developed countries' commitment to support developing countries in their contribution to the Paris Agreement goals (Article 9).

Moreover, despite the relevance assigned to central banks and financial regulators to address climate change - as reinforced in the Sharm el-Sheikh Implementation Plan – climate-related development finance to monetary institutions did not involve significant volumes over the 2014-2019 period.

Box 10.3. Initial assessment of trends and flows for climate-related support to financial systems in developing countries

Climate-related support to formal sector financial intermediaries (FSFI) such as banks and insurance companies from bilateral sources and multilateral funds reached an average of USD 433 million per year from 2014 to 2019. This was followed by support to financial policy amounting to USD 185 million per year on average (Figure 10.4).

Figure 10.4. Climate-related development finance (Rio market methodology) provided to sectors relevant for financial systems development

Rio Market methodology, 2-year averages, commitments in USD 2019 prices

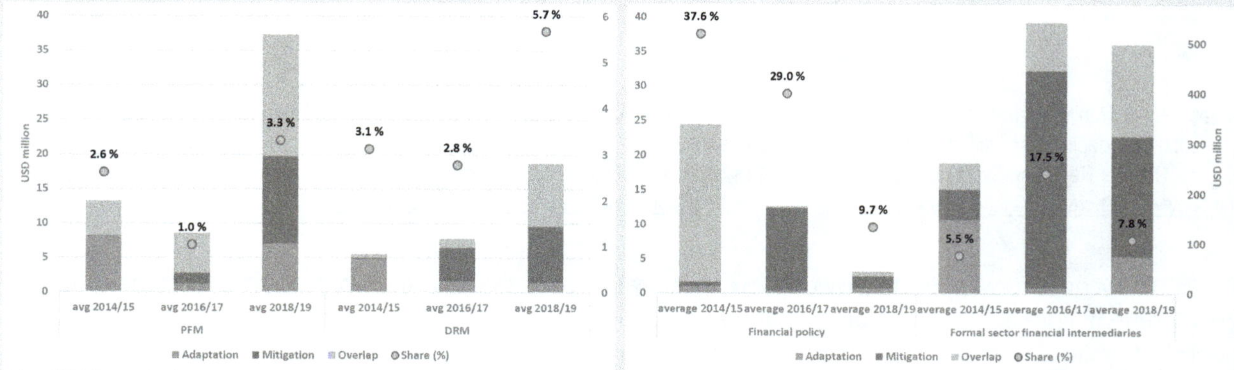

Note: PFM = Public finance management; DRM = Domestic revenue mobilisation; FP = Financial policy; FSFI = Formal sector financial intermediaries; avg = average. Climate-related support to monetary institutions not depicted as limited in absolute and relative terms.
Source: Creditor Reporting System (database), https://stats.oecd.org/; Climate Change OECD DAC External Development Statistics (database), http://www.oecd.org/dac/financing-sustainable-development/development-finance-topics/climate-change.htm.

In relative terms, however, the share of climate-related finance supporting financial sector policy overall was the highest over 2014-19, with 25% on average. Relevant support to public finance management (PFM), domestic revenue mobilisation (DRM) and support to monetary institutions was much less pronounced, reaching respectively USD 20 million, USD 11 million and USD 3 million on average per year over the same period. Although climate-related support in PFM and DRM increased overall from 2014 to 2019, climate-related support for financial policies decreased significantly in absolute and relative terms.

Across sectors, support targeted mitigation and adaptation objectives, while support to FSFI focused on mitigation only.

Multilateral development banks (MDBs) focused their support to green financial systems over 2014 to 2019 both in absolute and relative terms on support to formal sector financial intermediaries (FSFI).

Following a steep increase after 2014/15, climate-related support to FSFI reached on average USD 1 billion, or 11% of support to these institutions overall. This is likely based on the business model of development banks that relies on the provision of loans – for example in the form of green credit lines – and less on the provision of policy and regulatory support and capacity building.

Climate-related support to PFM and DRM by MDBs increased over 2014-2019 in both absolute and relative terms, with particularly steep increases from 2016/17 to 2018/19. Across sectors and years, support from MDBs to green developing country financial systems focused on mitigation (Figure 10.5)

Figure 10.5. Climate-related development finance provided by multilateral development banks to sectors relevant for financial systems development

Support provided by MDBs, 2-year averages, commitments in USD 2019 prices

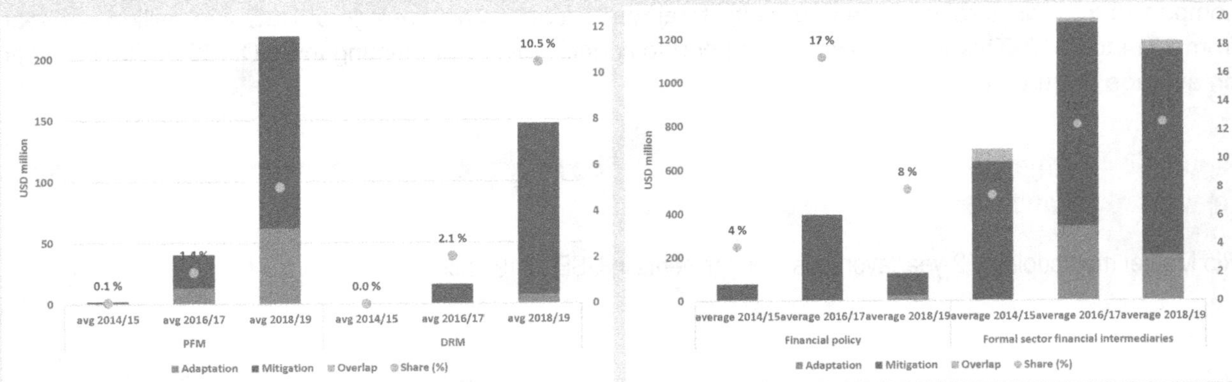

Note: PFM = Public finance management; DRM = Domestic revenue mobilisation; avg = average . Climate-related support to monetary institutions not depicted as limited in absolute and relative terms.
Source: Creditor Reporting System (database), https://stats.oecd.org/; Climate Change OECD DAC External Development Statistics (database), http://www.oecd.org/dac/financing-sustainable-development/development-finance-topics/climate-change.htm.

As is the case for support provided by bilateral providers and multilateral funds, climate-related development finance to monetary institutions did not involve significant volumes over the 2014-2019 period, despite the relevance assigned to central banks and financial regulators in promoting climate-related risk management in the financial sector, strengthening financial stability in a changing climate, and mobilising finance for climate outcomes.

Support to green financial systems in different country groups and via different instruments

Between 2014 and 2019, support to green financial systems was mostly provided to middle income countries (MICs). FSFI were almost exclusively supported in MICs. Low-income countries (LICs) rely more on informal and semi-formal financial institutions than FSFI, such as microfinance institutions ((Demirgüç-Kunt and Singer, 2017[27])). Support from bilateral providers and multilateral funds in 2014-2019 reflects this, with 62% of climate-related development finance to financial institutions supporting the latter institutions.

Bilateral providers extended their support to green financial systems in LICs exclusively through grants, including in the areas of PFM and DRM. MDBs used both loans and grants in their support to LICs, with a stronger focus on loans. Importantly, in 2014-2019 support to green financial systems in LICs targeted to a larger degree adaptation objectives than in other income groups (44% of support focused on adaptation). Interestingly, support to green financial systems in SIDS focused largely on mitigation objectives.

Source: OECD.

Chapter conclusions

Development processes and climate policy action are inextricably linked. The systemic integration of climate priorities into development processes and policy can drive alignment and help to communicate the developmental interest of countries' climate action. This has the additional benefit of embedding a multidimensional approach to climate policy action – a critical component to strengthening the resilience of the global net zero transition.

Understanding and responding to the interconnections between both development and climate transitions requires a strong focus on the energy sector. While developing countries have different starting positions to their energy transitions, they generally face two main challenges: Insufficient access to capital and insufficient capacities for the transition. This lends itself to "a common approach" to how development co-operation is provided by developed countries in the context of energy sector transitions.

Further to the energy sector focus, greening the financial systems of developing countries is essential to aligning development and climate objectives – including and beyond the energy sector, and enabling a resilient global transition to net zero. The Sharm el Sheikh Implementation Plan for the first time expressly referenced the need to transform the financial system in order to deliver on the Paris Agreement's objectives.

While support to developing countries' public and private financial system is a major focus of development co-operation, there is no positive trend in climate-related support to these systems and relevant sectors. In particular, despite the importance attached to central banks and regulators in enabling and driving the transition, no significant support – in absolute terms – can be detected from initial analyses.

Notes

[1] This support includes delivering the commitment of providing and mobilising USD 100 billion per year and the broader support of development co-operation providers such as the commitments outlined in the OECD DAC Declaration on a new approach to align development co-operation with the goals of the Paris Agreement on Climate Change.

[2] Excluding the People's Republic of China.

[3] The fall in costs is particularly important for utility-scale solar PV which can now compete with the cheapest new fossil fuel generation capacity, reaching a weighted average LCOE of USD 0.057/kWh (against costs for new coal power plants in the range of USD 0.055/kWh and USD 0.148/kWh). Other technologies such as concentrated solar power, onshore and offshore wind are also competitive or cheaper than fossil fuel-related electricity generation, without taking into account positive externalities.

[4] Outlined in OECD background paper on "Greening financial systems in developing countries".

References

Ameli, N. et al. (2021), "Higher cost of finance exacerbates a climate investment trap in developing economies", *Nature Communications*, Vol. 12/1, https://doi.org/10.1038/s41467-021-24305-3. [19]

Burke, P., D. Stern and S. Bruns (2018), "The Impact of Electricity on Economic Development: A Macroeconomic Perspective", *International Review of Environmental and Resource Economics*, Vol. 12/1, pp. 85-127, https://doi.org/10.1561/101.00000101. [9]

Demirgüç-Kunt, A. and D. Singer (2017), "Financial inclusion and inclusive growth: A review of recent empirical evidence", *World Bank Policy Research Working Paper*. [27]

IEA (2022), *Africa Energy Outlook 2022*, https://www.iea.org/reports/africa-energy-outlook-2022. [13]

IEA (2022), *For the first time in decades, the number of people without access to electricity is set to increase in 2022*, https://www.iea.org/commentaries/for-the-first-time-in-decades-the-number-of-people-without-access-to-electricity-is-set-to-increase-in-2022. [11]

IEA (2022), *World Energy Investment 2022*. [20]

IEA (2021), *Financing Clean Energy Transitions in Emerging and Developing Economies*, https://www.iea.org/reports/financing-clean-energy-transitions-in-emerging-and-developing-economies. [1]

IEA (2021), *The cost of capital in clean energy transitions*, https://www.iea.org/articles/the-cost-of-capital-in-clean-energy-transitions. [18]

IEA, IRENA, UNSD, World Bank, WHO (2022), *Tracking SDG 7: The Energy Progress Report*, https://trackingsdg7.esmap.org/data/files/download-documents/sdg7-report2022-full_report.pdf. [10]

IRENA (2022), *Renewable Power Generation Costs in 2021*, https://www.irena.org/publications/2022/Jul/Renewable-Power-Generation-Costs-in-2021#:~:text=Globally%2C%20new%20renewable%20capacity%20added,at%20least%20USD%2050%20billion. [17]

OECD (2022), *Climate Change: OECD DAC External Development Finance Statistics*, https://www.oecd.org/dac/financing-sustainable-development/development-finance-topics/climate-change.htm. [25]

OECD (2022), *Climate Finance Provided and Mobilised by Developed Countries in 2016-2020: Insights from Disaggregated Analysis*, Climate Finance and the USD 100 Billion Goal, OECD Publishing, Paris, https://doi.org/10.1787/286dae5d-en. [16]

OECD (2022), *OECD Creditor Reporting System*, https://stats.oecd.org/Index.aspx?DataSetCode=crs1. [15]

OECD (2021), *Investing in the climate transition: The role of development banks, development finance institutions and their shareholders*, https://www.oecd.org/dac/financing-sustainable-development/Policy-perspectives-Investing-in-the-climate-transition.pdf. [4]

OECD (2019), *Aligning Development Co-operation and Climate Action: The Only Way Forward*, The Development Dimension, OECD Publishing, Paris, https://doi.org/10.1787/5099ad91-en. [5]

OECD (2019), *Aligning Development Co-operation and Climate Action: The Only Way Forward*, The Development Dimension, OECD Publishing, Paris, https://doi.org/10.1787/5099ad91-en. [23]

OECD (Forthcoming), *Economic development and the climate transition: a review of the interlinkages between two transformative processes*. [2]

OECD (forthcoming), *Greening developing country financial systems: An overview of approaches and insights on the role of development co-operation*. [24]

OECD (forthcoming, 2023), *The role of the cost of capital in clean energy transitions*. [21]

Shahbaz, M. et al. (2018), "The energy consumption and economic growth nexus in top ten energy-consuming countries: Fresh evidence from using the quantile-on-quantile approach", *Energy Economics*, Vol. 71, pp. 282-301, https://doi.org/10.1016/j.eneco.2018.02.023. [8]

Stern, D. (2011), "The role of energy in economic growth", *Annals of the New York Academy of Sciences*, Vol. 1219/1, pp. 26-51, https://doi.org/10.1111/j.1749-6632.2010.05921.x. [7]

Sustainable Energy for All (2021), *Energesing Finance - Understanding the Landscape*, https://www.seforall.org/system/files/2021-10/EF-2021-UL-SEforALL.pdf. [12]

Taskin, Ö. (2022), *Supporting developing countries' net zero transition: An introduction to development co-operation providers' approaches, ONE*,. [3]

UNFCCC (2022), *Sharm el-Sheikh Implementation Plan*, https://unfccc.int/sites/default/files/resource/cma2022_L21_revised_adv.pdf. [22]

UNFCCC (2015), *Paris Agreement*. [26]

World Bank (2022), , https://data.worldbank.org/. [14]

World Bank (2020), *Transformative Climate FinanceA: A new approach for climate finance to achieve low-carbon resilient development in developing countries*, https://openknowledge.worldbank.org/bitstream/handle/10986/33917/149752.pdf. [6]

Part III Building resilience to climate impacts

11 Climate impacts, adaptation needs and limits

Despite concerted efforts to curb global greenhouse gas emissions, the impacts of climate change are intensifying and causing mounting losses and damages, some of them irreversible. This chapter reviews the current state of play of climate hazards, exposure and vulnerability as well as reviewing key projected impacts under current emissions reductions scenarios. It considers progress made on advancing adaptation efforts and highlights the urgent need to accelerate adaptation action and to build climate resilience systemically. However, it also shows that there are limits to adaptation that reinforce the need to overcome the compartmentalisation of climate policy into adaptation and mitigation.

This chapter draws on contributions to the horizontal project carried out under the responsibility of the Environment Policy Committee.

Despite concerted efforts to curb global greenhouse gas emissions, the impacts of climate change are intensifying and causing mounting losses and damages – some of them irreversible – for communities across the globe. This chapter briefly reviews the current state of play of climate hazards, exposure and vulnerability as well as key projected impacts under current emissions reductions scenarios. It underscores the urgent need to accelerate adaptation action and build climate resilience systemically.

Observed climate impacts

Despite efforts to mitigate global warming, climate change has already induced considerable costs and threatens the stability of many natural and human systems, including human health, terrestrial and aquatic ecosystems, cities, infrastructure, and food production. Average global surface temperature increased by 1.09°C in 2011-20 compared to the period 1850-1900, with larger increases over land (1.59°C) than the ocean (0.88°C) (IPCC, 2021[1]).

All regions of the world have suffered negative impacts from climate change (IPCC, 2021[1]). Flooding from storm surges combined with sea-level rise increasingly threaten the habitability and economic structures of coastal areas (OECD, 2021[2]; OECD, 2019[3]). Rising average and extreme temperatures, particularly in urban areas, are leading to increased heat-related morbidity and harm to human mental health (OECD, 2021[4]). Climate change is fuelling extreme wildfires, which increasingly threaten communities and cause irreversible environmental damage (OECD, Forthcoming[5]). Slow-onset impacts also threaten many parts of the world. Some 250 million people are affected by desertification (IPCC, 2019[6]) and more than 13% of the Earth's soils are affected by salinisation (FAO, 2021[7]). Other negative climate impacts include droughts, average temperature increase, land and forest degradation, ocean acidification, glacier melting and biodiversity loss.

Climate variability and climate-related events are responsible for increasing economic cost, but also human and environmental losses. The year 2022 saw the driest summer recorded in European history, inducing the loss of more than 660 000 hectares of land due to extreme wildfires and forecasted agricultural yield losses of up to 16% compared to the annual average of the past five years (Toreti et al., 2022[8]). In 2021 alone, the global direct costs of extreme climate-related events were estimated at EUR 265 billion (Munich Re, 2022[9]). Single events such as Hurricane Ida in the United States and catastrophic flooding in western Germany caused EUR 60 billion and EUR 40 billion in direct damages respectively (Munich Re, 2022[9]).

The impact of these events goes beyond their economic cost. They affect people's health and lives, and temporarily or even permanently disrupt the functioning of critical ecosystems. More recently, flooding in Pakistan caused more than 1 200 fatalities and displaced millions (Mallapaty, 2022[10]). Australian wildfires that ravaged the southeast of the country in 2019-2020 destroyed 18 million hectares of vegetation and killed an estimated one billion animals (UNEP, 2020[11]). Some experts argue that the destruction of the local biodiversity in this region of Australia has been so extensive that it may not be able to regenerate without human intervention (UNESCO, 2021[12]). Such extreme events can have significant and lasting mental health impacts, such as post-traumatic stress disorder (OECD, 2021[13]).

Figure 11.1. Mean annual change in the number of unusually warm days over the period 1979-2021

(a) Tmax > 95th percentile and (b) Tmin < 5th percentile over the reference period 1981-2010

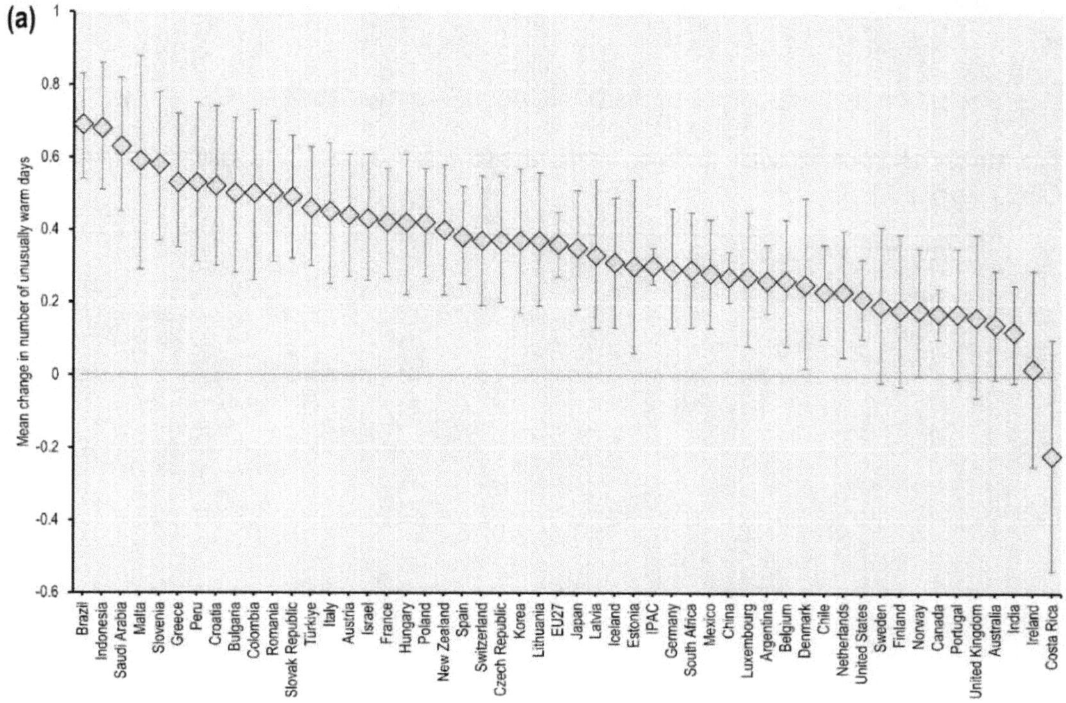

Source: (Maes et al., 2022[14]).

These climate impacts are the result of increasing climate risk caused by a combination of hazard, exposure, and vulnerability (Box 11.1) (OECD, 2021[13]). Advances in the understanding of climate systems strengthen the attribution of these impacts to climate change (IPCC, 2021[1]). For example, a recent study shows that climate change made the European drought of 2022 more than 20 times more likely (Schumacher et al., 2022[15]).

Climate change is characterised by an increase in global average temperatures, which in turn changes weather patterns, leading to an overall increase in the frequency and intensity of climate hazards. As illustrated in Figure 11.1 above, almost all countries experienced a significantly higher number of extremely warm days in recent years compared to the reference period 1981-2010. Similarly, the analysis also reveals fewer unusually cold days in recent years compared with the past reference period (Maes et al., 2022[14]). These climatic changes present risk affecting communities, disrupting economic activities and/or causing environmental damage and degradation. As shown in Figure 11.2 below, populations in each region of the United States, Chile, Mexico and Colombia have been significantly more exposed to heat stress in the last five years compared to the period 1981-2010 (Maes et al., 2022[14]).

The vulnerability of societies to climate impacts is a function of their exposure to the hazard in general, and their adaptive capacity or ability to cope with related impacts. The Intergovernmental Panel on Climate Change (IPCC) estimates that, at present, 3.3 to 3.6 billion people globally are highly vulnerable to climate change (IPCC, 2022[16]).

Climate change impacts are not evenly distributed. Developing countries, in particular least developed countries, are more exposed to climate hazards geographically and more vulnerable to their impacts (OECD, 2021[13]). Segments of populations that are marginalised due to gender, race, age, disability, income, or geographic location are particularly vulnerable, both globally and within countries (OECD, 2021[13]). Lack of financial and material resources to recover from climatic events; reduced awareness of the potential risks of climate change and adaptation options; greater dependence on climate-sensitive sectors such as agriculture and fisheries; and lower insurance coverage against risks are all factors that constrain capacity to adapt (Leichenko and Silva, 2014[17]). This inequality in the face of climate risk caused by highly variable exposure and vulnerability reinforces the link between climate action and social resilience.

Figure 11.2. Subnational variation of population exposure to heat stress

Level and growth of population exposure to strong heat stress or worse (UTCI > 32°C) over the period 2017-2021 for large OECD regions (TL2)

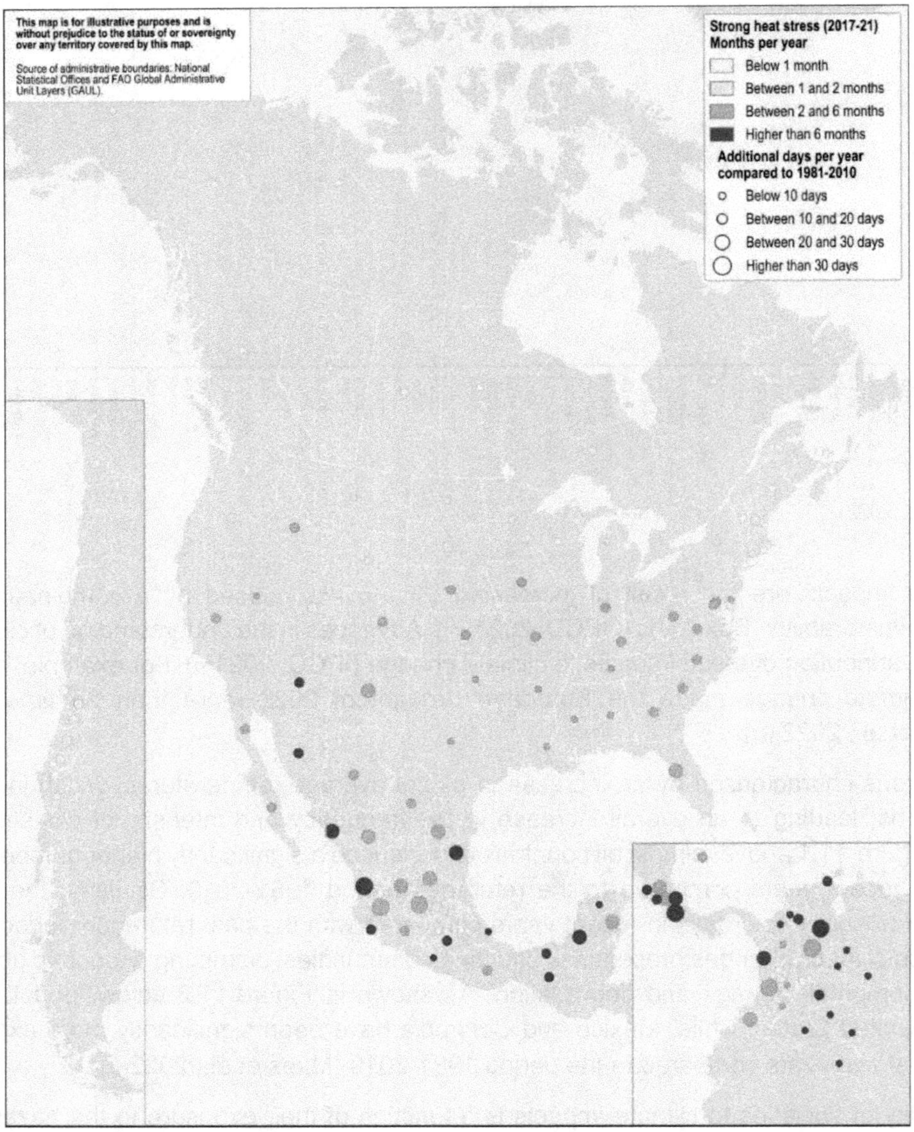

Source: (Maes et al., 2022[14]).

Significant progress has been made in the methods and tools used to assess climate exposure. Increasingly accurate weather satellite observation and better modelling tools are improving the capacity to assess local and regional hazards and populations' exposure to them. The OECD has recently developed country- and regional-level climate exposure indicators (Maes et al., 2022[14]).[1] Using a selection and combination of existing climate data, these homogenised indicators allow countries to better understand how climate hazards compare to one another and which regions and activities are most exposed, enabling the prioritisation of adaptation actions. For example, based on this new data, Figure 11.3 depicts the spatial evolution of soil moisture in Europe, Australia, Japan and Korea. The data show that Australia is already facing an increasingly dry environment in all regions, whereas in Spain and Italy some regions are getting wetter and others dryer. Understanding such spatial variation can help policy makers tailor policies to best suit local needs.

Despite this progress, climate risk assessments to date often give only a partial view, focusing exclusively levels of hazard and exposure without characterising vulnerability. Assessing the risk posed by climate change requires information on adaptive capacity or the ability of exposed entities to cope with identified potential negative impacts (Maes et al., 2022[14]).

There is some evidence that this is starting to change. For example, localities in the state of New York, including Orange County[2] and the city of Long Beach,[3] have included vulnerability studies in their climate risk assessments. These initiatives remain limited to a small number of localities, however. Moreover, vulnerability assessments must be regularly updated to include progress in adaptation but also because they rely on socio-economic and environmental dynamics. As such, comprehensive vulnerability assessments require considerable data and resources to carry out.

Figure 11.3. Soil moisture anomaly 2017-21 compared to 1981-2010

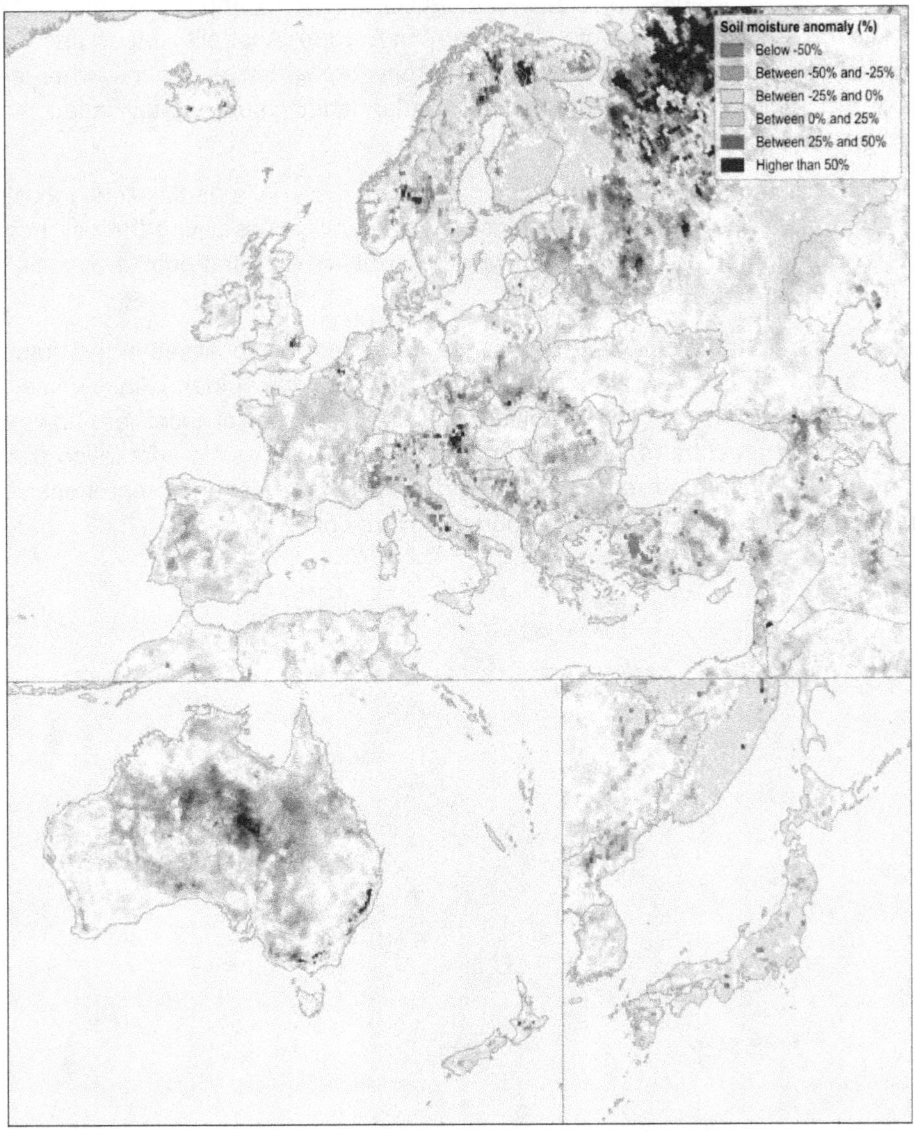

Note: A negative anomaly corresponds to drier soil (red), while a positive indicates an excess of humidity (blue)
Source: (Maes et al., 2022[14]).

Direct climate impacts are initially local, but their effects can spread well beyond the systems and regions originally affected. The interconnectedness of economic, social and natural systems can lead to cascading effects that propagate far beyond their initial impact (OECD, 2022[18]). For example, in 2011, Thailand was hit by remains the costliest flood to date for the insurance industry. The impact of this event, which caused USD 46 billion in damages, went far beyond Thailand's borders, however. Supplying about a quarter of all hard disk drives (HDD) sold in the world, the shutdown of Thailand's HDD industry led to a doubling of global HHD prices and only returned to normal more than a year after the shock (Swiss RE, 2021[19]). Assessing such indirect exposure and predicting likely cascading impacts is a new and major challenge.

Box 11.1. Key concepts surrounding climate change and adaptation

This report uses the Intergovernmental Panel on Climate Change's (IPCC) Fifth Assessment Report framework (2014) to describe risk. Risks are a function of the range of potential outcomes and the associated likelihoods of those outcomes materialising in a given period. In this context, risks arise from the interaction between hazards, exposure and vulnerability:

- **Hazards** are the potential occurrence of a physical event or trend (e.g. flooding, erosion) that may cause loss of life and injury, as well as damage and loss to property, infrastructure, livelihoods, service provision, ecosystems and environmental resources. Climate change will increase climate risk by leading to a global rise of three kinds of hazards: slow onset changes, extreme weather events and climate system tipping points (for more on climate system tipping points, see Chapter 2). At the same time, climate change will increase the intensity and frequency of extreme weather events (e.g. heatwaves, wildfires, flash flood and droughts), especially in places where they already occur.
- **Exposure** refers to the presence of people, infrastructure, housing and other tangible human assets in hazard-prone areas. A measure of exposure can include the number of people or types of assets in a coastal flood zone.
- **Vulnerability** is the degree to which natural or social systems are susceptible to, and unable to cope with, exposure to hazard.

Source: (IPCC, 2014[20])

Future climate impacts

While a number of climate change-induced impacts are already felt today, future projected climate change is set to intensify climate variability and extreme climate-related events. Even in the optimistic scenario of limiting global warming to 1.5°C above pre-industrial levels, all regions and systems will face a greater impact from climate change than today (IPCC, 2021[1]). With such warming, sea-level rise will continue and could reach 0.5 metres by the end of the century (OECD, 2019[3]). Although an average warming of 1.5°C will partially contain the increase in extreme weather events, it will not prevent the forecasted accumulation of smaller-scale weather events (IPCC, 2021[1]). What is more, the increase in the number of events makes it more likely that these events occur in combination, leading to more devastating compound events (Zscheischler et al., 2018[21]).

Reaching 2°C of global warming will increase the likelihood of many climate impacts and put the world at risk of several tipping points with potentially catastrophic impacts (see Chapter 2). Even without the increased risk of crossing tipping point thresholds, reaching 2°C of warming will result in considerable climate impacts, for example, almost tripling the number of people exposed to extreme heat at least once every five years (OECD, 2022[18]). Failure to meet the Paris Agreement goal of staying below 2°C of warming would have disastrous consequences. As shown in Figure 11.4, at 2°C of warming it is projected that residual damage due to flooding could cost between USD 1.7 trillion and USD 5.5 trillion over the 21st century (OECD, 2019[3]).

These projections show the clear risk of continued warming and the absolute necessity of meeting the Paris Agreement's mitigation targets. But even at current levels of warming, climate impacts are mounting. Building resilience to them is imperative, not only to avert, address, and minimise losses and damages, but also to enhance the resilience of mitigation efforts and ensure that future climate impacts are not exacerbated.

Figure 11.4. Global annual flood costs for different socio-economic and climate scenarios with and without adaptation

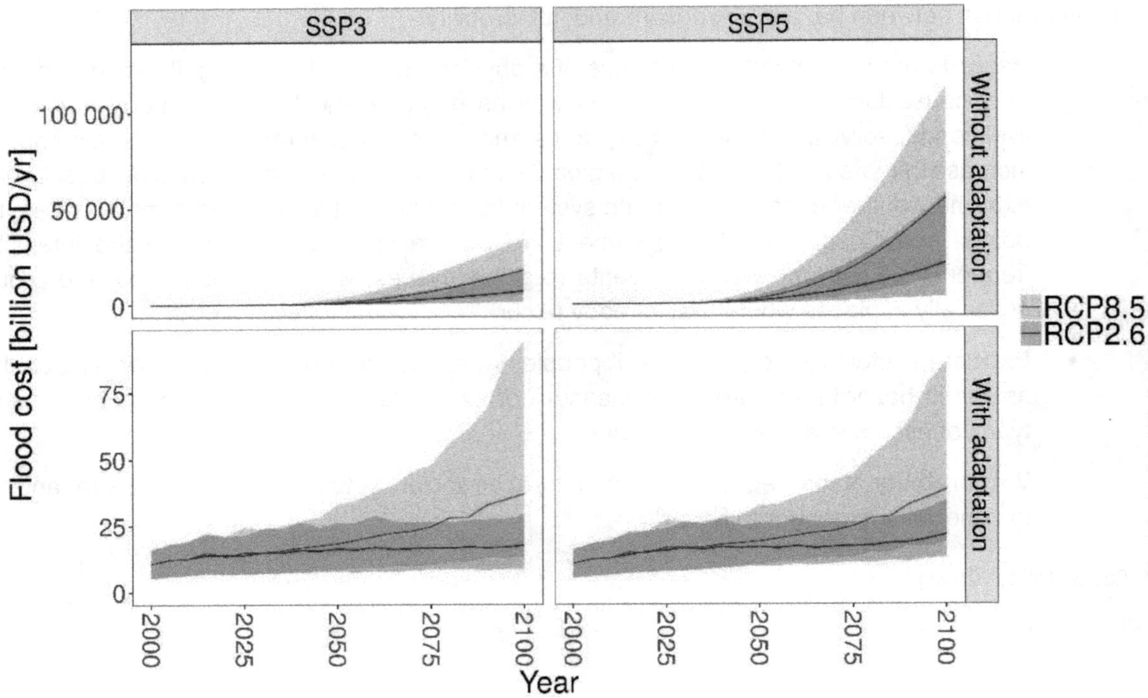

Note: The solid lines represent the median. The shaded area represents the range from the 5th to 95th percentile for a given scenario combination.
Source: (Hinkel et al., 2014[22]).

Aligning climate adaptation policies with expected climate impacts

Against the backdrop of significant observed climate-related losses and damages, and with future impacts projected to intensify, accelerated climate adaptation efforts are urgently needed. Managing climate risks and being prepared for losses and damages requires a broad range of policies at local, national and regional levels, co-ordinating across all areas of government and assessing policy options with regard to managing other socio-economic risks (OECD, 2021[13]). Recognising this, OECD countries and a growing number of non-OECD countries have made considerable progress in establishing comprehensive climate adaptation policies. For example, all OECD countries have adopted a National Adaptation Strategy (NAS) or Plan (NAP). Many are already moving into their second or third phase, adjusting adaptation objectives and actions according to evolving knowledge on climate risks.

National climate and impact assessments form the basis of National Adaptation Plan priority-setting in a growing number of countries. A recent OECD survey reveals that 73% of OECD countries have developed at least one risk assessment, whereas 60% assess both past and projected climate hazards. Even though 53% of countries report assessing vulnerability to the expected impacts of climate change, assessment methods and their quality (e.g. the degree to which environmental and socio-economic factors are considered) differ considerably.

Good practice NAS/NAPs have started formulating national adaptation objectives and identifying priority adaptation actions. For example, Costa Rica defines a broad adaptation objective for each of its six Axes of Action under its National Adaptation Plan. Each objective is detailed in several sub-objectives corresponding to a specific guideline (Ministry of Environment and Energy, 2022[23]). As another example, Austria sets an overarching objective for each of 14 identified sectors, with detailed sub-objectives needed to meet the main goal, including actions necessary for implementation, actors to be involved, and a time horizon (Austria, 2017[24]).

Some countries have also established indicators to measure progress and designate entities responsible for the implementation and monitoring of respective actions. For example, the United Kingdom's Climate Change Committee is developing cross-cutting indicators and a monitoring system for each of the 253 actions listed in England's second NAP.[4] The 133 cross-cutting indicators in NAP2 fall into three categories: i) robust assessment of trends in risk factors; ii) adaptation actions; and iii) climate impacts of adaptation actions. The indicators are classified according to each of the NAP areas (Natural environment, Health and the built environment, and Infrastructure and Business) and then grouped according to their adaptation priority; stage of the theory of change to which they relate (input, output, outcome, impact); and by one of three climate risk categories (hazard, exposure, vulnerability).

Recognising the important role of local communities and municipalities in building resilience to climate change impacts, a growing number of countries are strengthening co-ordination and collaboration with local stakeholders. Local governments are increasingly being consulted in the process of designing National Adaptation Plans and policies. National governments are facilitating knowledge sharing and information on climate risks and adaptation options with subnational governments. For example, Japan is sharing information about climate change impacts and adaptation solutions with subnational stakeholders through a Climate Change Adaptation Center (Japan, n.d.[25]). In Austria, the Natural Hazard Overview & Risk Assessment Austria (HORA) platform provides detailed information about local risk to various hazards (Austria, 2017[24]).[5] The United Kingdom's Local Adaptation Advisory Panel (LAAP) is a forum for local government, arm's-length bodies and national government to discuss climate adaptation. The LAAP helps to identify local adaptation priorities and shares good local adaptation practices among its members and with the national government (Department for Environment, 2018[26]). Colombia has created the *Comisión Internacional de Cambio Climático* (CICC) to co-ordinate climate action among the national government, territories, and actors in different sectors (Colombia, 2018[27]). National governments have also established guidelines to help all actors address the issue of adaptation.

Similarly, countries are fostering inter-ministerial co-ordination and collaboration to strengthen the mainstreaming of adaptation across government sectors. In Germany, for example, the Interdepartmental Working Group on Climate Change Adaptation (IMAA), composed of representatives from all federal ministries and led by the Federal Ministry for Environment, ensures that federal policies are consistent with climate change adaptation objectives. (BMUV, 2016[28]). The IMAA has been a key actor in developing Germany's adaptation policy framework and is heavily involved in the reporting system (preparation of progress reports, building adaptation action plans, and review and approval of monitoring). Similarly, the UK Climate Change Act established the Climate Change Committee (CCC) an independent statutory body that must provide independent advice to government on climate-related risks and opportunities every five years. The government assesses and responds to this advice in its Climate Change Risk Assessment (CCRA). By law, the government must then update its national adaptation programme every five years to set out government action in response to the risk assessment (DEFRA, 2022[29]).[6] The CCC then reports to Parliament on progress being made in preparing for climate change.

Despite the growing comprehensiveness of national adaptation policy frameworks and governance structures, progress on implementation remains insufficient. While limited knowledge and understanding of climate risks remains a major bottleneck to more comprehensive adaptation action, ownership, accountability and financial constraints are also clear barriers to making progress here. In particular, actions identified in National Adaptation Plans need to be implemented by different national, sectoral and subnational government stakeholders, requiring considerable co-ordination. Adaptation funding is rarely sufficient, if provided at all, and often hampers implementation efforts. In addition, most countries rely on soft policy to implement NAPs, without legally binding commitments and based on voluntary, informal or non-hierarchical co-operation. Overcoming this will require a stronger focus on introducing national adaptation laws (European Environment Agency, 2022[30]).

Progress on adaptation made to date often occurs in response to, rather than in anticipation of, weather-related disasters. For example, catastrophe funds created in Austria and France were the result of major preceding disasters. In Austria, an avalanche in 1951 first raised awareness of the need for federal-level support to help states finance recovery efforts. Subsequent flooding in 1965 and 1966 then led to permanent establishment of a national catastrophe fund. France's catastrophe fund was established following devastating floods in the country in 1981-1982.

Chapter conclusions

Considerable progress is still needed to build resilience to climate impacts. The lack of funding for adaptation shows that while the need for adaptation strategies and frameworks risk is increasingly recognised, implementing them remains challenging. Overcoming these gaps requires a more holistic approach to building resilience, one that considers the evolution of hazards, exposure and vulnerability and is tailored to regional variation within these categories. Adaptation efforts and overarching governance frameworks need to become proactive, anticipating future risks and building systemic resilience to them. This requires better knowledge of how future climate risks may develop, and an awareness that resilience building cannot focus only on preparing specific system components for specific impacts. A broader approach to systemic resilience is needed.

It should also be recognised that there are limits to adaptation. The IPCC defines these as "the point at which an actor's objectives or system needs cannot be protected from intolerable risks by adaptive action" (IPCC, 2022[16]). Two parameters define the limits to adaptation: the dynamics of climate change and the capacity available to adapt. The IPCC distinguishes between soft limits, those for which solutions are not available due to cost or technical limitations but may be available in the future, and hard limits, for which no additional options will be available.

The current increase in global average temperature is already pushing the world to certain limits of adaptation. Ecosystems and the biodiversity they host as well as some particularly vulnerable areas (small islands and mountainous areas) are experiencing both hard and soft adaptation limits. For example, species extinction and coral reef depletion in some regions is already considered irreversible and is severely impacting local economies and populations The decline of some species in the Arctic is already compromising food security in the region. Soft adaptation limits are being observed in the agriculture sector and in coastal areas, threatening the resilience of households, individuals and urban infrastructure (IPCC, 2022[16]). Increasing evidence that tipping point thresholds may be crossed sooner and at lower warming thresholds than previously thought intensifies the risk that further adaptation limits will be met. These limits reinforce the need for mitigation and exemplify the interlinkages between building resilience to climate impacts and the resilience of the net-zero transition itself.

Notes

[1] These OECD indicators detail exposure for seven hazard types: (1) extreme temperature, (2) extreme precipitation, (3) drought, (4) wildfire, (5) wind threats, (6) river flooding and (7) coastal flooding, and four exposure variables (1) built-up areas, (2) croplands, (3) forests and (4) population density.

[2] Effects of Climate Change in Orange County, NY (orangecountygov.com).

[3] long_beach_nyrcr_plan.pdf.

[4] NAP2 sets out key actions for the period 2018-2023. A third NAP for England is due for publication in 2023.

[5] For more information on the HORA platform visit https://www.hora.gv.at/.

[6] The Climate Change Act provides the legal framework for climate change adaptation and mitigation in the UK.

References

Austria (2017), *The Austrian strategy for adaptation to climate change Part 2-Action Plan*, http://www.bmnt.gv.at. [24]

BMUV (2016), *Adaptation to Climate Change: Initial Progress Report by the Federal Government on Germany's Adaptation Strategy*, Federal Ministry for the Environment, Nature Conservation, Building and Nuclear Safety (BMUB). [28]

Colombia (2018), *Plan Nacional de Adaptacion al Cambio Climatico*. [27]

Costa Rica (2022), *NAP 2022-2026*. [31]

DEFRA (2022), *Climate change adaptation: policy information*, https://www.gov.uk/government/publications/climate-change-adaptation-policy-information/climate-change-adaptation-policy-information#:~:text=The%20Climate%20Change%20Act%202008,those%20risks%20every%20five%20years (accessed on 18 November 2022). [29]

Department for Environment, F. (2018), *The National Adaptation Programme and the Third Strategy for Climate Adaptation Reporting : Making the country resilient to a changing climate*. [26]

European Environment Agency (2022), *Advancing towards climate resilience in Europe — Status of reported national adaptation actions in 2021*. [30]

FAO (2021), *Global map of salt affecte soils*, United Nations. [7]

Hinkel, J. et al. (2014), "Coastal flood damage and adaptation costs under 21st century sea-level rise", *Proceedings of the National Academy of Sciences*, Vol. 111/9, pp. 3292-3297, https://doi.org/10.1073/pnas.1222469111. [22]

IPCC (2022), *Climate Change 2022: Impacts, Adaptation, and Vulnerability. Contribution of Working Group II to the Sixth Assessment Report of the Intergovernmental Panel on Climate Change*, Cambridge University Press., Cambridge, UK and New York, NY, USA,. [16]

IPCC (2021), "Climate Change 2021: The Physical Science Basis. Contribution of Working Group I to the Sixth Assessment Report of the Intergovernmental Panel on Climate Change [Masson-Delmotte, V., P. Zhai, A. Pirani, S. L. Connors, C. Péan, S. Berger, N. Caud, Y. Chen,", *Cambridge University Press* In Press, p. 3949, https://www.ipcc.ch/report/ar6/wg1/downloads/report/IPCC_AR6_WGI_Full_Report.pdf. [1]

IPCC (2019), *Climate Change and Land: an IPCC special report on climate change, desertification, land degradation, sustainable food management, food security and greenhouse gas fluxes in terrestrial systems*, IPCC. [6]

Japan (n.d.), *Climate change adaptation plan*. [25]

Leichenko, R. and J. Silva (2014), "Climate change and poverty: vulnerability, impacts, and alleviation strategies", *WIREs Climate Change*, Vol. 5/4, pp. 539-556, https://doi.org/10.1002/wcc.287. [17]

Maes, M. et al. (2022), "Monitoring exposure to climate-related hazards: Indicator methodology and key results", *OECD Environment Working Papers*, No. 201, OECD Publishing, Paris, https://doi.org/10.1787/da074cb6-en. [14]

Mallapaty, S. (2022), "Why are Pakistan's floods so extreme this year?", *Nature*, https://doi.org/10.1038/d41586-022-02813-6. [10]

Ministry of Environment and Energy (2022), *National Plan for Adaptation to Climate Change of Costa Rica, 2022 - 2026*. [23]

Munich Re (2022), *Hurricanes, cold waves, tornadoes: Weather disasters in USA dominate natural disaster losses in 2021*, https://www.munichre.com/en/company/media-relations/media-information-and-corporate-news/media-information/2022/natural-disaster-losses-2021.html. [9]

OECD (2022), *Climate Tipping Points: Insights for Effective Policy Action*, OECD Publishing, Paris, https://doi.org/10.1787/abc5a69e-en. [18]

OECD (2021), *Adapting to a changing climate in the management of coastal zones*. [2]

OECD (2021), *Managing Climate Risks, Facing up To Losses And Damages*, OECD. [13]

OECD (2021), *Strengthening Adaptation-Mitigation Linkages for a Low-Carbon, Climate-Resilient Future*. [4]

OECD (2019), *Responding to Rising Seas: OECD Country Approaches to Tackling Coastal Risks*, OECD Publishing, Paris, https://doi.org/10.1787/9789264312487-en. [3]

OECD (Forthcoming), *Adapting to a Changing Climate in the Mangement of Wildfires*. [5]

Pachauri, R. and L. Meyer (eds.) (2014), *Synthesis Report*, IPCC. [20]

Schumacher, D. et al. (2022), *High temperatures exacerbated by climate change made 2022 Northern Hemisphere droughts more likely*. [15]

Swiss RE (2021), *A decade on, learning from Thailand's devastating 2011 floods*, https://www.swissre.com/risk-knowledge/mitigating-climate-risk/decade-on-thailand-devastating-2011-floods.html. [19]

Toreti, A. et al. (2022), "Drought in Europe August 2022", *Publications Office of the European Union*, https://doi.org/10.2760/264241. [8]

UNEP (2020), *Ten impacts of the Australian bushfires*. [11]

UNESCO (2021), *Australia: After the bushfires*. [12]

Zscheischler, J. et al. (2018), "Future climate risk from compound events", *Nature Climate Change*, Vol. 8/6, pp. 469-477, https://doi.org/10.1038/s41558-018-0156-3. [21]

12 Beyond adaptation: Systemic interlinkages with mitigation and other natural systems

This chapter explores how approaches to systemic resilience can address interlinkages between mitigation and adaptation to climate change, for example protecting renewable energy infrastructure from mounting climate impacts. It highlights the importance of adaptation as well the role of other natural systems for climate policy. Specifically, examples of biodiversity and oceans, and concretely the use of nature-based solutions, are drawn on in demonstrating how synergies across these systems can be harnessed to produce win-win policy options.

This chapter draws on contributions to the horizontal project carried out under the responsibility of the Environment Policy Committee.

The rapid increase in climate change impacts necessitates not only mitigation and adaptation objectives to be pursed in tandem but consideration of other socio-economic and environmental objectives that intersect with these efforts. Climate risks pose considerable challenges to the net-zero transition itself, and resilience to climate impacts is key to a resilient transition. Furthermore, although the impacts of climate change are initially felt locally, the interconnectedness and interdependence of different economic sectors, communities, and ecosystems means that these impacts cascade across a number of different systems.

Exploring how approaches to systemic resilience can address these systemic interlinkages and integrate adaptation and mitigation, this chapter highlights the importance of other natural systems for climate policy. Specifically, examples of biodiversity and oceans, and the role of nature-based solutions, demonstrate how synergies across these systems can be harnessed to produce win-win policy options.

Mitigation and adaptation policies: Synergies and trade-offs

Both adaptation and mitigation policies have the potential to significantly reduce the impacts of climate change. In the long run, mitigation responses will shape future adaptation needs and influence climate resilience pathways. Synergies between adaptation and mitigation efforts can foster climate resilience effectively. For example, efforts to restore forests or mangroves can increase ecosystems' carbon storage capacity while also helping to reduce weather-related risks such as landslides or coastal storm surges. Fighting deforestation, reducing the risk of wildfires and encouraging afforestation preserve carbon sinks and soil stability while protecting communities. Similarly, agricultural soil management can promote carbon sequestration (Henderson et al., 2022[1]) while improved agricultural practices can preserve water run-offs or prevent droughts (OECD, 2014[2]). Agriculture, forestry and land management, water management and urban planning are key policy areas where synergies between mitigation and adaptation can be found.

In addition to these potential synergies between adaptation and mitigation objectives, building resilience to climate impacts is also integral to the resilience of the net-zero transition itself. For example, energy systems will need to be able to withstand extreme weather events to ensure a smooth transition to low carbon energy sources. Excessive losses and damages which could have been minimised through effective adaptation policies may divert funds from mitigation efforts. The distributional outcomes of climate impacts may further exacerbate inequalities and concerns about a just transition. These examples underline the need to consider adaptation and resilience together.

Figure 12.1. Mitigation and adaptation policies: Synergies and trade-offs

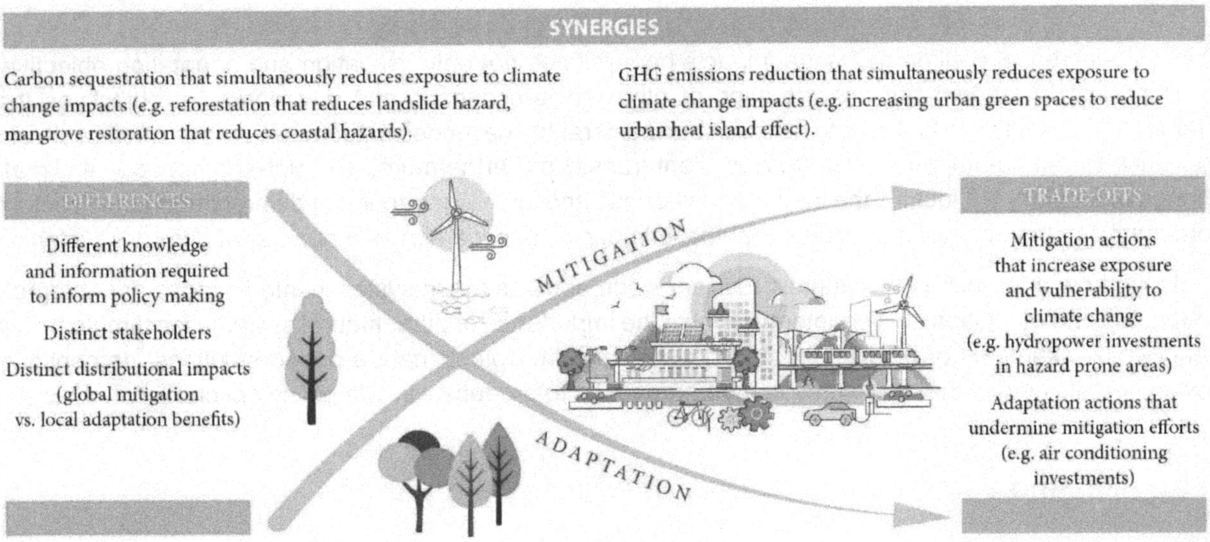

Source: (OECD, 2021[3])

Just as synergies between mitigation and adaptation actions can render climate policies more effective, there are also trade-offs that emerge from the complexity and diversity of adaptation-mitigation linkages across geographical scales. Some adaptation actions can exacerbate climate change, and reciprocally, mitigation actions can exacerbate climate risk if they increase the vulnerability and exposure of people, ecosystems and assets. As illustrated in Figure 12.1 above, growing investment in air conditioning to effectively combat heatwaves leads to higher energy consumption and thus increases greenhouse gas (GHG) emissions. Similarly, desalination plants are an important adaptation measure to cope with water shortages but their use increases energy demand and therefore, potentially, GHG-intensive sources of energy production. Paying for green set-aside in agriculture, i.e. land that is removed from food production, may have positive effects in terms of greenhouse gas emissions reduction and agricultural productivity but may negatively impact adaptation efforts (Lankoski, Ignaciuk and Jésus, 2018[4]).

There are also trade-offs between climate action and the achievement of other environmental objectives. Building a hydropower plant can support mitigation (renewable power generation) and adaptation (water reservoir for irrigation) but can also create new flood-prone zones, thereby hindering adaptation efforts. In addition, the construction of hydropower plants can lead to flooding and destruction of unique ecosystems and biodiversity (OECD, 2021[5]). These trade-offs are context-specific and define the long-term success of climate action.

Countries are increasingly recognising the importance of adaptation-mitigation linkages. A recent review by the OECD shows that almost all G20 countries mentioned adaptation-mitigation linkages in their NAPs or NDCs (OECD, 2021[5]). For example, Italy dedicates an entire section to adaptation-mitigation linkages in its National Climate Change Adaptation Strategy.[1] The UK's Environmental Land Management schemes, designed in consultation with farmers, promote good soil management practices to serve both mitigation and adaptation.

Notwithstanding these recent developments, climate change adaptation and mitigation policies have historically been largely addressed separately (OECD, 2021[5]). This is partly explained by the fact that limiting climate change through mitigation action has global public good benefits, while those of adaptation actions are mostly accrued locally (Swart and Raes, 2007[6]). This creates different needs and levels of co-ordinating action. The type of knowledge needed to inform adaptation and mitigation policies is also different. While mitigation policy is grounded in information on the source, type and amount of GHG generated, adaptation policy is informed by assessing the risks posed by different projected climate change impacts. As such, distinct stakeholders are involved in the design and implementation of adaptation and mitigation policies (Denton et al., 2014[7]).

While most countries mention the importance of exploiting synergies between adaptation and other environmental goals, often in the introduction to planning or strategy documents or in the context of co-ordination mechanisms, linkages are seldom discussed in depth and specific measures are rarely detailed. The recognition of linkages in national policy documents needs to be complemented with implementation strategies and clear actions. For example, better collaboration between mitigation and adaptation stakeholders could facilitate sharing of common background and knowledge about trade-offs and synergies. Strengthening reporting mechanisms of countries' climate actions could help better capture how countries incorporate these synergies, offering good-practice examples and enabling learning across countries (Adaptation Committee, 2022[8]). Future research could focus on developing or adapting decision-support tools to facilitate alignment considerations for project managers. Tools such as cost benefit analysis or multi-criteria analysis can support the analysis of complex and context-specific trade-offs (OECD, 2020[9]). Appraisals of climate risk should be mainstreamed within investment decisions. The "do no significant harm'" concept of the EU's sustainable finance taxonomy, which prevents an investment from being defined as sustainable if it harms any of six EU-identified environmental objectives, can be used as a framework to shed light on and manage possible trade-offs (OECD, 2020[9]).[2]

Systemic interlinkages across biodiversity and oceans and the potential for nature-based solutions to harness synergies

Biodiversity and climate change

A primary example of the complexity and interconnectedness of systems is the intertwined crises of biodiversity loss and climate change. Biodiversity is defined as the variability among living organisms from all sources including, among others, terrestrial, marine and other aquatic ecosystems and the ecological complexes of which they are part; this includes diversity within species, between species and of ecosystems (CBD, 1992[10]). Climate trends and extremes are pushing marine and terrestrial ecosystems closer to thresholds and tipping points (see Chapter 2) (Harris et al., 2018[11]). Allowing global average temperature to increase to 2°C above pre-industrial levels rather than holding it to 1.5°C could be catastrophic for some species (Smith et al., 2018[12]). Reciprocally, changes in biodiversity affect the climate system, especially through their impacts on nitrogen, carbon and water cycles (Pörtner et al., 2021[13]).

Biodiversity – an integral component of natural capital – provides critical ecosystem services upon which all life on Earth depends. These ecosystem services include pollination, nutrient cycling, erosion control, carbon sequestration and natural hazard protection. Biodiversity and ecosystem services underpin all economic and social systems, and so are fundamental for thinking around resilience.

Yet, biodiversity is declining at an unprecedented rate with one million plant and animal species facing extinction, and terrestrial, freshwater and marine ecosystems being driven towards tipping points (IPBES, 2019[14]). According to the literature on planetary boundaries, the biosphere integrity boundary that refers to the functional integrity of ecosystems, hence biodiversity, has already been transgressed, with considerable implications for the resilience of natural systems.

Numerous interlinkages exist between biodiversity loss and climate change. For example, marine and terrestrial ecosystems are natural carbon sinks, with an annual gross sequestration equivalent to about 60% of global anthropogenic emissions (IPBES, 2019[14]). But biodiversity loss is reducing ecosystems' natural capacity to store carbon and is contributing to greenhouse gas emissions, thereby aggravating climate change. Deforestation alone accounts for an estimated 10% of anthropogenic greenhouse gas emissions.

Tackling biodiversity loss could therefore make an important contribution to climate mitigation efforts. Conserving, restoring and improving the management of forests, grasslands, wetlands and agricultural lands could deliver an estimated 23.8 gigatonnes of cumulative CO_2 emission reductions by 2030 (OECD, 2021[15]). The ecosystem services delivered by healthy, intact ecosystems can help protect humans from slow onset and extreme climate events. For example, wetlands can absorb surplus water during floods and be a water source during droughts, while forests can help stabilise land, reducing the risk of erosion, desertification, and landslides. Biodiverse ecosystems are both more resilient and offer more climate benefits than growing monocultures.

Nature-based solutions (NbS) can play an important role not only in helping ecosystems, communities and industries build resilience to climate impacts but also by mitigating climate change through emissions sequestration and broadly improving human well-being. For example, wetland restoration, revegetation or reforestation in river deltas and along shorelines and the protection of coastal ecosystems such as mangroves, saltmarshes or shellfish would all increase biodiversity, enhance coastal resilience to extreme weather and natural disasters, provide other co-benefits such as water purification or soil enhancement, and sequester carbon emissions.

While obvious synergies between climate and biodiversity action exist, some actions to mitigate and adapt to climate change can negatively affect biodiversity (e.g. large-scale expansion of bioenergy and monoculture plantations, renewable energy infrastructure, and construction of dams and seawalls). This requires careful planning and management. The mitigation pathways countries choose will determine the extent of potential trade-offs between climate and biodiversity action (OECD, 2021[15]). These trade-offs highlight the importance of considering systemic interactions in climate policy making. The resilience of the transition will rely not only on the ability to safeguard climate-specific policies, but also the extent to which these policies trade off climate-relevant components of other systems.

These policy interlinkages are becoming increasingly acknowledged within the policy sphere. The Kunming-Montreal Global Biodiversity Framework, agreed in December 2022 at CBD COP15, includes four goals to be achieved by 2050 and 23 targets to be achieved by 2030. Target 8 specifically refers to climate change, stating that by 2030 Parties should: "Minimize the impact of climate change and ocean acidification on biodiversity and increase its resilience through mitigation, adaptation, and disaster risk reduction actions, including through nature-based solutions and/or ecosystem-based approaches, while minimizing negative and fostering positive impacts of climate action on biodiversity."

To ensure coherence and alignment of climate and biodiversity policies, the OECD report *Towards Sustainable Land Use: Aligning Biodiversity, Climate and Food Policies* emphases the need to:

- Strengthen coherence across relevant national strategies and plans (e.g. for biodiversity, climate and other key areas), and ensure that these have specific and measurable targets.
- Strengthen institutional co-ordination between different ministries related to climate, biodiversity and other key areas, including for examples via the creation of inter-ministerial committees.
- Better integrate spatial data into land- and sea-use decision making.
- Examine opportunities to harness synergies in the development of policy instruments so as to better address climate and biodiversity simultaneously, such as through payments for ecosystem services, among other policy instruments (OECD, 2020[16]).

Further concerted efforts are needed to identify and address potential trade-offs across policy objectives and instruments, e.g. between the expansion of renewable energy and grid infrastructure, and the protection of nature. As climate change is the fastest growing driver of biodiversity loss, transitioning away from fossil fuels is fundamental to achieving global biodiversity objectives. However, the growing demand for low-carbon electricity requires more land and sea to be dedicated to power infrastructure, posing new and growing risks to biodiversity.

The potential impacts of renewable energy and grid infrastructure are diverse. They include, among others, direct species mortality (e.g. collision of birds and bats with powerlines and wind turbines); habitat loss and degradation (e.g. from conversion of land for solar energy facilities and mining impacts); habitat fragmentation and barrier effects on species movement; behavioural impacts (e.g. avoidance behaviour), ecosystem services impacts and complex indirect impacts. These impacts can accumulate across projects and across time.

To ensure the transition to low-carbon electricity is nature-positive, decision makers must mainstream biodiversity into low-carbon pathways and renewable energy policy, planning, programme and project cycles. Adopting low energy demand pathways to achieve the Paris Agreement goals is fundamental for reducing conflicts between renewable energy and biodiversity. It is also important that countries consider biodiversity when developing their energy portfolios and determining where and how to deploy renewable energy and transmission infrastructure. Failure to mainstream biodiversity could further erode natural capital, thereby increasing economic and societal risks, and undermining efforts to achieve climate goals.

Conversely, when the low-carbon transition is planned in a systematic way that explicitly addresses biodiversity, synergies can be harnessed, enhancing resilience. For example, deploying solar photovoltaics in degraded land together with ecological restoration activities that generate habitat for pollinators could help meet climate and energy goals, while reducing climate impacts on biodiversity, promoting nature recovery and supporting agriculture.

Oceans and climate change

Another example of the interlinkages between different natural systems are the oceans and climate change. More than two-thirds of the Earth's surface is covered by oceans, which play an essential role in regulating global climate patterns, foods chains, and general ecosystem health. Climate change also has important consequences for oceans. Biological, chemical and physical feedback loops threaten to cross irreversible tipping points with catastrophic implications for ocean ecosystems, the climate system, and interlinked socio-economic and natural systems. At the same time, the ocean acts as a key carbon sink, and since the industrial revolution has absorbed 30-40% of emitted CO_2 and 93% of excess global warming (Seeger, 2021[17]).

This absorptive quality of the ocean, however, comes with considerable consequences. Ocean acidification, warming and deoxygenation have severe impacts on marine ecosystems. Marine species such as coral are sensitive to the slightest change in temperature and ocean warming has already led to wide-spread coral bleaching and will likely result in the irreversible loss of most coral ecosystems (OECD, 2022[18]). This in turn has profound knock-on effects, including a loss of key habitat for marine life with impacts felt along the ocean food-chain, and exposing coastlines to extreme weather. Deoxygenation has already led to the formation of large ocean "dead-zones" where low oxygen levels prevent the survival of aquatic life. Acidification compromises the survival of organisms sensitive to ocean Ph levels, such as shellfish, in turn, affecting ocean ecosystems and food-chains (Seeger, 2021[17]).

These impacts of global warming on ocean ecosystems have been labelled as "silent" tipping points due to a general lack of awareness of their existence (Heinze et al., 2021[19]). While tipping points literature points to the potential for a collapse in ocean circulation systems such as the Atlantic Meridional Overturning Circulation (AMOC) (see Chapter 2), warming, acidification and deoxygenation can also lead to irreversible changes with profound implications. However, the complex and heterogeneous effects of these climate impacts on marine life make it difficult to understand how climate change is affecting oceans, and what changes to expect in the future.

Ocean ecosystems play an essential role throughout socio-economic systems, and changes to these ecosystems, as brought about by climate change, can have a profound impact, socially and economically. Some 4.5 billion people (half the world's population) obtain more than 15% of their protein intake from the ocean (IPCC, 2019[20]). Fisheries and aquaculture employ around 60 million people globally, with coastal populations particularly reliant on the oceans for their livelihoods (FAO, 2020[21]). The impacts of climate change on fisheries differ across regions, and according to the scale of the fisheries, with some projected to increase catches, while others experience a significant decrease (FAO, 2020[21]).

Forty per cent of the world's population and 75% of its largest cities are located in coastal zones. As such, much of the world's population and urban infrastructure is exposed to increasingly severe weather and sea-level rise. From 2000-2019, storms killed over 200 000 people and caused USD 1.4 trillion in damage globally. This figure is projected to increase significantly due to climate change, with coastal flooding projected to threaten 360 million people and 4% of global GDP annually by 2100 (UNDRR, 2020[22]).

It is clear that climate change will have a profound impact on the ocean, its ecosystems, and the large populations and industries relying on them. In addition to climate pressures, local stressors such as overfishing, eutrophication, chemical pollution and habitat destruction further compromise the health of ecosystems and their resilience to climate impacts. Over half of coastal ecosystems have been lost since 1900, one-third of fish stocks are overexploited, and 90% of waste entering the ocean remains close to shore (Seeger, 2021[17]).

These pressures highlight the need to combine climate mitigation and adaptation policies with ocean specific measures in order to safeguard the health of ocean ecosystems. The highly complex global ocean network and its myriad of interlinkages with other natural and socio-economic systems requires systems thinking and the development of systemic resilience to design policies for a sustainable and resilient ocean.

Given the fundamental uncertainties surrounding ocean systems and the risk of crossing the thresholds of irreversible tipping points, policy makers should err on the side of caution in building ocean resilience. Adapting fisheries management policies to ecosystem changes, for example, would make fisheries more resilient to potential shocks. This requires reducing overall mortality rates and then maintaining flexible management practices that can be adapted to future events and emerging knowledge. Maritime special planning and marine-protected areas are two further policy tools with considerable promise for enhancing sustainability and resilience. Both, however, rely on robust scientific evidence in order to monitor ecosystems, adapt to ecosystems changes, and ensure special planning and protected areas are implemented in appropriate locations.

Given its interlinkages with the climate and socio-economic systems, the oceans hold considerable promise for marine nature-based solutions (NbS). However, in order to take full advantage of NbS in ocean systems, certain barriers to their implementation need to be overcome.

As with climate impacts generally, developing countries, especially small island developing states (SIDS) and coastal least developed countries (LDCs), are particularly vulnerable to shocks to ocean and coastal systems, and often lack the adaptive capacity and investment support needed to build resilience. Only 56% of overseas development assistance (ODA) channelled towards ocean-related sectors focuses on increasing climate change adaptation, mitigation or sustainability (USD 1.6 billion in 2019) (OECD, 2020[23]). However, the oceans, much like the climate, are a global system. Building systemic resilience is only possible if the international community works together to manage the risks of climate change and other local stressors.

Interlinkages between the ocean, climate, human and other natural systems highlight the importance of ensuring a sustainable and resilient ocean to avoid risks not only to marine ecosystems but also to the people and economic activities that depend on them. Policies for ocean resilience are highly specific in many ways but also bear strong parallels with climate policies that are discussed elsewhere in this report. This includes the importance of long-term thinking and integrated policies across systems; and social considerations such as the needs of coastal communities; the vulnerability of developing countries; the need for international co-operation; and the challenges of communicating science.

Reaching net-zero emissions alone will not be enough to steer humanity towards a safe planetary operating space. The climate system is inextricably linked with other systems such as biodiversity and the oceans. Such interlinkages require careful consideration and a systemic approach to building resilience that reaches across systems boundaries.

Nature-based solutions for aligned mitigation and adaptation action

Nature-based solutions (NbS) can play an important role in harnessing synergies between adaptation and mitigation, as well as with biodiversity (OECD, 2021[24]). NbS are defined by the OECD as "measures that can protect, sustainably manage, and restore nature, with the goal of maintaining and enhancing ecosystem services to help address a variety of social, environmental and economic challenges" (OECD, 2020[25]), such as protecting and restoring coastal habitats and upland forests or greening urban spaces (OECD, 2021[5]).[3] NbS can encompass a range of approaches; such as ecological disaster risk reduction, ecosystem-based adaptation, green infrastructure or natural climate solutions.

Although usually defined as opposite to "traditional" or "grey" infrastructure, NbS can be complementary and even combined with it (OECD, 2020[26]). Nature-based solutions can be an effective complement to existing or new infrastructure development to reinforce adaptation of the built environment through natural measures. For example, the creation of permeable surfaces around infrastructure assets reduces flood risk, and fuel breaks around infrastructure assets protect infrastructure in wildfire hazard areas. In an urban context, buildings can be retrofitted with NbS for cooling and to reduce the radiation effect during heatwaves (OECD, 2023[27]).

The potential of nature-based solutions to address the causes and consequences of climate change has been recognised by policy makers at the national and international levels. The Paris Agreement, the Sendai Framework, and the Kunming-Montreal Global Biodiversity Framework, as agreed at CBD COP15, all recognise the potential of NbS. Following these international statements, two-thirds of the signatories to the Paris Agreement have mentioned the development of NbS as a main objective to adapt to and/or mitigate climate change in their nationally determined contributions (NDCs) (Seddon et al., 2019[28]). The majority of OECD countries also make NbS an explicit priority in their National Adaptation Plans (OECD, 2021[5]). Similarly, almost half of 210 cities that submitted adaptation plans to the Carbon Disclosure Project in 2016 included measures related to NbS, such as the creation of green spaces for climate change adaptation (UNEP, 2021[29]).

In addition to effectively mitigating climate change and its future impacts, NbS can be win-win or no-regret adaptation options. This is true as long as strong social and environmental safeguards are applied in their planning, implementation and management, with special focus on the rights of local and indigenous populations and intersectionality. As NbS produce co-benefits such as ecosystem services, they remain beneficial even in the absence of the climate mitigation and climate resilience benefits that they provide (Hallegatte, 2009[30]). For example, Sweden has invested EUR 22 million in natural measures to drain the cities of Augustenborg and Malmö. These green solutions have reduced water run-off by 50% and have also led to a substantial increase in local biodiversity (OECD, 2020[26]).

As a cost-effective adaptation solution, nature-based solutions also generate significant economic benefits. For example, NbS interventions to restore riverbeds in Europe have increased flood protection while also enhancing agricultural production, carbon sequestration and recreation, for a total net economic benefit of EUR 1400 per hectare per year (Vermaat et al., 2015[31]).

The economic benefits of NbS often far outweigh those of grey infrastructure. In the United States, NbS as coastal defences are two to five times more cost-effective than grey infrastructure (Narayan et al., 2016[32]). When strategically planned, NbS can also enhance the resilience of traditional infrastructure to climate risks, reducing their vulnerability to climate impacts and their operational costs while also extending their lifetime (OECD, 2020[33]). Investments in NbS can also stimulate job creation.

Despite their potential, the use of nature-based solutions remains piecemeal (Kapos et al., 2019[34]; Browder et al., 2019[35]). Although NbS projects are multiplying, they are often limited to small-scale and pilot projects (Tremolet et al., 2019[36]). A recent OECD survey on the implementation of NbS to address water-related climate risks shows that less than 10% of water managers who responded believed that progress in the implementation of NbS is in line with their country's ambitions (OECD., 2021[37]).

The implementation of NbS is impeded by a lack of awareness of their uses and benefits. In addition, several practical limitations present obstacles. First, it is difficult to assess and quantify the benefits of NbS and thus prove their effectiveness as adaptation solutions, especially in comparison to the short-term and easily observable benefits of so-called "grey" solutions (OECD, 2020[26]). Some natural solutions such as mangroves or forests can be slow to develop and deliver their full adaptation benefits (Kabisch et al., 2016[38]). Moreover, current evaluation tools are not well suited for NbS, and often fail in assessing their benefits in comparison to "traditional" grey options (Tremolet et al., 2019[36]). Second, while the flexibility of NbS in the face of future climate variability is an asset, their sensitivity to their evolving environment, including climate hazards, can undermine their effectiveness. For example, droughts and rising temperatures can lead to wildfires. As reforestation takes time, communities will remain unprotected for many years, and the capacity of forest to store carbon will be altered for decades (Anderegg et al., 2020[39]). In implementing NbS it is of course critical to ensure they are aligned with existing planning and regulatory arrangements so as to safeguard local communities.

More broadly, nature-based solutions are also more difficult to implement than individual adaptation solutions because they rely on a wide set of environmental and socio-economic parameters (Calliari, Staccione and Mysiak, 2019[40]). For example, coral reefs are sensitive to rising ocean temperatures but also to water pollution (DUBINSKY and STAMBLER, 1996[41]). While 70 to 90% of coral reefs could disappear if global average temperature increase reaches 1.5°C (IPCC, 2021[42]), maintaining coral reefs also requires concerted management of diffuse pollution potentially emanating from a large number of sources, located over a wide geographical area.

Three main policy challenges to the implementation of NbS have been highlighted in the literature (OECD., 2021[37]). First, due to a lack of knowledge of their effectiveness, NbS are often overlooked by climate policy makers. Second, assessing the economic costs and benefits of NbS remains difficult, posing a barrier to policy makers wishing to justify NbS vis-à-vis other policy options as well as potential investors or funding institutions needed to finance NbS projects. Finally, NbS remain ill-defined within climate policy taxonomies and legal structures, posing significant regulatory challenges (Kabisch et al., 2016[38]; Kapos et al., 2019[34]; OECD, 2020[26]; Browder et al., 2019[43]).

A range of policy options can be implemented to overcome these problems (OECD, 2021[44]; OECD, 2020[26]). First, more information is needed to better assess the potential of NbS, especially in comparison to or in combination with grey solutions. Overcoming the perception that NbS are too expensive and technically too difficult to implement relies on international scientific co-operation to address knowledge and data gaps. Governments can support the generation of information by funding pilot programmes or subsidising research. Platforms or open data can then disseminate information to different stakeholders to share the knowledge produced. Second, public institutions can provide a space for technical assistance and knowledge sharing to help stakeholders better understand the role of NbS and co-ordinate their actions. Third, the revision of land use regulations and building standards should encourage the use of NbS. Fourth, while increased awareness of NbS as a cost-effective solution to adapt to climate change will encourage its implementation, dedicated funding for NbS will still be needed.

The implementation of NbS can also be supported by developing sustainable finance solutions such as ecosystem insurance products. Incorporating NbS into risk assessment frameworks and enhancing data and modelling capacity in order to quantify climate risks and the benefits of NbS in their management is essential. Finally, implementing NbS requires clear communication with local communities, building public support and buy-in.

Chapter conclusions

The examples of systemic interactions explored in this chapter underscore the need for a systemic approach to resilience. However, more often than not, policy efforts remain confined to individual systems or policy areas. This is well illustrated by as-of-yet minimal co-ordination across adaptation and mitigation actions despite clear synergies between the two. While efforts to address this are underway, the quickening pace of climate change necessitates an acceleration. Here, awareness of the importance of resilience to climate impacts for a resilient net-zero transition may offer an opportunity to enhance co-ordination. Systemic interlinkages with other natural systems such as biodiversity and the oceans, and the ability for nature-based solutions (NbS) to make the most of synergies between different policy objectives further highlight the importance of taking a broad approach. Given the cost-effectiveness of many NbS/ecosystems in sequestering carbon, biodiversity policies should look to climate mitigation finance for funding.

Notes

1 https://www.minambiente.it/notizie/strategia-nazionale-di-adattamento-ai-cambiamenti-climatici-0.

2 The six objectives are: (i) Climate change mitigation, (ii) Climate change adaptation, (iii) Sustainable use and protection of water and marine resources, (iv) Transition to a circular economy, waste prevention and recycling, (v) Pollution prevention and control, (vi) Protection of healthy ecosystems.

3 The United Nations Environment Agency has adopted a very similar definition of Nature-based Solutions, as "actions to protect, conserve, restore, sustainably use and manage natural or modified terrestrial, freshwater, coastal and marine ecosystems, which address social, economic and environmental challenges effectively and adaptively, while simultaneously providing human well-being, ecosystem services and resilience and biodiversity benefits." https://www.naturebasedsolutionsinitiative.org/news/united-nations-environment-assembly-nature-based-solutions-definition/

References

Adaptation Committee (2022), *Information paper on linkages between adaptation and mitigation*, https://unfccc.int. [8]

Anderegg, W. et al. (2020), "Climate-driven risks to the climate mitigation potential of forests", *Science*, Vol. 368/6497, https://doi.org/10.1126/science.aaz7005. [39]

Browder, G. et al. (2019), *Integrating Green and Gray : Creating Next Generation Infrastructure*. [43]

Browder, G. et al. (2019), *Integrating Green and Gray: Creating Next Generation Infrastructure*, Washington, DC: World Bank and World Resources Institute, https://doi.org/10.1596/978-1-56973-955-6. [35]

Calliari, E., A. Staccione and J. Mysiak (2019), "An assessment framework for climate-proof nature-based solutions", *Science of The Total Environment*, Vol. 656, pp. 691-700, https://doi.org/10.1016/j.scitotenv.2018.11.341. [40]

CBD (1992), *Convention on Biological Diversity*, https://www.cbd.int/doc/legal/cbd-en.pdf. [10]

Denton, F. et al. (2014), "Climate-resilient pathways: adaptation, mitigation, and sustainable development", in *Climate Change 2014: Impacts, Adaptation, and Vulnerability. Part A: Global and Sectoral Aspects. Contribution of Working Group II to the Fifth Assessment Report of the Intergovernmental Panel on Climate Change*, Cambridge University Press, Cambridge, United Kingdom and New York, NY, USA. [7]

DUBINSKY, Z. and N. STAMBLER (1996), "Marine pollution and coral reefs", *Global Change Biology*, Vol. 2/6, pp. 511-526, https://doi.org/10.1111/j.1365-2486.1996.tb00064.x. [41]

FAO (2020), *The State of World Fisheries and Aquaculture 2020*, FAO, https://doi.org/10.4060/ca9229en. [21]

Hallegatte, S. (2009), "Strategies to adapt to an uncertain climate change", *Global Environmental Change*, Vol. 19/2, pp. 240-247, https://doi.org/10.1016/j.gloenvcha.2008.12.003. [30]

Harris, R. et al. (2018), *Biological responses to the press and pulse of climate trends and extreme events*, Nature Publishing Group, https://doi.org/10.1038/s41558-018-0187-9. [11]

Heinze, C. et al. (2021), "The quiet crossing of ocean tipping points", *Proceedings of the National Academy of Sciences*, Vol. 118/9, https://doi.org/10.1073/pnas.2008478118. [19]

Henderson, B. et al. (2022), "Soil carbon sequestration by agriculture: Policy options", *OECD Food, Agriculture and Fisheries Papers*, No. 174, OECD Publishing, Paris, https://doi.org/10.1787/63ef3841-en. [1]

IPBES (2019), *Global assessment report on biodiversity and ecosystem services of the Intergovernmental Science-Policy Platform on Biodiversity and Ecosystem Services*, https://doi.org/10.5281/zenodo.6417333. [14]

IPCC (2021), "Climate Change 2021: The Physical Science Basis. Contribution of Working Group I to the Sixth Assessment Report of the Intergovernmental Panel on Climate Change [Masson-Delmotte, V., P. Zhai, A. Pirani, S. L. Connors, C. Péan, S. Berger, N. Caud, Y. Chen,", *Cambridge University Press* In Press, p. 3949, https://www.ipcc.ch/report/ar6/wg1/downloads/report/IPCC_AR6_WGI_Full_Report.pdf. [42]

IPCC (2019), *IPCC Special Report on the Ocean and Cryosphere in a Changing Climate*, https://www.ipcc.ch/srocc/chapter/summary-for-policymakers/. [20]

Kabisch, N. et al. (2016), "Nature-based solutions to climate change mitigation and adaptation in urban areas: perspectives on indicators, knowledge gaps, barriers, and opportunities for action", *Ecology and Society*, Vol. 21/2, https://doi.org/10.5751/es-08373-210239. [38]

Kapos, V. et al. (2019), *The Role of the Natural Environment in Adaptation, Background Paper for the Global Commission on Adaptation,*, Global Commission on Adaptation, Rotterdam and Washington, D.C. [34]

Lankoski, J., A. Ignaciuk and F. Jésus (2018), "Synergies and trade-offs between adaptation, mitigation and agricultural productivity: A synthesis report", *OECD Food, Agriculture and Fisheries Papers*, No. 110, OECD Publishing, Paris, https://doi.org/10.1787/07dcb05c-en. [4]

Narayan, S. et al. (2016), "The effectiveness, costs and coastal protection benefits of natural and nature-based defences", *PLoS ONE*, Vol. 11/5, https://doi.org/10.1371/journal.pone.0154735. [32]

OECD (2023), *Developing an Integrated Approach to Green Infrastructure in Italy*, OECD Public Governance Reviews, OECD Publishing, Paris, https://doi.org/10.1787/d84bb8e4-en. [27]

OECD (2022), *Climate Tipping Points: Insights for Effective Policy Action*, OECD Publishing, Paris, https://doi.org/10.1787/abc5a69e-en. [18]

OECD (2021), "Biodiversity, natural capital and the economy: A policy guide for finance, economic and environment ministers", *OECD Environment Policy Papers*, No. 26, OECD Publishing, Paris, https://doi.org/10.1787/1a1ae114-en. [15]

OECD (2021), "Enhancing the effectiveness of sub-national biodiversity policy: Practices in France and Scotland, United Kingdom", *OECD Regional Development Papers*, No. 22, OECD Publishing, Paris, https://doi.org/10.1787/1a8c77b7-en. [24]

OECD (2021), *Scaling up Nature-based Solutions to Tackle Water-related Climate Risks: Insights from Mexico and the United Kingdom*, OECD Publishing, Paris, https://doi.org/10.1787/736638c8-en. [44]

OECD (2021), "Strengthening adaptation-mitigation linkages for a low-carbon, climate-resilient future", *OECD Environment Policy Papers*, No. 23, OECD Publishing, Paris, https://doi.org/10.1787/6d79ff6a-en. [3]

OECD (2021), *Strengthening Adaptation-Mitigation Linkages for a Low-Carbon, Climate-Resilient Future.* [5]

OECD (2020), *Developing Sustainable Finance Definitions and Taxonomies*, Green Finance and Investment, OECD Publishing, Paris, https://doi.org/10.1787/134a2dbe-en. [9]

OECD (2020), "Nature-based solutions for adapting to water-related climate risks", *OECD Environment Policy Papers* 21. [25]

OECD (2020), *Nature-based solutions for adapting to water-related climate risks.* [26]

OECD (2020), "Nature-based solutions for adapting to water-related climate risks", *OECD Environment Policy Papers*, No. 21, OECD Publishing, Paris, https://doi.org/10.1787/2257873d-en. [33]

OECD (2020), *Sustainable Ocean for All: Harnessing the Benefits of Sustainable Ocean Economies for Developing Countries*, The Development Dimension, OECD Publishing, Paris, https://doi.org/10.1787/bede6513-en. [23]

OECD (2020), *Towards Sustainable Land Use: Aligning Biodiversity, Climate and Food Policies*, OECD Publishing, Paris, https://doi.org/10.1787/3809b6a1-en. [16]

OECD (2014), *Climate Change, Water and Agriculture: Towards Resilient Systems*, OECD Studies on Water, OECD Publishing, Paris, https://doi.org/10.1787/9789264209138-en. [2]

OECD (2009), *Integrating Climate Change Adaptation into Development Co-operation: Policy Guidance*, OECD Publishing, Paris, https://doi.org/10.1787/9789264054950-en. [45]

OECD. (2021), *SCALING UP NATURE-BASED SOLUTIONS TO TACKLE WATER -RELATED CLIMATE RISKS*, ORGANIZATION FOR ECONOMIC. [37]

Pörtner, H. et al. (2021), *IPBES-IPCC co-sponsored workshop report on biodiversity and climate*, https://doi.org/10.5281/zenodo.4782538. [13]

Seddon, N. et al. (2019), *Nature-based solutions in nationally determined contributions: synthesis and recommendations for enhancing climate ambition and action by 2020*. [28]

Seeger, I. (2021), *Resilience and the Ocean-Climate Nexus*, https://www.oecd.org/climate-change/net-zero-resilience/. [17]

Smith, P. et al. (2018), "Impacts on terrestrial biodiversity of moving from a 2°C to a 1.5°C target", *Philosophical Transactions of the Royal Society A: Mathematical, Physical and Engineering Sciences*, Vol. 376/2119, p. 20160456, https://doi.org/10.1098/rsta.2016.0456. [12]

Swart, R. and F. Raes (2007), "Making integration of adaptation and mitigation work: mainstreaming into sustainable development policies?", *Climate Policy*, Vol. 7/4, pp. 288-303, https://doi.org/10.1080/14693062.2007.9685657. [6]

Tremolet, S. et al. (2019), *Investing in Nature for European Water Security*, The Nature Conservancy, Ecologic Institute and ICLE. [36]

UNDRR (2020), *Human Cost of Disasters*, https://www.undrr.org/publication/human-cost-disasters-overview-last-20-years-2000-2019. [22]

UNEP (2021), *Adaptation Gap Report 2021 The Gathering Storm - Adapting to Climate Change in a Post-pandemic World*. [29]

Vermaat, J. et al. (2015), "Assessing the societal benefits of river restoration using the ecosystem services approach", *Hydrobiologia*, Vol. 769/1, pp. 121-135, https://doi.org/10.1007/s10750-015-2482-z. [31]

13 Financing adaptation amid increasing climate risks

Increased investment in adaptation will be a critical element in building resilience to the physical impacts of climate change and there is a crucial need to both align finance flows with climate-resilient development, as well as mobilising additional resources for necessary adaptation measures. This chapter provides an overview of adaptation finance, associated concepts and methods, and explores sources and mechanisms for increasing adaptation finance. This includes the importance of government policy in creating an enabling environment for aligning finance and investment flows with adaptation needs and the particular role of the insurance sector in this endeavour.

This chapter draws on contributions to the horizontal project carried out under the responsibility of the Environment Policy Committee, the Development Assistance Committee and the Insurance and Private Pensions Committee.

Increased investment in adaptation will be critical for building resilience to the physical impacts of climate change. Consistent with Article 2.1c of the Paris Agreement, there is a need to align finance flows with climate-resilient development and mobilise additional resources for necessary adaptation measures. Measures will be context-specific, but evidence suggests that there is a large unmet need for finance to implement necessary and urgent investments in adaptation.

Both public and private entities play a key role in financing adaptation. While additional public spending is essential to achieve adaptation goals, the adaptation investment gap cannot be filled by public funds alone. Beyond specific adaptation funding, all financial flows, whether public or private, domestic or international, will have important consequences for climate resilience. In addition to radically increasing spending on adaptation, financing adaptation also means aligning all finance flows and investments with resilience objectives to ensure they do not undermine adaptation efforts.

This chapter provides an overview of adaptation finance, associated concepts and methods, and explores sources and mechanisms for increasing adaptation finance, including the role of insurance.

Scaling up adaptation finance and aligning investment with climate resilience

The need to scale up adaptation finance

There is a large untapped potential for cost-effective investments in adaptation measures. (Neumann et al., 2021[1]) estimate that proactive adaptation can reduce the overall cost of climate change by a factor of 15. Looking at potential interventions, studies have found average benefit-cost ratios ranging from 2:1–10:1 for a sample of investments, including nature-based solutions (NbS) for flood risk management and climate-resilient infrastructure (Global Commission on Adaptation, 2019[2]) (Hallegatte, Rentschler and Rozenberg, 2019[3]). In terms of scale, the Global Commission on Adaptation has identified USD 1.7 trillion of potential investments across just five potential interventions.

Estimated adaptation financing needs for developing countries alone stand at between USD 140-300 billion per year by 2030 and USD 280-500 billion per year by 2050 (UNEP, 2021[4]). This covers a wide range of potential adaptation efforts, ranging from education and training to the building of protective infrastructure, as well as building evaluation tools and strengthening the monitoring capacity of institutions (NAP Global Network, 2017[5]). Evaluating climate risks and adaptation needs also requires funding of researchers and expertise, observational technologies and data creation. Finally, adaptation planning requires capacities to analyse adaptation needs and translate them into adaptation objectives and plans.

Increasing adaptation needs also create new market opportunities, such as new adaptation technologies, innovative insurance schemes or data observation and collection tools. Some estimates put the value of the market created by adaptation at USD 26 trillion.[1]

Aligning investments with resilience

Financing adaptation requires not only mobilising additional funding but aligning investments from private and public actors with resilience. National governments should ensure coherence of local adaptation spending across sectors and levels of governments, and their alignment with national adaptation goals. At the same time, the funds needed for adaptation often far exceed public budgets and require the private sector to fill the gap (The World Bank, 2021[6]). Strengthening the enabling environment is essential for influencing the direction of the trillions of euros of investments that are made each year. Representing more than 80% of the investments made each year in OECD countries,[2] the private sector constitutes an essential source of financing for adaptation. As companies experience or prepare for foreseeable effects of the impacts of climate change, they could autonomously finance part of their adaptation. The provision of private capital is especially key in financing large-scale projects such as building new infrastructure for which public-private co-operation is necessary (OECD, 2021[7]).

The need to align finance with climate-resilient development is embedded in article 2.1c of the Paris Agreement, yet efforts to define and operationalise this concept are at an early stage. A recent OECD paper defines the concept of "climate resilience-aligned investments" (Mullan and Ranger, 2022[8]), developing a framework for climate resilience financing based on three key principles. First is the identification and management of physical risks arising from climate impacts such as drought or floods. The analysis of these risks includes forward-looking information projecting future impacts and should take into account the intersection between hazards, exposure and vulnerability. The second "do no significant harm" principle is based on holistic risk management, which ensures that investments do not increase the risk faced by others (e.g. by increasing the risk of downstream flooding or damaging biodiversity). The third principle stipulates that investments must be aligned with adaptation strategies and objectives. The framework aims both to align all investments, i.e. to ultimately move away from financing projects that undermine resilience, and to increase "positively aligned" investments, which directly finance adaptation actions in line with relevant goals and plans (e.g. NAPs).

Aligning finance with adaptation and resilience goals does not necessarily mean divestment from activities that face higher physical climate risk. Indeed, this would risk drawing capital away from the most at-risk communities and potentially lead to maladaptation. Financial risk management without adaptation alignment would have negative outcomes for the most climate-vulnerable communities and particularly for lower-income countries and other developing countries with high vulnerability such as small island developing states (SIDS). Rather, alignment implies divestment from activities that create risk and proactively supporting adaptation and resilience efforts.

The public sector has an essential role in strengthening the enabling environment for adaptation aligned finance. First, governments can generate and share information on the risks and opportunities of climate change as well as promote guidelines and best practices to adapt to climate change. By investing in data sharing platforms and risk mapping tools (e.g. the Adaptation Support Tool from Climate ADAPT, a partnership between the European Commission and the European Environment Agency (EEA)),[3] public institutions share climate data and climate risk assessments as a public good, and enable businesses and civil society to better understand the challenges associated with their activities (Mullan and Ranger, 2022[8]). Moreover, the public sector can gather information about successes and failures in financing adaptation to then guide private investors. The availability of knowledge about both climate impacts and how to finance adaptation allows investors to better manage current and future risks of climate change for their assets. By raising awareness of the benefits and avoided costs of adaptation measures, knowledge accumulation can also lead to proactive and autonomous efforts by others to manage those risks.

Governments can also support alignment by communicating clear adaptation objectives and needs, and by defining appropriate measures and targets to achieve them (Mullan and Ranger, 2022[8]). Governments can go further by defining the actors responsible for these actions as well as identifying potential funding needs and sources. The more detailed and long-term the government's strategy is, the more the various actors will be able to integrate the risks and opportunities of climate change into their investment strategies.

Governments have a range of economic and regulatory instruments to influence investments in the real economy (Mullan and Ranger, 2022[8]):

- Grants: to support socially beneficial actions such as research and development of adaptation technologies, training, or changes in water use and agricultural practices. Subsidies are particularly useful for initiating changes in practice or usage. For example, the city of Linz, Austria helped residents to install green roofs by covering the cost of their installation up to 30%.[4] Similarly, France subsidises the energy retrofitting of buildings by granting tax credits.[5]

- Taxes and charges: to discourage negative externalities. These have the dual advantage of providing an incentive to reduce activities that cause social costs while generating revenues that could be spent on adaptation. For example, Germany has a rainwater tax that is charged based on the impermeable area of a property, thereby encouraging the use of nature-based solutions. Since 2012, French municipalities have also been allowed to apply a tax on soil sealing, which aims to limit soil artificialisation and encourage the use of permeable surfaces.[6]
- Regulation and standards: to make sure project holders incorporate resilience issues into new investments. For example, the FAST-Infra Sustainable Infrastructure label encompasses climate resilience, as does the prototype certification framework for the Blue Dot Network. At the local level, for example, by revising urban planning, municipalities can limit new investments in flood-prone areas. Similarly, new building code standards can be set to increase spending in buildings and make them more resilient to weather events.
- Risk transfer and insurance: the extent to which climate-related risks are held by the government creates incentives to invest in managing climate-related risks, and has distributional consequences. Reforms to provide transparency on risk ownerships can increase predictability and reduce moral hazard.

Governments can also act as catalysts for investment through innovative financial instruments such as blended finance instruments. The combination of low (perceived) return on investment and high risk remains a major barrier to private sector investment in most adaptation-related projects (The World Bank, 2021[6]). Mechanisms such as blended finance can include performance-based market incentives, provide technical assistance to project owners, and absorb some of the risk that investors incur through debt swaps or climate risk guarantees and insurance. By dedicating a small amount of domestic public funds or international multilateral funds, countries can remove investment barriers and raise large amounts of private capital for adaptation (OECD, 2021[9]).

In this regard, the strategic use of grant or concessional finance by multilateral development banks (MDBs) can be highly impactful. Institutional reforms in MDBs, including reducing shareholder expectations for return on equity and better targeting of performance indicators, can help to shift them from a role as sole financiers of projects towards a focus on mobilisation of broader financial flows and catalytic activities such as policy support and capacity development. In this manner, MDBs can help to create an enabling environment for the alignment of finance flows with climate-resilient development in developing countries (OECD, 2021[10]). This kind of catalytic activity can also be important for activities such as the greening of developing country financial systems.

Countries can also issue green bonds to finance specifically designated adaptation projects. Green bonds differ from regular bonds in their use, as they must only be used to finance "green" projects, which can be related to biodiversity, pollution, climate change mitigation, or adaptation (OECD, n.d.[11]). According to the Global Center on Adaptation, almost 1 300 green bonds (16% of all green bonds issued up to September 2020) included adaptation and resilience objectives (Global Center on Adaptation (GCA), 2021[12]). As an illustration of the growing need to finance adaptation, the first bond fully dedicated to climate resilience, was launched by the European Bank for Reconstruction and Development (EBRD) in 2019, raising USD 700 million. Although the value of green bonds issued increased four-fold between 2017 and 2021,[7] they still represented less than 1% of all bonds issued in 2022.[8]

Governments should also lead by example by ensuring that resilience is mainstreamed in all public spending and investments, particularly given that many of the relevant investment needs are within the competence of public authorities. The aim of this is to ensure that there are sufficient resources to achieve an acceptable level of risk while also aligning public spending with the reality of mounting physical climate risks. Key tools for achieving this include mainstreaming into budget planning, budget tagging (to identify trends in spending), and reform of procurement policies (such as using life-cycle costing) to reflect the benefits of adaptation. For a more detailed discussion of aligning public budgets and procurement with climate policy objectives, see Chapter 5.

Beyond the role for governments, investors and investor coalitions themselves can drive progress by demanding adaptation-aligned investment opportunities. They can also articulate frameworks and minimum standards for what information they require from investees. For example, The Institutional Investors Group on Climate Change (IIGCC) has released a set of investors' expectations on the management of physical risks and opportunities (IIGCC, 2021[13]).

Progress to date on financing adaptation

Despite the clear case for aligning public and private financial flows with adaptation needs, the extent to which this is taking place remains unclear. Information about domestic public spending on adaptation remains scarce. Few OECD countries highlight adaptation spending in their National Adaptation Plans (NAPs) or Adaptation Communications. Among those that do, Austria has estimated its spending for adaptation to be EUR 480 million per year (Austria, 2021[14]). South Korea has tracked and reported past spending for specific adaptation activities, for example, spending USD 3.5 million on developing crop-specific impact assessments, but does not provide broader aggregate figures (South Korea, 2021[15]). Similarly, the extent to which private investment contributes to climate resilience is unknown. One estimate suggests that private sector spending for adaptation is less than USD 1 billion per year (Buchner et al., 2021[16]) while the World Bank suggests that private sector financing for adaptation may already be substantial (The World Bank, 2021[17]). The OECD estimates that official development finance mobilised USD 4.4 billion of private finance for adaptation in 2020 (OECD, 2023[18]).

Multilateral development banks have made significant commitments to financing adaptation in recent years. In December 2017, together with the International Development Finance Club (IDFC), MDBs announced their vision for aligning financial flows with the objectives of the Paris Agreement, with one building block being dedicated to adaptation and climate resilience (Mullan and Ranger, 2022[8]). In December 2018, MDBs again declared their commitment to actively manage physical climate risks and co-operate to catalyse low-emissions and climate-resilient development.[9] As noted in Chapter 5, there have been calls for a reform of MDBs, including at COP27 in Sharm el-Sheikh, to better enable their implementation of these goals.

Finance flows for adaptation are only comprehensively measured as part of International public finance. Here, recent estimates show that while mitigation finance still represents the majority of all climate funding in 2020 (58%), adaptation finance almost tripled between 2016 and 2020, mostly due to investment in a few big infrastructure projects (OECD, 2022[19]; OECD, 2022[20]).

To date, the amount of funding mobilised by OECD countries in response to extreme weather events is likely to be considerably higher than funding for ex ante adaptation measures. For example, the German federal government set up a EUR 30 billion reconstruction fund to help victims of the 2021 flood (Reuters, 2021[21]). Compared to this, the third German Adaptation Action Plan (APA III) only allocated EUR 420 million to flood protection measures for the period 2020-2025. In Japan, central government budget data for both *ex ante* and *ex post* disaster management expenditure has been annually published since 1980 and shows a clear trend in increased funding for post-disaster recovery and reconstruction. In Colombia, post-disaster spending has grown on average by 65.26% per year (1998-2008), while pre-disaster spending only increased by 22.08% over the same period (OECD, 2018[22]).

Part of the challenge in accurately measuring adaptation finance flows is that defining what constitutes adaptation finance remains complex. Adaptation is often integrated into broader investments: in some cases, there will be identifiable marginal costs (e.g. raising a bridge) related to adaptation, but in others, adaptation responses are harder to quantify as they may involve broad changes in the way a project is implemented (e.g. relocating a planned infrastructure asset). Appropriate adaptation responses are also context-specific, so the contribution of an investment to adaptation will depend on a variety of factors.

A precise definition of adaptation finance is open to debate, particularly in terms of whether to count the marginal cost of adaptation measures or the entire value of projects. Recognising the need to clarify what is meant by adaptation finance, many entities have created their own definitions (see OECD (2020[23]) for a recent review). One of the first attempts to define adaptation finance was the Rio Markers, developed by the OECD to track flows of international finance for adaptation (OECD, n.d.[24]). Development agencies use these markers to track how their investments are allocated to one or several environmental objectives, including adaptation. Multilateral development banks have also joined forces to set "Common Principles for Climate Change Adaptation Finance Tracking" (MDB Climate Finance Tracking Working Group and the IDFC Climate finance Working Group, 2018[25]). This classification is used to measure the share of total project cost that belongs to adaptation.

Other efforts seek to elicit the adaptation part of private investments, such as taxonomies relying on process and sector-based classification of adaptation activities. For example, the recently released EU Taxonomy[10] and the Inter-American Development Bank's (IADB's) adaptation solutions taxonomy[11] can be used to characterise private finance as participating in one or more climate finance objectives. These taxonomies aim to change investor behaviour by making it mandatory to report investments according to these classifications, with the ultimate aim of influencing finance flows.

Despite the lack of quantitative information on adaptation spending, a review of OECD countries' NAPs, NASs and Adaptation Communications provides an insight into the importance that countries place on finance for effective adaptation to climate change. Financing is mentioned in almost all NAPs and several countries have dedicated sections to adaptation finance, while others identify adaptation finance as one of a small selection of top priorities for their adaptation strategies. Other initiatives have also been taken to enhance adaptation finance outside of the NAP process. For example, to support adaptation financing, Australia created a council of financial regulators to implement regulatory measures to help the financial sector better understand climate risk and address regulatory gaps undermining the consideration of climate risk.

There is growing interest in resilience issues within the financial sector itself as well, driven by the increasingly visible costs of climate-related extreme events and increasing financial opportunities offered by a changing climate. Several initiatives are underway to address this issue. For example, the recommendations and guidance issued by the Task Force on Climate-related Financial Disclosure (TCFD) are supported by over 3 000 organisations worldwide, representing USD 27.2 trillion in assets under management. The Coalition for Climate Resilient Investment brings together 120 public- and private-sector members to help increase private- and public-sector spending on resilience.

Some sectors, notably insurance, already have long-established procedures for managing physical climate-related financial risks. However, the focus here has been primarily on managing current risks rather than projected future risks even though it is clear that climate impacts will increase even if mitigation targets are met. This is due to the short timescale upon which asset and investment decisions are made. In addition, damages from physical climate risks to date, at least in more advanced economies, have been moderate compared to other sources of financial risks (Mullan and Ranger, 2022[8]).

To effectively harness growing interest from the financial sector in aligning financial flows with adaptation needs, initiatives such as environmental, social, and governance (ESG) criteria could play a considerable role, including by facilitating investment in resilient infrastructure. But such initiatives first need to overcome a number of issues. In particular, there needs to be measurement of financial flows and collection of data on how they align with adaptation efforts (Box 13.1). There is also the need to ensure financial sector commitments are implemented with integrity (see Chapter 9). Similarly, private sector-led adaptation efforts that align with responsible business conduct (RBC) guidelines can play an important role in enhancing climate resilience. They must first overcome challenges regarding the traceability of actions and accountability (see Chapter 9).

Box 13.1. Data for private investment in resilient infrastructure

One of the barriers to investment in resilient infrastructure is the lack of data. This data issue has been raised in various international discussions but, in particular, is reflected in Policy Message VII of the *Outcome Document of 2021 G20 Infrastructure Investors Dialogue Financing Sustainable Infrastructure for the Recovery* (October 2021). It calls to "[p]romote further **consistency in data collection** through improved methodologies and common terminologies, in particular in the ESG and new technologies area…". Having more data available is intended to address the information asymmetry in infrastructure financing. This leads to greater certainty and clarity for investors when they consider investments in sustainable infrastructure.

However, data availability on resilient infrastructure still faces multiple challenges. First, there is a need to define infrastructure to harmonise basic data collection as there is currently no internationally recognised definition of infrastructure for these purposes. The OECD's Working Party on National Accounts has developed an infrastructure definition to facilitate the data collection and comparison of statistics based on the System of National Accounts, which could be a useful starting point. A second challenge lies in defining what resilient infrastructure is. Despite extensive discussions on sustainable infrastructure to date, there is still no clear understanding of what it might constitute. The definition of sustainable infrastructure characteristics can be based on the many public and private sector initiatives on sustainable finance and infrastructure in recent years. A final challenge relates to the lack of availability of ESG data. While ESG-adjacent data exists, ESG-assessed data is not publicly available, and thus it is currently not possible to assess the performance of sustainable infrastructure. This lack of data is partly the result of the high cost of producing ESG data. Given the nature of infrastructure projects, infrastructure data is inherently expensive to produce and ESG data is even more resource-intensive. Greater implementation of existing sustainable infrastructure labels and the development of indicators could enable the dissemination of ESG data. Initiatives such as FAST-Infra, Blue Dot Network and the collection of QII indicators could contribute to and create a data repository for sustainable infrastructure in the future.

Source: OECD.

The role of the insurance sector in building resilience

The insurance sector plays a particularly notable role in enhancing efforts to align financial flows with adaptation and resilience needs.[12] While climate change poses physical and transition risks to the insurance sector, the sector can also significantly contribute to climate mitigation and adaptation through investment allocation and underwriting decisions (Figure 13.1).

In recent years, a number of international initiatives have been set up to support the sector in these efforts. These include the UN-convened Net-Zero Insurance Alliance, Insurance Development Forum, ClimateWise, the Sustainable Markets Initiative, the Munich Climate Insurance Initiative, the UN Principles for Sustainable Insurance, and the Global Shield against Climate Risks.[13] In line with these trends, many (re)insurance companies have also taken steps to withdraw or reduce the coverage they provide to companies involved in coal and (to a lesser extent) other types of fossil fuel activities.[14]

Figure 13.1. Contribution of insurance to climate change mitigation and adaptation

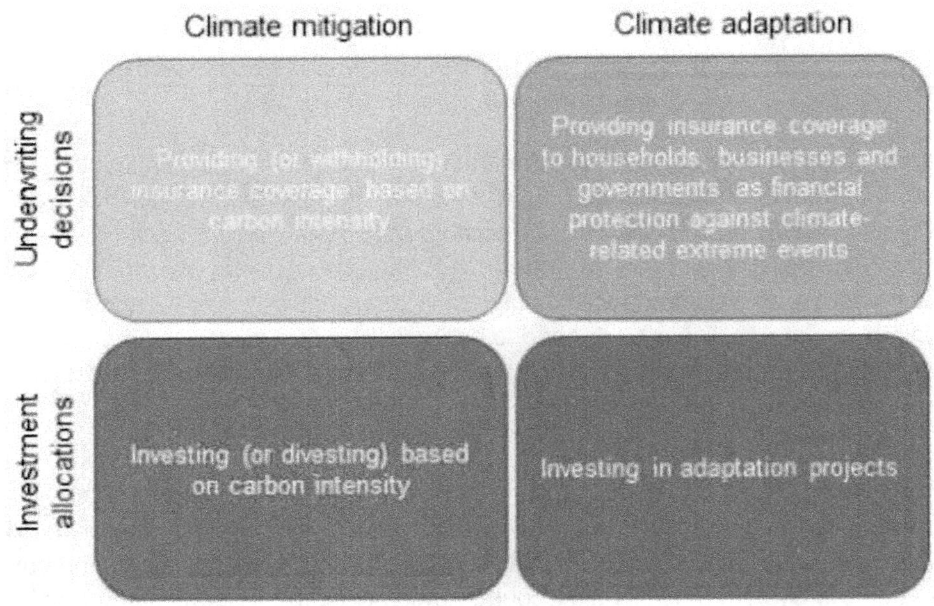

Source: OECD.

Climate risks and the resilience of the insurance sector

The physical, transition and liability risks of climate change pose significant risks to the insurance sector. These risks include those impacting insurers' assets (i.e. investments held to fund obligations to policyholders) and liabilities (i.e. the obligations created by the insurance coverage provided to households and businesses[15]). The types of risks as they apply to both liabilities and assets are outlined in more detail below (Figure 13.2).

Figure 13.2. Principle climate change risks to (re)insurance companies

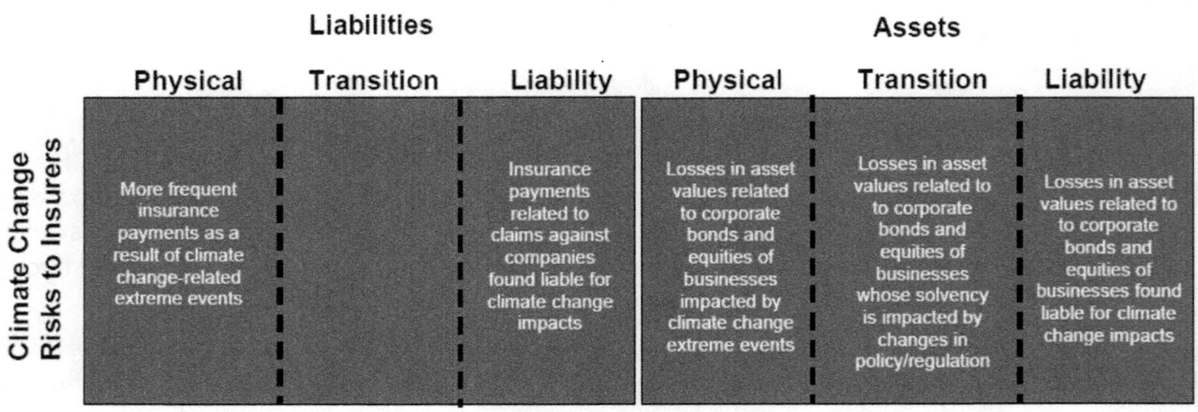

Source: OECD.

Monitoring these risks to insurance has been an important area of focus for international organisations, and individual regulatory and supervisory authorities overseeing risks to the insurance sector and broader financial system (Figure 13.3). International organisations and financial sector regulators are developing common tools (such as scenario analyses) to support the assessment of climate risks to insurance companies, with a particular focus on asset-related risks. The International Association of Insurance Supervisors has established a Climate Risk Steering Group with an initial focus on contributing to the development of scenario analysis and other supervisory tools for monitoring climate risks to the insurance sector. There have also been increasing efforts to collect data to assess liability risks for insurers as a result of the coverage they provide to households and businesses, although these risks have been more challenging to assess.[16]

Figure 13.3. Monitoring of climate change risks to the insurance sector and broader financial system

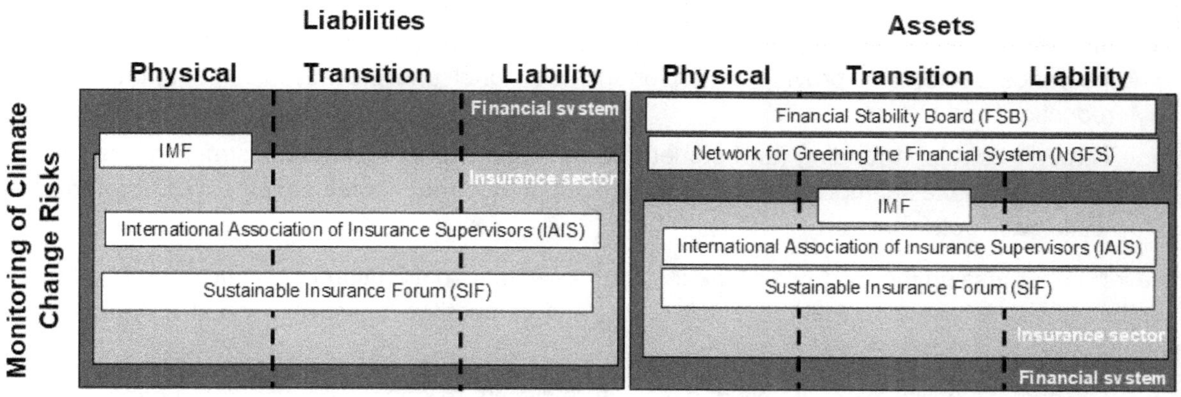

Source: OECD.

The level of financial protection provided by the insurance sector to other parts of the financial system (particularly banks) is also receiving increasing attention. For example, the Financial Stability Board's recommendations for enhancing supervisory oversight of climate-related risks to the financial sector includes a need to enhance the monitoring of risk transfers between the banking and insurance sectors (Financial Stability Board, 2022[26]).

Insurance sector contributions to climate change adaptation

Insurance coverage for climate perils can play a critical role in absorbing the costs of future climate damages and losses, supporting economic recovery in the aftermath of climate disasters, and ultimately building resilience. However, in many developed and developing countries, the level of insurance coverage for climate and other disaster-related damages and losses is relatively low, meaning that households, businesses and governments ultimately absorb a significant share of these costs. Increasing damages and losses from more frequent and/or more severe climate disasters could limit the availability of affordable insurance in the future and lead to larger uninsured losses for households and businesses. This will be the case if the amount of premiums needed to be collected to cover higher losses leads to a cost of coverage that is beyond the willingness (or capacity) of households and businesses to pay (EIOPA, 2021[27]). In this way, supporting adaptation measures to reduce the overall risk of climate impacts will be the only sustainable means to limit the increase in future climate damages and losses, and prevent potential disruptions to the availability of affordable insurance coverage that could result. In a number of countries and/or regions, increasing losses from climate-related impacts has led to concerns about the availability of affordable insurance coverage, such as for cyclone-related wind and flood damage in Australia, wildfires in California (United States) and floods in Ireland (OECD, 2021[28]).

The Insurance and Private Pensions Committee has developed an analysis of the potential contributions the insurance sector could make to climate change adaptation and ways to enhance that contribution. The insurance sector can play a role by identifying assets at risk, and encouraging and investing in risk reduction and adaptation (as a complement to government investment in adaptation):

- The insurance sector is at the forefront of developing sophisticated risk analytical tools such as catastrophe models. These tools can provide probabilistic estimates of the level of climate risk to homes, buildings and public assets in specific locations, taking into account individual building structural characteristics as well as any existing protections at the community level (e.g. flood barriers).
- Leveraging its claims experience and risk analytics, the insurance sector can provide expertise to climate policy makers, individual policyholders and wider communities on adaptation and risk reduction measures that can provide effective protection against climate perils;
- In applying premium pricing that reflects the level of risk at the level of individual policyholders, the insurance sector can provide an important risk signal and incentives for adaptation and risk reduction; and,
- Through its role in funding (and sometimes managing) post-event reconstruction, the insurance sector can make an important contribution to supporting resilient reinstatement (also referred to as "build back better").

However, in harnessing the full force of the insurance sector's contribution to climate change adaptation, a number of regulatory, technical, business model and competitive constraints need to be considered. These include:

- The sector's ability to accurately quantify future climate risk based on analysis of hazard exposure and vulnerability. The accuracy of risk information and signals can be impacted by uncertainties related to the level of future emissions (and resulting climate conditions); the impact of climate change on future hazard frequency and severity; and future changes in exposure and vulnerability as a result of economic and population growth in areas at risk, and levels of investment in adaptation and risk reduction. In addition, the demand for future climate risk analytics may be constrained by the short-term nature of insurance contracts, leading to a focus on near-term rather than longer-term climate conditions.
- While the insurance sector recognises the value of its risk management, risk reduction and adaptation expertise (and invests in sharing that knowledge with governments, communities and individual policyholders), the ability of the insurance sector to provide targeted advice – which could involve significant costs – is limited, particularly in the context of smaller insured risks (i.e. for which limited premiums are collected).
- There is only limited evidence that providing information on risk, including advice and services to support risk reduction, leads to the implementation of adaptation measures by policyholders. However, this may be partly due to regulation that limits (possibly inadvertently) the ability of insurance companies in some countries to provide risk management services (e.g. home sensors and monitoring services that can detect and/or prevent water or fire damage) to policyholders because of legal restrictions on the involvement of insurance companies in non-insurance commercial activities. Rules may also exist in countries where unfair trading practices that could undermine premium pricing requirements are restricted.
- Competitive factors, risk assessment capacity and regulation (in some countries) can impact the ability of insurance companies to charge premiums to individual policyholders that are truly reflective of the level of risk and therefore effectively incentivise risk reduction.[17]
- In addition, risk-reflective pricing may not sufficiently incentivise policyholders to undertake costly risk reduction or adaptation measures when it would be in exchange for premium discounts that take many years to fully recoup the cost of the adaptation investment. Longer-term insurance

coverage contracts could support better risk signalling and incentives, although they would lead to a significantly higher cost of premiums for policyholders and could be detrimental to market competition by impeding policyholders' ability to change insurance providers.

- While investing in risk reduction is usually most cost-effective during the reinstatement of a damaged property, insurance companies have little incentive to absorb the additional cost of resilience improvements – particularly where policyholders are free to seek coverage from a competitor who will then benefit from the resulting reduction in risk. Insurance companies are only obligated to repair an insured property to its pre-existing state and would have no way to ensure that any additional payments made to policyholders for betterment could be recouped through future premium earnings or reductions in future losses – as the policyholder could seek coverage from another insurance company.

Opportunities to enhance the role of the insurance sector

The underwriting and investment decisions of insurance companies – as providers of financial protection and significant portfolio investors (and, in some cases, as third-party asset managers) – can have important implications for driving climate resilience. This includes through the development of sophisticated risk analytical tools, leveraging the sector's expertise in risk analytics and risk reduction measures, providing important risk signals and incentives, and contributing to resilient reinstatement efforts.

Although there are challenges to harnessing the full potential of these efforts, there are also a number of opportunities to enhance the sector's contribution to adaptation, building on the above. These include the following:

- While not the main objective of insurance supervision, enhancing regulatory and supervisory efforts to ensure that insurance companies are appropriately monitoring climate risks is incentivising the development of longer-term climate risk assessments. For example, the Bank of England's 2021 Climate Biennial Exploratory Scenario exercise required certain insurers to provide a quantitative assessment of the impact of climate on future losses which led to the development of risk analytics to help insurers meet this requirement (Clarke and Latchman, 2021[29]).
- Policy and regulatory requirements that impede the provision of risk management and mitigation services, and the setting of risk-reflective premiums could be examined by governments to determine whether the benefits[18] of these restrictions outweigh the costs of restricting the insurance sector's role in advising on and incentivising risk reduction and adaptation[19] (or whether other (or modified) approaches[20] might be able to achieve these objectives while still contributing to climate adaptation). Insurance regulators or supervisors could encourage insurance companies to provide better and more targeted information on climate risk and potential adaptation investments that policyholders can make.
- The insurance sector and government could provide more co-ordinated support for resilient reinstatement (i.e. rebuilding damaged property to be more resilient) – which is likely a more cost-effective approach to managing the financial impacts of climate risks than providing compensation for damages and losses after an event. Insurers could also be encouraged to make coverage available (at an additional cost) for resilient reinstatement.

Chapter conclusions

A primary reason for the insufficient progress made on building climate resilience is the clear lack of finance for adaptation efforts. While progress has been made on setting national and subnational adaptation objectives, no comprehensive assessment of the financing needs of meeting these objectives exists. Challenges in defining what counts as adaptation efforts, and then measuring these, confound this problem. Overcoming barriers to scaling up adaptation finance is not only a task for governments. Rather, financial markets and the private sector also have an important role to play, as with mitigation efforts. In particular, the insurance sector holds considerable promise for advancing progress on financing adaptation.

Notes

1 https://www.ifc.org/wps/wcm/connect/publications_ext_content/ifc_external_publication_site/publications_listing_page/adapting-to-natural-disasters-in-africa?cid=IFC_LI_IFC_EN_EXT

2 https://www.oecd.org/governance/public-investment.htm

3 https://climate-adapt.eea.europa.eu/en/knowledge/tools/adaptation-support-tool

4 https://france-renov.gouv.fr/aides/credit-impot#:~:text=Cette%20aide%20fiscale%20s'%C3%A9l%C3%A8ve,euros%20par%20personne%20%C3%A0%20charge

5 https://france-renov.gouv.fr/aides/credit-impot#:~:text=Cette%20aide%20fiscale%20s'%C3%A9l%C3%A8ve,euros%20par%20personne%20%C3%A0%20charge

6 https://www.legifrance.gouv.fr/codes/article_lc/LEGIARTI000022494760/2010-07-14

7 https://www.climatebonds.net/market/data/

8 The Climate Bonds Initiative estimates the value of green bonds released in 2022 at around USD 1 trillion, while the International Capital Market Association estimates the value of global bonds at around USD 128 trillion. (https://www.icmagroup.org/market-practice-and-regulatory-policy/secondary-markets/bond-market-size/).

9 Joint Declaration MDBs Alignment Approach to Paris Agreement (worldbank.org)

10 https://finance.ec.europa.eu/sustainable-finance/tools-and-standards/eu-taxonomy-sustainable-activities_en

11 https://publications.iadb.org/publications/english/document/Adaptation-Solutions-Taxonomy.pdf

12 A global architecture for climate and disaster risk finance and insurance includes all financial instruments and corresponding institutional structures that can be used for the management and transfer of climate-related risks. Insurance solutions are a prominent example and thus the focus of this section. Besides insurance, risk financing also includes other instruments that can provide fast and reliable pay-outs in case of catastrophes, such as Contingent Credits, Contingency Reserves, or Credit Guarantees.

13 The UN-convened Net Zero Insurance Alliance is focused on encouraging low-carbon underwriting and investment decisions through a commitment by participants to achieve net-zero targets in underwriting and investment portfolios. The Insurance Development Forum (IDF) is focused on addressing climate-related financial protection gaps in developing countries. ClimateWise works to align underwriting and investment with climate goals. The Sustainable Markets Initiative (Insurance Task Force) focuses on

both sustainability in underwriting and investment decisions, and addressing climate-related financial protection gaps in developing countries. The Munich Climate Insurance Initiative aims to support climate resilience in developing countries through the implementation of climate insurance solutions. UN-convened Principles for Sustainable Insurance encourages sustainable underwriting and investment (including from a climate change perspective) through a commitment by participants to adhere to sustainable underwriting and investment principles. The Global Shield against Climate Risks is a joint initiative of the G7 and the Vulnerable Twenty Group of Finance Ministers (V20), which was officially launched at COP27 in Sharm el-Sheikh in 2022. The Global Shield will support instruments designed to strengthen resilience and provide rapid financial assistance when a climate-related disaster has impacted vulnerable communities. This includes various financial protection instruments such as social protection systems or insurance schemes tailored towards the needs of the country.

14 According to Insure our Future, an international campaign aimed at encouraging insurer exit from underwriting coal, and oil and gas activities, approximately 41 (re)insurers have placed restriction on providing coverage for the coal sector (representing 39.3% of the primary insurance market and 62.1% of the reinsurance market) while 13 (re)insurers have placed restrictions on providing coverage for the oil and gas sector (Insure Our Future, 2022[32]).

15 For example, a changing climate is expected to increase the frequency and/or intensity of a range of climate-related perils, including floods, storms and cyclones, wildfires and droughts. More frequent or more intense climate-related disasters – as well as continued development in hazard-prone locations – will lead to increasing damages to homes, businesses and public assets, and losses as a result of disrupted livelihoods and business interruption. To the extent that these losses are insured, insurance companies will face increasing losses as a result of the claims they pay.

16 A few individual insurance supervisors (e.g. France, United Kingdom) have undertaken stress tests or other types of analyses of the impact of climate change physical risks on insurance liabilities (see: (ACPR, 2021[30]) (Prudential Regulation Authority, 2022[31]).

17 In some countries, premium pricing is subject to a simplified pricing framework due to the existence of a catastrophe risk insurance programme that pools risks into a mandated pricing framework that requires that only certain criteria are considered in price-setting, thereby reducing the extent to which premiums fully reflect the level of underlying risk.

18 These types of restrictions are most often imposed in order to protect consumers, ensure broad affordable coverage or support competitive markets.

19 While risk-based pricing – and particularly the offer of premium discounts – should encourage policyholders to invest in risk reduction, there is mixed evidence on whether advice on risk reduction options and incentives through premium pricing are effective in leading to policyholder risk reduction investment. There are a number of other challenges that might impede policyholder risk reduction action, including the high cost of risk reduction measures relative to the potential benefits in terms of reduced premiums (among other challenges).

20 For example, in jurisdictions where risk-based pricing is limited by rating approval requirements or the presence of catastrophe risk insurance programmes that apply flat (or relatively flat) pricing frameworks, policyholders could be provided with information on what the risk-based (actuarial-based) premium would be if there were no impediments to risk-based pricing. This would at least provide a price signal to the policyholder related to the level of risk that they face even if the actual premium paid may not provide a significant incentive for risk reduction (a shift towards greater risk-based pricing would be more effective in creating such incentives). It could also provide a signal to governments on where risk

reduction or adaptation investments should be made (for example, if households in a specific community are facing unsustainable levels of current or future risk).

References

ACPR (2021), *A first assessment of financial risks stemming from climate change: The main results of the 2020 climate pilot exercise*, Banque de France. [30]

Austria (2021), *Austria's Adaptation Communication*. [14]

Buchner, B. et al. (2021), *Global Landscape of Climate Finance 2021*. [16]

Clarke, A. and S. Latchman (2021), *Helping Clients Respond to the Bank of England*, AIR Worldwide, https://www.air-worldwide.com/blog/posts/2021/8/helping-clients-respond-to-the-bank-of-englands-2021-climate-biennial-exploratory-scenario/ (accessed on 11 June 2022). [29]

EIOPA (2021), *Report on non-life underwriting and pricing in light of climate change*, European Insurance and Occupational Pensions Authority. [27]

Financial Stability Board (2022), *Supervisory and Regulatory Approaches to Climate-related Risks*. [26]

Global Center on Adaptation (GCA) (2021), *Green Bonds for Climate Resilience - State of Play and Roadmap to Scale*. [12]

Global Commission on Adaptation (2019), *Adapt Now: A Global Call for Leadership on Climate Resilience*, https://gca.org/reports/adapt-now-a-global-call-for-leadership-on-climate-resilience/ (accessed on 25 January 2023). [2]

Hallegatte, S., J. Rentschler and J. Rozenberg (2019), *Lifelines*, https://doi.org/10.1596/978-1-4648-1430-3. [3]

IIGCC (2021), *Building Resilience to a Changing Climate: Investor Expectations of Companies on Physical Climate Risks and Opportunities*, https://www.iigcc.org/download/building-resilience-to-a-changing-climate-investor-expectations-of-companies-on-physical-climate-risks-and-opportunities/?wpdmdl=4902&refresh=645bfff23a70c1683750898. [13]

Insure Our Future (2022), *2022 Scorecard on Insurance, Fossil Fuels & Climate Change*, Insure Our Future, https://global.insure-our-future.com/scorecard/. [32]

MDB Climate Finance Tracking Working Group and the IDFC Climate finance Working Group (2018), *Lessons Learned from Three Years of Implementing the MDB-IDFC Common Principles for Climate Change Adaptation Finance Tracking*, https://www.idfc.org/wp-content/uploads/2018/12/mdb_idfc_lessonslearned-full-report.pdf. [25]

Mullan, M. and N. Ranger (2022), "Climate-resilient finance and investment: Framing paper", *OECD Environment Working Papers*, No. 196, OECD Publishing, Paris, https://doi.org/10.1787/223ad3b9-en. [8]

NAP Global Network (2017), *Financing National Adaptation Plan (NAP) Processes: Contributing to the achievement of nationally determined contribution (NDC) adaptation goals*. [5]

Neumann, J. et al. (2021), "Climate effects on US infrastructure: the economics of adaptation for rail, roads, and coastal development", *Climatic Change*, Vol. 167/3-4, https://doi.org/10.1007/s10584-021-03179-w. [1]

OECD (2023), *Private finance mobilised by official development finance interventions*. [18]

OECD (2022), *Aggregate Trends of Climate Finance Provided and Mobilised by Developed Countries in 2013-2020*, Climate Finance and the USD 100 Billion Goal, OECD Publishing, Paris, https://doi.org/10.1787/d28f963c-en. [19]

OECD (2022), *Climate Finance Provided and Mobilised by Developed Countries in 2016-2020: Insights from Disaggregated Analysis*, Climate Finance and the USD 100 Billion Goal, OECD Publishing, Paris, https://doi.org/10.1787/286dae5d-en. [20]

OECD (2021), "Building resilience: New strategies for strengthening infrastructure resilience and maintenance", *OECD Public Governance Policy Papers*, No. 05, OECD Publishing, Paris, https://doi.org/10.1787/354aa2aa-en. [7]

OECD (2021), *Enhancing Financial Protection Against Catastrophe Risks: The Role of Catastrophe Risk Insurance Programmes*, OECD. [28]

OECD (2021), *Investing in the climate transition: The role of development banks, development finance institutions and their shareholders*. [10]

OECD (2021), *The OECD DAC Blended Finance Guidance*, Best Practices in Development Co-operation, OECD Publishing, Paris, https://doi.org/10.1787/ded656b4-en. [9]

OECD (2020), *Developing Sustainable Finance Definitions and Taxonomies*, Green Finance and Investment, OECD Publishing, Paris, https://doi.org/10.1787/134a2dbe-en. [23]

OECD (2018), *Assessing the Real Cost of Disasters: The Need for Better Evidence*, OECD Reviews of Risk Management Policies, OECD Publishing, Paris, https://doi.org/10.1787/9789264298798-en. [22]

OECD (n.d.), *Green bonds: Mobilising the debt capital markets for a low-carbon transition*. [11]

OECD (n.d.), *OECD DAC Rio Markers for Climate: Handbook*, https://www.oecd.org/dac/environment-development/Revised%20climate%20marker%20handbook_FINAL.pdf. [24]

Prudential Regulation Authority (2022), *Results of the 2021 Climate Biennial Exploratory Scenario (CBES)*, Bank of England, https://www.bankofengland.co.uk/stress-testing/2022/results-of-the-2021-climate-biennial-exploratory-scenario. [31]

Reuters (2021), *German cabinet backs 30 bln euro flood recovery fund*, https://www.reuters.com/world/europe/german-cabinet-backs-30-bln-euro-flood-recovery-fund-2021-08-18/. [21]

South Korea (2021), *3rd National Climate Change Adaptation Measures (2021-2025) Detailed Implementation Plan*. [15]

The World Bank (2021), *Enabling Private Investment in Climate Adaptation and Resilience : Current Status, Barriers to Investment and Blueprint for Action*. [6]

The World Bank (2021), *Enabling Private Investment in Climate Adaptation and Resilience: Current Status, Barriers to Investment and Blueprint for Action*. [17]

UNEP (2021), *Adaptation Gap Report 2021 The Gathering Storm - Adapting to Climate Change in a Post-pandemic World*. [4]

14 Building systemic resilience in practice: examples from key systems

This chapter explores how a systemic approach to building climate resilience requires in depth understanding of how individual systems and sectors. The chapter takes a deep dive into three key examples, namely food systems, energy and cities, to illustrate how taking a systemic approach to building resilience works in practice. Findings highlight what policy makers can learn from the experience of other systems, and what synergies exist across systems that can inform the broad approach.

This chapter draws on contributions to the horizontal project carried out under the responsibility of the Committee for Agriculture, the Regional Development Policy Committee and the International Energy Agency.

A systemic approach to building climate resilience requires in-depth understanding of how individual systems work as well as their interactions with other systems. How such an approach works in practice thus depends on the system in question. This chapter looks at food systems, cities, and energy systems to illustrate how a systemic approach to building resilience works in practice, how synergies can exist across systems, and what policy makers can learn from the experience of other systems.

Building resilience in food systems

Food systems are vulnerable to a wide range of climate shocks. In 2012, for example, a historic drought in the US Midwest led to a reduction in American maize production by 13% compared to the previous year. This had major repercussions for global markets, as the US typically accounts for some 40% of global maize production (USDA, 2013[1]). Climate change can also have indirect impacts on food systems. At the end of 2019, swarms of desert locusts infested Eastern Africa, destroying over 200 000 hectares of crop and pastureland and creating acute food insecurity for two million people in the region. This infestation can be traced back to climate change: warming of the western Indian Ocean has increased the frequency and intensity of cyclones, which has created desert lakes in Saudi Arabia, a suitable environment for desert locusts to breed. Swarms of locusts then spread via Yemen and Somalia across Eastern Africa (IPCC, 2022[2]).

Food systems around the world face a "triple challenge": ensuring food security and nutrition for a growing population; supporting the livelihoods of millions of people working along the food supply chain; and doing so in an environmentally sustainable way (OECD, 2021[3]).[1] As depicted above, climate impacts can disrupt the ability of food systems to meet these objectives, underscoring the importance of building resilience within food systems.

Figure 14.1 depicts some of the pressures affecting, and emanating from, food systems. The top of the diagram represents shocks which can affect food systems, many of which are related to climate change. Climate shocks affect all stages of the food supply chain: for example, droughts and floods directly impact farm production, but also disrupt transportation. The centre of the diagram shows the five stages of the food supply chain, with the arrows connecting them representing other economic activities, e.g. trade and logistics. These connections often cross international borders: some 20% of global calories consumed have crossed at least one international border (OECD/FAO, 2021[4]), and roughly one third of agri-food trade crosses more than one border (FAO, 2020[5]).

Figure 14.1. Food system resilience to shocks, including climate impacts

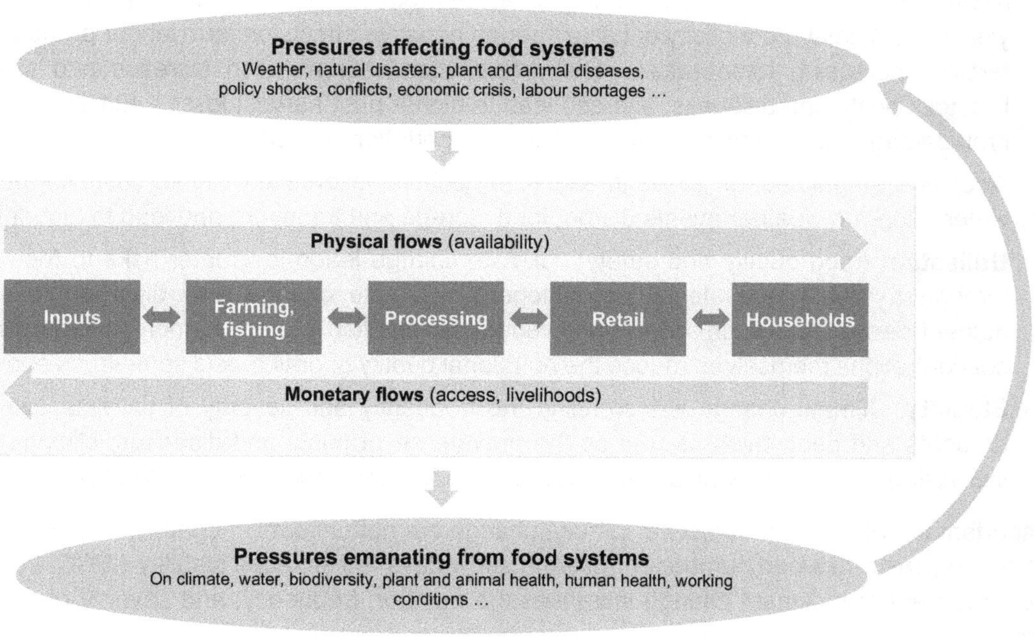

Source: (OECD, forthcoming 2023[6]).

The bottom part of the diagram highlights that food systems themselves can create pressures reducing resilience elsewhere. Food production (in particular land use and primary production) is a major source of environmental pressures including water use, biodiversity loss, eutrophication, acidification, and greenhouse gas (GHG) emissions (Poore and Nemecek, 2018[7]). Some of these in turn affect the inputs required for food production, thus creating a potentially detrimental cycle. For example, excessive water withdrawals create greater vulnerability to drought in the long run. More generally, food systems are uniquely vulnerable to climate change but also contribute an estimated one-third of anthropogenic GHG emissions (Crippa et al., 2021[8]).

Climate impacts on food security

Food security was defined at the 1996 World Food Summit as existing when "all people, at all times, have physical, social and economic access to sufficient, safe and nutritious food to meet their dietary needs and food preferences for an active and healthy life" (FAO, 1996[9]). In line with this definition, food security is often conceptualised in terms of availability, access, and utilisation. Complete food security thus requires stability across these three dimensions.

Food insecurity is most commonly caused by problems related to access, for example due to poverty, conflict, or other barriers, rather than problems related to the physical availability of food at the global level.[2] Nevertheless, the availability of food should not be taken for granted. Given population and income growth, the coming decades will see a steadily increasing demand for food while productivity growth is negatively affected by climate change (IPCC, 2022[2]). Since both food demand and supply are inelastic in the short run, even relatively small disruptions to global availability can lead to large price increases, which can reduce poor households' access to food. Moreover, availability and access are sometimes intertwined: shocks to food production can reduce the incomes of households working in the agri-food sector (especially in low- and middle-income countries), reducing their ability to buy food.

The Intergovernmental Panel on Climate Change (IPCC) provides a detailed overview of how climate change affects the different dimensions of food security.

- **Availability**. Increased heat and drought reduce productivity not only through direct effects on crop yields and animal productivity but also through negative effects on farm labour productivity and soil fertility. Increasing temperatures and precipitation changes also increase and shift crop and livestock pests and diseases, and can lead to higher post-harvest losses. Extreme events lead to crop damage, greater pest incidence, and transportation disruption.
- **Access**. Climate change poses threats to agricultural income and higher costs for inputs such as water. Extreme weather events disrupt food storage and transport, and lead to higher food prices.
- **Utilisation** (food quality and safety). Climate change leads to greater risks to food safety (e.g. through a greater prevalence of pathogens). Climate change also disproportionately affects nutrient-dense foods such as fruits and vegetables and fish. Moreover, increased atmospheric CO2 concentrations themselves reduce the nutritional quality of grains, and some fruits and vegetables.
- **Stability**. Climate change is increasing the frequency and severity of extreme events such as droughts and heatwaves as well as the prevalence of pests and diseases; climate change and increasing ocean acidity also lead to declines in fish populations. (IPCC, 2022[2]).

It is important to note that the effects of climate change are not uniformly negative. For example, in some temperate regions a reduced number of frost and snow days will increase stability (IPCC, 2022[2]). Yet on balance it is clear that climate change increases the number, frequency, and severity of shocks to food systems.

Climate impacts on food systems livelihoods

Food systems are also a key economic engine and provide livelihoods for millions of people. The food supply chain in Figure 14.1 involves physical flows moving towards the final consumer and monetary flows moving in the other direction.

Especially in lower- and middle-income countries, food systems account for a sizeable share of economic activity and employment. As countries develop, the relative role of agriculture typically lessens, but other activities along the food supply chain often gain in importance (e.g. wholesale, processing, food preparation, retail) ((World Bank, 2007[10]); (Barrett et al., 2022[11]) (Yi et al., 2021[12])). Climate shocks to food systems can therefore also have large economic effects. In addition, even in countries where the relative economic share of agriculture is lower, agriculture and the food industry often remain politically important, with a strong bearing on policy-making processes, including for climate change.

Most of the climate shocks affecting food security also affect livelihoods. Crop damage, post-harvest losses, and other reductions in food availability reduce revenues for farmers and others working in the food supply chain, as do disruptions in transportation.[3]

Principles for resilient food systems

The essential functions of food systems (food security and nutrition, and livelihoods) are too important to rely on a “reactive” approach of dealing with shocks after they occur. A proactive approach is needed. Here, building the systemic resilience of the food system is essential to enhance its ability to prepare and plan for, absorb, recover from, and more successfully adapt and transform in response to adverse events (OECD, 2020[13]).

It is useful to refine the definition of food system resilience by specifying to which outcome it pertains (e.g. livelihoods, food security) and at what level (e.g. individual consumer or farmer; food industry or retail sector; the local, national or global levels). Some actions (e.g. better education and training for farmers) might increase resilience in more than one way, creating synergies. Other actions might improve resilience in one way while reducing it in others, creating trade-offs. For example, a farmer can use groundwater irrigation to become less vulnerable to drought, but this may reduce the availability of water for other farmers (OECD, 2015[14]).

Moreover, climate change is not the only source of shocks to food systems. It is important to build resilience to multiple shocks (OECD, 2020[13]). An efficient and effective policy approach must therefore take into account the interactions and trade-offs between different risks, private adaptation strategies (by farmers and others), and government policies. Public policies must not accidentally encourage the adoption of riskier private strategies that undermine long-term resilience.

The next sections discuss broad approaches to food systems resilience in more detail. These are not mutually exclusive, and indeed often overlap.

Availability: Improving resilience of agricultural production

A wide range of actions can improve the resilience of agricultural production to climate shocks (IPCC, 2022[2]). These include actions by farmers themselves (e.g. changing the type and composition of crops and livestock; adjusting planting dates; investments in irrigation; using different crop rotations, etc.). Other actions require more coordinated efforts (e.g. R&D in improved crop varieties and breeds with greater resistance against extreme weather conditions; creating greater landscape-level biodiversity; provision of climate and weather information).

Actions that build resilience of production also tend to build resilience of livelihoods (Ignaciuk, 2015[15]). As such, it is often in farmers' best interest to invest in adaptation. This stands in sharp contrast with climate mitigation actions, where individual farmers bear the cost but benefits are spread globally.

There is a strong, though imperfect, correlation between the private and public benefits of investing in adaptation. Some actions help build the resilience of farmers' livelihoods but do not build resilience for production. This is the case for insurance products or exiting the sector in favour of other economic activities. Conversely, some actions could help build the resilience of production at a global level but without reducing uncertainty or volatility for an individual producer. For example, a greater diversity of crop varieties and livestock breeds at a global level could help build resilience to future shocks, but could still reflect a pattern where individual producers are highly specialised in one crop variety or livestock breed and hence subject to the same production risks as before.

In other cases, adaptation efforts by individual farmers might have positive externalities, e.g. through positive spillover effects on neighbouring farms or by generating knowledge about which strategies are most effective in a specific context. Identifying and harnessing these positive externalities should be prioritised (Ignaciuk, 2015[15]). Governments can play an important role through public and semi-public R&D as well as research on risks and vulnerabilities. Providing accurate and detailed information can help private agents make well-informed adaptation decisions. Training, education and extension services can similarly help farmers and others take more effective adaptation action.

Another important area for government action is to remove policies that discourage investments in adaptation. For example, some countries have distortions in input and output markets that lock farmers in to certain activities (by subsidising or stimulating production of certain crops over others). Poorly designed insurance schemes can also impede adaptation (by reducing incentives to change current practices) or even create maladaptation (by inducing farming in risky locations or with risky practices which otherwise would not be undertaken) (Ignaciuk, 2015[15]).

Investments in "no regret" policies that build resilience, such as R&D, account for only a small share of total support to agriculture or fisheries. For example, across the 54 countries covered by the OECD Agricultural Policy Monitoring and Evaluation 2022 report (OECD, 2022[16]), total support to agriculture was more than USD 817 billion per year in 2019-21, but only 13% of this went to investments such as R&D, biosecurity, or infrastructure, which could help build resilience and achieve sustainable productivity growth.

Instead, the bulk of support tries to raise farm revenues through higher prices, subsidies, or direct payments. In many countries these policies stimulate the production of specific commodities, thus reducing farmers' incentives to diversify or adapt.

Other policies can work against adaptation. For example, in many countries agricultural water use is not correctly priced, which, in the absence of quantitative restrictions, potentially contributes to over-reliance on irrigation and overuse. While there has been improvement in recent years, many countries are still far from meeting international commitments such as the OECD Council Recommendation on Water (2016) and the G20 Agriculture Ministerial Action Plan on water and food security (2017) (Gruère, Shigemitsu and Crawford, 2020[17]).

Access: Improving resilience through better safety nets

Higher incomes and better safety nets can be a powerful way of building greater food security. Household income is an important determinant of food access: where incomes are extremely low, even cheap food may be out of reach for many people. According to FAO estimates, even in the early 2000s, when international food prices were at all-time lows, more than 800 million people were undernourished (FAO, 2022[18]). By contrast, income growth typically leads to a decrease in childhood stunting, an indicator of chronic childhood malnutrition (Headey, 2013[19]). Recent research has shown that the cost of a healthy and nutritious diet exceeds per capita income for at least 1.6 billion people, while in high-income countries this cost represents only a fraction of income. While the cost of a healthy and nutritious diet itself varies by country, the main driver of affordability is income (Hirvonen et al., 2020[20]) (Bai et al., 2021[21]).

In addition to broad-based economic growth, better social safety nets could strengthen resilience against climate-related impacts on food security. In OECD countries, responses to food insecurity typically focus on livelihood assistance (such as increasing universal social security payments or providing cash transfers) or food assistance programmes (such as providing meals, food vouchers or food parcels to food insecure households) (Giner and Placzek, 2022[22]). While these policies themselves could be strengthened, they also provide useful lessons for low- and middle-income countries looking to create a stronger safety net to help citizens cope with climate-related shocks, e.g. higher food prices caused by disruptions to production.

Livelihoods: Improving farmer resilience

In the context of farm-level resilience, OECD work has identified three layers of risks (OECD, 2009[23]), (OECD, 2011[24]); (Glauber et al., 2021[25]). Each layer requires a different response:

- First, normal variations in production, prices and weather do not require any specific policy response: such frequent but relatively low-impact risks can be directly managed by farmers as part of their normal business strategy, for example by diversifying production or adapting their production technologies.
- At the other extreme, infrequent but catastrophic events can cause significant damage and can affect many or all farmers over a wide area, for example a severe and widespread drought or the outbreak and spread of a highly contagious disease. These will usually be beyond farmers' or markets' capacity to cope with and governments may need to intervene in such cases. Government action for these risks can include both ex ante efforts (e.g. to reduce disaster risk, or through the provision of public insurance) and ex post interventions (e.g. ad hoc assistance after a natural disaster strikes).
- Between the normal and the catastrophic risk layers lies a layer of "marketable risk" (e.g. hail damage) which can be managed through insurance and futures markets or through co-operative arrangements between farmers.

One effect of climate change is to modify the pattern of risks by increasing the frequency and severity of more extreme events. If countries continue with a business-as-usual approach to risk management, costs for governments will rise as they shoulder a growing share of the risk management burden.

For this reason, the division of labour based on the risk type should not be interpreted too rigidly, as all stakeholders have some role to play in managing various types of risks. For example, even for catastrophic risks farmers may be able to take proactive measures to reduce their exposure; and governments could also provide weather and market information to make it easier for farmers to deal with normal risks. These are two examples of broader strategies – building on-farm resilience capacity and the provision of public goods and no-regret policies – which can help build resilience across the risk spectrum. Figure 14.2 summarises these insights.

Figure 14.2. Risk management for agricultural resilience

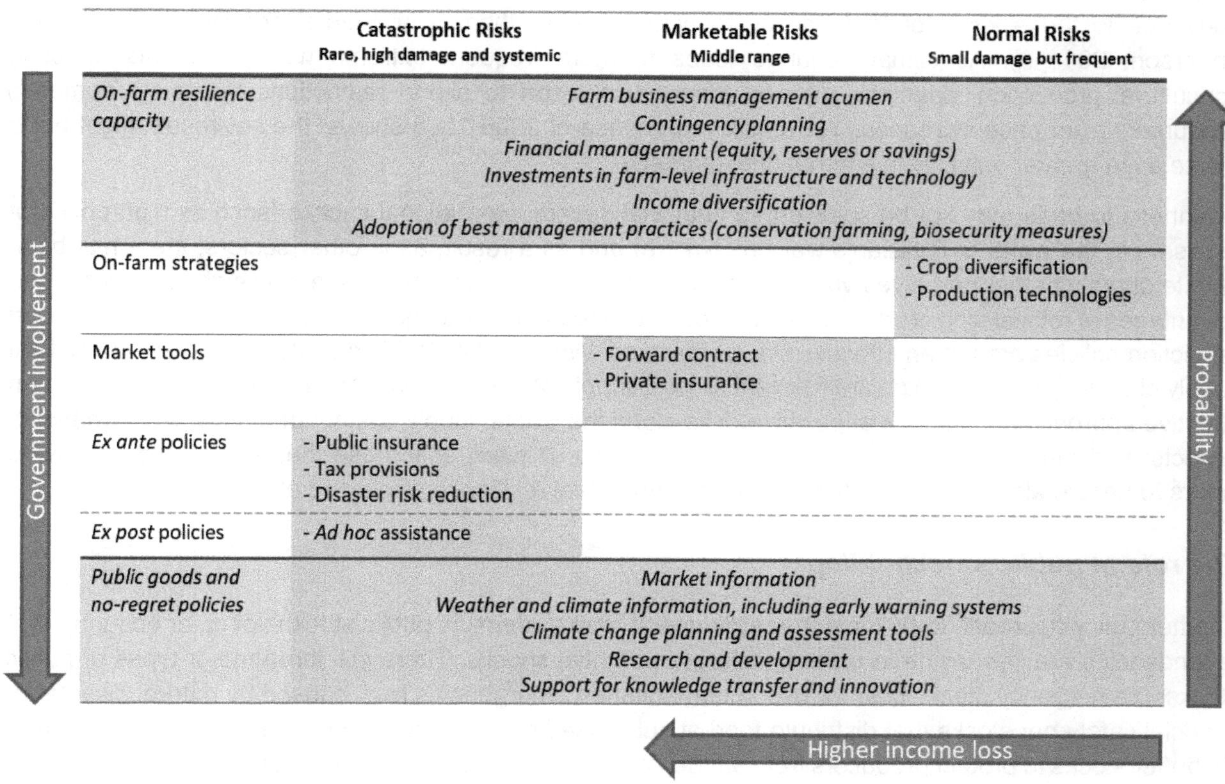

Source: based on (OECD, 2020[13]).

The role of trade

Trade has an important role to play in facilitating adjustments of food systems to climate change (Guerrero et al., 2022[26]); (Gouel and Laborde, 2021[27]); (Janssens et al., 2020[28]). While food production in a single country is vulnerable to many possible shocks, at a global level the supply of food is typically much less volatile. International trade thus often acts as a "risk pooling" mechanism, enabling countries to rely on international markets in the face of domestic shocks (Brooks and Matthews, 2015[29]). (Burgess and Donaldson, 2010[30]) provide a striking illustration of this mechanism at the intra-regional level in the context of colonial India. Prior to the spread of railroads in India, local rainfall shortages had large effects on famine intensity. As railroads spread, however, this link between local weather and famine disappeared almost completely. Such improvements in infrastructure (transportation and storage), as well as transparency regarding supply, demand, stocks, and prices, can contribute to the effectiveness of trade as a mechanism for coping with shocks. While the "portfolio diversification" aspect of trade leads to lower volatility, at the same time openness to trade also exposes countries to international price shocks. On balance, studies have concluded that although large international price spikes do occur occasionally (as occurred in the wake of Russian's war of Ukraine), the "buffering" effects of trade typically dominate (Brooks and Matthews, 2015[29]).

Trade can only play this buffering role if countries refrain from using policy instruments that undermine international markets. When global food prices increase, major exporting countries are often tempted to impose export restrictions or outright export bans in an attempt to stabilise domestic prices. This leads to even greater upward pressure on prices in the international market. In 2006-2008, when food prices were increasing rapidly, several major grain-exporting countries adopted export restrictions or bans. Some importing countries reacted by reducing pre-existing import restrictions such as tariffs (Jones and Kwieciński, 2010[31]). The result was additional upward pressure on world prices. Some 45% of the increase in international rice prices in 2006-2008 and almost 30% of the increase in international wheat prices was likely due to these kinds of trade policy responses rather than initial market conditions (Martin and Anderson, 2011[32]). As climate change leads to more frequent extreme weather events affecting agricultural production, countries may be tempted to resort to export restrictions to protect domestic consumers from price increases. Yet as the experience of 2006-2008 shows, the net result might be to create even greater volatility in international markets.

Openness to trade may not be sufficient to deal with severe international shocks (such as high prices of fertilisers in the wake of Russian's war on Ukraine) and as a result, as in other sectors, there has been debate about whether perceived vulnerabilities to global food supply chains are outweighed by perceived advantages of relocalising production. Countries need mechanisms to manage such risks; however, import restriction policies are not an effective way of doing so. Work by the OECD has identified "keys to resilient supply chains",[4] many of which are relevant to food supply chains. Importantly, this work highlights that an effective approach should look at possible risks along the whole supply chain, not merely its international aspects; and that governments should not try to handle all risks, only those that are too big for private actors to handle alone – echoing the lessons for farm-level resilience discussed above.

The role of public stockholding

Another policy approach to building the resilience of food systems is public stockholding, or ensuring that redundancies are kept aside in order to address potential shocks. There are three major types of public stocks: i) emergency stocks held for use in humanitarian emergencies (e.g. caused by natural disasters); ii) social safety net stocks that distribute food at subsidised prices to help food insecure households; and iii). buffer stocks to protect producers from sudden drops in producer prices and/or protect consumers from sudden consumer price spikes (Deuss, 2015[33]).

Climate change may increase the need for emergency stocks to be used in humanitarian emergencies. Such stocks are recognised as one option for disaster preparedness, alongside climate adaptation. Social safety net stock schemes are more akin to food assistance programmes. In developing countries, the importance of public stockholding programmes may be greater, as the relative number of the vulnerable poor is generally larger than in developed countries. At the same time, while food assistance in general can be an effective way of dealing with shocks to food systems, the performance of public stocks as a food assistance policy should be compared with other possible instruments, including providing income support or building a broader social safety net.

Buffer stocks, by contrast, aim to buy and sell in order to influence market prices. The goal of existing schemes has often been to reduce price volatility. As climate change increases the frequency and severity of shocks to food systems, and hence possibly price volatility, the political demand for buffer stock schemes may grow in coming years. However, it is not clear whether buffer stocks actually reduce domestic price volatility. Even when they do, it is at a high cost. First, these schemes are almost always implemented through other policy instruments such as price regulations, trade restrictions, and import and export monopolies, creating economic inefficiencies. Second, even though these schemes in theory should buy low and sell high, this often does not work in practice and countries end up with a fiscal deficit and/or excessively large stocks. Third, the accumulation and release of stocks can create instability in global markets (Deuss, 2015[33]) (OECD, 2018[34]). A greater reliance on buffer stocks in response to climate change could thus worsen, rather than improve, the resilience of food systems.

Better policies for resilient food systems

An important consideration in the resilience of food systems is that any intervention to improve one objective may create synergies and trade-offs with several others (OECD, 2021[3]). For example, modelling suggests that green set-aside payments may help with mitigation but could reduce adaptation, while investments in adaptive capital (e.g. drainage) might help with adaptation but could negatively affect mitigation (Lankoski, Ignaciuk and Jésus, 2018[35]). Actions may also improve the resilience of only some actors at the expense of others. Conversely, some actions (e.g. better education and training for farmers) might increase resilience in more than one way, creating synergies. This calls for coherent policies that strengthen, or at least do not actively counteract, each other.

Because of these synergies and trade-offs, it is important to take a systems view to building resilience (see also Chapter 4) (OECD, 2021[3]). In the context of food systems, one interesting example is the use of a territorial approach to food security and nutrition (OECD/FAO/UNCDF, 2016[36]). Historically, food security and nutrition policy has often been developed in a top-down fashion, designed and implemented at the national level without much consideration for (or involvement of) local stakeholders, resulting in one-size-fits-all outcomes. Moreover, policies have often taken a sectoral approach (focusing almost exclusively on agriculture). A more bottom-up and multisectoral approach, where different levels of government and different policy communities (agriculture, poverty, education, public health, etc.) work together, may be more effective.

Policy making for resilient food systems also means keeping a long-term focus in mind and planning for a range of possible scenarios and adverse events, including various climate change scenarios. Identifying possible trends and risks, and thinking through possible consequences and how to deal with them can be done through participatory processes involving policy makers, researchers, farmers, other industry leaders, and the financial sector (OECD, 2020[13]). This improved understanding not only helps in developing better policies but can also help individual stakeholders to better prepare themselves.

Finally, building resilience in food systems is also made difficult by disagreements over facts, interests, and values (OECD, 2021[3]). Many areas of food systems are characterised by evidence gaps, including on trade-offs and synergies, and on policy effectiveness (Deconinck et al., 2021[37]). In other areas, vested interests may be successful at blocking policy reforms; a large literature has documented these political economy pressures in agricultural and food systems policy (Swinnen, 2018[38]).

Understanding these dynamics is helpful in making policies themselves resilient to future shocks. Building on earlier work by OECD and others, (OECD, 2021[3]) identifies policy processes that can help navigate around these obstacles. Strategies include building a shared understanding of the facts (for example, through scientific advisory bodies and stakeholder input into regulatory impact assessments); balancing diverging interests (for example, by creating a more level playing field through greater transparency, or by providing compensation); and overcoming differences over values (for example, through deliberative democracy approaches).

Even where policies improve overall outcomes, they may impose costs on specific interest groups. Shocks to food systems may then lead to calls for relaxing or abolishing these policies, threatening the resilience of the policies themselves. For example, in the wake of Russian's war on Ukraine, several countries have considered relaxing environmental constraints on agriculture to boost output. As the discussion in this section has shown, however, if food security is the objective, several other policy instruments can be used, such as providing financial assistance to consumers to cope with higher food prices and specific support to countries facing high food import bills. Policy makers should keep in mind that once measures are relaxed they may be hard to reinstate, and that relaxing these environmental constraints may at any rate provide only marginal relief to the current pressures, at significant costs to biodiversity and other environmental goals (OECD, 2022[16]).

Building systemic climate resilience in cities

Cities are especially vulnerable to climate shocks

Cities are at increased exposure to climate risks (IPCC, 2022[39]). They concentrate people, infrastructure, and economic activities, and this concentration comes with risks. Cities are home to more than half the world's population and their inhabitants are the most exposed to climate shocks such as floods, storms, and heatwaves. Low-income and socially marginalised urban populations, which may include the elderly and children, often live in areas that are prone to climate change hazards or that are ill-equipped to face climate risks. Pregnant and breast-feeding women in these areas are also especially vulnerable. As such, they are more likely to be affected by climate shocks, and have a lower capacity to recover from them (OECD, 2017[40]). For example, in the United States, a recent study found that extreme heat is disproportionately affecting Black and Hispanic workers, who are more likely to live in areas where air pollution is already increasing childhood asthma diagnoses (United States Environmental Protection Agency, 2021[41]; Adrienne-Arsht Rockefeller Foundation Resilience Center, 2022[42])

The urban heat island effect – a phenomenon that results from high building density, heat from human activities, building materials and limited vegetation – has a significant impact on temperatures in cities. Its intensity varies depending on the population size and climate zone. Between 2017 and 2021, almost half of OECD cities experienced urban heat island effects of more than 5°C and even more than 7°C in some cases. Cities with more than 250 000 inhabitants are on average 3°C warmer than their surrounding areas, with temperatures almost twice as high as in cities with fewer than 100 000 inhabitants (Figure 14.3). Policy frameworks to address urban heat island challenges must take specific local contexts into account.

Sea-level rise also impacts cities disproportionately. It is estimated that 75% of the world's largest urban agglomerations are located in coastal zones. Two-thirds of cities with more than 5 million inhabitants are located in low-lying coastal areas, which are especially exposed to risks of a changing climate (OECD, 2021[43]). By 2050, over 570 low-lying coastal cities are projected to face sea-level rise of at least 0.5 metres (C40, n.d.[44]). Average global losses from floods could reach USD 52 billion by 2050 in 136 of the world's largest coastal cities, even in the absence of climate change (OECD/Bloomberg, 2014[45]).

Figure 4.3 . Urban heat island intensity in Europe (summer, daytime, 2017-2021)

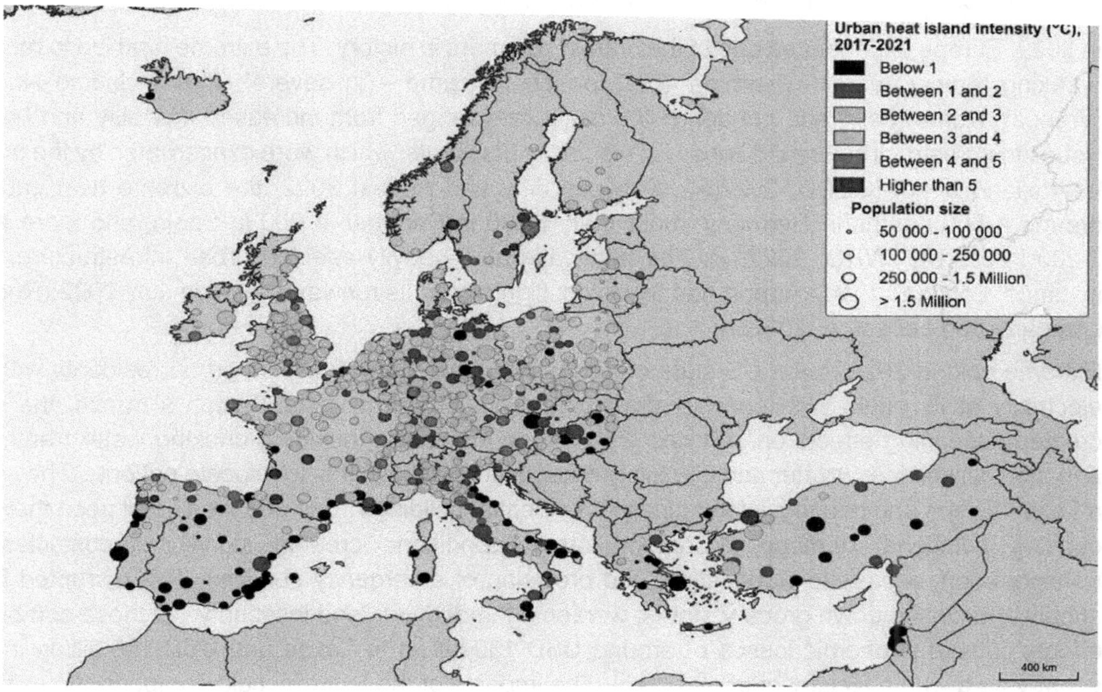

Source: (OECD, 2022[46]) based on MODIS Aqua and Terra land surface temperature, and MODIS land cover data.

Cities can generate solutions to improve climate resilience

Despite their particular vulnerability to climate change, cities are an essential part of the solution to addressing climate change and its impacts. First, they are responsible for critical policy domains that influence climate outcomes. Many of the domains that fall under the jurisdiction of cities – land-use planning, zoning, water provision, sanitation and drainage, housing construction, urban renovation, regulation, economic development, public health and emergency management, transport, environmental protection – are directly vulnerable to climate change impacts. At the same time, they also represent opportunities to develop adaptive capacities and strategies, making cities well-positioned to integrate different policy sectors relevant for climate action on the ground. Second, cities generate a large share of climate-significant investment that goes towards the implementation of mitigation and adaptation strategies. In OECD countries, subnational governments are responsible for 69% of climate- and environment-related public investment (OECD, 2019[47]) (IPCC, 2022[39]) (OECD, 2022[48]).

Against this backdrop, geographical scale becomes a key element in understanding and addressing the complexity of climate shocks and their impacts. The complexity of urban climate dynamics is related to urban systems and to cities as an open system themselves. A city can be conceived of as an urban system in which multiple systems interact, but also as part of a wider open system in which many cities and other systems influence each other.

Defining systemic climate resilience in cities

Major climate shocks and their impacts in cities

Climate change affects many interconnected systems in cities, including economic systems (e.g. production, jobs), social systems (e.g. housing, health, education), ecological systems (e.g. vegetation, water basins) and urban infrastructure systems (e.g. transport, energy, water and sanitation).

Recent major climate shocks in cities around the world illustrate the variety of climate impacts and the varying effect of these impacts on specific locations and people:

- In 2022, Europe experienced one of the hottest summers in history. The extreme heat led to record-breaking temperatures – reaching 40°C for the first time – in several cities including Nantes (France), Rome (Italy) and London (UK). Outcomes ranged from increased mortality and health issues to infrastructure breakdowns and electricity blackouts, which were exacerbated by the urban heat island effect (OECD, 2022[46]). Between July and August 2022, the extreme heat caused around 4 500 deaths in Germany, more than 1 000 in Portugal, 4 000 in Spain, and more than 3 200 in the UK (WHO, 2022[49]). The heatwave also heavily affected urban infrastructure. For instance, London's Luton Airport had to restrict flights after its runway melted in July 2022 (Rodas, Lombardi and Ledesma, 2022[50]).
- Extreme cold in 2021 in the US state of Texas left more than 10 million urban residents without electricity at its peak. With energy infrastructure not built to withstand such a freeze, the cold created cascading effects on services that rely on electricity, including drinking water treatment and medical services. Water and electricity outages forced hospitals to relocate patients. They also affected boilers and heating. Water pipes in residential buildings froze and then burst upon thawing causing additional damage. Moreover, storm conditions created significant obstacles to transportation, access to workplaces, and provision of emergency services. This disrupted food supply and closed down grocery stores, worsening underlying food insecurity. All these combined effects caused economic losses of around USD 130 billion in Texas and USD 155 billion in the country as a whole (Busby et al., 2021[51]). The impacts of the extreme cold compounded existing vulnerabilities. For example, homeless shelters were already out of capacity due to COVID-19 restrictions, with shortages then exacerbated by power failures and burst pipes (Pezenik and Ebbs, 2021[52]).
- A massive flood in Pakistan in 2022 left one-third of the country under water and affected 33 million people. Half of the districts (first tier of local government) in the country declared themselves "calamity hit", including cities in the Sindh province such as Mehar, Qambar, Larkana, Sukkur, Sehwan, and Khairpur Nathan Shah. (Bhargava et al., 2022[53]) (Union, 2022[54]). The impacts of the flood cascaded into different sectors including education, healthcare, and energy and transport infrastructures, leading to total economic losses of about USD 15.2 billion. Preliminary research suggests that the flood was a compounding crisis that started with the phenomenal heatwave experienced in April and May 2022. During that period, temperatures reached above 40°C for long periods in many places. In the city of Jacobabad, the temperature reached 51°C. Such unusual and extreme heat melted glaciers in the northern mountainous regions, increasing the amount of water flowing into tributaries that eventually make their way into the Pakistan's Indus River. - which crosses the country from north to south, flowing through towns, cities and large swathes of agricultural land along the way (Mallapaty, 2022[55]).

Cities are home to 3.5 billion people, accounting for 48% of the world population, and this number is estimated to reach 55% by 2050 (OECD, 2020[56]). As the urbanisation trend continues, the impacts of climate change are likely to increase and become much more complex. Furthermore, climate-induced migration can generate additional pressures on urban systems such as energy, water and sanitation, transport, and housing. A recent study found that climate disasters caused by weather-related hazards in 2021 triggered the displacement of 30 million people, more than three-quarters of new displacements recorded worldwide (Internal Displacement Monitoring Centre, 2021[57]). With many of those displaced moving to urban centres, cities need to be better prepared to accommodate increasing numbers of migrants (Khanna, 2022[58]).

The various impacts of major climate shocks illustrated above can be characterised by type of shocks (floods and storms, heatwaves, droughts, biodiversity losses, and sea-level rise) and by type of impacts (direct/single impacts, indirect, cascading and compound impacts, and impacts across places and/or people) (Table 14.1).

Table 14.1. Major climate shocks and their impacts in cities

Climate shocks (from fast to slow onset)	Direct (single) impacts	Indirect, cascading and compound impacts	Impacts across places and/or people
Floods and storms	Damage to urban infrastructure (e.g. roads, energy) and housing Damage to schools and public health facilities Disruption of urban services (e.g. water, energy, transport) Damage to agricultural land Degrading coastal ecosystems, such as mangroves or coastal reefs	Disruption of services (e.g. health, food supply) due to damaged urban infrastructure (e.g. energy, transport) Impacts on manufacturing supply chains (e.g. hard-disk drive manufacturing; food supply chains) Locational and investment decisions of firms (in the long term) Emergence of waterborne diseases Changes in the demand of goods and services A disruption in manufacturing supply chains may affect places other than those hit by flood/storm. Loss of cultural assets, artefacts and places Loss of sense of security among citizens Displacements due to climate migration create higher demand for public services and increased population living in informal settlements.	Economically and socially marginalised communities may be more vulnerable to floods and damaged urban infrastructure. Migration induced by floods affecting the most vulnerable Children affected and more vulnerable to waterborne disease Where mangroves are already affected, there is increased vulnerability of coastal communities.
Heatwaves	Heat stress on human health Pressure on energy, water infrastructure and supply Damage to urban infrastructure	Decrease of general labour productivity for both manual and cognitive tasks Extended fire weather seasons (i.e. periods of time where weather conditions are conducive to the outbreak of wildfires) Increased morbidity from vector-borne diseases	Children and the elderly are more vulnerable to heat stress Low-income households most likely living with inadequate housing conditions (e.g. without air conditioning) are more vulnerable. Psychological or mental health impacts on the most exposed population
Droughts	Impacts on food supply system in cities Water shortages affecting population's access to safe drinking water	Limiting the hydropower capacity of dams Changes in ecosystems' functioning Changes in labour and agricultural productivity Land degradation Impacts on food production leading to rise in food prices	Disruption of agricultural production leads to severe and more chronic food insecurity, increasing the propensity of malnutrition, as well as rise of food prices. This problem is strongly concentrated in vulnerable populations.
Biodiversity loss	Loss of ecosystems services, such as carbon sequestration and the capacity to further adapt to climate change	Limitations for discovery of potential treatments for diseases and health problems	Food and nutritional security impacts may disproportionally affect vulnerable populations.

Sea-level rise	Potential damage to urban assets in coastal areas Impacts on urban land use and infrastructure investment strategies Accelerated coastal erosion	Coastal defenses become increasingly expensive to adapt and to maintain over time. Decrease of tourism-related activities	Vulnerability is higher in Small Islands Development States, where the most vulnerable area is the low-lying coastal zone

Source: Author's elaboration based on (OECD, 2020[59]).

The impacts of global crises on climate challenges in cities

While climate shocks affect social, ecological and health systems (Table 14.1), shocks in other systems (e.g. financial or health crises) also affect climate challenges. The COVID-19 pandemic started as a public health crisis before escalating into an unprecedented social and economic crisis, demonstrating the complex interaction of different systems. It also demonstrates how over-emphasis on efficiency and cuts in public expenditures over the past years (e.g. health infrastructure and staff) has jeopardised the resilience of key systems to shocks, allowing failures to cascade from one system to others (OECD, 2020[60]).

In cities, the COVID-19 pandemic generated not only socio-economic impacts, disproportionately affecting people, firms and places, but a wide range of environmental ones. These threaten or slow the progress of cities towards building systemic resilience to climate change. At the same time, the COVID-19 pandemic has shown the potential of cities in building long-term resilience by using a systems approach. Cities were hit hardest by the pandemic but they were also at the forefront of the response. They played a key role in implementing nation-wide measures and providing laboratories for innovative, bottom-up recovery strategies (OECD, 2020[61])

A framework for understanding and enhancing systemic climate resilience in cities

The examples discussed above illustrate the complexity and uncertainties of climate risks in cities. This underlines the need for applying a systems approach to building resilience. As discussed in Chapter 4 of this report, the OECD defines resilience from a systems point of view as the capacity of a system to recover in the midst of shocks and stresses over time.

Due to the inherent complexity of a systems approach, it is important for policy makers to have a clear understanding of what such an approach would entail and how it could be applied in the urban policy context. Figure 14.4 offers a framework for policy makers to better understand and build systemic climate resilience in cities.

Figure 14.4. A policy framework to enhance systemic climate resilience in cities

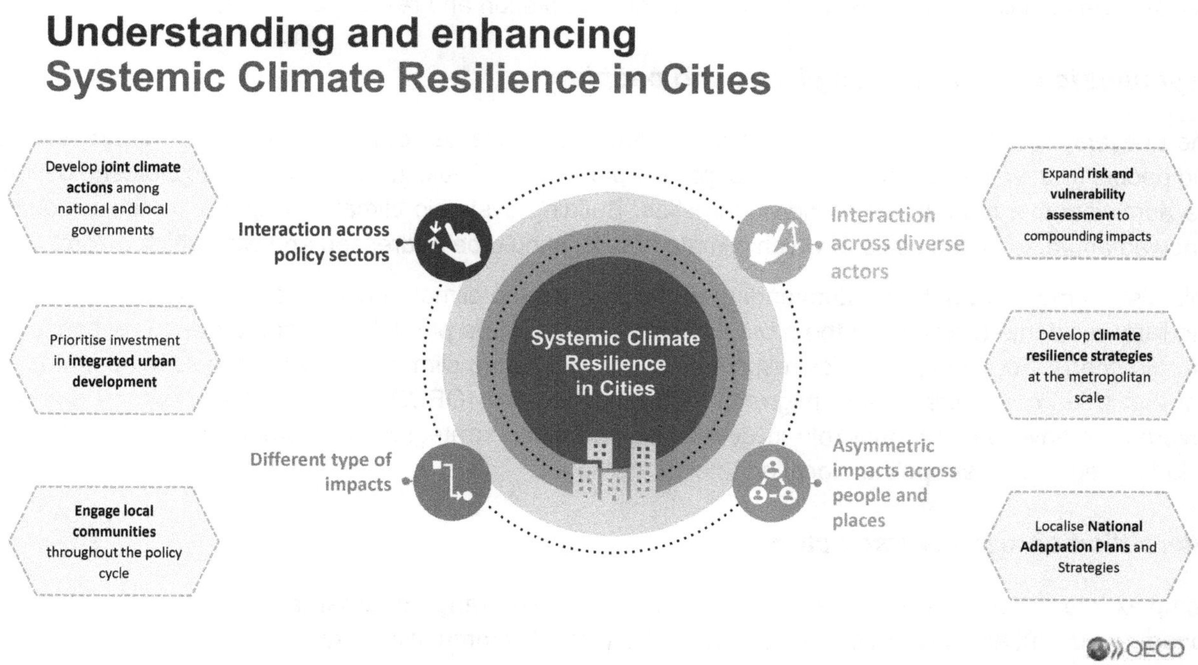

Source: Authors' elaboration.

Understanding systemic climate resilience in cities

Interactions across urban policy sectors, from infrastructure to services

Complex interactions take place across policy and governance scales and often imply trade-offs between policy objectives (Bai et al., 2017[62]). However, current policy practice often ignores the complexity of urban systems by designing and implementing measures that serve individual systems (e.g. transport, water management) instead of considering the interactions between or among them. Climate shocks can add more complexity and uncertainty to how different systems interact in cities. Systemic climate resilience in cities thus requires a better understanding of the interaction between various dimensions, enabling policy instruments to address multiple objectives together, generating synergies and co-benefits and minimising trade-offs. Cities should explore interactions between the impacts of climate shocks and other societal challenges such as health, social marginalisation and labour productivity. Proper identification of such interactions would allow cities to prioritise climate actions that also benefit other social objectives. For example, greening urban spaces can boost cities' resilience to extreme weather while providing health benefits.

Diverse types of impacts, from direct to cascading and compounding

Systemic resilience in cities means a better understanding of diverse types of impacts, in particular, cascading and compounding impacts of climate change. Cascading impacts in cities are observed when a climate shock damages buildings and urban infrastructures and leads to a disruption of services such as transport, energy, water, and food provision, resulting in impacts that are significantly higher than the initial impact. Compounding impacts in cities are observed when the impacts of a climate shock interact with pre-existing inequalities and vulnerabilities of urban residents, thereby exacerbating the impacts. For instance, this occurs when low-income households living in homes without adequate insulation are hit both by extreme cold weather and an increase in energy prices. As the cascading and compounding impacts of climate change on other systems span a wide range of policy areas, assessing each type of risk and identifying solutions to minimise their negative impacts is critical. This can help increase preparedness for diverse types of climate impacts, and develop better adaptation and resilience policies.

Asymmetric impacts across places and people

The unevenly distributed impacts of climate change across places (e.g. low-lying areas, urban centres) and people (e.g. vulnerable population groups) are particularly visible in cities. The impacts extend beyond the administrative boundaries of individual cities. Building systemic climate resilience in cities requires renewed appraisal of the scale at which climate shocks should be addressed and with which actors.

This also demands a better understanding of the asymmetric climate impacts across urban, peri-urban, and rural residents (particularly the most vulnerable) to facilitate place-based and targeted responses to specific needs. For example, policy responses to address urban climate resilience should account for the fact that cities concentrate more migrants than other regions (OECD, 2022[63]). Therefore, all levels of government have an important role in developing resilience strategies at different geographical scales, including regional, metropolitan, local and neighbourhood.

Interaction across diverse actors

Complex interactions across systems in cities involve a wide range of urban and rural actors – not only governments, but also the private sector, civil society, local communities, city networks, etc. Co-ordination mechanisms for climate-resilient planning and investment across multiple sectors and among national, regional and local governments are often lacking or not clearly defined. Local communities are not always offered opportunities to engage with the early stages of disaster risk management strategies and frameworks, although they are the first responders in the event of a disaster. This underlines the need for policy co-ordination to align goals and incentives across different levels of government and across society at large. Systemic resilience in cities requires diverse urban actors to collaborate, identify and implement appropriate solutions to address the complex interaction of climate and other economic, social and health systems.

Policy approaches for enhancing systemic climate resilience in cities

Prioritise investment in integrated urban development that benefits multiple systems

A key policy option is to prioritise investment in integrated urban development by breaking sectoral silos and encouraging horizontal co-ordination. Local governments are well positioned to implement integrated urban development, with a growing number of cities integrating complementary measures (Box 14.1). To carry out such investments, subnational governments can use a mix of public sources of revenue including grants, subsidies, user charges and fees, and tax revenues, as well as external sources including loans, loan guarantees, and bonds, among others. The OECD Compendium of Financial Instruments for Subnational Climate Action[5] provides an overview and analysis of some climate-related public revenue sources provided to subnational governments from national governments, and state governments in federal countries. It includes grants, climate funds and loans, as well as information on contractual arrangements as an innovative way to link funding to climate action.

Box 14.1. Medellín Green Corridors, Colombia

Medellín's Green Corridors (*Corredores Verdes*) is an ambitious initiative to add to and further connect existing green spaces, improve biodiversity, reduce the city's urban heat island effect, soak up air pollutants and sequester a significant amount of CO2. The Green Corridors received investment through Colombia's participatory budgeting process, which allows citizens to select projects to invest in through a democratic popular vote. Since 2016, 30 Green Corridors have been implemented in Medellín, demonstrating how integrated, nature-based policies can benefit the local and global environment, as well as significantly improve citizens' lives and well-being. The project targets some of Medellín's busiest and most polluted streets to increase potential environmental returns.

Some of the project's specific benefits include offering residents from disadvantaged backgrounds training to become city gardeners and planting technicians as well as investing USD 16.3 million in ecosystem services. It is estimated that the programme has already reduced Medellín's heat island effect by 2°C. A bioclimatic study also estimates that in just one corridor, the new vegetation growth would absorb 160 787 kg of CO2 per year in the initial phase of the plants' lives. The study projects that the plants' biomass will absorb around 2 308 505 kg of CO2 over 100 years.

Source: (Agencia de Cooperación Internacional Medellín, 2019[64])

Expand risk and vulnerability assessment to cascading and compounding impacts

Given the growing uncertainty underlying local climate risks, climate and urban development policies need to be better equipped to address such uncertainty. This requires assessing all dimensions of climate risks, including how they may cascade or compound with other climate and non-climate risks and across different geographical scales. In turn, this can help policy makers set their policy priorities, and design and implement their climate action more effectively. However, in practice, although climate risk and vulnerability assessments are increasingly becoming a common exercise at the city level, such assessments do not always cover different systems (e.g. economic, social) or different geographical scales (e.g. regional, national and international).

Against this backdrop, some cities are increasingly using systems approaches for the development of their resilience strategies. In 2022, Paris, France started a process to review its Resilience Strategy and is currently carrying out several new climate risk assessments, including on social and environmental fragility. Similarly, Rotterdam, Netherlands analysed seven major crises (climate, biodiversity, pollution/natural resources depletion, inequality, cyber, health and unknown and potential crisis) to expand the scope of its resilience strategy from solely climate risks to economic, social, energy, ecological and digital readiness.

Develop climate adaptation and resilience strategies at the metropolitan scale

Urban and rural areas are spatially and functionally interconnected and dependent on each other through, for example, their labour markets, production and consumption of food and energy, and water management. Without co-ordination with neighbouring communities and towns, a city alone cannot address climate-related hazards. Leveraging the spatial continuity and functional relationships between urban and rural areas, is thus a key strategy to build systemic climate resilience. However, better definitions of geographical scope are needed. For example, the OECD-EU Functional Urban Area (FUA) looks at the economic and functional extent of cities based on people's daily movements (Dijkstra, Poelman and Veneri, 2019[65]). These tools can help subnational governments coordinate policy actions at the relevant scales.

Engage local communities throughout the policy cycle

Systemic resilience requires engagement from a wide range of stakeholders, in particular, local communities affected by specific policy measures. Resilience measures can create tensions among communities. For example, policies to conserve ecosystem services that limit or prevent specific land uses (e.g. housing) may be interpreted by citizens as a barrier to urban development. When planning resilience policies and strategies, policy makers need to ensure that there is a shared understanding of the problem, a shared vision, and shared responsibility among affected citizens.

To overcome such potential tensions, policy making should implement participatory approaches to guide national and local adaptation planning and implementation. In addition to overcoming tensions, such participatory approaches can help cities draw on community knowledge, including from vulnerable groups that are disproportionally affected by climate change. Community engagement can help governments identify the specific needs of each community; target/adapt policy responses more effectively; and fairly distribute the costs and benefits of climate adaptation actions. When securing citizen/community participation in adaptation and resilience planning, governments can also build a sense of ownership and garner community support (e.g. for the maintenance of green roofs).

Box 14.2. Preparing Australian Communities Program – Local stream

The "Preparing Australian Communities Program – Local stream" has supported locally identified and locally led projects to improve the resilience of communities against natural hazards. Round One (2021-22 to 2024-25) has funded 158 projects to improve the resilience of communities against bushfires, flood and tropical cyclones through the following activities: i) Planning – assessment of risk and vulnerability; resilience and disaster risk reduction activities; investment/business case; technical feasibility; ii) Awareness and capacity – increasing disaster risk and resilience awareness and capacity-building activities; iii) Infrastructure – delivery of built and/or natural infrastructure, including new or upgraded infrastructure.

Source: (National Emergency Management Agency, n.d.[66]) https://nema.gov.au/programs/preparing-australia-program/preparing-australia-communities-program-local

Localise National Adaptation Plans, National Adaptation Strategies and Nationally Determined Contributions

Although National Adaptation Plans and Strategies (NAP/NAS) are unlikely to guide adaptation processes at the city level, it is important for cities to be aware of their goals, targets and priorities and reflect them in city-level adaptation plans (UN-Habitat, 2019[67]). Similarly, efforts should be made to align adaptation targets in Nationally Determined Contributions (NDCs) and action taken at the local level. It is essential that national governments coordinate action and ensure policy alignment, taking into account territorial disparities in climate risks.

National governments can use the NAP, NAS and NDC processes to engage regions and cities, clarify the roles and responsibilities of each level of government, and align national and subnational climate adaptation targets and policy instruments to achieve the targets. To do this, various national-level authorities and different levels of governments need to be consulted in the NAP, NAS and NDC formulation process. Some countries are already advancing these localisation processes (Box 14.3.

Box 14.3. National adaptation planning mainstreaming local climate action in Australia, Ireland and Portugal

Australia's National Climate Resilience and Adaptation Strategy 2021-2025

The National Climate Resilience and Adaptation Strategy (hereinafter "the Strategy") positions Australia to better anticipate, manage and adapt to climate change. The Strategy is designed to support governments, communities and businesses to better adapt, recognising that adaptation is a shared responsibility that requires sustained and ongoing action. The Strategy operates across four domains – natural, built, social and economic – to drive adaptation. It recognises that effective adaptation must be informed by the best available science and information; delivered through partnerships and investments; and guided by effective governance and coordination.

The Strategy recognises that all levels of government, businesses, communities and individuals have important, complementary and differentiated roles in adapting to the impacts of climate change. While regional governments have influence through their planning laws and investments in public infrastructure, local governments are well-positioned to inform regional and national governments about the on-the-ground needs of local and regional communities; communicate directly with those communities; and respond to local challenges.

Ireland's National Adaptation Framework and Local Authorities Climate Action Plans (LACAPs)

In 2018, the Government of Ireland launched its National Adaptation Framework, which is complemented by sectoral plans covering key sectors (e.g. natural, and cultural capital, critical infrastructure, water and flood risk management, public health). This national framework has also encouraged cities to prepare their own adaptation and resilience strategies. By 2018, all 31 municipalities in Ireland had prepared local adaptation plans.

In 2023, new legislation will enter into force, requiring all municipalities to prepare Local Authorities Climate Action Plans (LACAPs) to cover both adaptation and mitigation measures. To support the preparation and implementation of LACAPs, the national government will provide financial support through the Climate Action Regional Offices (CAROs). The CAROs were initially established in 2018 to support municipalities in the preparation of local adaptation plans. They have received funding of up to USD 10 billion since 2018, and funding will be renewed in 2023 for the development of LACAPs.

Portugal's National Climate Change Adaptation Strategy (2020-2025)

The National Climate Change Adaptation Strategy (ENAAC) sets objectives and the model for the implementation of solutions for adapting different sectors to the effects of climate change, namely agriculture, biodiversity, economy, energy and energy security, forests, human health, security of people and goods, transport, communications, and coastal areas.

The ENAAC has a strong focus on the territorial dimension of climate adaptation. To this end, it aims to improve the level of knowledge on climate issues of subnational governments and promote the integration of adaptation to climate change into sectoral policies and territorial planning instruments. ENAAC also aims to support regional and local administrations to implement adaptation solutions based on technical-scientific knowledge and the best practices available.

Source: (Australian Government, 2021[68]) (Government of Ireland, 2018[69]) (Agência Portuguesa do Ambiente, 2020[70])

Develop joint climate actions among national and local governments

In addition to consulting subnational governments in national adaptation planning, effective coordination across government levels will also require aligning policies and funding structures across sectors, as well as with private actors. While national governments have a key role to play in setting and implementing national policy and investment frameworks for climate adaptation and resilience, subnational (regional and local governments) hold competences in many policy areas that are key for climate adaptation and resilience, such as land use, water and disaster risk management. Establishing institutional frameworks for effective co-ordination and integration can result in better policy outcomes.

A means of engaging both national and local governments (and other relevant stakeholders) is through the development of joint climate actions, for instance, in the form of partnerships, contracts or joint programmes. Such actions can include common targets, allocation of roles and responsibilities, and financing arrangements (Box 14.4). Similar arrangements can be made to promote knowledge sharing across and within levels of governments (e.g. capacity-building programmes, city-to-city collaboration programmes).

Box 14.4. Examples of collaborative climate action across levels of government

Flemish Local Energy and Climate Pact (LEKP), Belgium

In 2022, the Region of Flanders (Belgium) adopted the second version of the Local Energy and Climate Pact (LEKP 2.0) to align with the EU's Fit for 55 objectives. The LEKP 2.0 encompasses nearly 300 municipalities and has four pillars: i) nature-based solutions, with a focus on urban greening; ii) mitigation policies, with a focus on energy efficiency and renewable energy sources; iii) mobility and development of shared, active, and sustainable solutions; iv) water management, including re-use and up-use. It sets concrete objectives to tackle the global climate challenge at the local level. These include, for example, at least one tree per inhabitant by 2030; 50 collective renovations per 1 000 housing units; one electric charging point per 100 inhabitants; and one cubic metre of extra rainwater collection per inhabitant. Through the LEKP 2.0, municipalities can access grants to implement local climate actions in 2023 on condition that they provide co-funding of at least two times the awarded grant.

The Climate Adaptation City Deal, Netherlands

Running from the beginning of 2016 to the end of January 2021, the Climate Adaptation City Deal was a collaboration agreement between 37 partners, including 10 cities. The cities that participated in this City Deal were The Hague, Amsterdam, Eindhoven, Dordrecht, Rotterdam, Breda, Zwolle, Amersfoort, Deventer and Groningen. Partners in this City Deal worked together intensively, learning from each other, and experimenting and innovating together. The collaboration took place via pilot projects in which experts and administrators worked together on activities to achieve the goals of the Delta Decision on Spatial Adaptation of making the Netherlands water-robust and climate-resilient by 2050.

The Administrative Agreement on Climate Adaptation, Netherlands

In 2018, the Dutch national government, provinces, district water boards, and municipalities signed the Administrative Agreement on Climate Adaptation, under which they give impetus to the implementation of measures scheduled in the Delta Plan on Spatial Adaptation. Taking effect from 2021, the national government made available a maximum of EUR 300 million, matched by another EUR 300 million from local and regional authorities. Out of the total amount, the national government set aside EUR 200 million for the Climate Adaptation Incentive Scheme. This scheme qualifies municipalities, provinces, and district water boards for national government grants to implement climate adaptation measures.

Source: (Vlaanderen, 2022[71]) (Global Covenant of Mayors for Climate & Energy, 2022[72]) (Kennisportaal Klimaatadaptatie, 2021[73]) (Kennisportaal Klimaatadaptatie, n.d.[74])

Building systemic resilience in the energy system

Risks to energy supply due to climate impacts

Climate change is putting global energy infrastructure at risk. More frequent and intense extreme weather events can affect energy supply by damaging assets and infrastructure for fuel supply, power generation, transmission and distribution. Rising temperatures can damage oil and gas production in arctic regions and reduce power generation and the efficiency of power plants. Changes in hydrological patterns with more frequent droughts and floods have critical impacts on mining, biofuel production and hydropower generation, which are all heavily dependent on water availability. Wildfires can damage electricity grids and refineries in some areas while reducing solar power generation. Tropical cyclones can also destroy overhead electricity lines and poles; prompt automatic shutdown of wind power plants; and damage refineries in coastal areas.

Some of the major energy supply disruptions seen in 2022 resulted from extreme climate events. Heatwaves in Europe raised electricity prices to a record-breaking level with soaring cooling demand (Bloomberg, 2022[75]). Massive floods from monsoon rains and glacial melt in Pakistan damaged power stations and gas pipelines (Arab News, 2022[76]). A record-breaking 13-year drought in Chile is severely reducing the production of copper, which is used in key clean energy technologies such as solar photovoltaics (PV), wind, electricity networks and battery storage (Euronews, 2022[77]). Hurricane Ian in the United States and Cuba destroyed electricity networks, leaving over 13 million people in the dark for hours to weeks (CNN, 2022[78]).

Disruptions to oil and gas-based power production

Oil and gas refineries are facing growing risks of climate impacts. Over 25% of refineries are exposed to tropical cyclones and over 10% are under threat of intense tropical cyclones (above Category 3) (IEA, 2022[79]). In August 2021, for instance, Hurricane Ida shut down around 96% of crude oil production and 94% of natural gas production in the Gulf of Mexico, which accounts for 47% of total petroleum refining capacity and 51% of natural gas processing capacity of the United States (EIA, 2021[80]). The strong winds, torrential rains and associated landfall of the hurricane prompted the evacuation of 288 offshore oil platforms and curtailed production from at least nine refineries (SPG Global, 2021[81]) (EIA, 2021[80]) As a result, US crude oil production fell by 1.5 mb/d (around 14% of total daily production), and exports fell by 698 000 b/d in the week of Hurricane Ida, raising oil prices to their highest levels in three years, with an increase of 10% in the following month alone (Forbes, 2021[82]). Hurricane Ida also affected several oil and gas pipelines in Louisiana, causing widespread power outages. In the two weeks after Ida, the National Oceanic and Atmospheric Administration issued a total of 55 spill reports, demonstrating that the concentration of pipelines, platforms and wells in the area have become increasingly affected by tropical cyclones (CNBC, 2021[83]) (New York Times, 2021[84]).

In some oil production sites, such as western North America and southern Australia, wildfires are a major threat to energy infrastructure. In May 2016, wildfires in northern Alberta, Canada halted production in the oil sands and cut Canada's daily oil production by as much as 1mb/d (Bush and Lemmen, 2019[85]) (Canada Energy Regulator, 2017[86]). In 2017, a wildfire in California burned through six oil fields (Fractracker

Alliance, 2018[87]). Given that climate change could increase the probability of wildfires in certain regions, wildfires may disrupt oil production more frequently by forcing pre-emptive shutdowns and loss of stored resources. According to IEA analysis, more than half of the world's refineries are currently exposed to more than 50 fire weather days per year (according to the Fire Weather Index, a meteorologically based index to estimate fire danger). One-quarter of refineries are experiencing meteorological conditions favourable to wildfires for over 200 days per year. More than 10% of refineries are under the risk of wildfires during the entire year (IEA, 2022[79]).

Rising temperatures could also have adverse impacts on oil and gas pipelines and ports. In the United States, for instance, roughly 14 000 km of active oil and gas pipelines are not sufficiently monitored against extreme weather events (U.S. Government Accountability Office, 2021[88]). Temperature rise resulting from climate change may influence the integrity and reliability of existing oil and gas pipelines, leading to expansion in pipelines and increased risk of rupture. Increasing temperatures leading to ice and permafrost melt could threaten fossil fuel transport and storage in the Arctic region, which is heating twice as fast as the global average (IPCC, 2021[89]). In Alaska, permafrost thaw and subsequent ground instability could lead to an estimated USD 33 million in damages to fuel pipelines in a high-emissions scenario (RCP 8.5) by the end of the century. To address this problem, the Alaska Department of Natural Resources has approved the use of about 100 thermosyphons to keep the permafrost directly below the pipeline frozen and prevent further damage to the pipeline's support structure (NBC News, 2021[90]).

Disruptions to electricity systems and renewable energy production

Electricity systems are also under increasing pressure from climate change impacts. These range from shifts in generation potential and output, and physical damage to electricity grids to the increasing likelihood of climate-driven outages.

Tropical cyclones, which have increased in intensity over the last four decades, are already one of the major causes of climate-induced disruptions in some countries. In Japan, for instance, Tropical Cyclone Faxai destroyed the country's biggest floating solar plant (13.7 MW) in 2019 by tearing the modules off and causing fires (EnergyTrend, 2019[91]). In Puerto Rico, Tropical Cyclone Maria destroyed a 100 MW solar PV system near Humacao in 2017 (Krantz, 2020[92]). In Malawi, Tropical Cyclone Idai caused two major hydropower plants to go offline due to flooding and excessive debris, prompting widespread disruption in electricity supply for several days (IEA, 2020[93]). In the Philippines, Typhoon Odette (Rai) broke distribution and transmission lines, and deprived more than 3 million families of electricity (Inquirer, 2021[94]). In 2023, 29% of nuclear power-installed capacity, 19% of wind, 15% of solar PV, 14% of hydro and 11% of grids are exposed to tropical cyclones. Eighteen percent of nuclear, 12% of wind, 6% of solar PV, 7% of hydro and 5% of grids may face major tropical cyclones above Category 3 (with a higher wind speed of over 177km/h) (IEA, 2022[79]). Climate projections show that the intensification of tropical cyclones may continue in the coming decades if GHG emissions are not mitigated, exposing more power plants.

Another rapidly increasing climate risk is heavy precipitation and floods. In 2080-2100, over 55% of installed capacity of hydropower, coal power, nuclear power, gas power and electricity grids are projected to be exposed to more than a 10% increase in one-day maximum precipitation compared to 1850-1900 in a low-emissions scenario (SSP1-2.6). Under a high-emissions scenario (SSP5-8.5) the share soars to over 90% (IEA, 2022[79]). Although power plants are generally equipped with flood protection structures that work in most cases, severe floods could prompt disruptions, including pre-emptive shutdown. For example, five gas-fired power stations in Sylhet, Bangladesh, were shut down pre-emptively when flood water engulfed the stations in June 2022 (Business Insider, 2022[95]). Increased river flow in the aftermath of record rainfall from Hurricane Florence prompted a shutdown of the L.V. Sutton natural gas power plant in the United States because the excessive water flow brought waste into the plant's cooling lake (Wall Street Journal, 2018[96]). Excessive rainfall and floods can also halt project development. Viet Nam's Thua Thien

Hue hydropower project in 2020 and Lao People's Democratic Republic (Lao PDR)'s Xe-Pian Xe-Namnoy Dam in 2018 were halted after landslides resulting from excessive rainfall (IEA, 2021[97]).

Meanwhile, some power systems are projected to face a drier climate, which may raise potential risks of water shortage to some electricity generation technologies such as hydro, oil, gas and nuclear power. Globally, around one-third of existing thermal power plants using freshwater cooling are located in areas of high water stress. This share is set to increase as the changing climate turns today's low-risk sites into high-risk ones (IEA, 2021[98]). Some thermal power plants in South Africa and the United States are currently exposed to water shortages so are switching to dry or hybrid cooling systems (IEA, 2022[79]). Hydropower plants in drought-prone regions, such as the Mediterranean and southern Africa, are also experiencing disruptions owing to droughts. For instance, the power supply in Zambia, where more than 80% of electricity supply comes from hydro, is significantly affected by declining water availability attributable to more frequent droughts and a shorter rainy season. In February 2016, the water level of the Kariba Dam, one of the biggest electricity sources for Zambia and Zimbabwe, dropped to near-record lows (12%), prompting blackouts and power rationing. This occurred again in August 2019, with the Kariba station forced to cut output and impose daily blackouts (IEA, 2020[93]).

In addition to water shortages, climate change poses challenges to electricity supply. Higher temperatures could lead to lower voltages and less electricity generation, as solar PV and wind power plants generally work best in a 25°C environment or lower. Extreme heat can increase electrical resistance in circuits, damage battery cells and lower the viscosity of lubrication oil for wind turbine gearboxes, causing grinding in the gears. As such, electricity generation from solar PV and wind turbines could significantly drop or even stop under extreme heat. For instance, if surface temperature goes above 35°C and raises solar panel temperature to 70°C, solar PV efficiency can drop by 13.5-22.5%, leading to a notable reduction in generation output if no adaptation measures and technological enhancements are undertaken. Extreme heat can also damage power lines, poles and substation equipment while causing the thermal derating of overhead lines.

Heatwaves leading to higher intake or discharge water temperatures can challenge conditions for water cooling water necessary for thermal power plants. High intake water temperatures can reduce operating efficiency and maximum generation capacity, and by regulation are forbidden in some countries. In France, for instance, heatwaves in June and July 2019 forced the power utility *Électricité de France* to curb or entirely stop output of some nuclear reactors based on government regulations that power generation must be cut when water temperatures rise above 28°C (ASN, 2019[99]).

As with oil and gas power production, wildfires also pose threats to power systems, particularly solar PV and the electricity network. Over 60% of today's solar PV plants and around 50% of electricity networks are located in regions with more than 50 days of fire weather per year. Around one-quarter of solar PV and some 18% of electricity grids are exposed to more than 200 fire weather days annually (IEA, 2022[79]). Wildfires can cause physical damage to solar PV plants and significantly reduce solar power generation by emitting large amounts of smoke particulates into the atmosphere and absorbing solar radiation. In the United States, roughly 50% of all claims for solar asset damage owing to extreme weather were caused by wildfires (PV Magazine, 2021[100]). Wildfires in September 2020 in the United States were considered responsible for a 10-30% decrease in solar power generation during peak hours (Juliano et al., 2022[101]). Wildfires can also cause multiple simultaneous faults in various parts of the electricity grid such as lines, poles and substation equipment, while derating overhead lines. In Australia, wildfires in 2019-2020 caused unplanned power outages, mainly because flames damaged transmission and distribution lines. In New South Wales alone, the two main electricity suppliers reported the destruction of 4 000 power poles, leaving 158 000 people without electricity (Department of Premier and Cabinet (New South Wales), 2020[102]).

Risks to energy demand due to climate impacts

Several factors influence energy demand related to climate change. Higher cooling requirements in buildings may result in higher electricity demand during summer peak hours, adding additional stress to the electrical infrastructure. At the same time, milder winters may result in a decrease in the amount of energy needed to heat buildings. Depending on the overall temperature increase, world energy consumption is projected to rise by 7–17% by 2050 as a result of climate change. The severity of this effect varies by region, with developing economies in the tropics seeing the majority of the rise in energy consumption. Rising temperatures cause cooling degree days (CDD) to increase and heating degree days (HDD) to decrease. Under a high-emissions scenario (SSP5-8.5), CDDs are projected to increase by 732 days between 2081-2100 with respect to 1850-1900. Increases in global energy demand increases as a result of the noticeable increase in cooling demand are projected to offset a decline in heating demand. As much as two-thirds of all households are projected to own an air conditioner by 2050 as a result of rising average temperatures, expansion in building floor areas, improved living standards and policies to broaden access to essential energy services. The projected growth in peak electricity demand for cooling is expected to put significant stress on electricity systems (IEA, 2022[79]).

Increased frequency or intensity of extreme weather events can increase energy demand in some industries, for example by increasing the demand for building supplies needed for reconstruction of damaged infrastructure (e.g. cement, iron and steel). Long-lasting droughts can also raise energy needs in some regions by increasing the usage of energy-intensive desalination of seawater for drinking, farming, cooling of power plants, and other uses. On the other hand, more frequent and severe precipitation events may increase demand in the chemicals industry owing to increased fertiliser production needs. Such climate-related stresses may increase the demand for synthetic nitrogen fertilisers, which are currently used in approximately half of the world's food production and are projected to increase by nearly 40% by 2050, mainly driven by the need to increase food production due to economic and population growth (IEA, 2022[79]).

Systemic approaches for improving climate resilience in the energy system

As climate change impacts all means of energy supply and demand, it is necessary to take a systemic view of the climate resilience of energy systems. A climate-resilient energy system implies the ability to anticipate and prepare for changes in climate, adapt to and withstand slow-onset changes in climate patterns, continue to operate under immediate shocks caused by extreme weather events, and restore the system's function after climate-driven disruptions.

A systemic approach to energy sector resilience requires action by all stakeholders. Energy suppliers, consumers and authorities are key actors, while science communities, international organisations, civil society and businesses in other sectors all have important roles to play.

Energy suppliers have primary responsibility for and direct interest in protecting their own assets and providing reliable energy services to their customers. The IEA recommends five priorities for energy suppliers to improve climate resilience and identifies climate risk and impact assessments as the first step (IEA, 2022). Although more energy-related companies are conducting climate risk and impact assessments and disclosing the results following the guidelines of the Task Force on Climate-related Financial Disclosures (TCFD), many of these assessments remain incomplete. As of 2020, only 44% of the 267 energy companies participating in the TCFD submitted climate-related metrics, which include information on the physical risks of climate change (TCFD, 2021[103]).

Energy suppliers have a number of options for enhancing the resilience of energy systems. For example, they can implement physical system hardening (e.g. floodwalls for generation assets, improved electricity networks with underground lines or galvanised steel poles, enhanced reservoir capacity of hydropower and coastal barriers against sea-level rise) that can help energy systems withstand climate impacts. They can also consider switching to more water-efficient and heat-resilient production processes, such as using alternative water sources (e.g. wastewater, seawater, produced water); dry or hybrid cooling systems for thermal power plants; innovative cooling technologies for solar PV; and better design of wind power turbine ventilation.

In addition, energy suppliers can diversify the energy supply chain so that they can continue operation despite shocks to one production site. For instance, in North Africa, where hydropower is likely to see a significant drop in generation output and an increase in variability, raising the share of other power generation technologies would help enhance climate resilience (IEA, 2020[93]). Better climate monitoring systems with innovative technologies (e.g. smart metering, real-time monitoring devices, unmanned aerial vehicles, high-resolution video cameras with automatic alert systems, and Internet of things (IoT) solutions supported by satellite imagery) can help energy suppliers minimise damage from climate impacts and fix problems rapidly (IEA, 2022[79]).

Energy consumers can contribute to climate resilience by adopting demand-side measures in the main end-use sectors (e.g. buildings, industries, transport). Although demand-side measures may seem to have only indirect impacts on the resilience of the energy system, they actually play a key role in enhancing the flexibility of demand and managing peak load in power systems. Energy consumers can ensure climate resilience by adopting climate proofing in the design of key infrastructure and when conducting regular performance assessments. They can also help energy systems better cope with climate change impacts by changing their behaviour patterns and shifting to energy-efficient alternatives. For instance, smart ACs and thermostats, cool roofs and a shift to more energy-efficient transportation help manage electricity demand in summer during peak hours. In addition, nature-based solutions such as green roofs and restoration of riverbed and coastal wetlands can reduce risks from heatwaves and floods. Energy consumers can also consider using alternative materials which will be more resilient to extreme weather events and gradual changes in temperature (IEA, 2022[79]).

Energy authorities, including national and subnational governments and regulators, have a critical role to play in building energy-sector climate resilience by establishing an enabling policy and market environment. Energy authorities can facilitate action on the part of energy suppliers and consumers by addressing barriers such as high up-front costs versus long-term benefits; uneven distribution of costs and benefits; and limited knowledge and awareness about climate impacts and risks. In addition, monopolistic market conditions may require greater policy and regulatory measures to enable climate resilience actions and investments among energy suppliers. Energy authorities can catalyse actions by enhancing knowledge about climate risks and impacts. For instance, the United States' Climate Resilience Toolkit and a guide for climate change vulnerability assessments support electricity utilities in assessing vulnerabilities to climate change and offer a portfolio of resilience solutions.

Establishing appropriate policy frameworks and mainstreaming climate resilience into relevant regulations, standards and guidelines are also crucial. A policy framework that provides clear goals, strategies and commitments while setting clear responsibilities for various actors encourages actions for climate resilience. The European Union has required that climate risks be considered in environmental impact assessments since 2014 and provides a guidance document to raise understanding of climate change adaptation (EU, 2022[104]). In addition to EU-level requirements, some European countries (e.g. Spain, Italy) and the United Kingdom have conducted climate change risk assessments and developed adaptation programmes for the entire or certain parts of the energy sector.

In addition to providing clear policy frameworks, energy authorities can support energy stakeholders by mobilising public financing and investment, and providing adequate risk-sharing mechanisms to facilitate private financing. For example, public investment played a major role in financing rehabilitation and modernisation of the Yacyretá hydropower plant, funded by the governments of Paraguay and Argentina (IEA, 2021[105]). Energy authorities also have a major role in ensuring an efficient and co-ordinated disaster risk preparedness and response system. Once a disaster occurs, energy authorities connect recovery efforts among various actors to minimise the magnitude of interruptions and restore normal operation as quickly as possible (IEA, 2022[79]).

In summary, climate impacts pose clear risks to energy systems at the supply and demand levels. Given energy system interlinkages, addressing these risks requires a systemic approach. Figure 14.5 below summarises different actions various energy system stakeholders can take in order to enhance resilience, categorised in four areas.[6] The table illustrates that building resilience remains a complex endeavour, with individual measures by themselves unlikely to suffice. Rather, co-ordination across groups of actors and encompassing the whole spectrum of resilience areas will be necessary to address climate risks in the energy system.

Figure 14.5. Measures to build climate resilience for energy security by stakeholder

Types	Measure	Readiness	Robustness	Resourcefulness	Recovery
Supply side	Conduct climate risk and impact assessment				
	Implement physical system improvement				
	Switch to water-efficient and heat-resilient production process				
	Diversify energy supply chain				
	Better monitor for early warning and emergency response				
Demand side	Ensure climate proofing in design and performance				
	Increase awareness and promote behavioural changes				
	Improve energy efficiency				
	Use smart and advanced technologies for better management				
	Adopt nature-based solutions				
	Switch to climate-resilient materials				
Authorities and governments	Enhance knowledge about climate risks and impacts				
	Establish appropriate policy frameworks				
	Mainstream climate resilience into relevant regulations				
	Mobilise financing and investment				
	Support adequate climate insurance				
	Ensure emergency preparedness				

Source: (IEA, 2022[79])

Chapter conclusions

The examples detailed in this chapter highlight the complexity of building systemic resilience. Each system has different particularities, involving different actors, at different spatial scales, and with different needs. Climate impacts are not evenly distributed across systems, meaning that careful risk assessment is required both across and within systems boundaries. Perhaps most importantly, systems are not static, but evolve dynamically in tandem with broader global events. As such, strategies to build systemic resilience must be able to react and adapt to global changes, as for example in the transition to net-zero emissions.

Considering the examples given, a few overarching lessons emerge. First, building systemic resilience requires an understanding of how each system functions, the interactions between systems components, the stakeholders and institutions involved, and how these relate to other systems. In particular, policy actions should aim to harness synergies across systems and avoid trade-offs. Second, systemic resilience requires a better understanding of climate risks and how these are distributed across space, time and people. In particular, policy actions should be targeted to specific needs to be most effective. Finally, building systemic resilience requires broad co-operation across government levels, economic sectors and communities. Only a comprehensive and inclusive approach to policy making will ensure that systemic resilience efforts are truly effective.

Notes

1 The term "food systems" refers to all the elements and activities related to producing and consuming food, and their effects, including economic, health, and environmental outcomes.

2 The problem of access to food is not confined to poor countries, but understanding the true extent of food insecurity in OECD countries is difficult in part because most OECD countries do not routinely measure food (in)security, and those who do rarely use internationally comparable methodologies and instruments (Giner and Placzek, 2022[22]).

3 There may be distributional effects, however. For example, lower output in one region due to drought may push up global food prices, benefitting producers elsewhere.

4 https://www.oecd.org/trade/resilient-supply-chains/

5 https://www.oecd.org/regional/compendiumsubnationalrevenue.htm

6 As defined by the IEA (IEA, 2022[108]), the climate resilience of an energy system depends on its ability to prepare for changes in climate (readiness); to adapt to and withstand the slow-onset changes in climate patterns (robustness); to continue to operate under the immediate shocks from extreme weather events (resourcefulness); and to restore the system's function after climate-driven disruptions (recovery).

References

Adrienne-Arsht Rockefeller Foundation Resilience Center (2022), *Extreme heat: the economic and social consequences for the United States*, https://onebillionresilient.org/2021/08/31/extreme-heat-the-economic-and-social-consequences-for-the-us/ (accessed on 13 December 2022). [42]

Agencia de Cooperación Internacional Medellín (2019), *Corredores verdes, corredores de vida en Medellín*, https://www.acimedellin.org/corredores-verdes-corredores-de-vida-en-medellin/. [64]

Agência Portuguesa do Ambiente (2020), *Estratégia Nacional de Adaptação às Alterações Climáticas 2020 (prorrogado até 2025)*, https://apambiente.pt/clima/estrategia-nacional-de-adaptacao-alteracoes-climaticas. [70]

Arab News (2022), *Massive outages hit Pakistan's north after flash floods damage over 20 power houses*, https://www.arabnews.pk/node/2147616/pakistan. [76]

ASN (2019), *Rapport de l'ASN 2019*, https://www.asn.fr/annual_report/2019fr/12/. [99]

Australian Government (2021), *National Climate Resilience and Adaptation Strategy 2021-2025*, https://www.awe.gov.au/sites/default/files/documents/national-climate-resilience-and-adaptation-strategy.pdf. [68]

Bai, X. et al. (2017), "Defining and advancing a systems approach for sustainable cities", *Environmental Sustainability*. [62]

Bai, Y. et al. (2021), "Cost and affordability of nutritious diets at retail prices: Evidence from 177 countries", *Food Policy*, Vol. 99, p. 101983, https://doi.org/10.1016/j.foodpol.2020.101983. [21]

Barrett, C. et al. (2022), "Agri-food Value Chain Revolutions in Low- and Middle-Income Countries", *Journal of Economic Literature*, Vol. 60/4, pp. 1316-1377, https://doi.org/10.1257/jel.20201539. [11]

Bhargava, A. et al. (2022), *Reuters.* [53]

Bloomberg (2022), *Europe Braces for Extreme Heat as Power Infrastructure Wobbles*, https://www.bloomberg.com/news/articles/2022-08-08/europe-braces-for-extreme-heat-as-power-infrastructure-wobbles?leadSource=uverify%20wall. [75]

Brooks, J. and A. Matthews (2015), "Trade Dimensions of Food Security", *OECD Food, Agriculture and Fisheries Papers*, No. 77, OECD Publishing, Paris, https://doi.org/10.1787/5js65xn790nv-en. [29]

Burgess, R. and D. Donaldson (2010), "Can Openness Mitigate the Effects of Weather Shocks? Evidence from India's Famine Era", *American Economic Review*, Vol. 100/2, pp. 449-453, https://doi.org/10.1257/aer.100.2.449. [30]

Busby, J. et al. (2021), "Cascading risks: Understanding the 2021 winter blackout in Texas", *Energy Research & Social Science*, https://doi.org/10.1016/j.erss.2021.102106 (accessed on 13 December 2022). [51]

Bush, E. and D. Lemmen (2019), *Canada's Changing Climate Report; Government of Canada*, https://natural-resources.canada.ca/sites/www.nrcan.gc.ca/files/energy/Climate-change/pdf/CCCR_FULLREPORT-EN-FINAL.pdf. [85]

Business Insider (2022), *5 power plants shut down in Sylhet*, https://www.businessinsiderbd.com/national/news/24119/5-power-plants-shut-down-in-sylhet. [95]

C40 (n.d.), *Sea Level Rise and Coastal Flooding: A summary of The Future We Don't Want research on the impact of climate change on sea levels.* [44]

Canada Energy Regulator (2017), *2016 Review: Short-lived effect on crude oil exports due to the Fort McMurray wildfire*, https://www.cer-rec.gc.ca/en/data-analysis/energy-markets/market-snapshots/2017/2016-review-short-lived-effect-crude-oil-exports-due-fort-mcmurray-wildfire.html. [86]

CNBC (2021), *Floods and outages stall oil firms' efforts to restart after Ida*, https://www.cnbc.com/2021/08/31/floods-outages-stall-oil-firms-efforts-to-restart-after-ida.html. [83]

CNN (2022), *Ian left a trail of destruction stretching from the Caribbean to the Carolinas. Here's a closer look*, https://edition.cnn.com/2022/10/03/us/hurricane-ian-trail-destruction/index.html. [78]

Crippa, M. et al. (2021), "Food systems are responsible for a third of global anthropogenic GHG emissions", *Nature Food*, Vol. 2/3, pp. 198-209, https://doi.org/10.1038/s43016-021-00225-9. [8]

Deconinck, K. et al. (2021), "Overcoming evidence gaps on food systems", *OECD Food, Agriculture and Fisheries Papers*, No. 163, OECD Publishing, Paris, https://doi.org/10.1787/44ba7574-en. [37]

Department of Premier and Cabinet (New South Wales) (2020), *Final report of the NSW Bushfire Inquiry*, https://apo.org.au/node/307786. [102]

Deuss, A. (2015), "Review of the performance and impacts of recent stockholding policies", in *Issues in Agricultural Trade Policy: Proceedings of the 2014 OECD Global Forum on Agriculture*, OECD Publishing, Paris, https://doi.org/10.1787/9789264233911-5-en. [33]

Dijkstra, L., H. Poelman and P. Veneri (2019), "The EU-OECD definition of a functional urban area", *OECD Regional Development Working Papers*, No. 2019/11, OECD Publishing, Paris, https://doi.org/10.1787/d58cb34d-en. [65]

EIA (2021), *Hurricane Ida disrupted crude oil production and refining activity*, https://www.eia.gov/todayinenergy/detail.php?id=49576#:%7E:text=As%20a%20result%20of%20the,of%20Safety%20and%20Environmental%20Enforcement. [80]

EnergyTrend (2019), *Typhoon Faxai Destroys Japan's Biggest Floating Solar Plant*, https://www.energytrend.com/news/20190911-15190.html. [91]

EU (2022), *Law and Governance Policy - Library*, https://circabc.europa.eu/ui/group/3b48eff1-b955-423f-9086-0d85ad1c5879/library/94b9394e-cc9e-4859-94ca-95ccecb43422?p=1&n=-1&sort=name_ASC. [104]

Euronews (2022), *Chile's parched mines race for an increasingly scarce commodity: Water*, https://www.euronews.com/2022/05/07/us-chile-drought-mining-focus. [77]

FAO (2022), *The State of Food Security and Nutrition in the World 2022*, FAO, https://doi.org/10.4060/cc0639en. [18]

FAO (2020), *The State of Agricultural Commodity Markets 2020*, FAO, https://doi.org/10.4060/cb0665en. [5]

FAO (1996), *Rome Declaration on World Food Security*, https://www.fao.org/3/w3613e/w3613e00.htm. [9]

Forbes (2021), *Oil Prices Surge To Three-Year Highs After Hurricanes And Unexpected Demand—How Much Higher Can They Go?*, https://www.forbes.com/sites/jonathanponciano/2021/09/27/oil-prices-surge-to-three-year-highs-after-hurricanes-and-unexpected-demand-how-much-higher-can-they-go/?sh=4313bbc354c3. [82]

Fractracker Alliance (2018), *California's Oil Fields Add Fuel to the Fire*, https://www.fractracker.org/2018/12/california-wildfires-oil-fields/. [87]

Giner, C. and O. Placzek (2022), "Food insecurity and food assistance programmes across OECD countries: Overcoming evidence gaps", *OECD Food, Agriculture and Fisheries Papers*, No. 183, OECD Publishing, Paris, https://doi.org/10.1787/42b4a7fa-en. [22]

Glauber, J. et al. (2021), "Design principles for agricultural risk management policies", *OECD Food, Agriculture and Fisheries Papers*, No. 157, OECD Publishing, Paris, https://doi.org/10.1787/1048819f-en. [25]

Global Covenant of Mayors for Climate & Energy (2022), *A local energy and climate pact in Flanders of inspiration for all Europe*. [72]

Gouel, C. and D. Laborde (2021), "The crucial role of domestic and international market-mediated adaptation to climate change", *Journal of Environmental Economics and Management*, Vol. 106, p. 102408, https://doi.org/10.1016/j.jeem.2020.102408. [27]

Government of Ireland (2018), *National Adaptation Framework: Planning for a Climate Resilience Ireland*. [69]

Gruère, G., M. Shigemitsu and S. Crawford (2020), "Agriculture and water policy changes: Stocktaking and alignment with OECD and G20 recommendations", *OECD Food, Agriculture and Fisheries Papers*, No. 144, OECD Publishing, Paris, https://doi.org/10.1787/f35e64af-en. [17]

Guerrero, S. et al. (2022), "The impacts of agricultural trade and support policy reform on climate change adaptation and environmental performance: A model-based analysis", *OECD Food, Agriculture and Fisheries Papers*, No. 180, OECD Publishing, Paris, https://doi.org/10.1787/520dd70d-en. [26]

Headey, D. (2013), "Developmental Drivers of Nutritional Change: A Cross-Country Analysis", *World Development*, Vol. 42, pp. 76-88, https://doi.org/10.1016/j.worlddev.2012.07.002. [19]

Hirvonen, K. et al. (2020), "Affordability of the EAT–Lancet reference diet: a global analysis", *The Lancet Global Health*, Vol. 8/1, pp. e59-e66, https://doi.org/10.1016/s2214-109x(19)30447-4. [20]

IEA (2022), *Climate Resilience for Energy Security*, https://www.iea.org/reports/climate-resilience-for-energy-security. [79]

IEA (2022), *Climate Resilience for Energy Security*, https://www.iea.org/reports/climate-resilience-for-energy-security. [108]

IEA (2021), *Climate Impacts on Latin American Hydropower*, https://www.iea.org/reports/climate-impacts-on-latin-american-hydropower. [105]

IEA (2021), *Climate Impacts on South and Southeast Asian Hydropower*, https://www.iea.org/reports/climate-impacts-on-south-and-southeast-asian-hydropower. [97]

IEA (2021), *World Energy Outlook 2021*, https://www.iea.org/reports/world-energy-outlook-2021. [98]

IEA (2020), *Climate Impacts on African Hydropower*, IEA, https://www.iea.org/reports/climate-impacts-on-african-hydropower. [107]

IEA (2020), *Climate Impacts on African Hydropower*, https://www.iea.org/reports/climate-impacts-on-african-hydropower. [93]

Ignaciuk, A. (2015), "Adapting Agriculture to Climate Change: A Role for Public Policies", *OECD Food, Agriculture and Fisheries Papers*, No. 85, OECD Publishing, Paris, https://doi.org/10.1787/5js08hwvfnr4-en. [15]

Inquirer (2021), *3 million families affected by power outages due to Odette; floods stalling repairs*, https://newsinfo.inquirer.net/1529357/3m-lost-power-floods-stalling-repairs. [94]

Internal Displacement Monitoring Centre (2021), *Internal displacement in a changing climate*. [57]

IPCC (2022), *Climate Change 2022 Impacts, Adaptation and Vulnerability: Summary for Policy Makers*, https://www.ipcc.ch/report/ar6/wg2/. [39]

IPCC (2022), *Food, Fibre, and Other Ecosystem Products*, Cambridge University Press, https://doi.org/10.1017/9781009325844.007. [2]

IPCC (2021), “Climate Change 2021: The Physical Science Basis. Contribution of Working Group I to the Sixth Assessment Report of the Intergovernmental Panel on Climate Change [Masson-Delmotte, V., P. Zhai, A. Pirani, S. L. Connors, C. Péan, S. Berger, N. Caud, Y. Chen,”, *Cambridge University Press* In Press, p. 3949, https://www.ipcc.ch/report/ar6/wg1/downloads/report/IPCC_AR6_WGI_Full_Report.pdf. [89]

Janssens, C. et al. (2020), “Global hunger and climate change adaptation through international trade”, *Nature Climate Change*, Vol. 10/9, pp. 829-835, https://doi.org/10.1038/s41558-020-0847-4. [28]

Jones, D. and A. Kwieciński (2010), “Policy Responses in Emerging Economies to International Agricultural Commodity Price Surges”*, OECD Food, Agriculture and Fisheries Papers*, No. 34, OECD Publishing, Paris, https://doi.org/10.1787/5km6c61fv40w-en. [31]

Juliano, T. et al. (2022), “Smoke from 2020 United States wildfires responsible for substantial solar energy forecast errors”, *Environmental Research Letters*, Vol. 17/3, p. 034010, https://doi.org/10.1088/1748-9326/ac5143. [101]

Kennisportaal Klimaatadaptatie (2021), *City Deal Klimaatadaptatie*, https://klimaatadaptatienederland.nl/overheden/city-deal/klimaatadaptatie/. [73]

Kennisportaal Klimaatadaptatie (n.d.), *Policy and programmes*, https://klimaatadaptatienederland.nl/en/policy-programmes/. [74]

Khanna, P. (2022), *COGITO*. [58]

Krantz, D. (2020), “Solving Problems like Maria: A Case Study and Review of Collaborative Hurricane-Resilient Solar Energy and Autogestión in Puerto Rico”, *Journal of Sustainability Research*, Vol. 3/1, https://doi.org/10.20900/jsr20210004. [92]

Lankoski, J., A. Ignaciuk and F. Jésus (2018), “Synergies and trade-offs between adaptation, mitigation and agricultural productivity: A synthesis report”*, OECD Food, Agriculture and Fisheries Papers*, No. 110, OECD Publishing, Paris, https://doi.org/10.1787/07dcb05c-en. [35]

Mallapaty, S. (2022), “Why are Pakistan’s floods so extreme this year?”, *Nature*, https://doi.org/10.1038/d41586-022-02813-6. [55]

Martin, W. and K. Anderson (2011), *Export Restrictions and Price Insulation During Commodity Price Booms*, The World Bank, https://doi.org/10.1596/1813-9450-5645. [32]

National Emergency Management Agency (n.d.), *Preparing Australian Communities Program - Local*, https://nema.gov.au/programs/preparing-australia-program/preparing-australia-communities-program-local. [106]

National Emergency Management Agency (n.d.), *Preparing Australian Communities Program - Local*, https://nema.gov.au/programs/preparing-australia-program/preparing-australia-communities-program-local. [66]

NBC News (2021), *Trouble in Alaska? Massive oil pipeline is threatened by thawing permafrost*, https://www.nbcnews.com/news/us-news/trouble-alaska-massive-oil-pipeline-threatened-thawing-permafrost-n1273589. [90]

New York Times (2021), *After Hurricane Ida, Oil Infrastructure Springs Dozens of Leaks*, https://www.nytimes.com/interactive/2021/09/26/climate/ida-oil-spills.html. [84]

OECD (2022), *Agricultural Policy Monitoring and Evaluation 2022: Reforming Agricultural Policies for Climate Change Mitigation*, OECD Publishing, Paris, https://doi.org/10.1787/7f4542bf-en. [16]

OECD (2022), *OECD Regions and Cities at a Glance 2022*, OECD Publishing, Paris, https://doi.org/10.1787/14108660-en. [46]

OECD (2022), *OECD Regions and Cities at Glance 2022*, https://doi.org/10.1787/26173212. [63]

OECD (2022), "Subnational government climate expenditure and revenue tracking in OECD and EU Countries", *OECD Regional Development Papers*, No. 32, OECD Publishing, Paris, https://doi.org/10.1787/1e8016d4-en. [48]

OECD (2021), "Adapting to a changing climate in the management of coastal zones", *OECD Environment Policy Papers*, No. 24, OECD Publishing, Paris, https://doi.org/10.1787/b21083c5-en. [43]

OECD (2021), *Making Better Policies for Food Systems*, OECD Publishing, Paris, https://doi.org/10.1787/ddfba4de-en. [3]

OECD (2020), *A systemic resilience approach to dealing with Covid-19 and future shocks*. [60]

OECD (2020), *Cities in the World: A New Perspective on Urbanisation*. [56]

OECD (2020), *Cities policy responses*. [61]

OECD (2020), *Cities policy responses*. [59]

OECD (2020), *Strengthening Agricultural Resilience in the Face of Multiple Risks*, OECD Publishing, Paris, https://doi.org/10.1787/2250453e-en. [13]

OECD (2019), *An Integrated Approach to the Paris Agreement: The role of regions and cities*, OECD Publishing, https://doi.org/10.1787/96b5676d-en. [47]

OECD (2018), *The Economic Effects of Public Stockholding Policies for Rice in Asia*, OECD Publishing, Paris, https://doi.org/10.1787/9789264305366-en. [34]

OECD (2017), *OECD Champions Mayors for Inclusive Growth: Seoul Implementation Agenda*. [40]

OECD (2015), *Drying Wells, Rising Stakes: Towards Sustainable Agricultural Groundwater Use*, OECD Studies on Water, OECD Publishing, Paris, https://doi.org/10.1787/9789264238701-en. [14]

OECD (2011), *Managing Risk in Agriculture: Policy Assessment and Design*, OECD Publishing, Paris, https://doi.org/10.1787/9789264116146-en. [24]

OECD (2009), *Managing Risk in Agriculture: A Holistic Approach*, OECD Publishing, Paris, https://doi.org/10.1787/9789264075313-en. [23]

OECD (forthcoming 2023), *Building system-wide resilience in agro-food value chains*. [6]

OECD/Bloomberg (2014), *Cities and Climate Change: National governments enabling local action*, https://www.oecd.org/environment/cc/Cities-and-climate-change-2014-Policy-Perspectives-Final-web.pdf. [45]

OECD/FAO (2021), *OECD-FAO Agricultural Outlook 2021-2030*, OECD Publishing, Paris, https://doi.org/10.1787/19428846-en. [4]

OECD/FAO/UNCDF (2016), *Adopting a Territorial Approach to Food Security and Nutrition Policy*, OECD Rural Studies, OECD Publishing, Paris, https://doi.org/10.1787/9789264257108-en. [36]

Pezenik, S. and S. Ebbs (2021), *ABC News*. [52]

Poore, J. and T. Nemecek (2018), "Reducing food's environmental impacts through producers and consumers", *Science*, Vol. 360/6392, pp. 987-992, https://doi.org/10.1126/science.aaq0216. [7]

PV Magazine (2021), *Wildfires could lead to millions in solar losses, insurer warns*, https://pv-magazine-usa.com/2021/07/20/wildfires-could-lead-to-millions-in-solar-losses-insurer-warns/. [100]

Rodas, M., A. Lombardi and M. Ledesma (2022), *Cogito Blog*. [50]

SPG Global (2021), *Producers shut in 95% of US Gulf oil volumes; refiners close plants as Hurricane Ida makes landfall*, https://www.spglobal.com/commodityinsights/en/market-insights/latest-news/natural-gas/082921-producers-shut-in-95-of-us-gulf-oil-volumes-refiners-close-plants-as-hurricane-ida-makes-landfall. [81]

Swinnen, J. (2018), *The Political Economy of Agricultural and Food Policies*, Palgrave Macmillan US, New York, https://doi.org/10.1057/978-1-137-50102-8. [38]

TCFD (2021), *Task Force on Climate-related Financial Disclosures 2021 Status Report*, https://assets.bbhub.io/company/sites/60/2021/07/2021-TCFD-Status_Report.pdf. [103]

U.S. Government Accountability Office (2021), *Offshore Oil and Gas: Updated Regulations Needed to Improve Pipeline Oversight and Decommissioning*, https://www.gao.gov/products/gao-21-293. [88]

UN-Habitat (2019), *Addressing urban and human settlements issues in National Adaptation Plans*. [67]

Union, T. (2022), *Pakistan floods 2022 Post-Disaster Needs Assessment*. [54]

United States Environmental Protection Agency (2021), *Climate Change and Social Vulnerability in the United States: A focus on Six Impacts*, https://www.epa.gov/system/files/documents/2021-09/climate-vulnerability_september-2021_508.pdf. [41]

USDA (2013), *Crop Production Down in 2012 Due to Drought, USDA Reports*, https://www.nass.usda.gov/Newsroom/archive/2013/01_11_2013.php. [1]

Vlaanderen (2022), *Local Energy and Climate Pact (LEKP)*. [71]

Wall Street Journal (2018), *Flood Shuts Down N.C. Power Plant, Sweeps Waste Into River*, https://www.wsj.com/articles/flood-shuts-down-n-c-power-plant-sweeps-waste-into-river-1537555052. [96]

WHO (2022), *World Health Organisation*. [49]

World Bank (2007), *World Development Report 2008*, The World Bank, https://doi.org/10.1596/978-0-8213-6807-7. [10]

Yi, J. et al. (2021), "Post-farmgate food value chains make up most of consumer food expenditures globally", *Nature Food*, Vol. 2/6, pp. 417-425, https://doi.org/10.1038/s43016-021-00279-9. [12]

Part IV Policy recommendations

15 Policy recommendations for building climate and economic resilience in a changing world

The diversity of material across the three parts of this report exemplifies the complexity of the challenge policy makers face in tackling climate change in parallel with other challenges. This chapter collects key policy recommendations drawn from across the report, identifying commonalities and interlinkages across policy domains to help policy makers navigate this complexity. The recommendations focus on embedding resilience into climate mitigation and adaptation policy making, on safeguarding the resilience of the net-zero transition and on building systemic resilience to climate impacts. Together, these recommendations serve as a guide for how to integrate systemic resilience across climate relevant issue areas.

This chapter brings together policy recommendations stemming from the full range of work carried out for the Net Zero+ project. It is structured around the key themes explored in this report, highlighting priority policy areas and related actions for governments in driving transformative and effective climate policy in a changing world.

Responding to increasing climate risks and concurrent global crises

Act urgently to avert catastrophic impacts from climate system tipping points (Chapter 2)

In light of increasing evidence that thresholds for climate system tipping points may be crossed earlier and at lower warming thresholds than previously thought, governments should:

- Take all possible measures to limit global warming to 1.5°C with limited or no overshoot. This includes:
  - Strengthening Nationally Determined Contributions (NDCs) before 2025 and ensuring that well designed policies are implemented urgently, with frequent review and evaluation.
  - Prioritising accelerated emissions reductions now rather than balancing out continuing emissions with negative emissions later, and not over-relying on CO2 removal technologies.
- Prepare for the possibility of climate system tipping points being triggered even if 1.5°C is achieved. This includes:
  - Considering "transformational adaptation" strategies, including potentially drastic actions such as the relocation of at-risk communities and industries should tipping point thresholds be crossed (e.g. coastal communities at risk of sea-level rise).
  - Enhancing monitoring and early warning systems of climate system tipping points as well as modelling of their likely impacts. This includes advancing Earth-system monitoring technologies and supporting further research, innovation and international collaboration.

Make climate action resilient to unpredictable and overlapping global disruptions (Chapter 3)

Recognising the likelihood of future global socio-economic shocks or disruptions such as those caused by the COVID-19 pandemic and Russia's war on Ukraine, governments should:

- •Continue to prioritise climate policy making in the face of unpredictable and overlapping global shocks, focussing not only on accelerating the transition to net-zero emissions but making the transition itself resilient to future shocks.
  - Ensure that any recovery spending in response to future shocks is fully aligned with the net-zero transition, avoiding support to fossil fuels and emissions-intensive activities.
  - Extend recovery spending to climate technology diffusion and innovation, and implement complementary science, technology and information (STI) policies.
  - Responding to high costs of living and energy prices, support to households should be via income support rather than price support where possible, and targeted to those most vulnerable. Governments should avoid blanket measures that may disincentivise households from reducing emissions, thereby undermining climate objectives.

Embedding resilience into climate mitigation and adaptation policy making[1]

Adopt a systemic approach to climate and economic resilience (Chapter 4)

Climate and economic resilience necessitates a systemic approach to mitigating climate change and adapting to climate impacts while simultaneously grappling with other, sometimes overlapping, socio-economic crises. To this end, governments should:

- Ensure that sufficient resources and functional redundancies are maintained in order to adequately intervene in case of crises. For example, as climate change increases extreme weather events, governments should retain the necessary resources to provide emergency assistance to affected communities and rebuild critical infrastructure.
- Look beyond short-term efficiency in order to better absorb future shocks and limit the need for emergency intervention. For example, a more diversified energy system in Europe may have been better able to absorb the shock of a halt in Russian gas imports brought on by the war in Ukraine. This would have minimised the need for emergency support to households and businesses.
- Ensure that measures to bolster resilience to climate impacts do not trade off, but enhance, other socially desirable objectives such as funding basic social services and reducing inequalities.
- Focus policy making on rethinking overall systems, rather than individual components or outcomes, to bring them in line with climate goals (for example, considering overall needs for sustainable mobility rather than a sole focus on replacing thermal vehicles with electric ones).

Future-proof climate action (Chapter 4)

Given the possibility of future disruptions to the net-zero transition, governments should:

- Carry out stress testing of net-zero strategies using a strategic foresight approach. This includes:
  - Identifying a diverse range of possible disruptions to net-zero strategies that could occur across the economy.
  - Assessing and exploring the interlinkages between disruptions and their interactions with local/national/regional contexts to develop plausible future scenarios that can inform policy design.
  - Developing anticipatory strategies to respond to multiple potential challenges and ensure resilience of the net-zero transition should they occur.

Get policy basics right (Chapter 5)

Well-aligned climate policy basics covering mitigation and adaptation should be paramount irrespective of the particularities of overlapping global crises and their implications for climate policy making. Governments should:

- Establish long-term climate policy frameworks setting overarching policy objectives such as emissions reductions trajectories and interim targets, and regularly monitor and assess them.
  - Set up mechanisms to track progress on implementation of policies to meet these ambitions and use the information to compare and evaluate potential alternative policy options to optimise the policy mix for each context. Such assessments can draw on the work of the OECD's Inclusive Forum on Carbon Mitigation Approaches (IFCMA).

[1] This section diverts from the structure of the rest of the report, collating recommendations that span the adaptation-mitigation divide, demonstrating the need to address both priorities simultaneously.

Recognising that no single policy instrument can sufficiently address climate-related challenges, governments should:

- Consider the full range of policy tools, including price-based and non-priced-based instruments, and employ a mix of measures appropriately tailored to regional, national and local contexts. Governments could use the following criteria to assess the appropriateness of different policy instruments within the context they are to be applied:
  - mitigation potential/cost effectiveness;
  - administrative cost;
  - innovation co-benefits;
  - predictability and ability to deal with uncertainty;
  - trade compatibility (non-restrictiveness/non-discriminatory);
  - distributional outcomes;
  - public acceptability.
- Establish complementary policies to provide enabling conditions for effective climate policy implementation. This includes, for example, education policies to ensure that civil society remains informed and engaged or a regulatory environment that enables, or at least does not obstruct, climate policy implementation.

Promote transformative climate policy making across all of government (Chapter 5)

Recognising the multidisciplinary nature of climate policy, the urgency for action and importance of public trust and consensus for durable policies, governments should:

- Take a genuinely whole-of-government approach to policy making, recognising the important role of "centres of government" in driving a co-ordinated approach.
- Reinforce integrity standards for policy making, including through strengthened public consultation processes across all institutions responsible for designing and implementing climate policy.
- Harness innovative public governance tools to drive effective and efficient public governance processes and practices, including:
  - Adopting green budgeting, assuring that expenditures align with objectives to accelerate a resilient net-zero transition and resilience to climate impacts, as well as other environmental objectives.
  - Set an example for other countries by transforming public buildings and transport fleets, using green public procurement, strengthening responsible supply chain requirements, and encouraging suppliers to implement robust responsible business conduct (RBC).
  - Integrate strategic foresight into climate policy-making processes and take behavioural insights into account.
  - Reinforce the capacity of the justice system to resolve environmental claims and enforce environmental commitments, including through dispute resolution mechanisms.
- Involve subnational governments in the design of national climate policies and facilitating knowledge sharing and information exchange.

Strengthen research, monitoring and evaluation, and communication with the public (all chapters)

To support resilient and more effective climate change policy across other policy domains, governments should:

- Advance research and data collection. Increase information sharing across countries and institutions, and the transparent dissemination of results to policy makers and the public in order to continuously assess climate policy progress and the suitability of climate policy plans to changing circumstances.

Safeguarding the resilience of the net-zero transition

Identify and address potential bottlenecks (Chapter 5)

- In addition to stress testing overarching climate policy strategies through strategic foresight, governments should stress test key systems, in particular identifying how bottlenecks across sectors might slow the net-zero transition.
- Governments should anticipate and address potential bottlenecks, for example, by creating the conditions for a stable and scaled-up supply of electricity (e.g. by facilitating permitting procedures and investing in transmission and distribution) and addressing potential dependencies in the supply of critical minerals by diversifying supply chains and/or creating appropriate incentives for local manufacturing where conditions to do so exist.

Address public finance implications of the net-zero transition (Chapter 6)

Given the potentially large public finance implications of the net-zero transition, in particular the revenue potential of carbon pricing being diminished by indirect effects on other sources of public revenue such as e.g. fossil fuel taxes, governments should:

- Employ careful fiscal planning to ensure a resilient net-zero transition. This implies considering both direct and indirect effects of policy instruments on emissions. For instance, while policies can directly alter tax rates, they also lead to changes in tax bases. Most indirect effects put a downward pressure on public revenues.
- Thoroughly analyse the implications of national policy mixes for public finance, keeping in mind that non-price-based policies generally imply increased government expenditure and that national economic structure plays a key role in determining fiscal outcomes.
- Plan for the gradual introduction of alternative tax instruments such as distance-based fuel charges to address the risk of tax base erosion. Base erosion is a considerable risk for countries' fiscal balances, particularly with regard to excise duties on fossil fuels in the transport sector, which will decrease as the transition to net-zero accelerates.

Accelerate innovation (Chapter 7)

Given the clear need for accelerated, cost-effective technological innovation to achieve net-zero emissions, governments should:

- Adopt a mission-oriented, outcome-based approach to innovation and technology deployment to deliver on the scale of technological changes needed, driving the whole innovation ecosystem from research, development and demonstration (RD&D) to full commercialisation.
- Prioritise technology development and diffusion as part of science, technology and innovation (STI) policies.
- Focus additional policy measures on RD&D with support that is targeted rather than horizontal, for example focusing on breakthrough technologies that are integral to the transition but have low market readiness.

- Reach beyond traditional STI policies to include complementary pricing and regulation; set technology standards (e.g. on electric vehicle charging infrastructure compatibility); and implement related education and skills development policies.
- Work to reduce barriers to external funding for innovation, for example through favourable tax schemes, low-interest loans, and government venture capital.

Ensure a net-zero transition that is fair, equitable and publicly supported (Chapter 8)

Build public acceptance for climate policies through careful design and communication.

Recognising that widespread public acceptance of policies is essential to a resilient transition, governments should:

- Provide clear, accurate and easily accessible information to the public about how policies will be implemented and their distributional impacts (i.e. not only about why they are needed).
- Support timely and effective data and information sharing. Take all measures to address disinformation about climate change and other environmental pressures.
- Combat dis- and misinformation by agreeing on common data standards to monitor climate change. Provide unrestricted access to climate change data for analysis and re-use, identifying the provenance of both trusted and untrusted data sources.

Address the distributional outcomes of climate policies

Governments should carefully assess the distributional outcomes of climate policies before they are implemented and ensure that any revenues generated from climate policies are redistributed to minimise adverse outcomes. Such assessments should:

- Include direct and indirect impacts of climate policies and account for behavioural responses.
- Carefully consider multiple options for revenue recycling and tailor these to national/local contexts, taking into consideration the distributional implications of different revenue recycling mechanisms and their role in bolstering or deterring public support of climate policies. For example, governments could consider targeted capital subsidies based on household vulnerability or region.
- Clearly communicate the uses of revenue generated as well as funding sources for policies.
- Address all labour market implications of the net-zero transition

Address all labour market implications of the net-zero transition

Recognising that the net-zero transition will entail employment shifts across and within sectors and require new skills profiles, governments should:

- Ensure labour market flexibility and mobility while also promoting job quality and protecting workers from unfair hiring and firing. Labour market flexibility can be increased in a publicly acceptable manner if generous benefits are coupled with non-restrictive dismissal regulation.
- Pursue active labour market policies such as offering compensation to laid-off workers in emissions-intensive industries. Design such policies in close collaboration with social partners in order to identify worker needs and preferences. Collective bargaining can play a role in enhancing innovation and reallocating displaced workers.
- Prioritise up- or re-skilling workers, offering targeted rather than horizontal support. Include skills needs within long-term planning and reform of curricula in initial education.
- Enhance research, monitoring and modelling of skills needs to address the lack of data on and understanding of key skills bottlenecks.

Align finance and private sector action with climate goals (Chapter 9)

Track climate alignment of finance

Recognising that tracking and assessing the climate alignment of finance flows is critical to measuring and driving progress on climate objectives and the resilience of the net-zero transition, governments should:

- Prioritise further research, improved data collection, and strengthened co-ordination among ongoing initiatives to improve accuracy and consistency across the methodologies used to assess the climate alignment of finance.
- Consider the development of a range of complementary metrics to provide a more nuanced and comprehensive view of the contribution of finance to reaching climate policy goals.

Strengthen financial market practices

Recognising the role of market practices in accelerating the mobilisation and reallocation of capital towards net-zero-aligned investments, governments should:

- Foster global collaboration, interoperability and comparability across environmental, social, and governance (ESG) investing approaches; strengthen the availability and use of reliable and comparable metrics and data to assess physical and transition climate risks and opportunities; and harness ESG approaches to focus more on the alignment of real economy investments with climate objectives rather than rewarding disclosure practices.
- Design and implement measures to enhance the accountability and comparability of financial sector net-zero commitments to better track progress.

Maintain investment flows despite rising costs of capital (Chapter 5)

Recognising the challenges that current rising costs of capital create for the net-zero transition and that current investment conditions may threaten the economic viability of low-carbon projects, governments should:

- Maintain ambition and stringency of core climate policies to send a strong signal to investors and financial institutions about the future role of low-carbon assets.
- Continue fiscal support for low-carbon investments where possible and approach phase-outs of clean technology subsidies with caution.
- Implement policies to reduce investor risk, for example by encouraging the incorporation of risk insurance or guarantees in finance for renewable energy projects; shoring up high-quality and predictable governance; and reducing permitting barriers to renewable energy projects.
- Support the evolution of market products and measurement methodologies to allow investors to better align portfolios with climate objectives. Approaches should be carefully designed to avoid the risk of redirecting investment away from developing countries.
- In addition to government policies, central banks can consider “green” monetary policies to shield low-carbon investments from challenging investment conditions. This could include the creation of lower rates of refinancing for low-carbon technologies or green quantitative easing (purchase of green bonds only) in order to keep interest rates low for climate-friendly sectors specifically.

Harness key finance flows

In harnessing key finance flows to advance action towards a resilient net-zero transition, governments should:

- Align existing foreign direct investment (FDI) flows with net-zero objectives.
- Create enabling conditions and policies to attract additional FDI, using governance, regulation and targeted support measures to ensure that it contributes to a resilient net-zero transition; prioritise measurement and tracking of the impact of FDI on emissions reductions to help identify appropriate policy responses.
- Align investment treaty policies with the Paris Agreement, recognising the potential for well-designed investment treaties to channel massive finance flows into activities aligned with a resilient net-zero transition.

Drive responsible private sector-led action

Recognising that a resilient net-zero transition requires: (i) the credible implementation of net-zero commitments, and (ii) resilient supply chains, governments should:

- Ensure that private sector-led net-zero transitions are implemented with integrity, in line with relevant responsible business conduct (RBC) recommendations as outlined in the OECD Guidelines for MNEs and related OECD due diligence guidance, including for small and medium-sized enterprises.
- Embed safeguards, including through RBC, to strengthen responsible and sustainable sourcing and supply – especially of minerals and materials critical to low-carbon technology, often concentrated in areas with governance challenges.

Mobilise synergies between the net-zero and development transitions (Chapter 10)

Development co-operation providers should draw on policy support, capacity building and direct provision of financial resources to align development and climate objectives, and leverage the momentum afforded by development transitions.

Recognising that a resilient net-zero transition necessitates a globally co-ordinated response that takes differing developing country contexts into account, a 'common approach' can support developing countries' energy transitions. It will be important for development co-operation providers to:

- Support the integration of ambitious climate objectives into national and subnational development plans and sectoral policies, connected with Nationally Determined Contributions (NDCs) and Long-Term Strategies.
- Support the integration of climate change in national development financing strategies in order to leverage broader resource flows for development aligned with climate mitigation and adaptation objectives.
- Support the inclusion of climate objectives in national budgeting frameworks and tax systems.
- Support the development of effective green financial systems across developing countries.
- Recognise that a resilient global net-zero transition requires developing countries' net-zero transitions to reflect and respond to energy sector development priorities (i.e. access to secure and affordable energy).

Building systemic resilience to climate impacts

Assess climate impacts and adaptation needs (Chapter 11)

Recognising that even with ambitious emissions reductions pathways some climate impacts remain unavoidable, and that comprehensive assessments of climate risk, including disaggregated data on gender and vulnerable populations, are necessary to identify and align adaptation needs and build resilience to climate impacts, governments should:

- Continue to mainstream adaptation throughout national policy processes, including budget processes and government investments; establish comprehensive adaptation planning to build resilience to climate impacts; carry out careful monitoring and review of implemented policies.
  - National climate risk and impact assessments (CRA) should form an important part of National Adaptation Strategies (NAS), Plans (NAP), or other.
- Recognise that limits to adaptation reinforce the need for urgent emissions reductions, especially given the increased risk of crossing tipping point thresholds, and that delayed mitigation action will only further limit adaptation options.
- Develop appropriate measurement tools, and make and regularly update assessments of hazards, exposure and vulnerability.

Build climate resilience using a systems approach (Chapter 12)

Recognising the reciprocities between adaptation and mitigation action – notably, that healthy ecosystems can effectively reduce exposure and vulnerability to climate impacts while constituting important carbon sinks – governments should:

- Conduct careful analysis to exploit synergies and minimise trade-offs between interlinked mitigation and adaptation policy objectives, including biodiversity and other natural systems.
- Enhance institutional and governance frameworks to involve all stakeholders in the process of identifying and managing these synergies and trade-offs.
- Identify opportunities for and implement nature-based solutions (NbS) to effectively foster adaptation-mitigation synergies.
- Ensure that monitoring of ecosystem services and NbS employed to support them is commensurate with the complexity of, and interlinkages between, natural and other systems, allowing policies to be adapted to changing circumstances.
  - Fund pilot programmes and subsidise research in order to better assess the potential of NbS and their continued suitability in evolving contexts.
  - Enable technical assistance and knowledge sharing to help stakeholders better understand the role of NbS and co-ordinate actions.

Finance adaptation to mounting climate impacts (Chapter 13)

Scale up adaptation finance

- Governments should scale up funding for the wide range of adaptation measures needed to respond to the climate change impacts. This includes funding for risk assessments and evaluating adaptation needs, planning processes and implementation of adaptation plans.

Align financial flows with adaptation needs

To encourage and leverage growing interest from the financial sector in aligning financial flows with adaptation needs, governments should:

- Strengthen the enabling environment for investment in adaptation:
  - Mainstream physical climate risk into financial sector regulation and practice in order to enhance transparency about risk exposure and increase the incentive to invest in adaptation actions.

- Provide public goods (such as climate data and tools) to support investments in adaptation.
- Examine policy frameworks for climate-sensitive sectors to ensure that they are conducive to investment in adaptation (e.g. flood management).

- Increase and align public expenditure on climate change, including through allocation of adequate funding for National Adaptation Plans and integration of climate adaptation in budgeting and procurement processes.
- Develop and deploy a range of financial instruments to support the management of climate-related risks.

The role of the insurance sector in driving climate resilience

Given the unique double role that the insurance sector provides in improving climate resilience as both investor and provider, governments should:

- Ensure that current regulatory and supervisory efforts strengthen the capacity of the insurance sector in monitoring climate risks and incentivising the development of longer-term climate risk assessments.
- Examine policy and regulatory requirements that impede the provision of risk management and mitigation services provided by the insurance sector as well as the setting of risk-reflective premiums to determine whether the benefits of these restrictions outweigh the costs.
- Consider providing more co-ordinated support together with the insurance sector in addressing resilient reinstatement (i.e. rebuilding damaged property to be more resilient to climate impacts).

Build resilience across systems and sectors – three key examples (Chapter 14)

Recognising that any intervention to support the achievement of a given policy objective may create synergies and trade-offs with others, governments should:

- Employ a systems approach to ensure policy coherence in building resilience to climate impacts, recognising that specific approaches will depend on sector and local contexts.
- Include all relevant stakeholders in the design and implementation of policies to build systemic resilience, ensuring that policies fit system-specific needs and are met with the necessary support of systems actors. For example:
    - System-wide resilience in the energy sector requires awareness and action throughout the energy supply chain including energy suppliers, transporters, consumers and civil society. Governments can support this by facilitating adaptation actions by energy suppliers and consumers and overcoming barriers such as high up-front costs with diffuse benefits. Governments should work to enhance knowledge and awareness about climate impacts and risks, and have the means to step in when energy systems are hit by natural disasters, funding reconstruction that is more resilient than before.
    - Building resilience in food systems requires governments to recognise the "triple challenge" of ensuring food security and nutrition for a growing population; supporting the livelihoods of those who work in the food supply chain; and doing so in an environmentally sustainable way. Governments should provide information, education and training to farmers on effective adaptation actions and avoiding maladaptive practices, encouraging actions that can be taken by farmers themselves. Policy approaches should take into account the interactions and trade-offs between different risks, private adaptation strategies (by farmers and others), and government measures. It is important that public policies do not accidentally encourage the adoption of riskier private strategies that undermine long-term resilience.

- Building the resilience of cities requires the engagement of diverse population groups across the entire policy cycle in order to develop climate adaptation and resilience strategies at a metropolitan scale. This includes breaking sectoral silos within city systems and encouraging horizontal co-ordination. Adaptation plans and strategies should be developed jointly across national and local governments to take advantage of knowledge spillovers and synergies.

Contribution from Youthwise, the OECD's youth advisory board

Box 15.1. A just, green and inclusive future. six proposals from Youthwise

This contribution was written by Youthwise, the OECD's youth advisory board. The opinions expressed and arguments herein do not necessarily reflect the official views of the OECD or its member countries.

Underscoring the critical importance of integrating youth perspectives into all areas of policy making, in 2021 the OECD launched Youthwise, an internal programme to provide a youth perspective on OECD policies.

Youthwise is a diverse group of 24 young people representing views from across OECD member countries. Throughout 2022, Youthwise has consistently demonstrated the necessity of including youth perspectives in responses to global challenges. This has never been more urgent than in the case of climate action. Youthwise sees the climate crisis as not just a policy theme; it is a threat to our future.

To ensure a resilient climate and economy, Youthwise has identified the following six priorities for policy makers:

1. Make policymaking diverse, inclusive and equitable

"Governments could open up and diversify the spaces of environmental decision making. Involving youth, indigenous communities and marginalised regions in real collaboration – not only contribution – is possible if policy serves to break down structural oppressions."

Xananine Calvillo
Youthwise member from Mexico

All young people, regardless of their physical or mental abilities and educational, social and/or economic backgrounds, should be given equal opportunities to participate in policy making and implementation. Young people's voices are sometimes marginalised on essential topics such as climate change, social justice and equality, and usually it is only young people from privileged backgrounds who are given opportunities to have a say. In certain cases, young people face systemic violence and opposition that not only excludes them from decision-making processes but also puts them at legal risk if they speak out. These young people should be included in a fair, collaborative policy-making process.

We propose that:

- Climate policy be developed with the meaningful involvement and consultation of young people, with particular attention given to including youth from under-represented and marginalised groups that are regularly excluded.
- Policies are drafted in simple language, supported with clear summary documents, and distributed using a range of platforms to allow diverse and equitable participation from all young people.

- Policy development processes build capacities, educate, empower and include protection mechanisms to ensure all young voices are heard.
- Youth are remunerated for their involvement in policy development and stakeholder consultation.

2. Build a culture of imagination and exchange

"The green transition is not simply found in the building of a singular solar farm, the insulation of a home, or the banning of diesel vehicles; it will be found in a great structural reform to society and the economy as we know it."

Michael Bakare
Youthwise member from England

The results of systemic change can be hard to conceptualise. Countless generations, including today's youth, have been raised within an economic model that puts growth and profit over long-term well-being. To build a resilient future, we must envisage alternative life-centric systems around mitigating and adapting to climate change, encouraging the use of fewer resources while maintaining – and even improving – living standards.

Other possibilities already exist. We must learn from other ways of living, like those of indigenous communities that help preserve the world's biodiversity. Systemic change will require interculturality, interdisciplinary initiatives, and global collaboration at all levels of society to account for the needs of all.

We propose that:

- Climate policy integrate post-growth mechanisms not only encouraging a transition between extraction sources but a transformation in production principles, consumption and distribution patterns.
- Measures be adopted to reduce absolute resource consumption in a just manner.
- Capacity development for policy makers on alternative ways of thinking to imagine alternative futures and communicate these clearly.
- Nature and its protectors are institutionalised as crucial stakeholders.

3. Provide the right financing and investment to fight climate change

Multiple reports, including from the IPCC, have noted serious deficiencies in climate financing. Most funds are inaccessible to young people at the local and grassroots levels; indeed, Youthwise members have often had difficulty securing funding for climate action in our own experience as activists, advocates and researchers. Meanwhile, investment in fossil fuels continues to rise, partly aided by poorly regulated carbon offset mechanisms that allow emissions to continue unabated. Youth from developing countries have unequal access to finance for climate-related investments, which has increased the disadvantage faced by the global south, already the region most exposed to climate-related damages and financial stress. Developed countries have still not met their financial responsibility to the global south due to a lack of adequate indicators and limited political will to repair historical losses, damages and environmental costs.

We reiterate that:

- Financial market regulation is necessary for carbon neutrality strategies. These strategies should focus on net-emissions reduction, considering carbon capture or compensation offsetting only as a last resort.

- The unmet financial responsibility of developed countries towards the global south regarding climate must be addressed by governments, international organisations, and private entities.
- Processes for directing climate finance should be transparent and democratic, with instruments for disclosure, monitoring and reporting of information to the public, including measures to sanction greenwashing.
- Climate finance should be directed into investments to benefit the communities and territories most affected by the crisis.
- Climate finance support should be provided to communities and territories in the global south that are already working on emissions reduction.

4. Prepare youth for the future through climate education

"We have been told we will need to engage in re- and upskilling and adopt a mindset of lifelong learning to ensure long-term employability. But training and lifelong learning is not free, nor is it inclusive by default. And a failure to prepare the workforce for a green transition or adapting their skills accordingly will delay progress."

Marine Marty
Youthwise member from Switzerland

To better inform young people and make them better stewards of the Earth, young people should be formally educated about sustainability and ecology in local, regional and global ecosystems. This will allow all youth to be equipped with the substantive knowledge and practical skills needed in the green economy. Education does not and should not stop once youth have left formal education. Governments must provide accessible opportunities for lifelong learning to ensure that the youth of today and the future can upskill and reskill in an ever-changing job market.

We propose that:

- Governments provide training in the skills required for the green economy, both for youth about to enter the workforce and those already in it.
- Curricula promote innovation, creativity and digital fluency, with a keen focus on sustainability.
- Accessible modes of education delivery are developed to break the economic, geographic and personal barriers that inhibit access to quality education.
- Schools favour alternative modes of education, such as mentoring, and create time and space for informal learning.

5. Embed institutionalisation and accountability

Ambitious green and inclusive policies are too often treated as bold, new ideas rather than as fundamental parts of an integrated system of governance. This leads to a siloed approach that can hinder the development of genuine long-term strategies. Strong commitment to whole-of-government, long-lasting green and inclusive policies is often lacking, influenced by party politics and a lack of accountability.

We propose that:

- Government policies are forward-thinking, for example as demonstrated by Wales's Well-being of Future Generations Act, which requires cross-sectoral planning and consideration of future generations.
- Cross-departmental panels advising on climate related policy that include youth representatives should be created and integrated into centres of government.

- Governments hold stakeholder forums every five years to assess a policy's effectiveness, resilience, and usefulness for future generations.
- Mechanisms for ensuring youth voices are systematically included in decision-making be developed that include clear and meaningful quotas.

6. Remember, tackling climate change requires a mix of solutions

We know that no approach in isolation can solve the problem of climate change. We must implement a mix of solutions to tackle this challenge, including ones that seem difficult. Current approaches too heavily emphasise efficiency and techno-solutionism, while sufficiency and systemic approaches are underutilised. For instance, policy responses often focus on reducing emissions from cars and vehicles, with little consideration of systemic impacts such as a lack of public transport, affordable housing, or factors that make it unsafe for people to walk or ride a bike. Technology is but one part of a much larger whole systemic change that addresses the climate crisis.

We propose that:

- Technological innovation and implementation incorporate social justice, human rights and life-centred approaches.
- A systemic view of climate change, including multifaceted and slow onset impacts that cannot be easily quantified be adopted.
- Climate change policies also focus on sufficiency and associated behaviour changes to reduce consumption within planetary boundaries, even if it means reducing our comfort.

www.ingramcontent.com/pod-product-compliance
Lightning Source LLC
Chambersburg PA
CBHW061203240926
51846CB00006B/1103